A Most Fortunate Ship

A Most Fortunate Ship

A Narrative History of Old Ironsides

REVISED EDITION

Tyrone G. Martin

Naval Institute Press   Annapolis, Maryland

Naval Institute Press
291 Wood Road
Annapolis, MD 21402

First Naval Institute Press paperback edition, 2003

Library of Congress Cataloging-in-Publication Data
Martin, Tyrone G.
        A most fortunate ship : a narrative history of Old Ironsides / Tyrone G.
Martin.—Rev. ed., 1st Naval Institute Press pbk. ed.
        p. cm.
        Includes bibliographical references (p.) and index.
        ISBN 1-59114-513-9 (alk. paper)
1. Constitution (Frigate)—History. I. Title.
VA65.C7 M33 2003
359.3'22'0973—dc21

                                                              2002041052

Printed in the United States of America on acid-free paper ∞
10 09 08 07 06 05 04 03   9 8 7 6 5 4 3 2 1

"I feel a strong predeliction for the Constitution. I think . . . she will be a most fortunate ship; and I am sometimes good in my predictions. . . ."

Tobias Lear, consul general to the Barbary Regencies
IN A LETTER TO CAPT. JOHN RODGERS (16 OCTOBER 1804)

"It is seldom, indeed, that men have ever come to love and respect a mere machine as this vessel is loved and respected, . . . and we hope the day may be far distant when this noble frigate will cease to occupy her place on the list of the marine of the republic. It is getting to be an honor, of itself, to have commanded her, and a long catalogue of names belonging to gallant and skillful seamen has already been gathered into the records of the past, that claim this enviable distinction. . . . Neither disaster nor disgrace ever befell any man who filled this honorable station. . . ."

James Fenimore Cooper
PUTNAM'S MONTHLY (MAY 1853)

Contents

Preface   IX

ONE
A Legend Is Born   1

TWO
Shaky Shakedown   23

THREE
Talbot Takes the Helm   41

FOUR
The Ship and Life Aboard Her   67

FIVE
The Barbary War   82

SIX
The Barbary War, Climax and Aftermath   102

SEVEN
Prelude to Glory   127

EIGHT
The Great Chase   143

NINE
"The Americans Were Our Masters"   152

TEN
Lightning Strikes Twice   166

ELEVEN
Stewart's Trials and Triumph   181

TWELVE
Mediterranean Sojourn   208

THIRTEEN
Rebirth and Brouhaha   233

FOURTEEN
The Mediterranean, Pacific, and Home Squadrons   247

FIFTEEN
Around the World   266

SIXTEEN
Mediterranean Finale   290

SEVENTEEN
African Adventure   300

EIGHTEEN
Second-Rate Ship   311

NINETEEN
The Long Road Back   339

TWENTY
The Second Century Completed   356

Afterword   373
Notes   375
Glossary   381
Bibliography   389
Index   405

Preface

The unexpected opportunity that resulted in the earlier edition of this work turned out to be an enduring research project; so many unanswered questions were still there when the original manuscript was submitted. That that effort was so well received was my good fortune; that I should have an opportunity to amend it, doubly so.

For those readers who made the first cruise with me, in the pages to follow you will find a more detailed description of how *Constitution* came to be. You also will find that the discussions of her three major War of 1812 battles have been revised in varying degrees. Study and analysis of the materials left by nine participants on both sides—most of which were unknown to me before—has resulted in a battle with HMS *Guerriere* that is markedly different from the tale handed down by earlier historians, and which I had largely followed. In the *Java* fight, I have included the startling new information that *Constitution* actually was raked from astern in a surprise maneuver that caught Bainbridge unready. Also present is a battle diagram based on identical ones from two opposing participants. Elsewhere, later research has permitted me to describe more clearly events previously only dimly known, and to add still more to this fabled frigate's story.

All the new or more accurate information has resulted in a longer work, but in order that it not be unwieldy I have had, regretfully, to greatly reduce the number and length of quotations from participants; to eliminate some background and "color" material and the myths; and to abridge the notes and the bibliography. The complete manuscript of this work as written, with the foregoing material, plus all informational endnotes and a full bibliography, is available for study at the USS *Constitution* Museum.

None of this effort was done in isolation, of course. First and foremost, my wife, Mary, has endured more than two decades of my fascination with this ship with only occasional chiding. Mr. W. Davis Taylor, who created the original opportunity more than fifteen years ago, is a man whose friendship and support I continue to acknowledge. I wish to express my appreciation to Mr. and Mrs. Gordon Abbott, Jr., Judge and Mrs. Levin Campbell, Mr. Ronald M. Egalka, Mr. and Mrs. Barry Hoffman, Mr. Robert W. Selle, and Mr. and Mrs. Harvey Steinberg, of the USS *Constitution* Museum's Bicentennial Coordinating Committee, latter-day benefactors who made this edition possible. I must especially acknowledge the true friendship of artist John Charles Roach. His creation of the battle diagrams was accomplished while he, a navy combat artist, momentarily expected the arrival of orders to Bosnia. Another artist-friend to acknowledge is Briton Ken Grant, whose pencil study of the *Guerriere* fight graced the endpapers of the first edition and whose fine rendering of that episode illumines the current dust jacket. Among academicians and fellow aficionados, a number have aided and abetted my effort through most of these years and have my deepest gratitude: Virginia Steele Wood, author of *Live Oaking* and now a research specialist at the Library of Congress, has thoughtfully kept me in mind while pursuing her own researches and regularly surprised me with unexpected "finds." Dr. David F. Long, author of a number of naval biographies, including one of William Bainbridge, victor over *Java,* and another of John "Mad Jack" Percival, the ship's commander during her circumnavigation, with whom I have exchanged my "salty talk" for his knowledge of naval officers as diplomats; Dr. William M. Fowler of Northeastern University, from whose lectures and friendly discussions over the years I have learned much; Dr. Christopher McKee, from whose expertise in the maze of the National Archives I have benefited and for whose wholehearted advocacy I shall ever be indebted. Newer members of my circle of correspondence include Dr. Spencer C. Tucker, History Chair at Texas Christian University, who has been an immense help with continuing research; and Mr. Patrick Otton, Mr. Richard Eddy, and Mr. Stephen W. H. Duffy, all of whom are fishing the same waters and with whom I happily exchange "catches." Their contributions will be readily recognizable to them; any errors are mine. Mr. Burt Logan, director, and Ms. Margherita M. Desy, associate curator, of the USS *Constitution* Museum were singularly helpful in the final rush to publication of this edition. At the Naval Institute Press, production editor Ms. Linda O'Doughda made me feel there was a firm and friendly hand on the tiller, while proofreader Ms. Jeanne Pinault was a steady influence on an increasingly jaded writer. Two other persons have been staunch helpers in this effort: Mrs. Jody Leshua, senior librarian at the Landrum Branch of the Spartanburg Library, gave me virtually unlimited access to a microfilm reader for years before I finally managed to get my own; and Mr. Robin Michaels, the local computer whiz who has rescued me more than once from electronic oblivion as my database, The Captain's Clerk, mushroomed.

A MOST FORTUNATE SHIP

CHAPTER ONE

A Legend Is Born

WHY A NAVY?

On a hot, sultry day in August 1785, at the Merchants' Coffee House in Philadelphia, an eight-year-old ship was auctioned off for $26,000; *Alliance* was her name. During the American Revolution she had served well as a 32-gun frigate. Some in government had hoped to keep her as a symbol of national honor and as a deterrent to those who would interfere with American commerce on the high seas. But the terrible and costly Revolution was over. The expense of maintaining even a single frigate was a luxury the straitened economy of the weary young country could do without. With the sale of *Alliance*, the Continental Navy ceased to exist.

The few who sought to maintain a sea service were aware that the Barbary pirates of North Africa had pounced with delight on the merchantmen of the new nation as soon as they sailed the length and breadth of the Mediterranean. In their last years as colonials, Americans annually sent 80 to 100 ships, carrying some 1,200 seamen, to the Middle Sea in this trade—under the protection of the Royal Navy. The Revolution ended that protection.

Within a week of *Alliance*'s sale in Philadelphia, there occurred two seizures of interest in the Mediterranean. The first was the schooner *Maria*, out of Boston, by an Algerine xebec of fourteen guns. One of the seamen enslaved was James Leander Cathcart, who would play an influential role in the Barbary Wars two decades later. The second was the ship *Dauphin* of Philadelphia, whose captain, Richard O'Brien, also would serve his country well in the solution of the pirate problem. Shocking and outrageous as these acts of piracy were, they stirred no national commotion in the United States.

In 1793 there occurred an event, involving no Americans, that ultimately would bring about the creation of the United States Navy and relief to the long-suffering captives taken in the Mediterranean. British diplomat Charles Logis, on his own, concluded a truce in the seven-year war between Algiers and Portugal. This, in turn, resulted in the termination of Portuguese naval activities in the Strait of Gibraltar, where they had been the "cork in the bottle," holding the Algerines in the Middle Sea. Thus, in no time at all, the corsairs were active in the Atlantic. The last three months of the year gave Americans a jolt: eleven merchantmen taken by pirates and more than one hundred crewmen held for ransom. Now they understood why a navy was needed.

THE ENABLING LEGISLATION

The Algerine piracies that spurred the Third Congress into action heralded the beginning of the successful legislative effort to create a navy, but it was not the first effort. In 1789, immediately after the House of Representatives was organized, James Madison introduced a revenue bill that considered, in part, the collection of revenue to be used to strengthen the country's maritime defenses. In 1790, such considerations led to the creation of the Revenue Marine, precursor to the modern Coast Guard. And in November 1791, Secretary of War Henry Knox submitted several estimates concerning the maintenance costs of different types of warships to a Senate committee. None of these actions resulted in any positive moves toward a navy.

The Third Congress convened on 2 December 1793. On the 8th, the newspapers of Philadelphia carried the first stunning accounts of the Algerine depredations in the Atlantic. President Washington sent Congress a message on the subject on the 16th, together with a State Department report on foreign trade. The House adopted by a narrow margin three resolutions on 2 January 1794 to (1) appropriate additional money for diplomatic expenses; (2) provide a naval force sufficient to protect American commerce from the Algerine corsairs; and (3) establish a committee to determine the size and cost of this force.

The Select Committee, composed of six Federalists and three Republicans, was heavy with pro-shipping people. Its report, delivered on the 20th, was based upon the earlier estimates from Secretary Knox, in addition to those documents most recently provided by the president and the secretary of state. The committee recommended that four 44-gun (18- and 9-pounders) and two 20-gun ships be constructed for the optimistically small sum of $600,000.

The House debate on this report began on 16 February and split along predictable North-South, inland-tidewater lines. Opponents argued that the proposed naval force was too expensive, constituted a menace to democratic government, was inadequate, and that its development could both upset the British and render negotiations with the Algerines more expensive in itself. Proponents argued that this naval force would cost less than the inflated insurance rates being paid by the merchant marine and that a defenseless government was equally in danger of being overthrown. Furthermore, they argued that the proposed force was adequate for the intended limited purpose, and for this reason, too, would be less of a burden than a full-blown navy and less of a menace to civil liberties.

The debate had been going on for nearly a month when Washington sent over additional supporting documents. More help for the proponents came on 5 March in the form of a petition from Baltimore merchants for an adequate naval force. And final impetus was gained when news of the British Orders in Council prohibiting all neutral trade in the French West Indies outraged the congressmen just two days later.

The complete bill was brought to a vote in the House on the 10th and passed 50 to 39. The opposition had been further weakened by the addition of an article providing for the termination of construction should a peace treaty with Algiers be signed. Senate action seems never to have been in doubt, and on 19 March the bill was approved without a division. President Washington signed "An act to provide a naval armament" on 27 March 1794. It called for the construction of four 44-gun and two 36-gun frigates, stipulated their crew composition, set pay scales, and detailed the weekly food ration.

THE DESIGNER AND HIS DESIGN

While there is no extensive file of correspondence available to detail his activities in this regard, existing letters indicate that Secretary Knox had been considering the problem of beginning a naval force for some time before the bill became law. It is known that he was corresponding with naval veterans of the Revolution within a year after the establishment of the federal government. One of those contacted was John Foster Williams, one-time captain of the Massachusetts state frigate *Protector*. Others known to have been consulted by Knox were James Hackett of Portsmouth, New Hampshire, who had built the Continental Navy's *Alliance*; Capt. John Barry, who had commanded both *Alliance* and the brig *Lexington* during the Revolution; and John Wharton, a shipwright of Philadelphia whose firm had built the Continental frigate *Randolph, 32.** The following letter to Robert Morris, from Joshua Humphreys, Wharton's cousin and one-time business partner, is further evidence of the tight little group in consultation with Secretary Knox and, in light of later developments, is a good summation of the consensus of their advice. It is dated 6 January 1793, but the opening statement seems to indicate that Humphreys meant to date it "1794."

> From the present appearance of affairs I believe it is time this country was possessed of a Navy; but as that is yet to be raised I have ventured a few ideas on that subject.
>
> . . . [A]s our navy must for a considerable time be inferior in numbers, we are to consider what size ships will be most formidable and be an over match for those of an enemy; such Frigates as in blowing weather would be an over-match for double deck ships, and in light winds to evade coming to action, or double deck ships as would be an over match for common double deck ships and in blowing weather superior to ships of three decks, or in calm weather or light winds to outsail them. Ships built on these principles will render those of an enemy in a degree useless, or require a greater number before they dare attack our ship. Frigates, I suppose, will be the first object and none ought to be built less than 150 feet keel to carry 28 32-pounders or 30 24-pounders on the gun deck and 12-pounders on the quarterdeck. These ships should have scantlings equal to 74's. . . . [T]hey should be built of the best materials that could possibly be procured.

Who was Joshua Humphreys and how did he come to be selected as the designer of the authorized frigates? He was born in Haverford, Pennsylvania, on 17 June 1751, the son of Welsh Quakers who first arrived in the colonies in 1682. At the age of about fourteen, he was apprenticed to James Penrose, a well-known Philadelphia shipwright and builder. When Penrose died in 1771, shortly before Humphreys completed his apprenticeship, the Widow Penrose remitted his time and hired him as master shipwright to complete a vessel then building at her late husband's yard.

In 1774, young Joshua, now twenty-three, went into a partnership with his older cousin, John Wharton. Wharton was a close friend of Robert Morris, a politician on the inside track to both Continental and provincial shipbuilding. It

---

* Warships were rated according to the number of long guns they were expected to carry; "32 guns" indicates a small frigate.

was the firm of Wharton and Humphreys that built the frigate *Randolph* in 1776. The design, on which Humphreys may have worked, was of a sharp frigate of conventional layout in the British pattern, but larger than the standard for the rate, in the French manner. Clearly, the design reflected elements found in both contemporary French and British construction, but these were combined with peculiarly American requirements—e.g., a greater emphasis on speed.

Whatever his role as a ship designer and builder during the Revolution, in the years following the war's end Humphreys became an established shipbuilder in Philadelphia. The reason he had access to the secretary of war undoubtedly was due more to his connections and his residence in Philadelphia than to any preeminence in his chosen field.

Further evidence as to Humphreys's readiness to design the new ships is inferred from the fact that, when hired for the job in June, his pay was made retroactive to 1 May 1794, since it was during this period he created a half model illustrating his concept. As was the case with *Randolph*, the half model contained features found in both French and British frigates, blended with native ideas to produce a uniquely American man-of-war. These ships were very large for 44s, being 175 feet between perpendiculars and with an extreme beam of 44 feet, 2 inches. That made them 2 to 3 feet wider and 20 feet longer than their British contemporaries and 13 feet longer and 1 foot wider than the French. Strengthening and widening the gangways connecting the forecastle and quarterdeck created the "spar deck," capable of accommodating great guns anywhere along its length. The framing was so close that the designed interval between pairs was two inches, compared with two to four times that amount of space in other frigates of the day. And while this great strength of deck and hull permitted the mounting of heavier armament, the better length-to-beam ratio and the comparative fineness of the bow resulted in ships capable of sailing with the fastest and most maneuverable in the world.

The most innovative elements of Humphreys's design, however, were not to be seen in his half model; rather, they were found in different places in his materials requirements list and evident only when the ship's structure took shape. Original with Humphreys was the development of what one might call an inverted cantilever system built into the hull. His design called for three parallel pairs of pre-stressed diagonal riders rising forward from the sides of the keelson to be joined to the opposite ends of berth deck beams four, six, and eight from the bow, and another three pairs rising aft to join with the fourth, sixth, and eighth berth deck beams from the sternpost. The lower ends of the aftermost

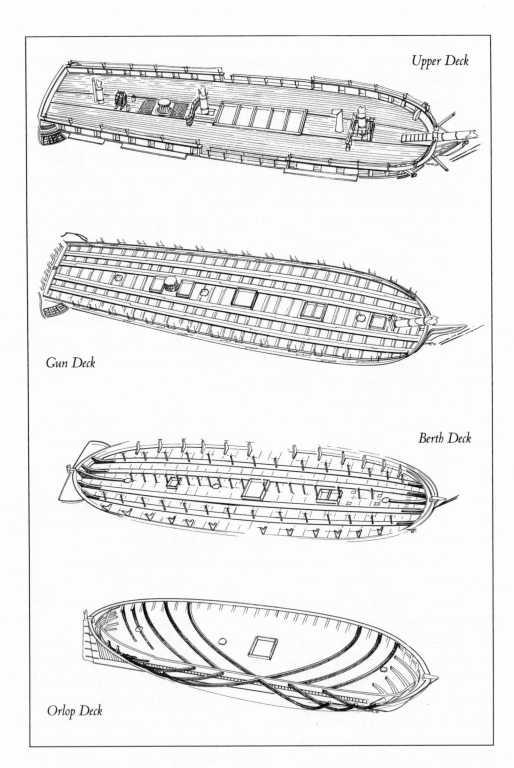

Upper Deck

Gun Deck

Berth Deck

Orlop Deck

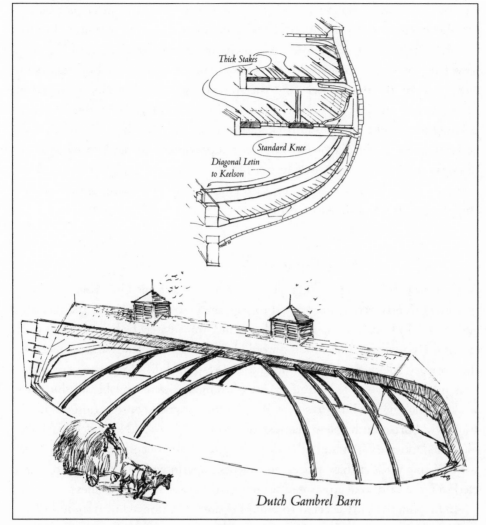

Thick Stakes

Standard Knee

Diagonal Letin
to Keelson

Dutch Gambrel Barn

Joshua Humphreys is not known to have recorded the source of his idea for diagonal riders. One may have been the roof structure of the Pennsylvania Dutch barn (above). The deck level sketches (facing page) show the principal element of Humphreys's original system: from bottom to top, the diagonal riders themselves on the orlop; the twelve standard knees, three rows of stanchions, four pairs of interconnected "thick" planks providing longitudinal unity, and the interconnected spirketting framing the deck's perimeter, on the berth deck; the thick planks and spirketting repeated, together with a single row of stanchions on the gun deck; and, finally, the conventionally constructed spar deck. A transverse cutaway (top) provides another view of the interrelationship of the various parts of Humphreys's system. *Original sketches by John Charles Roach in the author's collection* pair of the forward diagonals and those of the forwardmost after pair butted together at the keelson. The berth deck structure was, in turn, connected to the gun deck structure by three lines of stanchions running the length of the ship. Two pairs of lock-scarphed "thick planks" ran the lengths of both decks on either side of the main hatch, and the spirketting of both decks consisted of pieces hooked and joggled together. The result was an integrated system that distributed the weight of the gun deck and its armament evenly to the berth deck and ultimately via the diagonals to the central portion of the keel, thereby greatly diminishing those forces mostly responsible for a ship "hogging" (bowing down at either end) and the resultant keel distortion. This was something new in warship design.[1] It was a stroke of genius.

Preparing to Build the Ship

At the time the "Act to provide a naval armament" was signed by President Washington, no funds were appropriated to pay for the construction of the six ships authorized. Indeed, nothing existed that could immediately be put to use in their creation. Recognizing that funding would be forthcoming, Knox and Secretary of the Treasury Alexander Hamilton, who had responsibility for letting contracts, took preliminary steps to be ready to act when monies were available. Within three weeks of signing the bill, President Washington assigned construction of the six frigates to Portsmouth (New Hampshire), Boston, New York, Philadelphia, Baltimore, and Gosport (Portsmouth today), Virginia. Subsequently, contracts were let with existing yards at these places, and agents, superintendents, constructors, and clerks of the yard were appointed to oversee the government's business.

In Boston, the yard selected to build Frigate "B" belonged to Edmund Hartt and was located near where Coast Guard Base Boston stands today, north of Copp's Hill. Gen. Henry Jackson was hired as naval agent and charged with hiring artisans and laborers, purchasing materials not otherwise contracted for, supervising the clerk of the yard, paying wages, and maintaining accounts. The prospective commanding officer of the ship, Capt. Samuel Nicholson, appointed to that rank on 5 June 1794, was ordered to report as superintendent, to exercise overall supervision, and provide naval expertise to the builders. Col. George Claghorn joined the organization as constructor, controlling the work force on the ship and ensuring Humphreys' design was followed. Clerk of the Yard Caleb Gibbs maintained the accounts and inventories for the naval agent.

On the 9th, $688,888.32 were appropriated for initial construction costs. That same day, a contract was let with John T. Morgan, a master shipwright of Boston, to proceed to Charleston and Savannah to procure the necessary live oak, red cedar, and pitch pine timbers.

A week after this, the Treasury Department directed its collector of customs at New London, Connecticut, Jedidiah Huntington, to procure sixty axmen and thirty ship carpenters from Connecticut, Rhode Island, and the "western coast of Massachusetts" to be sent south to cut the trees. Huntington also was required to arrange for the procurement and shipment of supporting supplies and provisions from New London, New York, and Philadelphia, wherever the goods could be had at the most economic price.

Secretary of the Treasury Hamilton, on the 25th, received estimates of the composition metal, sheathing copper, bolts, nails, bunting, and iron kitchens ("cambooses") needed. Many of these were to be ordered in Europe, through our minister in London, as such items were not readily available in the new United States. Suitable anchors could be procured on this side of the Atlantic.

In the interests of economy, it was decided that the naval agents previously appointed by Secretary Knox also would attend to local treasury interests concerning contracts. Accordingly, on 5 and 7 July instructions were sent to the agents by the Treasury Department to procure in their immediate areas all white oak, yellow pine, and treenails meeting specifications. On the 15th, they received further instructions to procure masts, blocks, ironwork, cooperage, cordage, and sailcloth from local sources.

On the 17th, an itinerant English Quaker, Josiah Fox, was hired as a clerk in the War Department and given duties assisting Joshua Humphreys in the preparation of the first building plan for the 44s. Fox, ten years Humphreys's junior, had apprenticed for about three and a half years as a shipwright in England at private yards at Plymouth and Deptford. He had been in America since October 1793 and may have secured the clerkship through the influence of his cousin, Andrew Endicott, then surveyor general of the United States. From the outset, Fox sought to make alterations to the design contrary to Humphreys's directions, leading the latter, who was under pressure from Knox to "expedite this work," to make the initial drawing himself. He gave the design the name "Terrible," meaning "awesome." It was completed by September. Copies for the building yards, together with moulds, were finely drawn from Humphreys's original by Fox and William Doughty, clerk at Humphreys's yard, and were distributed by the end of November. Doughty's copy of Humphreys's master draught went to Boston.[2]

A contract, the second of the program, for sixty 24-pound naval cannon, was signed on 8 August with the Furnace Hope foundry in Providence, Rhode Island. Delivery was to be completed by 1 May 1795 at a price of $106.66 per ton. During September, the Boston Manufacturing Company received a contract to manufacture "one entire suit of sails" for each frigate, contrary to earlier directives to the naval agents. The agreed-upon price reportedly was between $13 and $15 per thirty-nine-yard bolt. Production was completed before the year ended.

John Barry, of Revolutionary War fame and captain-designate of the frigate building in Philadelphia, was sent to Georgia on 5 October in the brig *Schuylkill* to learn firsthand the situation and to get things begun expeditiously. On the 23rd, the cutting of live oak for the frigates was begun on St. Simon's Island. By the 28th, Morgan reported to Barry that he thought the first shipload of timbers, consigned to the Philadelphia frigate, would be ready to be put aboard ship about 4 November; others would be ready as the ships could be hired and brought to the island for loading. Barry, satisfied with the initial effort, was back in Philadelphia by the 10th, and in an 18 December letter to the secretary of war, he reported that one shipload already had been delivered to that city and that others were soon to follow, bound for Philadelphia and the other building sites.

On Christmas Eve 1794, Nathaniel Cushing received a contract to forge anchors for delivery to Boston. One of these, weighing 6,116 pounds, went aboard the new frigate there in January 1798.

BUILDING PROBLEMS

The winter of 1794–1795 proved to be a bad one. Incessant rain occurred in Georgia, inundating the already swampy areas where the live oak grew and bringing cutting operations to a standstill. Persistent efforts resulted in some moulded timbers being shipped out by spring, but the quantities were small, and of these, one shipload (bound for New York) was lost in a storm en route. By June 1795, all but three of the axmen had given up and returned North. These three hardy souls, with a gang of black laborers, strove to keep the supply coming. They reported to Humphreys that they hoped to complete their operations by May 1796.

With this dim outlook for supplies, and yet recognizing the need to get a navy in being, it was decided by Secretary of War Timothy Pickering to concentrate

A moment early in the shipbuilding process. Stem and stern posts have been raised, floor timbers are in, and another frame is being hoisted into position, joining a number of others already in place. *Courtesy of artist Samuel F. Manning and the* USS Constitution *Museum*

the earliest deliveries of live oak, cedar, and yellow pine in the yards at Philadelphia and Baltimore. Slow communication partially aborted this plan, in that shipments already had been made by the cutters in Georgia to Boston, Portsmouth, and Gosport. In addition, suppliers in Massachusetts and New Hampshire already had provided the Boston yard with white oak for the frigate's hull planking and tall white pines for her masts.

On 14 March 1795, two months after he succeeded Henry Knox, Secretary Pickering gave President Washington a list of ten names "such as have occurred in my conversations with gentlemen on the subject." Five of these ultimately were selected for hulls then building, *Constitution* among them.[3] Work proceeded through 1795 at a leisurely pace, as the supply of materials allowed. White oak keel timbers arrived in Boston from New Jersey late in May. By early December, Humphreys was able to report to Pickering about the frigate to be named *Constitution:*

> The keel is completed and laid on the blocks. The [four] pieces are scarfed and bolted to each other in the best manner. The stern frame is now completing, and will be soon ready to raise. The stern is also putting together, every part being worked to the moulds. About two-thirds of the live oak timbers have

been received, and are all worked agreeable to the moulds; great part of those timbers are bolted together in frames, and are ready to put into the ship, but some of the principal pieces for the frames have not yet arrived. All the gun deck and lower deck beams are procured and ready for delivery, and the plank for those decks are received into the yard. The plank for the outside and ceiling are also received and are now seasoning. The copper is all in the public stores. The masts, bowsprit, yards, and other spars, all are ready for working. The bits [sic] for the cables, coamings for the hatchways, partners for the masts, are all ready. The caboose, with a forge, hearth, armorer's tools, spare coppers, boilers, etc., are all complete. Most of the ironwork is in great forwardness. All the necessary contracts are entered into by agent, and the articles contracted for are arriving daily.

Humphreys's terse report did not take note of the suppliers of the many materials being assembled. Aside from the woodcutters in a half-dozen states, foundries in Maryland and Rhode Island were producing cannon. In Boston, Paul Revere had provided the copper bolts and fastenings from his own works; the Skillens brothers, John and Simeon, were carving the Hercules figurehead at their shop on Skillens Wharf; Ephraim Thayer was preparing "fire engines" and gun carriages; and the flaxen sails were being cut and sewn at the Old Granary Building, the only loft in the city large enough for the task.

It will be recalled that an article of the authorizing Act of 1794 provided for the cessation of all construction should an Algerine peace treaty be secured. Early in March 1796, word was received from the consul, Joel Barlow, that such a treaty had indeed been signed. On 15 March, President Washington sent Congress a letter noting the treaty and suggesting, in view of work already accomplished, that three of the building frigates be continued. In the Senate, a committee headed by Federalist William Bingham of Pennsylvania received the president's letter for consideration and recommended only two days later that the president's proposal be approved using such of the monies as remained from the original appropriation (about $229,000) as well as any available from some $80,000 appropriated for the construction of galleys. The committee also proposed that the president be given discretionary powers to complete the other three frigates "having due regard to the existing price of labor and materials." The Senate passed a bill with all these provisions on the 28th, and it was on the House calendar for debate the next day. That body passed an amended version on 19 April. None of the Bingham committee proposals had been altered. On the 20th, President Washington directed completion of the three frigates "building at Philadelphia, Boston, and Baltimore."

When the second session of the Fourth Congress met late in 1796, a naval committee was appointed in the House to look into the state of the building program and whether or not *any* navy was necessary. Headed by Federalist Josiah Parker, its first step was to ask Secretary of War (since 27 January 1796) James McHenry for a report. His response, dated 11 January 1797, said of *Constitution:*

> The whole of the frame is raised, and is ready for planking; the wales are prepared, and it is expected will be on and fastened this month; the keelsons are now in their places and bolted off; the masts are now in hand, and the boats are building; all the dead eyes for lower and topmast shrouds are made and strapped; the knees for all the decks are procured, as well as the beams, carlings, ledges, etc.; iron ballast sufficient is in store, and the necessary materials for completing the hull are procured and received.
>
> The hemp for the cables, rigging, etc., and blocks, are in the hands of the respective tradesmen, manufacturing, and if the winter should prove favorable, there is no doubt but this frigate may be launched in July next.

Events that hitherto had been divorced from the building program at long last were coming to a head and would provide the final impetus to the rebirth of an American navy. In late spring 1794, Washington had sent Chief Justice John Jay to England to try to put an end to the British practice of taking prize a neutral ship carrying any French property whatsoever, a course of action resorted to when the French Revolution began to spill outside national boundaries. Jay also was to settle certain questions that had caused friction since the American Revolution. He succeeded admirably.

As soon as the French learned the provisions of the Jay Treaty, Franco-American relations began a downward course. In July 1796, the French resolved to retaliate with essentially the same policy, but practiced far more brutally by their privateers in the West Indies than by the Royal Navy. The policy was formalized by decree on 2 March 1797. On the 25th, President John Adams, in office slightly more than three weeks, called for a special session of Congress to convene on 15 May to settle the nation's maritime problem with France. A happy circumstance occurred on 10 May when *United States* at long last was launched at the nation's capital. President Adams addressed the full Congress on the 16th. He reviewed the course of events in our relations with the French and urged that some defensive measures be implemented. He recommended that the frigates be completed, that American merchant ships be convoyed, but that the building of privateers in America be banned. Clearly, it *was* a defensive program, one whose provisions might encourage negotiation by the French.

For the next six weeks, the arguments waxed hot and heavy in both houses of Congress, between Anglophile and Francophile, between Federalist and Republican. In the midst of it, on 16 June, Josiah Parker received still another report from Secretary McHenry concerning the frigates. Of *Constitution* he wrote: "The bottom of this ship is squared off, and the calkers are at work. The various decks are laying; the breasthooks, diagonal riders, and counter timbers, are all in and secured, and the mast makers are employed on the masts and yards. All the boats excepting the pinnace are built. The riggers are at work on the rigging, which will be soon ready; the water casks are in hand; sails are preparing, and the constructor reports the ship may be launched about the twentieth of August next—the Captain is of the opinion she may be completely equipped in one month after."

As had been the case earlier, the secretary indicated that more money would be needed—$197,636 more—for the three men-of-war. Oh yes, and pay and subsistence for their crews was now estimated at $220,938 a year.

A hot debate was fueled by this announcement of further expense, but on 1 July 1797 a bill was approved. The first section authorized completion of the frigates and provided $200,000 for that purpose. Later sections dealt with manning, pay, and rations. Proposals for a navy yard and a live oak preserve again were turned down.

Building of the two frigates still on the ways now pressed forward to a conclusion. The final chore on *Constitution*'s underwater body was the application in August of the copper sheathing provided through purchases from British mills. In that same month, the battery of 24-pounders was delivered from Furnace Hope. On 5 September, two days before *Constellation* was launched at Baltimore, *Constitution*'s anchor cable, borne by 293 men and accompanied by flags, fife, and drums, was marched from Jeffrey and Russell's ropewalk into the Hartt shipyard. At long last, launching seemed imminent.

LAUNCHING, AT LAST

For months, the burgeoning bulk of the frigate dominated the Boston waterfront just down the hill from Old North Church. The citizenry had evinced considerable pride in her from the earliest days of her construction, and now that both *United States* and *Constellation* had been launched, they were most anxious that "their" ship likewise be afloat. The two major newspapers discussed her design and building progress according to their political preference: the Federalist *Columbian Centinel* waxed poetic about her form and strength; the Republican *Chronicle* assailed Federalist bungling and sloth in the pace of construction.

The day selected for the launch was 20 September 1797. President Adams and his suite were invited, as were the governor of the Commonwealth, Increase Summer, and Boston's selectmen. Enterprising nearby property owners and boatmen sought to capitalize on the occasion by erecting viewing platforms for paying customers on the one hand and hiring out their boats to well-heeled rubberneckers on the other. People even were expected to gather on Noddle's Island across the way to see the mighty *Constitution* "launch forth into that element which connects the world together." In town, dinners, dances, and dramatics would celebrate the occasion.

Constructor Claghorn took note of this growing enthusiasm and published a circular on 18 September advising that, because of the limited space in the Hartt yard and a concern for public safety, only the president, governor, lieutenant governor, and their respective suites and the invited select few would be permitted "inside the fence" to watch the spectacle.

The 20th of September 1797 dawned cold but bright, and was altogether a pleasant day. At 11:20 A.M., the calculated moment of high tide, Colonel Claghorn gave the order to knock out the blocks, and a hush fell over the crowd as it gathered itself to cheer the frigate's first moments afloat. Soon, all the blocks were gone—but the ship failed to move. A mortified Claghorn ordered the use of screws to get her going, and she did. After twenty-seven feet, she would move no farther. A portion of the ways had settled half an inch and left her stuck. The blocks and shores were replaced, and the disappointed throngs went home. *Constitution*'s first moment in the sun had been a fizzle. Predictably, the *Columbian Centinel* commiserated with Claghorn while the *Chronicle* used the occasion to take swipes at its political foes. Mishap notwithstanding, the Haymarket Theatre presented a musical play by John Hodgkinson entitled "The Launch, or Huzza for the Constitution," that evening. It is said to have been a box office success.

The next day, after taking measurements and laying his plans carefully, Claghorn wedged the ship up two inches in a fifty-minute operation, and set

At about noon on 21 October 1797, *Constitution* slides into the water on the third try in a month. This particular image is the product of an unknown artist's not very accurate imagination, but it is the only one known. *Official U.S. Navy photo*

about correcting the defects in the ways as he saw them. By evening, all again appeared to be in readiness.

On the 22nd, with almost no one the wiser, the launch sequence again was started. This time the ship moved thirty-one feet and was about to enter the water when she stopped abruptly. Claghorn was sorely tempted to try and force her on in, but he recognized the real possibility of her becoming hung up, half in and half out, and wisely desisted. The settling of another portion of the ways, this time by one and five-eighths inches, had frustrated the plan. Claghorn decided to make the launching ways steeper and try again at the next period of spring tides.

A cold, overcast day was 21 October 1797. An east wind swept across the Hartt yard. Early that morning, Claghorn caused one of *Constitution*'s cannon, which were not yet on board, to be fired as an announcement to anyone interested that he was ready to try again at high tide. By noon "a very numerous and brilliant collection of citizens assembled at the spectacle." Among those on board for the occasion were Capt. Samuel Nicholson, prickly as a porcupine and eager to have sole authority over the frigate; Capt. James Sever, visiting from his post in Portsmouth, New Hampshire; Mr. George Ticknor; and Mr. Benjamin Russell (of the *Columbian Centinel*) and his guests, the Duc de Chartres (later King Louis Philippe of France), Duc de Montpensier, Comte de Beaujolais, and Prince Talleyrand, together with a number of ladies. A few moments later, Claghorn gave the order to knock out the blocks and shores, and this time the large frigate moved promptly and swiftly into the harbor waters. As she went, Sever broke a bottle of Madeira on the heel of her bowsprit, declaring her to be named *Constitution.*

Once anchored, the yard was signaled and *Constitution*'s cannon on shore "announced to the neighboring country that CONSTITUTION WAS SECURE." For all the satisfaction he must have felt that day, Nicholson was frustrated in the exercise of what he considered one of his prerogatives: the breaking of the Stars and Stripes aboard the new ship. Two shipyard workers, Samuel Bently and a man named Harris, in return for the many occasions when Nicholson had vented his spleen on the workforce, slipped aboard while the captain was at a post-launch dinner ashore, and hoisted the colors. Nicholson, of course, was furious when he returned and found that he had been preempted. But the flag remained, fluttering in the damp, chill air.

COMPLETION AND OUTFITTING

At the time *Constitution* was launched, there was an atmosphere of watchful waiting in Philadelphia. Our free trade upon the high seas was being affected by the belligerents in Europe, Britain and France—principally the latter. The country seemed ready to take some defensive measures, but hoped the situation could be resolved without bloodshed.

As the talks drifted along in Paris, so, too, did governmental efforts at defense preparations. By late December 1797, the frigate at Boston had had virtually all her joiner work completed (the installation of interior bulkheads, etc.), all the lower masts had been stepped, and the riggers were busy rigging them. In January 1798, Congress once again was investigating the cost of the frigates and Secretary McHenry's request for a deficiency appropriation of $396,212 to get on with that program and other naval matters. In the absence of funds, completion and outfitting proceeded slowly.

On 5 March, President Adams relayed to Congress a letter he had received from his emissaries in France that said, in part, "We can only repeat there exists no hope . . . that the objects of our mission will be in any way accomplished." As a result, defense legislation began to move. The Federalists and Republicans spent two weeks in attacking one another's honor and exchanging vituperations before finally appropriating the requested monies. When the famous "XYZ" papers, delineating French diplomatic machinations, were passed to the Congress on 2 April, money ceased, for the time being, to be a serious problem to the embryonic navy.

Secretary McHenry, on the 9th, directed Intendent of Military Stores Samuel Hodgdon to have "transported to the Frigate Constitution at Boston in the safest and most expeditious manner" a long list of materials, including 100 pairs of pistols, 100 boarding axes, 200 cutlasses, 2,957 24-pounder shot, 750 stools of 24-pounder grape and cannister, 450 24-pounder double-headed and chain shot, 60 muskets (for Marines), 3,000 flannel cartridges for 24-pounders, and a host of other weapons-related items. A 242-pound bell was provided by Paul Revere for $108.90. On the 21st, Secretary McHenry informed Nicholson that "The Medecine Chest . . . and a complete Sett of instruments . . . will be sent as soon as possible." He also approved of Nicholson's proposal to have Paul Revere cast "Canonades" for the ship, subject to "the usual Proofs and Examinations." This same letter directed Nicholson to select "proper Characters for Boatswain, Gunner, Carpenter, Sailmaker, and Midship-Men."

With the need apparent and the way now cleared for a navy *in fact*, Congress acted to end the War Department's stewardship of the new force. Events set afoot by the president's announcement on 5 March of French persiflage resulted, on 27 April, in a bill authorizing expansion of the navy by not more than twelve vessels carrying no more than twenty-two guns each, and on the 30th in the establishment of a Department of the Navy in the executive branch of the government. George Cabot of Massachusetts was nominated by the president to be the first secretary of the navy on 1 May and confirmed by the Senate two days later; on the 11th, Cabot declined to serve because he felt unqualified. On a second try, President Adams nominated Benjamin Stoddert of Georgetown, Maryland, who also was confirmed, and who accepted, and whose first day in office was 18 June 1798.

Meanwhile, *Constitution's* outfitting went on. On 5 May, Nicholson was directed "to repair on board . . . and to lose no Time in completing, equipping, and manning her for Sea." He was to "open houses of Rendezvous in proper Places" and engage 150 able seamen and 103 midshipmen and ordinary seamen "all certified healthy by the Surgeon, for twelve Months unless sooner discharged."

Throughout May, as recruiting went on, stores were arriving in ever greater quantities for the ship: 1,792 pounds of musket and pistol balls, 2 bales of bunting, 1,755 gallons of brandy, 48 capstan bars, chaldrons of sea coal, thirty 24-pounder cannon, a grindstone, over 500 handspikes, 90 lanterns, 2,143 gallons of rum, 6 speaking trumpets, a chest of carpenter tools—the variety and numbers of items necessary to the small, seagoing community was staggering to the imagination. Congress finally agreed on "An Act more effectually to protect the commerce and coasts of the United States" on 28 May. Not indicated in the title was the fact that it was directed solely at "armed vessels sailing under authority or pretense of authority from the Republic of France." Some congressmen had hoped Great Britain would be included, but there was insufficient support for it. President Adams issued his instructions to the navy the very same day, for his captains "to seize take and bring into any Port of the United States . . . any Armed Vessels sailing under Authority . . . from France" off our coasts attacking, or waiting to attack, our merchantmen. Those taken by the French were to be recaptured when encountered. The orders were rushed to the Delaware Capes, where the sloop of war *Ganges,* a converted merchantman carrying twenty-six guns under the command of Capt. Richard Dale (John Paul Jones's first lieutenant in *Bon Homme Richard* during the Revolution), was waiting eagerly to be first out.

Congressional action made it imperative that the navy, for which so many had striven so long, get in action as soon as possible to demonstrate its worth. The secretary of war, in the absence of the new secretary of the navy, took positive steps to overcome equipment and supply deficiencies. On the 30th, Secretary McHenry took the unusual step of writing to the governor of Massachusetts for help. Noting the "failure of a Contract" for 12-pounders, he requested that fourteen or sixteen of the nineteen iron 18-pounders the Commonwealth had on Castle Island be loaned to the federal government, together with a quantity of shot. (Nicholson had inspected the guns and had suggested this course of action.) The loan was to terminate when the correct guns were available for the frigate. The governor agreed. In the meantime, however, someone located some 12-pounders and got them to the ship. *Who* is a mystery, as is the source, although Furnace Hope is a good possibility. The upshot of all this activity was that, by mid-June, *Constitution* had been armed with thirty 24-pounders from Furnace Hope, the sixteen borrowed 18-pounders, *and* the windfall of fourteen 12-pounders.

Nicholson had a reputation for being a tough, abrasive character who often acted before having all the facts pertinent to the action in hand. There is extant a letter from Stephen Higginson, General Jackson's successor as naval agent in Boston, presumably to the secretary of war, that sheds contemporary light on *Constitution*'s first commanding officer and some of his subordinate officers during this outfitting period. In it, Higginson terms the captain "a rough blustering Tar merely" but a good seaman; 2d Lt. John Cordis is "deficient at every point" and "said to be intemperate"; and as for the surgeon, William Read, "there is not a man in this town who would trust the life of a dog in his hands."

Constellation began her first cruise the last week in June. *United States* was out early in July. Because of Nicholson's unpopularity, and because those Bostonians so patriotically inclined had the option of enlisting with Sever in the eighteen-gun ship *Herald, Constitution* remained in port. On 2 July, Nicholson managed to set a few sail for the first time and moved the ship out to King's (now President's) Roads, from whence his crew would be less likely to attempt desertion, and where he completed loading powder and shot from Castle Island, and provisions from the city.

Secretary of the Navy Stoddert's first written comment concerning the frigate was made to Higginson on the 5th: "I wish I knew the exact situation of the frigate Constitution." On the 12th, he sent Nicholson his orders. He was to patrol off the coast "to secure from the Depradations of the French Cruisers, the principal Ports of New Hampshire, Massachusetts, & Rhode Island, & to pay some attention to that of New York." He was authorized to capture French armed vessels anywhere on the high seas, as well as in territorial waters. Dale in *Ganges* had the next patrol south, from Long Island to Cape Henry. Nicholson was to check at Newport, Rhode Island, at ten- to twelve-day intervals to receive any later communications. Detailed instructions relative to prizes and relations with ships of other than French registry were included.

Constitution finally was ready for sea on the 22nd. It was not an auspicious beginning. Evidence was strong that she was jinxed: It had taken three tries to launch her. Her captain had an abysmal reputation, and the officers were, in the main, drunks and libertines—and probably professionally second rate, to boot. The crew was unhappy and demoralized. Only the bright, breezy weather augured well for this, the newest warship of the young United States Navy.

TALLYING UP THE BILL

Constitution's gestation period had lasted for more than four years. In the appropriation providing initial monies for her construction, approximately $115,000 had been provided. When all was said and done, her final bill was $302,718.84 —in modern terms, a cost overrun of some 260 percent. Quite predictably, Congress had called for an inquiry into the matter even before any of the "original three" had gotten to sea.

One of Secretary McHenry's last tasks before turning over the navy reins to Benjamin Stoddert had been to respond to this inquiry. He ascribed the "extraordinary expenditures" to five causes: (1) the building of the ships in different places; (2) the size of the ships; (3) the quantity of live oak used in their construction; (4) the rise in the price of materials and labor; and (5) certain losses and contingencies. He straightforwardly admitted that "had it been determined to build the ships in one place, and in succession, instead of each in a different place, and all at the same time, it is certain that a considerable savings would have thereby accrued to the public." But, he noted, the law passed by Congress had required that the ships be ready for operations "with little delay as possible." As it was doubtful that any one city was capable of accomplishing the task, it was decided to allocate construction to widely separated sites whose local economies could support the effort. Finally, in a particularly relevant barb to the politicians, the wealth was spread in this way to a half-dozen constituencies.

Upgrading the characteristics of the ships from normally armed frigates of standard construction to heavily armed, heavily built "super frigates" was another cause of price rise. Not only were the characteristics changed, said McHenry, but the decision was made to use large quantities of live oak in lieu of white oak. Growing in a tidewater habitat, live oak had been infinitely more difficult to procure. This, in turn, was exacerbated by the fact that not all timbers cut for shipment proved to be usable.

The rising costs of labor and materials has a modern ring to it. The secretary reported that "the rise of wages alone, between the date of the first estimate and the time the frigates were launched, taking Philadelphia for the example, was from nine shillings to fifteen shillings per day; the rise in wrought iron and hemp, about forty percent; and on freight, one hundred percent."

Under the heading of "certain losses and contingencies" in McHenry's report, those which appear to have applied to *Constitution* include the loss of about fifty tons of hemp in a Boston fire, the interyard transfer of materials in 1796 when the program was cut back, and finally, the fact that timbers shipped generally were of a larger dimension than needed, upping the freight charges and increasing the work needed to fit them into the ship.

The secretary informed Congress that he considered it "unfair" to have *Constitution, Constellation,* and *United States* bear the full onus of the inflated cost. The account included expenses incurred in efforts aborted in the years since 1794, such as those relating to the expected establishment of shipyards, in the safeguarding of assembled materials, and in the commencement, stoppage, and dismemberment of three hulls. These costs, he wrote, should be considered as peculiar to the day and not to be expected whenever a ship was built.

In concluding his report, McHenry observed that "after wisdom" is always better, and offered a thought for the future: "The great delay that has occurred in the present undertaking must always be more or less experienced, when heavy ships of war are required to be suddenly built, and the Government not previously possessed of the necessary timber and materials. It is certainly an unfit time to look for these, and prepare a navy yard, when the ships are required for actual service." Pregnant words that have not always been heeded.

CHAPTER TWO

Shaky Shakedown

"Steady Breezes fine & Pleasant Weather. At 8 P.M. Took my departure from Boston Light."

The operational history of the most famous ship ever to have served in the United States Navy begins. After nearly three weeks of provisioning at anchor off Castle Island in Boston Harbor, Captain Nicholson got *Constitution* under way in the evening of 22 July 1798.

THE FIRST CAPTAIN

Samuel Nicholson, a fifty-five-year-old Marylander, was no stranger to warships. He and his brothers James and John all had seen service in the Continental Navy. Middle brother Samuel was commissioned in December 1776 and initially commanded the sloop *Dolphin*, 10, in European waters; he subsequently commanded the frigate *Deane* and captured three British sloops-of-war. When a navy was recreated in 1794, he was second in seniority among the six captains commissioned.

The first days at sea passed uneventfully in stowing gear and exercising the men at the guns. Nicholson proceeded first to the eastern end of his patrol area. On 29 July, *Constitution* spoke her second ship: the *Industry*, bound to Boston from Turks Island. Moving to the southwest, *Louisa* was spoke on the 30th, three days out of New York for "Hamburgh." The next midnight, the frigate encountered a squall during which time she "Shipt. much Water Thro' the ports."

Taking a new ship to sea can be a trying experience. The workings of the hull in a seaway can disclose improperly fastened planking, and lines can be stiff and balky. People are still learning their ways about. In *Constitution*, the first problem of note was the fact that the ship's compasses did not agree. The causes for such a condition are many; here, it was found to be that the binnacles had been assembled with iron nails. Under the direction of Midshipman James Pity, these compass stands were disassembled and refastened with copper nails.

On 6 August, *Constitution* arrived in the Newport-Block Island-Montauk Point area and patrolled those waters for two weeks, speaking a number of American merchant ships and seeing nary a Frenchman. Shaking down continued, although exercising at the great guns occurred less frequently than it had.

Nicholson brought the frigate to anchor off Fort Wolcott at Newport late on the 20th to take aboard provisions and water and to learn if there were further orders for him. There were: In a letter dated 30 July, Secretary Stoddert informed the captain that, as two additional units now were available in Boston, they would be assigned the northern patrol and Nicholson was to "[p]roceed more Southward, & consider your Cruising Ground, for the present, to extend from the Eastward of [L]ong Island, to Cape Henry" and "There will be two Revenue Cutters [*Governor Jay* and *General Greene*] . . . to cruise under your command." These were the first of many orders that would make *Constitution* a flagship.

In a second letter, dated 13 August, the secretary superseded these orders by informing Nicholson that since frigate *Constellation* (Capt. Thomas Truxtun), had been "ordered on different service," *Constitution* was to "proceed without delay to the southward, and consider your Cruising Ground to extend from Cape Henry to our Southern Extremity." As in the earlier orders, two revenue cutters were to be subordinated to him. His communications rendezvous were to be Cape Henry and Charleston, South Carolina. Nicholson got under way on the 26th, after waiting several days due to adverse winds, and cleared the eastern end of Long Island heading south at noon the next day.

The first recorded instance of *Constitution* beating to quarters for cause was on the 31st, when what appeared to be an armed ship was sighted to the northwest. The frigate was then some 174 miles east of "Cape Henery." Two warning shots brought the chase to. She proved to be an American schooner en route from Savannah to Boston.

Friday, 31 August 1798, also included the first recorded instance of disciplinary measures being carried out in the frigate. Sometime earlier, Irish seamen Dennis Carney, John Brown, and Richard Sullivan had given vent to "Mutinious [*sic*] Expressions" and had fought with the master-at-arms. As a result, at 3:00 P.M. the boatswain's mates well and truly laid twelve lashes of the cat-o'-nine-tails on each man's bare back as their shipmates bore witness.

Capt. Samuel Nicholson, first captain of USS *Constitution* and later first commandant of the Boston Navy Yard. *Official U.S. Navy photo*

The following Monday, the ship again beat to quarters, this time having sighted a ship and a schooner in company acting suspiciously. A half-hour's chase and two warning shots brought the pair to heel. The schooner was a British privateer mounting ten guns; her sailing mate, the *American,* was transporting Yankee captains whose ships had been captured and condemned by the French home to Baltimore from St. Bartholomew.

IMPROPER PRIZE

Cruising slowly southward, *Constitution* had almost reached the latitude of Charleston when, at 7:00 A.M. on 8 September, a masthead lookout reported seeing a ship dead ahead "Looking like a Cruizer [*sic*]." Nicholson crowded on sail, beat to quarters, and cleared the guns "fore and aft" for action. At 11:30, he hoisted his colors and fired a warning shot. The chase responded by hoisting the Union Jack and firing a gun to leeward (usually a signal of surrender), but she would not heave to. *Constitution* closed to within pistol shot (less than fifty yards) and Nicholson hailed her. The chase hove to and sent two boats to *Constitution*, as ordered, with her papers. As Nicholson later reported to Secretary Stoddert, "I was convinced they were pirates. . . . [T]hey said they were french—Royalists and bound from Jamaica to Philadelphia & had a commission from the British Government . . . which I believe to be Counterfeit. . . . The Ship is called Niger . . . and . . . mounts twenty four nine & twelve pounders."

By midafternoon, Nicholson had the officers and crew of *Niger* removed to *Constitution* and the latter put in chains. A prize crew was placed aboard the privateer to bring her safely into port in company with the frigate. The two ships reached Hampton Roads, Virginia, late afternoon of 12 September, and Nicholson dispatched his report. The attention to irrelevant detail and the use of rather lurid adjectives in it lead one to suspect that *Constitution*'s captain had serious doubts about the correctness of his actions and how his superiors would view it.

Constitution's arrival in Norfolk was totally unexpected. Pending the completion of appropriate arrangements ashore, the prisoners remained in chains, all linked together by a messenger, down below. Finally, on the 16th, they were herded into a revenue cutter and taken ashore, where they were incarcerated in the fort. George du Petit-Thouars, who commanded *Niger*, set forth his version of the capture and subsequent events in a statement dated the 17th, endorsed by five other officer witnesses. It is in marked contrast to Nicholson's report. Later portions of the Frenchman's statement detail instances of calculated insult to the British flag, Nicholson denying that he had seen any *Niger* log, and the theft of money from a locked trunk belonging to one of the *Niger* officers. The picture painted is one of a bunch of bullying schoolboys being given their head by a petty tyrant of like stripe. And Nicholson's assertion that he was ignorant of the existence of French Royalists serving other nations rings like a lead penny: His own volunteer midshipman Louis Alexis was exactly that.[1]

Constitution unmoored on the 17th and moved closer to Norfolk in order to reprovision. The ship settled down once more to normal routine. The carpenters busied themselves with alterations to the fore channels to improve support of the mast. On the 20th, Acting Master's Mate Ward was broken for abusing the ship's steward; and having done that, Nicholson departed for Williamsburg.

Meanwhile, at the Navy Department, Secretary Stoddert anxiously was awaiting Nicholson's report of his activities in order to set a course through the shoal of rumors he had been receiving. As Nicholson was proceeding to

Williamsburg, the secretary was writing to President Adams at his home in Quincy of his hope the prize could be added to the navy.

Nicholson's 12 September report of his actions was not received by the secretary until the evening of Saturday, the 22nd. The causes for the delay are not apparent. His report certainly did little to help his case for, after mulling it over through the weekend, Stoddert wrote again to the president on Monday and systematically picked Nicholson's story apart. The crux of his analysis was that the captain had been less than truthful and accurate in his report.

First Casualty

In *Constitution*—which Secretary Stoddert presumed had returned to her cruising area—there transpired another event that caused Nicholson more immediate, and personal, grief. The log for 21 September noted "Doctor [William] Read and Mr. Nicholson taken very sick." When the captain returned on the 24th, he found Dr. John Minson Galt of Williamsburg on board attending to the sick. Twenty-four hours later, Midshipman Samuel Nicholson, Jr., aged sixteen years, died "of the prevailing epidemic fever." He had been ill just four days. His was the first death to be recorded in *Constitution*'s log. The carpenters quickly made a coffin, and that afternoon the youth was buried in a Hampton churchyard. The ailing Dr. Read was sent ashore that evening; he died the next morning. Master's Mate Dorant, also stricken, survived. Dr. Galt remained aboard as the new surgeon.

At the seat of government, Secretary of State Pickering, now aware of the *Niger* affair and the apparent debacle, on the 28th requested that Attorney General Charles Lee ensure a speedy adjudication of the case "to vindicate the Government and fix the blame."

On 4 October, Secretary Stoddert finally learned that, as of 27 September, *Constitution* still was at Norfolk. He was, he told the president, mortified and was ordering Nicholson "to proceed instantly to sea." But the latter had decided that going to sea was what he ought to do without prodding from his superiors. On the 28th and 29th of September, he had retrieved his men from *Niger*. After a week of calms and adverse winds, *Constitution* finally cleared Cape Henry, bound for her cruising station, the revenue cutter *Virginia* in company. The secretary's scolding letter was dated 8 October and so largely was overtaken by events, although it directed Nicholson to terminate the cruise at Boston "about the 20th Novr."

Between 8 and 19 October, the two "cruisers" spoke but nine ships, none of them French. Nicholson took advantage of the situation by resuming efforts to correct deficiencies in his new ship, both material and operational. He had the carpenters rig and install new topgallant and royal masts at the fore and the main. The sailmakers were set to stitching new topsails. The spritsail, that troublesome appendage on the bowsprit, Nicholson had struck below, never to be used again. After the 15th, sloop-of-war *Baltimore* (Isaac Phillips), 18, was a member of the patrol.

On the 19th and 20th, *Constitution* stood off and on near the Charleston bar. Nicholson brought her to anchor there at 10:00 A.M. on the 21st. Provisions were ordered from the city, and the arrival of a schooner full of water casks on the 23rd put an end to four days of short rations.

Baltimore and *Constitution* got under way early on the 24th on orders to convoy eleven merchantmen to Havana. Everything went routinely until 6:30 A.M. on the 28th, when *Constitution* sprung her bowsprit. All hands quickly were called to secure it. In consultation with his officers, Nicholson decided to head north and leave *Baltimore* to see the ships safely to Havana.

Squally weather appeared before the day was out to bedevil the frigate as she sought safety. As the weather increased, fewer and fewer sails could be set because of the weakness of the top-hamper. To add to the problem, it was found that the fish on the foremast also was sprung. At times, the bowsprit worked dangerously, threatening to wrench itself and the bows to pieces. The weather moderated somewhat on the 29th, but the squalls returned with the dawn the next day. The carpenters were busy raising the height of the hatch coamings to help reduce the amount of water getting below. Still worsening conditions on the 31st led to the securing of all gun ports.

The afternoon of that last day of October found *Constitution* laboring badly, and after attempting to scud before the blast, the captain resigned himself to heaving to and riding it out. At 3:00 P.M. "James Johnson Odd. Seaman was lost overboard by Accident but it was impossible to give him any assistance and poor fellow he found a watry grave." At the beginning of the evening watch, the gale seemed to abate.

For the next week, the frigate struggled northward. The crew was on constant call, adjusting the rigging to hold the damaged spars in place. Frictions grew. On 7 November, an altercation in the main rigging resulted in James Bates falling to the deck and being badly injured. At 4:00 that afternoon, Robert Sharkey was punished with twelve lashes for having caused Bates's fall. Bates died at 5:00 the next morning and was buried at sea, *Constitution* then being about a hundred miles east-southeast of Cape Ann.

First Cruise Ends

At noon on 10 November 1798, Nicholson anchored his ship in six fathoms of water south of George's Island in Nantasket Roads east of Boston. The first cruise of *Constitution* was done. It had lasted 111 days and had been completely inglorious.

If the voyage was over, the affair of the *Niger* was not. On 22 October, as *Constitution* was reprovisioning off Charleston, Secretary of State Pickering was writing to the U.S. District Attorney for Virginia, Thomas Nelson, that "the eagerness of Captain Nicholson to procure a condemnation savoured of rapacity. And in the very letter in which he informed of the death of his son (the consequence of this unfortunate capture) his thoughts seemed wholly engrossed with this prize and the means of ensuring, if possible, a condemnation. . . . I am inclined to think that there is not another captain in the American Navy who . . . would have imagined the Niger a subject of capture." Pickering called for a trial to assess conflicting claims—Nicholson's for prize money and the British Minister's concerning *Niger*'s British identity—and direct appropriate settlement. It was quickly done: Payment of $11,000 in damages was made to the British by the United States.

Nicholson moved *Constitution* into King's Roads on 11 November, and preparations began for the removal of the damaged bowsprit despite signs of an impending gale. At 11:00 A.M. on the 16th, the weather having abated, the bowsprit was hoisted out and towed to George's Island, where the cap could be removed. One-third of the Marine detachment, as well, was put ashore for small arms practice.

Repairs and normal ship's routine proceeded apace until the 20th, when another gale bore down on the ship, making life miserable with blowing snow and pelting hail. The storm screamed about the ship for twenty-four hours, bringing all topside work to a halt.

Personnel Problems

The poor morale and lack of leadership in *Constitution* boiled to the surface the next day in a series of unseemly incidents. Acting Master's Mate Ward was placed in irons for "Speaking Seditious Words tendg. to Stir up the Minds of the People." James Connell, the boatswain, likewise was clapped in irons for "abusing

Mr. Cordis 2d, Lieut. for Inspecting the Store Room." The storeroom was the boatswain's particular responsibility, and Cordis, erratic and often drunk, presumably had gone there without taking the trouble to have the boatswain along. This undoubtedly was not the first time Cordis had acted in this manner, but this time Connell had reached his limit. In a third incident, Nicholson himself ordered Midshipman Pity arrested and confined to his stateroom for "unofficer-like Conduct." In the absence of further elaboration in the records, it appears that Pity's offense involved nothing more than an excess of the capriciousness characteristic of teenagers. All three offenders evidently were dismissed from further service in the frigate about 1 December. But Pity, ashore in Boston, received reinstatement orders on the 22nd and, after performing several official errands in town, repaired on board five days later.

On 26 November, the secretary wrote to Nicholson expressing the hope that the ship would again be ready for sea in a week or so, and stressing that the captain should ensure having "sufficient quantity of Ball" and that his powder was good. Furthermore, Stoddert forwarded the regulations concerning the delivery of crewmembers' pay (up to half of it) to designated dependents, and directed Nicholson to attend to it. (He had neglected to do so when *Constitution* first sailed in July, and a number of families had been left destitute.)

Sailing Master Nathaniel Haraden reported aboard for duty on 1 December, the one positive event to occur in *Constitution*'s wardroom during this unhappy time. He replaced Charles Swain, to whom Nicholson had refused to deliver his warrant as sailing master. This native of Massachusetts would serve in the ship until late 1804 and would provide posterity with many of the intimate details of the frigate's service during the decisive part of the Barbary War.

Secretary Stoddert penned Nicholson's new orders on the 5th. He was directed to "proceed without delay . . . to Prince Ruperts' bay in the Island of Dominica, where it is probable you will find Captain Barry of the Frigate United States; under whose command you will then be."

The secretary's hopes and urgings notwithstanding, Nicholson was nowhere near ready to sail. On the 8th, the new bowsprit was towed out to the ship and taken aboard. Later that same day it snowed, heralding a period of generally very cold weather that would hamper the rerigging of the ship, an evolution that begins at the bowsprit and works aft. It snowed again on the 9th and on the 11th. Throughout the period, stores were being brought aboard and efforts made to improve the ship's trim. Finally, on the 25th the crew began clearing the ship for sea.

If the ship was nearing operational readiness, the wardroom officers were coming apart at the seams. Second Lieutenant Cordis finally exceeded even Nicholson's patience and was discharged "for oppression and disobedience of orders" on the day before *Constitution* sailed, to await the pleasure of a court-martial. That same day, First Lt. Charles C. Russell* and 2d Lt. of Marines William Amory "left the ship and went on shore . . . without giving any reason why" and were declared discharged by Nicholson. The captain, it seems, had denied them their commissions on the grounds that they needed further experience. In any event, Russell was made lieutenant commandant of the ship *Herald*, 18, less than a month later, and Amory subsequently served in *Constitution* again during the Quasi-War after Nicholson's detachment.

Early on the morning of the 29th, *Constitution* was under way on her second cruise. Within a few hours, she was in the midst of a howling gale; driving snow made watch standing a misery. And it soon became apparent that the efforts to correct her trim had been inadequate, for she "plunged and rowled" and shipped great amounts of water. The number fifteen gun port lid to starboard, in Nicholson's cabin, was stove in; all the gun port lids leaked. A fire couldn't be kept in the camboose, so the crew was victualed with bread and cheese. Two gallons of rum were expended in one day just to sustain the "Wheelmen." Life became a wet, lurching misery for all hands, above and below, and stayed that way until the closing hours of 1798. But in one twenty-one-hour period the ship averaged ten to twelve knots despite her poor trim.

Moderating weather welcomed in the new year and made it possible to restore some semblance of order in the storm-tossed ship. On the morning of 2 January 1799, Nicholson had ship's company mustered and the Articles of War read—the first opportunity to do so since leaving Boston. It also was time to reorganize his shattered wardroom, and he took the opportunity to announce his new appointments. Lts. Richard C. Beale and Isaac Hull, originally the third and fourth, moved up two numbers. Philip Jarvis became acting third and Joseph Torrey, until then the gunner, was named acting fourth. Sgt. Cotton Thayer became the second lieutenant of Marines. James Moore, who had been enlisted as a seaman just the preceding July, was appointed the ship's gunner.

As *Constitution* continued her way southward, a surprised secretary of the navy learned that she had been in Boston as recently as Christmas day. Nicholson

* For clarity, the numerical adjective denoting a naval lieutenant's *position* in the ship is spelled out; that forming part of a Marine lieutenant's *rank* is digitized.

certainly must have been sensitive to the secretary's growing dissatisfaction in deciding to sail when he did despite his officer personnel problems.

Nicholson's string of misfortunes continued to plague him. On the afternoon of 6 January, someone noticed that the foremast tended suspiciously to starboard. Closer inspection revealed it to be sprung fourteen feet above the spar deck. In short order, sail was shortened and the foretopgallant mast sent down. The injured mast was stayed so that no further damage could occur before the boatswain's and carpenter's crews could make temporary repairs. Working until late the following morning, they skillfully fished and woulded the injured stick.

For the next week or so, life aboard followed the normal routine. As a part of the crew cleaned and fumigated between decks, others were busy making splinter netting to be strung over the quarterdeck in battle to prevent falling spars and rigging from injuring personnel there. Following its completion and trial installation, awnings for inport use were cut and sewn. On the afternoon of the 11th, a "crossing the line" ceremony was performed with great hilarity "Vizt. Blackg. Ducking Shaving &c. which among 400 People produced a Set of Devils equal to any ever Seen." The occasion was the fact that the ship had reached the Tropic of Cancer, not the Equator. On the 10th, 11th, and 14th, the crew was exercised at the great guns and with small arms. After the last exercise, the guns were "loaded for Service," for they were now near their destination in the Leeward Islands.

BUNGLED CAPTURE

Early in the afternoon of the 15th, in fine weather, two sail were sighted to the northwest. Nicholson ordered *Constitution* in chase. As the first dogwatch was taking over, one of the strangers was seen to be a warship, but her sole response to both American and British recognition signals was to crowd on more sail. Nicholson accepted the challenge, believing her to be the French frigate *L'Insurgente*, 36, and clearing for action as he went. Rain squalls complicated the chase as the sun set and caused the lee guns to be bowsed in, but intermittent contact was maintained until seven bells of the evening watch, when the stranger was lost to sight.

When Hull took the deck for the midwatch, *Constitution* still was standing to the north-northwest, reluctant to give over the chase. At twenty minutes into the new day, contact was regained. Nicholson bore up and fired two warning guns, to which the chase responded by wearing around to the south and loosing more sail. Nicholson followed suit, fired two more guns, and soon brought her to heel. She proved to be *Spencer*, a British merchant that had been on passage from Shields, England, to Barbados at the time she was captured and made prize to *L'Insurgente*. In effect, *Spencer* was a French vessel. Nicholson removed the French prize crew to *Constitution* and sent an officer and nine of his sailors to handle her.

But Nicholson did not gloat over his prize this time. In fact, he wondered if he hadn't again blundered. Study of his orders reminded him that he was not authorized to capture anything other than French or French-captured *American* ships. At 9:00 that evening (the 16th), "bro't too and took out of the Ship Spencer the Officers & Men we Sent on board her." He returned the Frenchmen to the ship and gave her up because "it was tho't prudent." For the second time in five months, Nicholson demonstrated that he had no clear understanding of his orders.

The West Indies *Author's collection*

Parting company with *Spencer*, whose Frenchmen took her to Guadeloupe, Nicholson sailed for Dominica. Rounding the south end of that island, he arrived off Prince Rupert's Bay at 9:00 A.M. on the 17th and immediately went in his gig to report to Commodore Barry in *United States*, *Constitution*'s sister ship. The captain returned to his waiting frigate at 4:30 P.M. His orders were to proceed on patrol to the north and east of Dominica.

For the next four days, *Constitution* conducted an uneventful patrol, sometimes in company with *George Washington*, 32, and sometimes with *United States*. These frigates really were much too big for the work of trying to catch swift, small privateers. They were forced to provide the "outer screen" against the advent of similar French units while the brigs and schooners pursued their elusive quarry inshore. On the 21st, there was brief excitement when the main topgallant yard carried away, but the damage soon was repaired.

The weather turned squally on the 23rd, and it became evident that the woulding and fishes on the injured foremast were working loose. Shortly thereafter, "Carried away our Main T. Mast Cross Tree & Main T. Mast Stay." *Constitution*'s whole top hamper was in danger of collapse. Quickly, the topgallant yards were sent down to reduce the strain. At 4:00 P.M., a signal was made to the commodore alerting him of the frigate's plight, to which he responded by ordering *Constitution* into Prince Rupert's Bay, under escort of *United States*.

At 4:00 A.M. on the 24th, Ordinary Seaman Cornelius Howard died of "a putrid and nervous fever." He was buried at sea at four bells of the morning watch. Deaths occurred often at sea, of course, but note is taken of Howard because he was black. Despite the Department's injunction against the enlistment of Negroes and mulattos, he, at least, had been enlisted on 19 July 1798, and so had been one of *Constitution*'s "plank owners" (original crew members).

As *Constitution* worked her way into Prince Rupert's Bay on the afternoon of the 28th, her jib boom carried away, leaving her a bedraggled sight as she anchored by her best bower in seventeen fathoms of water. Nicholson went immediately on board *United States* to apprise Barry of his problems in detail and to make a formal request for a board of survey. This board, conducting its inspection at first light the next morning, found the foremast serviceable, with repairs, and work began immediately "to expedite the Business."

One week was spent in effecting the repairs. At the same time, water was taken aboard, stores shifted and more ballast jettisoned to improve trim and lessen draft, and the hull was painted and blackened. Despite the welter of activity, the crew found occasion to show their low morale. Seaman James Carey was given twelve lashes on the 29th for "Striking his Superior Officer on Shore." The next day, six others were made to run the gauntlet of their shipmates for being thieves. William Brook (or Brooks) received twelve lashes for fighting on the following morning, while five others each received like amounts for "Leaving the boat without leave." At least ten of these thirteen men had been aboard since the ship first sailed, and one was a master's mate.

Barry returned from a brief patrol on the morning of 1 February, and almost before his anchor had set was ordering *Constitution* and the other ships present (*George Washington* and *Merrimack,* 28) to prepare for sea. Between 3:00 and 4:00 P.M., the men-of-war, together with seven American merchant ships to be convoyed by *Merrimack,* made sail and stood out of the bay. At two bells in the night watch, Nicholson parted company from the rest to resume patrolling in the vicinity of Guadeloupe.

Constitution patrolled the area until the 21st. During these three weeks, she went in chase but eight times; four proved to be British, two were Americans, and two eluded her. Four crew members died, one having fallen overboard from the main topgallant yard. Nicholson continued to be plagued by spar problems. On the 16th, the recently installed jib boom was found to be sprung. And three days later, "found the Bowsprit to work very much owing to the Badness of the Bobstays & Gammoning." A week passed before he could get out his flying jib boom and make use of jibs and fore staysails. If Nicholson's first problem with his forward spars stemmed from poor materials used in the ship's construction, most of his subsequent ones might be laid to indifferent repairs by a disgruntled crew.

The frigate's stay in Prince Rupert's Bay on the 21st lasted just 9.5 hours. Further efforts were made to set up the gammoning while a large detail was busy getting more fresh water on board. On this occasion, the crew filled 40 butts, 70 gang casks, and 4 leaguers—some 16,000 gallons, or 66.7 tons—in less than 8 hours.

Constitution returned to her patrol station for another three-week stint. It differed little from the earlier one—eight chases, of which three eluded her close to shore—except that it was blessedly free of troubles with spars or rigging. In fact, that effective repairs finally had been made clearly was demonstrated. Early in the evening of 1 March, a strange sail was sighted bearing northwest ½ north, and the chase began. The frigate was then about twenty-five miles northeast of Deseada Island. At 7:00 P.M. contact was lost, but at 7:30 the contact was seen standing *toward Constitution.* Nicholson immediately brought his ship to and cleared for action. In the course of doing so, "Mr. Jno. Hancock (Boatswain) was Accidentally shot thro' the Head with a pistol & expired Immediately." The confusion this bizarre incident undoubtedly caused had no lasting effect, for the chase turned out to be HMS *Santa Margaretta*, 36, and no engagement ensued. Nicholson sent an officer to the Briton to exchange private signals so they would know one another during the night. The boatswain was buried with appropriate honors at 10:30 P.M.

A RACE WON

At two bells of the next forenoon watch, Captain Parker of *Santa Margaretta* called upon Nicholson. In less than an hour, they exchanged pleasantries and agreed to a sailing duel. At 10:00 A.M., both ships were under way once more. The log proudly but laconically noted the outcome thusly: "[A]t 3 PM parted company with the Santa Margaretta. Capt Parker after sailing in company 16 hours . . . being sensible of Inability."

Thus *Constitution* won her first race against a peer. It appears to have been the same race whose winning early writers credited to Capt. Silas Talbot and Lieutenant Hull. Hull was there, all right, but let's give the devil his due: This was one thing that Samuel Nicholson did right.

In the main, the days of this patrol passed slowly. The crew was kept busy cleaning and painting, and the victory over the British frigate gave them a unity hitherto unknown. Various units of the American squadron occasionally were seen and spoke—*Santa Margaretta* again, too. In addition to the unfortunate boatswain, Seaman Philip Paine fell overboard from the mizzen topsail yard and drowned. On the 5th, his clothing and personal gear, together with that belonging to eight others who had died earlier in the cruise, were sold at auction at the main mast to improve the lot of some of their surviving mates. On the 14th, *Constitution* anchored once again in Prince Rupert's Bay in the company of *United States, Herald,* brigs *Pickering* and *Eagle,* schooner *Scammell,* and a stores ship—a major portion of our navy of the day.

Back in Philadelphia, Secretary Stoddert was busy penning two documents that would affect directly Nicholson and *Constitution.* The first was a circular to all commanding officers that must have made the captain blanch when he saw it. It was intended to clarify and emphasize the authority of commanding officers in making captures. As a preamble to its operative sections, it said point blank: "A Misconstruction of his authority by Captain Nicholson in relation to a Vessel of friendly Nations, captured by the French renders it necessary that I should make some explanatory observations on the Subject." In the second missive, Stoddert wrote directly to Barry "to order, to Boston without delay, the Constitution." Once the ship was in Boston, the secretary could remove Nicholson to a less sensitive post.

The entire squadron spent the six-day inport period watering, taking on supplies from chartered stores ship *Polly*, and making minor repairs. Nicholson used the time to set up his rigging and ensure continued support for his wounded foremast. Barry busied himself reporting to Secretary Stoddert on the squadron's activities and his plans for the future. Coincidentally, these two gentlemen's letters, dated but one day apart, show a remarkable unanimity in that one saw the need to have the heavier ships off the U.S. East Coast in the spring and the other announced his intention to place them there for the same reason. Lt. Robert W. Hamilton of *United States* transferred to *Constitution* as third lieutenant at about this time to bolster her inexperienced wardroom.

Barry got his squadron under way at 10:00 A.M. on the 20th in squally weather. Proceeding slowly to the northward, he spoke a British war sloop escorting two transports on the 21st. The next morning, *United States, Constitution, Merrimack,* and *Eagle* came to off Basse-Terre, Guadeloupe, in order to determine French maritime forces present. What were thought to be two frigates were seen at anchor among lesser shipping. After noon, Barry sailed his ships "down the bay" for a better look: Ten schooners, all armed, and seven sloops, three armed, were counted on his reconnaissance. No reaction was noted from the French, and the American squadron moved back out to the southwest before turning northward and eastward to a position beyond Antigua on Sunday, the 24th. At the end of the afternoon watch that day, *Constitution* was detached to resume her previous station while Barry and the rest proceeded northward.

PROBLEM CAPTAIN

On the 26th, back in Philadelphia, Stoddert was writing once again to Boston Navy Agent Higginson concerning the navy's needs as they related to that area. But Capt. Samuel Nicholson was very much on his mind: "I am afraid to trust him with a separate command.—and to keep such a Frigate as his under the command of Barry . . . is to make her of no more use or importance than a Ship of 20 Guns." The man had to be transferred.

The next day, Nicholson once again did something right: Sighting two strange sail to windward, he gave chase and four hours later recaptured the American sloop *Neutrality* of New Haven, which was then a French prize. Removing the Frenchmen, he sent an officer and five seamen to sail her to "Martinico," then in British hands. Another chase on the 28th turned out to be British, and a third on the 29th and 30th was given over.

Proper Prize

The carpenter's mates' busywork building an eight-oared cutter was the principal activity for two days before *Constitution* once again went in chase at 9:00 A.M. on 2 April. At 10:00 A.M., the chase tacked southward, and then northward a half hour later. She was estimated to be sixteen miles off. Shortly after noon, the quarry was seen to lose her main topmast, but she continued to run. All afternoon the race continued. At 6:30 P.M., she was last seen "East by South 9 Miles." Nicholson ordered the frigate to maintain a position to windward of the chase's likely course until midnight, then steer west by south. His estimate of the chase's intentions was good, for at 5:30 the next morning contact was regained at twelve miles and the race resumed. As the day wore on, the breezes moderated, and in the light and variable airs Nicholson resorted to "wetting the Sails with firemen and Engines." (*Constitution* carried two portable "fire engines," which were pumped in much the same manner as an old kitchen pump.) A gun at 5:00 P.M. finally brought the thirty-two-hour chase to an end. In hand was the French prize *Carteret*, late His British Majesty's Packet. Twelve Frenchmen came aboard the frigate as prisoners, replaced by an equal number of Americans. Nicholson took his prize in tow and headed for Martinique. He must have been a happy man: two good prizes in a week.

Constitution arrived off St. Pierre, Martinique, on the morning of the 5th and sent *Carteret* in to be placed in the custody of merchant John Gay, who would act as Nicholson's agent. All day long, the big frigate stood off and on, awaiting the return of its prize crew. Finally, the boat returned at 6:00 P.M. The boat officer, Hull, reported that seamen Thomas Jones, Edward West, and John Connally apparently had deserted. (West had been one of those punished for "leaving the boat without leave" on 31 January.) Nicholson made sail and headed back to his station.

On the 12th, *Constitution* returned to Martinique to pick up a convoy of seventeen sail bound for Prince Rupert's Bay and points northward. All arrived safely at mid-morning the next day. Barry in *United States* arrived on the 14th. For a few days, ships' crews were busy watering, scrubbing hammocks, painting, and generally getting squared away for sea again.

United States, Constitution, and *Eagle* went out on the afternoon of the 17th, escorting a convoy of thirty American merchantmen. In light and variable airs, they made their way northward, *United States* in the van, *Constitution* in the rear (and occasionally towing the slowest civilians), and *Eagle* the busy terrier, sniffing at every scent along the way. The number of merchantmen waxed and waned during the next six days as the convoy wended its way past St. Kitts, thence to St. Thomas, and passing north of Santa Cruz. Taking his departure from the northeast point of Puerto Rico, at 5:30 on the afternoon of the 23rd, Nicholson "spoke with the Como. and cheer'd him . . . and made sail with Convoy in Co." He was homeward bound, with seventeen merchants to protect.

The days passed uneventfully as they sailed northward. As she had done before, *Constitution* occasionally towed a laggard to ensure the unity of the convoy. On the 24th, Nicholson reduced the crew's meat allowance by one-third when much of the beef and pork remaining on board was found to have spoiled. On the 26th, two British ships in the convoy left it for Bermuda and Nova Scotia, considering themselves to be clear of dangerous waters. At 8:30 A.M. on the 29th, Nicholson dispersed the convoy for the same reason and headed for Boston alone.

NEW CAPTAIN SOUGHT

As the ship proceeded northward under easy sail, Secretary Stoddert was busy arranging for the ship's early refitting for another cruise—and for a new commanding officer. On 2 May, he wrote to Talbot: "The Frigates United States and Constitution, are both expected to arrive in the course of fortnight . . . and you will be called upon to take the Command of one of them."

At sea, *Constitution* continued her uneventful voyage to Boston. On the 8th, a freshening gale caused her topgallant yards to be sent down as she continued under close-reefed topsail. By the afternoon, she could do little more than lie to, some seventy-five miles southeast by south of Nantucket Shoal. The gale abated considerably by the following dawn, so that the foresail and foretopsail could be set. At 6:00 that evening, the topgallant masts were swayed up. At 7:00 "Pitching into a heavy head beat Sea. Sprung our fore Mast in the wake of the partners on the gun deck." Working through the night, the crew got the situation under control. By 6:00 the morning of the 10th, a hawser had been run from the mast head to the main hatch to support the mast enough to permit setting the foresail. For the third time in the cruise, the carpenters were employed in fishing and woulding the foremast. Working her way northward around Cape Cod, *Constitution* endured two days of adverse winds and calms in Cape Cod Bay before finally reaching Nantasket Roads and anchoring at 5:00 P.M. on the 14th. Thirty minutes later, Nicholson went ashore, no doubt relieved that the blighted cruise was at an end and yet anxious about what the future might hold for him.

In Philadelphia, Secretary Stoddert had hit upon a scheme that would remove Nicholson from sea duty without causing a stir. Congress, in its last session, had approved the addition of six 74-gun ships of the line and six 18-gun brigs to the navy. Senior officers had to be appointed to supervise the gathering of materials and the construction of these ships. Nicholson already had experience of this sort in overseeing the building of the prototype heavy frigate *Constitution*. Who would be better fitted to undertake a similar task with another, larger design than he? The secretary penned his orders on the 15th, citing Nicholson's year of sea duty and separation from his family and telling him that he would suffer no reduction in pay upon coming ashore. What a sugar-coated pill! No loss of pay, and the implication that he would command the liner when she was commissioned, just as he had done *Constitution*.

It was never to be, however, for the building of ships of the line was canceled before any were fairly begun. Nicholson became the first commandant of the Boston Navy Yard, built the commandant's house, and never built or repaired a ship in the yard in the twelve years he was there before going galley west.

CHAPTER THREE

Talbot Takes the Helm

PERSONNEL PROBLEMS

On 15 May 1799, Secretary Stoddert wrote to Captain Talbot, confirming his intention to have Talbot take command of *Constitution*. Talbot, a native of Dighton, Massachusetts, was forty-eight years old. He had behind him an unimpeachable record of service to his country. He began the Revolution as a militia captain in Rhode Island. Joining the Continental Army in 1776, he served first in command of a fire ship on the Hudson River, with which he attempted to set fire to HMS *Renown*, 50. Severely burned in the act, he nonetheless got away. For this, he was promoted to major. Late in 1777, in New Jersey, he was wounded in the wrist and hip while assisting in the defense of Fort Mifflin, on the Delaware River. On 27 October 1778, with the small coaster *Hawke*, 2, he captured the British tender *Pigot*, 3, for which he was promoted to lieutenant colonel and awarded a sword by Rhode Island. In 1779, in command of the sloop *Argo*, 12, he captured at least ten enemy ships, including privateers *Lively*, 12; *King George, Dragon*, 14; *Hannah*, 14; and *Dublin*. Finally, on 17 September 1779, he was commissioned a captain in the Continental Navy; then, because no ships were available, he took command of the Rhode Island privateer *General Washington*, 20. After two captures, he lost this ship to a British squadron and was captured and imprisoned until the war's end. He had been wounded a total of thirteen times (five balls he carried for life) and received a pension of $300–400 a year. A tall, attractive man, Talbot was said by his contemporaries to have been zealous, dignified, a "thorough" disciplinarian, and "although impulsive by temperament, his will was firm and consistent."

With the advent of the new navy, Talbot was commissioned as the third senior captain, after Barry and Nicholson. In accepting his appointment, Talbot resigned his seat in the House of Representatives as congressman from New York. During the summer of 1798, as the disagreement with France boiled over and Congress acted to expand the navy, merchant John Brown of Rhode Island offered his ship *George Washington* for conversion to a man-of-war. On 29 August, Secretary Stoddert wrote to Talbot requesting he go to Providence from New York, where he was supervising the completion of the frigate *John Adams*, 28, to inspect the *George Washington*, make a recommendation as to its utility as a warship, and provide an estimate of the cost of conversion.

This Talbot did. On 20 September, Stoddert again wrote to Talbot to advise him that *George Washington* would be acquired and to request him to return to Providence as naval agent to oversee its conversion to a 24-gun ship.

Throughout the turbulent months of expansion, "expediency" was the watchword. Frictions resulted from the almost willy-nilly issuance of captains' commissions. These frictions were particularly strong in the cases of Talbot and Richard Dale, both of whom had been senior to Thomas Truxtun in 1794, but because he had been lucky enough to have been assigned to one of the frigates completed (*Constellation*), they now found themselves his junior. Strongly worded correspondence ensued, with the harassed secretary trying to mollify the feisty contenders and retain such men of value in the service. In December, he managed to keep Talbot in service with the "plum" of commanding *Constitution*.

REFIT

At 5:00 P.M. on 14 May 1799, *Constitution* anchored in Nantasket Roads, Boston's outer harbor. Finally, on Sunday the 19th, *Constitution* was able to enter King's Road and anchor off Castle Island just before midnight. Nicholson shortly had in hand orders from the secretary to pay off his old crew, settle all accounts, send out the lieutenants recruiting—and be prepared to be relieved. In line with Stoddert's desire to have the ship ready for further service as soon as possible, Nicholson created a flurry of activity, made preparations for watering ship, overhauling rigging and sails, landing powder for rotation, and sending out the recruiters.

Talbot's formal orders were issued on 28 May. Aboard *Constitution*, postvoyage repairs and paying off the year-old crew were going slowly. The sails had been unbent and the running rigging unreeved, and all had been sent ashore at Castle Island for overhaul. On the 24th, the powder was placed in the fort's magazine, and the casks, leaguers, and butts empty of water landed on Spectacle

A wounded veteran of both Continental Army and Navy service, Capt. Silas Talbot proved to be the exemplary leader *Constitution* needed early in her career. Following his unfortunate early resignation from the navy, he dabbled in land speculation in Kentucky. He died of old age at New York on 30 June 1813. *Official U.S. Navy photo*

Island. Monday, the 27th, found one party caulking the quarterdeck under cloudy skies as another prepared to raise shears at the plaguey foremast. Three days later, and almost two weeks after her return, *Constitution*'s disenchanted crew finally began to be paid off. The foremast was got out on the last day of the month and later was towed ashore at Hartt's shipyard.

CHANGE OF COMMAND

"Moderate breezes and cloudy" noted the log in the entry for noon, 4 June. At 1:00, Talbot came aboard. All hands were assembled and heard him read his commission as *Constitution*'s new commander. Nicholson then formally resigned his command. The two captains then went below to the cabin, where Nicholson turned over the logs and journals, the magazine keys, and such unexecuted orders as were in his possession. The crew went back to work, caulkers resuming their tattoo upon the spar deck, another party of seamen receiving and stowing boatswain's stores below. At 6:00 P.M., Nicholson and Talbot went ashore.

Preparations on the ship proceeded slowly, recruiting even more so. The new foremast was stayed adequately enough by the 12th to permit the return of the shears to Hartt's. On the 14th, the fore top was emplaced. The next day, twenty Marines were received on board. Talbot gave as one reason for the lack of progress the fact that he was anchored in an open bay some four miles from the source of supplies. The foretopmast was restepped on the 17th; the caulking was completed a day later.

Beginning on the 20th, and almost daily through 14 July, the ship's log records the arrival of endless supplies, listed in such arcane and varied quantities as leaguers, butts, gang casks, firkins, puncheons, tierces, pipes, hogsheads, chaldrons, bags, and buckets. Time has blurred the precise amounts involved (indeed, many never were standardized). But discernible in the inventory are 18 tons of salt beef and a like quantity of pork, over 37,500 gallons of water, 5,880 pounds of flour, almost 3,000 gallons of rum, nearly as much vinegar, 250 gallons of molasses, and about 20 tons of coal for the camboose. Other supplies included bread, rice, beans, raisins, pease (peas), candles, potatoes, oil, butter, cheese, and a barrel of "suett."

With the passing of time, Secretary Stoddert came to realize that his plan to have *Constitution* patrol the Cayenne coast and the West Indies before the hurricane season began was not possible. His thoughts perhaps turned upon memories of the Revolution and the striking psychological effects of the operations of Gustavus Conyngham and John Paul Jones in European waters, for on 25 June he wrote to President Adams concerning a new plan of operation. He was thinking, he said, of having *Constitution* and *United States* sail together to Cape Clear, Ireland, then head south to patrol off the French, Portuguese, and Spanish coasts before heading to Caribbean waters and returning home in November.

THE NAVY'S FIRST COURT-MARTIAL

During the preceding December, it will be remembered, Second Lt. John Cordis had been ordered from the ship by Nicholson as a result of alleged intemperance, sleeping on watch, and improper punishment of his inferiors. Charges to this effect were forwarded to the secretary of the navy, but the sailing of the frigate shortly thereafter had prevented assembly of a court-martial to try the case. But at long last, at 8:00 A.M. on 27 June 1799, the signal was hoisted to assemble the court, the first to be held in the navy under the two-month-old Articles of War.

At 10:00 it convened; Talbot sat as president. Capt. James Sever, prospective commander of the frigate *Congress*, building at Portsmouth, New Hampshire, Capt. George Little of the frigate *Boston*, Lt. Cmdt. Cyrus Talbot, and Lt. Michael Titcomb were members. Noahdiah Morris, Captain Talbot's clerk, sat as judge advocate *pro tem.* Nicholson appeared in person as prosecutor.

After a number of the prosecutor's proffered documents were rejected, Nicholson paraded a series of witnesses whose testimony indicated that Cordis was not a model officer. Many of the witnesses were vague in their recollections, and some were such obvious toadies to Nicholson that their words were damaging to his case. Cordis's defense keyed on the fact that the majority of prosecution witnesses were beholden to the captain in one way or another. In a surprise move, Cordis called Nicholson as a witness and led him to admit he could not provide a single instance when the lieutenant had failed to do his duty.

The court did not deliberate long. The verdict: that, although Cordis had given a man a beating (but not "cruelly") in violation of regulations, he had done so on orders from the first lieutenant and was therefore acquitted; and that the charge of sleeping on watch was not supported by the evidence. The court was dissolved at 9:00 P.M. on 28 June. Nicholson once again had demonstrated his ineptitude and inability to earn the respect and loyalty of subordinates. Cordis, concerning whom there are many indications that the actions charged were completely typical of his character, survived in the service until 1801, when the peacetime reduction of the navy ended his career.

PERSONALITIES AGAIN

Outside the captain's cabin, the frigate was a beehive of activity. Blacking the yards and tarring rigging required two days, then the running rigging reeved. Three days were spent in painting the lower parts and blacking the hull. (Above the yellow ocher gun streak, the ship was painted black; below it, it was smeared with a mixture of pitch and lamp black.) Offsetting all this very dirty work, about half the growing crew at a time was set ashore for the day on Spectacle Island to wash their clothing and themselves. A spare main topmast, three topgallant masts, and three topgallant yards were swayed aboard and stowed on the skid beams between the nested boats in the waist.

On 3 July, Secretary Stoddert wrote Talbot's orders, telling him only to call at Hampton Roads for further orders, and hoping *Constitution* could be at sea within a week. It is curious that the secretary said nothing about a European cruise, as it could have affected the ship's load-out.

The log entry for that day records, "At 12 fired a salute of 16 guns in celebration of the glorious 4th of July. The 16 guns represented one for each state in the Union, Vermont, Kentucky, and Tennessee have joined the original thirteen." It was the first of many such national birthday salutes *Constitution* would fire.

Talbot continued to ready *Constitution* for sea as quickly as possible. The carpenters were employed cutting a hatchway in the spar deck forward of the ship's wheel in order to improve communication with the gun deck. All of the ship's sails, new or refurbished, were brought aboard and stored. The 'tween decks' bulkheads were whitewashed. Watering, necessarily, continued on an almost daily basis.

The crew was nearing its sailing number of 398, and the lieutenants were busy making quartering and stationing assignments. And discipline was meted out: On the 19th, Seaman Luther Eddy was punished with twelve lashes for theft and for having drawn his knife on a "Centry." The latter offense may have represented a thwarted desertion. Indeed, Seaman James Watson swam away successfully the very next night, one of twenty-one to desert in seven weeks.

West Indies Flagship

At 2:00 A.M. on the 23rd, with a moderate breeze from the west-southwest, Talbot got *Constitution* under way and began working his way to sea. Once clear, the frigate headed for Hampton Roads.

It proved to be a long voyage thanks to adverse or fitful winds and the effects of the Gulf Stream. *Constitution* actually reached the latitude of her destination in one week, then was forced by nature into a giant "zig-zag" that took her first as far south as Cape Hatteras and north to the Delaware capes in order to make her westing. Talbot exercised his crew at the great guns and small arms three times and read them the Articles of War. The day after leaving Boston, a general muster was held for stolen clothes; Seaman John Robinson received twelve lashes for thievery. Seven contacts were chased and spoke, and all were Americans. On the 30th, the foretopsail yard was found to be sprung and was replaced. Two days later, the same occurred with the maintopsail yard. Seaman Thomas Williams was given twelve lashes on 6 August for "riotous behavior" (probably roaring drunk). On the 10th, the jib boom was sprung. Cape Charles, marking the north side of the entrance to Chesapeake Bay, finally was sighted on the 13th. Talbot subsequently came to anchor in Lynnhaven Bay at 7:00 the next evening. By that time the boatswain, Benjamin Brackett, had been suspended from duty and confined to his stateroom—another case of "riotous behavior."

While Talbot struggled south, Secretary Stoddert in Philadelphia had faced up to the fact that the time for his hoped-for raid on French coastal shipping had passed. Accordingly, on 27 July he penned Talbot's next orders: Proceed to the area of Cayenne on South America's north coast along a route "you shall judge most likely to fall in with French Armed Vessels" and there seek out some large French privateers that have been preying on American commerce. On 20 September, he was to proceed to patrol the route to Guadeloupe, get the latest intelligence from our squadron there, and continue on to the north coast of Haiti to take command of that squadron. Talbot received these orders on 15 August. Three days later, he was able to take *Constitution* into Hampton Roads and fill up his stores in earnest. Desertions continued to be a problem, and in one instance involved two Marine sergeants.

The second leg of *Constitution*'s voyage proceeded no more speedily than the first, and the days were occupied with ship's routine. Small "Keggs" were issued to the messes in which to keep their water allowance, set at two quarts per man daily. In three weeks, the great guns were exercised twice and the small arms thrice. The ship went in chase on the 31st and 2, 5, 7, 8, and 14 September: four Americans, one Briton, and one Dane. Both the maintopsail yard and the main topgallant yard sprung and were replaced.

AMALIA

By 15 September, *Constitution* still was somewhat north and east of the Leeward Islands. At 8:00 A.M., a sail was seen to the east, and she went in chase with "all sail by the winds." In three hours, the chase had been brought to. She proved to be the Hamburg ship *Amalia*, which had been made prize by a French corvette ten days earlier. Ten Frenchmen were taken aboard as prisoners. Acting lieutenant Nathaniel Bosworth was placed aboard the "prize" with a quartermaster and sixteen crewmen and was directed to make for New York.

The big frigate quickly was on her way southward once more. The days passed in occasional battle exercises, including firing all thirty 24-pounders on the gun deck, and in thoroughly cleaning the ship. A fore topgallant yard was sprung and replaced, as was the main topgallant yard (for the second time). Day after day, "moderate breezes" were recorded in the log, the steadfast "trades." On 28 September, a sounding finally was gotten with the 120-fathom leadline, and a current setting to the west-northwest was observed. That afternoon, Seaman Eddy was given twelve lashes for theft.

After a night of wearing and tacking and taking soundings every half hour, at 5:00 A.M. on Sunday the 29th, land was sighted bearing from southwest to west-southwest, supposed to be the "High Land of LaGabriel [Pointe Behague?] which is about 18 or 20 miles from Cayenne to Windward [i.e., eastward]." A sage observation entered in the ship's log on this occasion states, "A Lucky circumstance for the safety of Navigation on this coast is Your soundings is very regular."

Talbot proceeded to patrol to the north and west, feeling his way cautiously with the leadline in order to keep the shore in sight as much as possible. On the 30th, he chased and spoke HMS *Syrene*, 32, from whose captain he learned that the British had taken possession of Surinam. On 1 and 2 October, three British merchantmen were spoke and HMS *Invincible*, 74, sighted, and all were seen to anchor off the Surinam River (Paramaraibo). With that, Talbot took his departure from South America and headed for his ultimate station via the Windward and Leeward Islands.

On Station

This time, the trip was quickly made. After sighting Deseada shortly after dawn on the 8th, Talbot headed for the western side of Guadeloupe in order to look into Basse-Terre Roads. Finding nothing, he passed between Montserrat and Rodondo Rock back into the Atlantic. Although the American ships covering Guadeloupe were based upon St. Kitts, Talbot ignored the opportunity to exchange information and passed on. At 11:00 A.M. on the 15th, *Constitution* rendezvoused with frigate *Boston* (Captain Little), 28, about twenty-three miles north of Monticristi, Santo Domingo. In the offing were frigate *General Greene* (Capt. Christopher R. Perry), 28, and brig *Norfolk* (M.Cmdt. William Bainbridge), 18, two other units of the squadron then to come under Talbot's command. Perry and Bainbridge came aboard *Constitution* during the afternoon and, together with Little, briefed Talbot on the current local situation. After dining together and receiving Commodore Talbot's instructions, each returned to his ship and all proceeded to patrol stations. The Santo Domingo Squadron came into being with this meeting. *Constitution*'s station primarily was between the longitudes of Cape Francois (Cape Haitien today) and Monticristi. With generally fair weather and tranquil seas, life settled into tedious routine. In the forty-seven days that followed, the frigate went in chase forty-six times. Almost all turned out to be neutral or friendly vessels, although on a couple of occasions Talbot saw fit to beat to quarters until what were seen to be men-of-war were identified as British or American.

One small break in the routine occurred on the evening of 12 November, when *Norfolk* rejoined. Bainbridge came aboard and reported he had captured a French armed boat carrying several swivel guns, small arms, and twenty-four men. Talbot had the prisoners transferred to the larger ship and took the prize in tow while Bainbridge went into Cape Francois to check with the American consul, Dr. Edward Stevens, as to its disposition. When he returned two days later, the prize was stripped and scuttled, and the prisoners returned to their original captors, as *Norfolk* was departing for duty at Havana.

For the crew, life largely was humdrum. The 18th of October was a bad day, however: Marine Lieutenant Amory, who had been confined to his stateroom by illness for some time, was sent ashore in hopes he would recover; at noon, Seaman John Robinson was killed in a fall from the main yard; and Marine Peter Allen died of a "stomach cramp" three hours later. On the 22nd, Seamen James Collins died of "several disorders." Master's Mate John Sprague passed away from consumption three days later. In the following month, the crew was diminished further by the deaths of Seamen Archibald Thompson (1 November) and Francis Bouldfern (29 November, of yellow fever). But if the Grim Reaper was active during this period, the cat-o'-nine-tails was not: The awarding of twelve lashes each to Seamen John Bennett and Jesse Defield stands as the lone disciplinary entry in the ship's log.

On two occasions, at least, Talbot was able to relieve the monotony of the situation by having informal sailing contests with the smaller frigate *Boston*. At 9:00 A.M. on 1 November, "Wore and Steerd down for her [*Boston's*] wake allowing her to pass nearly 2 miles a head, we then Tried on a Bowling which brought us parrallel to her course with an Equal proportion of Canvass we found her far from Equability in sailing, @ 11 we Tacked on her weather Bow In order to Give her a fair Tryal at sailing @ 12 Shortend sail and brought too the Boston a Stern nearly one mile." And a day-and-a-half later, "@ 5 wore and came to the wind to the Northward under all plane sail In order to give the US Ship Boston another fair Tryal at Sailing @ 7 Shortend sail and parted company with the Boston this is now the second time we have Given Captain Little a trial at sailing he is now fully satisfied of the Constitution's superiority." Not a little pride there!

At 4:00 P.M. on Saturday, the 16th, United States ship *Herald*, 20, under the command of Lt. Charles C. Russell (*Constitution*'s first First Lieutenant), reported to Talbot for duty in the squadron. Successive chases, however, delayed his coming aboard the frigate to call on his senior until late Sunday afternoon. *Herald*, being a smaller vessel, was directed to remain on patrol within *Constitution*'s general area, but closer in shore and not actually "in company."

On the following Saturday, the 27th, both *Herald* and *General Greene* rejoined the flagship. Their captains conferred with Talbot over dinner late that afternoon, and the ships remained in the vicinity of one another through the night. At 10:00 the next morning, *Constitution* was alerted by a signal from *Herald* of a mutiny on board. Talbot "shorten'd sail Brout too and sent an officer and a Boats crew on board the Herald." Demon rum apparently had been at work; hangovers and the cat soon put things to rights.

As the days passed, and as his correspondence with our consul general, Dr. Stevens, flourished, Talbot gained a deeper understanding of conditions in the strife-torn land. Of great concern to Stevens was the fact that, as the "policing" actions of the American warships became known, the presence of these units in port for any reason might trigger overt attacks upon them by some of the numerous violence-prone factions vying for power. It was his desire that port calls be held to a minimum; so strong was his concern that he had written to the secretary of the navy recommending that the Santo Domingo Squadron be sustained, insofar as possible, at sea. In line with Stevens's wishes, Talbot wrote to naval agent Nathan Levy at Cape Francois on the 24th requesting that he seek to charter a "watering vessel" with which to supply squadron units that necessary commodity on station. He also ordered quantities of limes, oranges, onions, yams, plantains, beeves, goats, sheep, and Indian meal or oatmeal. Levy reported three days later that no ship was available. In consequence, Talbot evolved, in the weeks to follow, a practice of using the smaller units of the squadron and itinerant American merchantmen calling at Cape Francois to bring out supplies to the others, and especially to his immediate command.

On the 28th, Stevens came out by ship's boat to confer with the commodore. The two officials spent seven hours discussing the many aspects of the diplomatic monstrosity in which they were involved. Stevens later reported to the secretary of state, Timothy Pickering, that he found Talbot to be "a Man of Sense, Prudence & Candor" and "a Man of . . . Sense and Understanding," and that, because of the presence of the American Squadron, "the Privateers have entirely deserted this part of [the coast]."

At this point, *Constitution* literally had been scraping the bottom of the barrel for fresh water, so long had she been under way. Twice in recent days she had received small amounts from *General Greene*, but not enough to sustain so large a crew. Talbot thus was forced to leave his station and proceed westward to St. Nicholas Mole, where water could be had, and the presence of a naval agent offered the prospect of additional logistic support. A rare squall delayed his progress somewhat, but *Constitution* was towed into port by her boats on 2 December, coming to anchor in twenty-four fathoms just as eight bells struck in the dog watches. Noted the log: "From our last anchorage to this is one hundred days which time we have been at Sea three men we lost overboard and 6 died."

Just as Talbot had been wrestling with the problems of who the "enemy" was, so, too, were the officials in Philadelphia. Their problem was that the lucrative American trade with Santo Domingo was inadequate to the needs of the populace; this, in turn, led the favored Haitian leader, Toussaint L'Ouverture, to insist that such trade as was coming from France not be stopped and that French warships protecting said trade be privileged. Secretary Stoddert laid it out for the commodore thusly in a letter on the 4th:

> "1st That our Vessels shall not block up the [?] of Touissant, so as to prevent the French armed freely entering into, or departing from them—
>
> "2nd That our Vessels shall not leave Touissants ports until 24 hours have elapsed after the departure of a French armed Vessel on her return to France—
>
> "3rd That our vessels shall not capture within one league of the shores of Touissant French armed Vessels trading between France and Santo Domingo—
>
> "4th That our Vessels shall occasionally leave any particular port which Touissant may desire, and its vacinity [*sic*] for a certain number of days for the purpose of affording to the French armed Vessels trading as aforesaid, a fair opportunity of returning to France, without danger of capture near the Island—"

What a way to fight a war: "quasi," indeed!

Overhauling the rigging and watering ship proceeded. The ground tier of 90 leaguers, 46 butts, and 30 gang casks was filled before noon on the 5th. The whole watering operation ended on the afternoon of the 6th, with 191 tons of water stowed below—45,840 gallons. She was on her way back to patrol station at 6:00 A.M. on the 8th.

The routine known in October and November was reestablished, with one change: Fresh water was strictly controlled. The chases almost always turned out to be Americans; none were French. On 15 December, *Boston* and *General Greene* rejoined *Constitution* for a periodic conference of commanders. A new unit arrived on the scene as well: schooner *Experiment*, 12, newly commissioned under Lt. Cmdt. William Maley, and on her maiden voyage. Her shallow draft made her well adapted for work in shoal waters and would enable Talbot to extend the sphere of influence of his squadron. Two days later, *General Greene* was sent into Cape Francois for a badly needed overhaul period, while *Boston* moved to a station east of Monticristi. *Experiment* remained with *Constitution* for nearly two weeks "learning the ropes" before Talbot sent her to the Bight of Leogane via St. Nicholas Mole to protect the American interests off the west end of Santo Domingo.

Not long after resuming his patrol station, Talbot began experiencing some of the top-hamper problems that had plagued his predecessor nearly a year before. The foremast trestletrees were found to be sprung on 14 December and had to be replaced—this only two days after having had to redo the gammoning on a loosened bowsprit. But on the 17th, Talbot became aware of a much more serious problem: "Observed the Mainmast to labour very much about 10 or 12 feet below the Treeletrees [*sic*]." Further observation revealed severe checking in the mast. For the next month, the carpenter strove to ensure that the mast would not be lost completely, ultimately fitting it with two 32-foot-long oaken fishes woulded in place with 120 fathoms of 6-inch hawser.

The days passed quietly for *Constitution*'s crew. Talbot exercised them just twice at the guns. During December, they averaged a chase a day; but with the coming of the new year, such occurrences were halved—and all proved to be friendly. On the 27th, Seamen Thomas Williams, Thomas Moody, and William Cooper were given six lashes each for neglect of duty (the boredom of seemingly endless watches?). For the same offense, as well as insolence, Seaman William Shaw received twelve lashes on 9 January 1800. In January, too, Sailmaker Samuel Cavalier died of a bilious complaint and Marine Asa Haskins of "a complication on the lungs." Both were buried at sea.

Underway Replenishment

The Navy Department-chartered schooner *Elizabeth* (Master Thomas Hughes) of Philadelphia rendezvoused with *Constitution* at 10:00 A.M. on 30 December, laden with stores for the Santo Domingo Squadron. In an early example of underway replenishment, a technique that is a particular talent of the modern U.S. Navy, Talbot took the merchantman in tow (to keep her close by) and commenced the transfer of stores by ship's boats. In twelve hours, the frigate took aboard 260 barrels of bread, 30 of potatoes, and 8 of cheese, as well as 4 tierces of rice and one of pease, another "small cask" of pease, and 6 kegs of butter. A heavy swell from the northward brought a halt to the operation until daylight. Another ten hours of heavy labor completed the task, and at eight bells of the afternoon watch *Elizabeth* was ordered to replenish *Boston*.

On 15 January, Secretary Stoddert wrote Talbot that two additional units were being added to his command: sloop *Patapsco* (Capt. Henry Geddes), 20, and brig *Richmond* (M.Cmdt. Richard Law, Jr.), 16. These were intended to improve Talbot's ability to respond to any changing circumstances.

On the afternoon of Sunday the 19th, the squadron broke up to carry out their several orders. Talbot took *Constitution* to the northwest and spent nine days reconnoitering the waters south of "Heneaga" (Great Inagua) Island. Only three contacts, all American, were made in the area. The return to the old station off Cape Francois was marked by outsailing HMS *Maidstone*, 32, in a 10.5-hour run.

Three days after resuming patrol, Talbot chased and brought to an American "polacky." Perry in *General Greene* joined for a few hours at about the same time and reported "all quiet" in the Turks Island Passage before beginning his circumnavigation of Santo Domingo.

Constitution's log for this period bears witness to the continuing good health and generally high morale of Talbot's crew. Discipline was exercised for only the second time in the new year on 10 February, when the commodore suspended from duty Midshipman John Longley and Carpenter Pliny Davidson "for fighting." A week later, only the third death of the year occurred when Ordinary Seaman Dennis Murray went "galley west" and was buried at sea "with the usual custom."

Just a few hours earlier, the brig *Richmond* had joined. Captain Law awaited the commodore and received orders to join forces already in the Bight of Leogane, where there was a constant demand for escorts by American merchantmen. At two bells of the first dogwatch on the 19th, Law parted company and headed for his new duties.

On the afternoon of the 20th, *Constitution* again had company: a supply sloop from New York, which was kept in tow through intermittent heavy weather over the two days stores were transferred. As this operation was concluding, Talbot discovered to his dismay that the heel of the foretopmast had sprung and had to be woulded. He must have been most thankful that the hurricane season was not upon him, with two injured masts.

A flurry of excitement occurred on the 25th when *Constitution* overhauled a chase. It turned out to be a Danish ship "In Great distress by her crew being mutinous and the Ship so leaky." At the captain's request, Talbot took the mutineers in *Constitution* and towed the unfortunate vessel to Cape Francois, where it could be repaired and the mutineers punished.

Lt. Cmdt. Maley appeared in *Experiment* on the morning of the 27th, escorting two prize schooners laden with stores for the flagship. Through the day, the boats plied back and forth, restocking the frigate's hold and storerooms with some of the things required by the large crew: 110 barrels of bread, 28 bags and 2 barrels of potatoes, 17 barrels of beans, 26 casks of brandy, 42 firkins of butter, 58 boxes of candles, and 20 dozen shirts. That evening, *Augusta* also rejoined.

Talbot long had been vexed by the fact that he had no small, light draft vessels to work in *Constitution*'s patrol area. One of *Experiment*'s prizes, *Amphitheatre*, appeared to be just what he needed, and so, replenishment completed, he set about fitting her out for her new role. For three days, *Constitution*'s carpenters and gunners labored to strengthen decks and bulwarks and install "Cannonades [*sic*] and Swivels sent out of" the frigate. And she was laden with stores for a thirty-day cruise. Lt. David Porter, first lieutenant of *Experiment*, was detailed to command her as she patrolled inshore of the flagship. (Talbot ordered *Constitution*'s fourth lieutenant, Edward Boss, to *Experiment* as a replacement, together with his volunteer midshipman son.) Both *Experiment* and *Augusta* sailed again for the Bight on the 28th.

The days passed quietly, with the new inshore patrol uncovering nothing. Periodically one of the subordinate units would appear, report to Talbot, and go off again—*Boston* on 6 March and *Experiment* nearly a week later. On the 13th, Talbot decided to run in to St. Nicholas Mole for water; he arrived there at noon the next day. *Constitution* had been at sea for 195 of the previous 201 days.

The frigate completed her watering in rapid order and was under way for her well-remembered station at 9:00 A.M. on the 17th. A welcome last-minute acquisition undoubtedly looked upon with delight by the crew: a precious supply of coffee and sugar. *General Greene* rejoined on 4 April, having completed her cruise around the island; Perry had with him two prizes taken along the way. The next day, Talbot directed that one be released as not being a proper prize. On that day and the next, Talbot sent sixteen invalided seamen and Marines to Perry in exchange for twenty-three seamen, prior to issuing orders to the latter to proceed to New Orleans and Havana, and then back to America. *General Greene* parted company at four bells of the midwatch on the 6th.

For more than three weeks, the humdrum patrolling went on. *Constitution* received stores from *Enterprize* on the 6th, a chartered stores ship on the 13th (both Sundays), *Amphitheatre* on the 24th ("6 cords of wood"), and *Herald* on the 28th.

ACTION AT LAST

As he had done two weeks earlier, Talbot worked once more to windward as the month of May opened to check out any activities going on in or near the ports of Isabella and Puerto Plata, some ninety to one hundred miles east of Cape Francois. Three vessels were seen in the latter port, one of which was found to be Danish when she came out at noon on the 2nd.

Talbot, rendered curious by the activity that three ships in that small harbor represented, sent in a cutter to reconnoiter. At 7:00 P.M. on the 3rd, it returned with the information that the harbor was bounded by reefs to the east and west and was defended by a small fort on a point of land that apparently mounted four guns. The waters of the harbor were insufficient for the likes of the big frigate. Talbot moved off to consider the situation.

Several days went by, and then, at 11:30 A.M. on the 8th, "spyed a sail Close in shore which appeared to be coming to an Anchor In a large Bay to leeward [i. e., westward] of Old cape francois, Tacked and ordered the Amphitheatre to stand in and see what that Sail was." At 2:00, Porter returned with the news that two privateers and a prize were anchored close inshore. An augmented *Amphitheatre*, together with four armed boats, was sent in to do battle. In mid-afternoon, the force succeeded in capturing the privateer schooner *Esther* and the prize, American brig *Nymph* of Newburyport, laden with $7,000 and a cargo of dry goods. A privateer barge managed to escape. The ship's log included the information that *Esther* carried three guns and had had a crew of forty-three. Three had been killed, and several of the prisoners were "badly wounded." In the brief engagement, *Amphitheatre* had lost her rudder and had had three men wounded. At 7:30 P.M., "Lieutenant [Isaac] Collins with two arm'd boats was order'd in shore to a bay call'd Laragee Salle bay In order to cruize for [the] barge." *Esther* was taken in tow; a prize master took charge of *Nymph*.

Collins and his little force were nowhere in sight when the sun rose on the 9th. At 1:30 P.M., the large cutter returned, but the midshipman in charge didn't know what had become of his senior's craft. Anxiously, Talbot sent *Amphitheatre* and *Esther* looking for it. They returned as night was coming on, empty-handed. Through the night, an alert watch sought a sign of their missing mates. At 7:00 the next morning (10th), *Herald* joined, and Russell reported he had spoke Collins the evening before: He had cut a sloop out of the harbor at St. Iago! At 9:00, the triumphant Collins appeared in the fifty-eight-ton sloop *Sally*, an American trafficker that recently also had called at Puerto Plata.

Collins' adroit adventure not only brought him the commodore's compliments, but it also gave the squadron commander the means to get at what he knew to be a privateer in Puerto Plata: that one vessel had not come out in the week since he had seen three together in there. *Sally* had been one of them; she and her master, Thomas Sandford, were known there; his ship could call again without suspicion. Talbot had in mind "the wooden horse at Troy."

CUTTING OUT A PRIVATEER

By the evening of the 10th, lying out of sight from the shore, *Sally* was ready for her big moment. Talbot ordered First Lieutenant Hull, Marine Capt. Daniel Carmick and his lieutenant, Amory (recently returned from sick leave at Cape Francois), together with ninety seamen and Marines, to board the sloop as a cutting-out expedition. They were to sail into Puerto Plata with Sandford and only a few of *Constitution*'s crew (enough to handle the vessel) visible, innocently make for an anchorage near the French privateer, and then . . .

With the morning sun came a steady breeze. The raiders entered Puerto Plata with no one suspecting *Sally*'s changed character. Hull guided her straight to his objective. Carmick wrote what happened next: "We all remained below until we received orders from the officer [Hull], the only one of us who remained on deck of the sloop, whose business it was to lay us on board, which he did on the starboard bow. The men went on board like devils, and it was as much as the first lieutenant and myself could do to prevent blood being spilt. I believe it was not

An assault force of sailors and marines from *Constitution* swarms aboard a French privateer at Puerto Plata, Hispaniola, April 1800, from the previously captured sloop *Sally*. The privateer, formerly the English packet *Sandwich*, later was found to be an improper prize because she was taken in what was a Spanish-controlled port. The painting by Robert Salmon is dated 1836 and was presented to Hull by an admirer. *Courtesy Boston Athenaeum*

half an hour before the ship was take [*sic*], that I had possession of the fort and all the cannon spiked, and returned again on board the prize before they could get any succours from the city."

Hull's lightning attack had stunned both the privateer crew and the town's inhabitants. And a good thing, too, for he found his prize had had all but its lower masts unshipped and the rigging coiled in the hold. Calmly, he told off gun crews to place the ship's battery in readiness and had the Marines stationed to repel boarders. With the remaining seamen, Hull set about rerigging the ship. By sunset, the ship was "in every respect ready for service." At midnight, *Sally* and her prize sailed out in perfect order on an offshore breeze without the loss of a single man. Shortly before noon on the 12th, they rejoined *Constitution* and *Nymph*.

The prize had once been the British packet *Sandwich*, but for the previous three or four years had been a French privateer. She was a fast, copper-bottomed ship mounting six-pounders and two nines and laden with coffee and sugar. As events finally turned out, Talbot, Hull, et al., would receive heartiest congratulations from Secretary Stoddert for this daring and skillful operation, but no prize money. The ex-*Sandwich* had been cut out of a Spanish, and therefore neutral, port, and ultimately was returned to the French by the diplomats with apologies. Nice try, *Constitution!*

Buoyed by the activity and apparent success of the past several days, Talbot took *Constitution* on a sweep to Samana Bay at the east end of Hispaniola after provisioning ex-*Sandwich* and *Sally* and sending them northward. No privateers or traffickers were found. On the 17th, back off Monticristi once more, the frigate was joined by brigs *Richmond* and *Augusta*, whose captains conferred with Talbot. At 10:00 the next morning, *Augusta* was on her way to the Bight of Leogane for more convoy duty. On the 19th, *Richmond* was ordered in the Cape Francois for provisioning. *Constitution* settled in once again to the familiar routine. On the 30th, Seaman Thomas Smith received twelve lashes for disobedience of orders and drunkenness. The seemingly endless days at sea were having their effect on the crew.

If Talbot had found no targets on his sweep eastward, he had been made suspicious about what might be going on at the little village in Baie Citron, about fifteen miles west of Cape Samana, and he returned once more to the east end of the island. On the morning of 3 June, the barge, the pinnace, and a cutter were laden with ninety-five seamen and Marines under Hamilton and Amory, and sent in on a "search and destroy" mission. As they ruefully reported the next morning when they returned, surf had pooped their boats and wetted all their powder, causing Hamilton to abort the plan and return to *Constitution* for a fresh supply. He reported, however, seeing what appeared to be a privateer at anchor off the village and two more on stocks being built.

The commodore decided to try again, but this time he would move his big flagship in to provide gunfire support, the element of surprise probably having been lost. At 2:00 P.M. on the 4th he had *Constitution* at anchor as close to the village as he could, the boats nearby, awaiting the cover of a bombardment by the batteries of 18- and 24-pounder long guns. But in this, too, was the plan frustrated: A few salvos soon showed Talbot that the range was too great for an effective cannonade. At 5:00 P.M., with the surf still running high, he gave up the attempt, called in the boats, and hauled off shore.

As the ship patrolled slowly westward once more, additional signs of growing fatigue of ship's company became evident. At 6:00 P.M. on the 6th, Pvt. Rufus Montor "died of a fever." Hot weather was coming on, which only would exacerbate the difficult conditions under which these men lived and worked. Despite the efforts to supply the proper provisions regularly, scurvy became a problem. Tempers grew short as frustrations grew long. Talbot, as any captain would, kept a tight rein and reacted promptly to each infraction. On the 7th, in the morning, Seaman Daniel Flynn received twelve lashes for mutinous language and disobedience of orders; that same afternoon, Seaman Daniel (or Andrew) Freeman got a "dozen o' the cat" for theft and insolence to his superior officer.

Immediately after Freeman's punishment, Talbot ordered out two boats with forty armed men to go with the tender, *Amphitheatre*, into a bay to the west of Old Cape Francois to cut out a privateer and barge he believed to be lurking there.

At dawn on the 8th, Talbot found *Amphitheatre* in chase of the privateer, heading westward, and the boats pursuing a schooner. He closed the latter, which came to at 8:30 A.M. after a volley of small arms fire from the boats and three rounds from the frigate's 18-pounders. Leaving the schooner in the charge of the redoubtable Hamilton, the commodore pressed after the tender and her quarry. The Frenchman, however, was able to gain the safety and protection to be found near the fort at Puerto Plata.

Constitution and *Amphitheatre* took up a vigil off the port. At 3:00 P.M., Hamilton joined with his boats and the schooner, a Danish slaver. Talbot made preparations to cut out the privateer, intending to anchor *Constitution* close in shore where her long guns could make a suitable impression on the fort while the boats gained the prize. But soundings by one of the boats proved the impracticability of the scheme, and at 7:00 all were hoisted aboard and the ships headed west once more.

The brig *Richmond* joined the commodore the next morning in the vicinity of Monticristi. Lying to there, Talbot sent over thirty-five French prisoners he had been carrying, together with twenty-one seamen and Marines whose enlistments had expired and who desired to be put ashore. At eight bells of the afternoon watch, *Richmond* headed for Cape Francois.

Seaman Eddy died "with a complication of diseases" shortly after daylight on the 10th and was buried at sea. *Amphitheatre* was sent in to Cape Francois, and Talbot decided to take *Constitution* to St. Nicholas Mole for watering. En route, he was joined by schooner *Experiment* and ship *Trumbull*. He anchored at the Mole as the afternoon watch was ending on the 11th and sent the watering party ashore immediately.

What a relief it must have been to all hands to be riding at anchor again— only the third time in ten months—and not be constantly alert to the watch officer's hail or the mate's "starter." One, at least, relaxed too much. The next morning, Pvt. Simeon Cook took twelve lashes for neglect of duty and sleeping on post.

THE ODYSSEY ENDS

Watering was completed at 3:00 A.M. on Saturday, the 14th, and after taking aboard coffee and sugar with which to supplement ship's fare, Talbot was to sea again at 6:00. *Amphitheatre* was in attendance as well. Patrolling off Cape Francois, it soon was apparent that ship and crew alike were coming to the end of their endurance. Since the preceding August, they had been in port just nine days—and those all too brief periods involved the back-breaking labor of watering and supplying the ship. The log on the 16th noted thirty sick with fever, and scurvy was becoming prevalent. On the 17th, Seaman Thomas Nash was given twelve lashes for quarreling with his superior officer. Many a man's term of enlistment was about done.

Richmond, brig, 18, appeared late on the afternoon of the 21st. Talbot issued Law orders to proceed to the Bight to operate against rebel General André Rigaud's armed barges in defense of American shipping operating to and from Port Republicain. Law was on his way in an hour, having first delivered the French prisoners he had received eleven days earlier.

For the next several days, *Amphitheatre* was kept close to *Constitution*, systematically being stripped of her war stores and supplies. Talbot had determined to send her to Philadelphia. Porter was to take home some of the men whose time had expired. *Amphitheatre* began her voyage at 3:00 P.M. on the 24th.

Once more, the crew could begin to measure their patrol time in weeks. Ship *Ganges* appeared briefly on the 26th, having escorted four American merchantmen from Philadelphia. She soon departed, heading for Havana and a return convoy. Heavy squalls on the 29th must have reminded the commodore that this was the start of the hurricane season in these waters—another worry for a commander with a tired ship and weary crew. Two days later, a log entry read: "Our principle sails except a foresail has actual service become worn out so much as to be unserviceable, on a lee shore, or pursuing an enemy under a press of sail. We have repeatedly split the fore and main topsails when every effort would have been useless to bend others. Notwithstanding, forty bolts of canvas has been on them."

Talbot did his duty relentlessly. *Constitution* held her station, although others came and went. *Trumbull* appeared for a few hours on 2 July. *Augusta* reported back from the south coast and was ordered into Cape Francois for overhaul and resupply. Chaplain William Austin took advantage of the commodore's stoppage of a homeward-bound American sloop to end his term of service on the 6th. Ironically, it was a Sunday; the log makes no mention of divine services. *Augusta* came back a week later, bringing to the frigate some badly needed supplies.

Real trouble came for the commodore on the afternoon of the 13th, when the sprung main mast, which he had been nursing for nearly seven months, sagged forward and threatened to carry away. Now they *had* to go into port. At 6:00 A.M. on the 15th, the pilot boarded, and just before noon they were safely anchored in Cape Francois. There, *Herald* was waiting. Also present were thirty-seven merchantmen and an armed French ship. *Constitution* was in no condition to fight, but the Frenchman apparently was awed by her size. Repairs began immediately. By midafternoon, both main and maintopsail yards had been sent down. A stores party brought aboard thirty barrels of pork and five of flour, which *Herald* had loaded to take out to the patroller. In return, *Herald* received the peripatetic French prisoners.

On the 16th, the maintopmast was gotten down before noon, double runners were rigged fore and aft of the injured mast, and "by Degrees" it was hove straight once more. While the carpenters began fitting fishes as splints to the mast, others took advantage to overhaul the rigging that had been taken down. By midnight of the 21st, the upper masts had been swayed up once more, the rigging rigged, and the sails bent on. Talbot was ready for sea: In the last three days, Seamen Moody, William Smith, Jacob and William Brown, John Handy, Henry Phillips, Nehemiah Warner, and Jonathan Hardison had deserted ship.

At six bells of the midwatch on the 22nd, Talbot hove short and fired a gun to signal waiting merchantmen that their escort was ready to sail. At daylight, with two pilots aboard, *Constitution* entered the narrow channel, outward bound. A dead calm forced her to anchor until 7:00, when a westerly breeze let her stand along the reef. Suddenly near the outer fort, the big frigate was taken aback by a northerly wind, which quickly shifted to the east. Before she could come to anchor, *Constitution* went aground stern first on the reef "which Shock was Sensibly felt and Violently repeated." By shifting guns forward, running out a stream anchor and heaving around, she was brought off and anchored once more in mid-channel. She was aground only forty-seven minutes. "The ship makes no more Water than Usual." At 5:00 that afternoon, the wind came again fair. Talbot was to sea and stowing anchors by 7:00.

When the sun rose the next morning, *Constitution* was joined by *Constellation*, Capt. Alexander Murray, just arriving as her relief, and by *Trumbull*. All day they remained in company, the commanding officers conferring as the merchantmen slowly worked out of harbor. On the afternoon of the 24th, Murray formally relieved Talbot as commander of the Santo Domingo station. At 6:00 P.M., with twelve merchants under her wing, *Constitution* headed for Caicos Passage and home.

It was a long, slow trip for the frigate's worn crew. Merchant ships were a notoriously motley lot as sailors, and generally skippered by men prone to *not* taking orders. At times, *Constitution* had as many as three of the dullest in tow. On the 29th, the sighting of what was obviously a man-of-war caused Talbot to beat to quarters, but it proved to be HMS *Andromache*, 38, which sent an officer to wait upon the commodore. Carpenters had to be sent aboard a sloop that sprang a leak on 1 August.

The convoy arrived off Charleston, South Carolina, on the 6th. There, seven members went their way while Talbot received supplies and let the shipping in harbor know a northbound escort was available to anyone interested. *Constitution* resumed her homeward journey at four bells of the night watch on the 7th. The convoy headed first to the east to enter the Gulf Stream, then north in light showers.

Off the Capes on 3 August, *Constitution*'s convoy had dispersed for Baltimore and Philadelphia. Now, the weather willing, Talbot could take advantage of his ship's speed to gain an early return to Boston. It could be none too soon: "[O]ur State of Provisions being as follows Viz. Beef none Pork 14 barrels Rum 60 Gallons put the Ships Company on half Allowance of Spirits."

It was eleven long days until Boston Light was raised. It was too long for Seaman Charles Leonard: He died of fever on the 15th. The thirteen-month deployment at last came to an end as *Constitution* anchored in President Roads at 2:00 P.M. on 24 August 1800. It had been an epic voyage that had demanded the utmost in leadership from Silas Talbot. The president clearly had been right in insisting that he was the man to be *Constitution*'s captain. Secretary Stoddert summed up Talbot's achievement thus:

> Your feeling as a military man, might have been more gratified had opportunities been afforded you of engaging in scenes of greater brilliancy—but no services you cd. have rendered, could have been more useful & more important to your country than those you have meritoriously performed, in protecting

with effect a great portion of our commerce in laying the foundation of a permanent Trade with St. Domingo & in causing the American character to be respected by the just, temperate judicious course by which your conduct had been marked, during the whole time of your command at St. Domingo.

THE WAR WINDS DOWN

Even before *Constitution* had begun her return voyage to Boston, Talbot was laying the groundwork for a thoroughgoing overhaul of the ship after her year of strenuous employment. As early as 14 July 1800, he had written to Naval Agent Higginson an order to prepare a new mainmast for the frigate. In Talbot's estimation, the continuing problem that had faced both Nicholson and himself stemmed from masts of inadequate dimension. The current mainmast, he wrote, was smaller than that in *United States* and was "not sufficient to bear up." The new mast was to be 101.5 feet tall (four feet shorter than the present one), but it was to be thicker at the cap and therefore better able to withstand the stresses of her large sail area.

Little time was wasted in setting about readying the ship for a return to Haiti. The exhausted crew quickly was paid off; the officers went on leave or were transferred to other duties. Talbot himself went on leave on 11 September, leaving Hull in charge of the overhaul. Among his orders to Hull was one to be sure that "no woman of Ill fame . . . be alow'd to take shelter on Board the Ship." The new mainmast and a new maintopmast were set up late in September and early in October. A new suit of sails was begun.

In Paris, at the end of September, Joseph Bonaparte and Oliver Ellsworth signed "A Convention of Amity and Commerce between the United States and France." When ratified, it would cause each side to return the other's public and private vessels not previously disposed of, exchange commercial agents, and guarantee each the freedom of the seas and trade.

Secretary Stoddert drafted Talbot's new orders on 18 November, at a time when rumors already were circulating in Washington (where the federal government had been since the preceding June) that the treaty had been completed. He was to resume command of the Santo Domingo Squadron and adopt a posture of watchful protectiveness, countering any overt attacks on American property but initiating no offensive actions against the French.

Talbot sailed *Constitution* from Boston on 17 December, two days after President Adams presented the draft treaty to the Senate for its advice and consent.

This time the voyage south took a mere twelve days. As 1801 dawned, the commodore was on his station again off Cape Francois. Other units under him included frigate *Adams*, 28, ship *Trumbull*, 18, and brigs *Richmond*, 18, and *Augusta*, 14. Except for the absence of cutting-out expeditions, the old routine continued in effect. *Constitution* herself remained on patrol off Cape Francois until the second week in February, when Talbot took her to St. Nicholas Mole for water and consultations with the naval agent there. He got under way on 6 March in escort of a convoy of merchantmen returning to the United States. The escort was to last until the convoy passed north of the Bahamas.

OUTFOXING A FRIGATE

The two-day voyage north through the Crooked Island Passage was a tedious one of repeated calms or head winds. Shortly after open waters had been reached, the Americans were approached by the remembered British frigate *Andromache*. Her captain on this occasion requested Talbot bring the entire convoy to so that it could be searched—whether for British deserters or for contraband wasn't specified. Talbot's hands were tied by the Navy Department general order of 16 January 1799, which forbade action against searches and seizures of merchantmen by other than French warships and privateers. If he was prevented from using *Constitution*'s guns, though, he could refuse to aid the Briton's purpose and, indeed, to render its attainment more difficult. He "immediately hove out a Signal for the [the convoy] to Disperse and shift for themselves as from what I could learn from the Several Masters when at the Mole, that if they were boarded by any of the British ships they expected to be Sent into a British port for adjudication." When *Andromache* realized the meaning of Talbot's signal, she made sail for the headmost ships in the convoy. Once she was well clear of *Constitution* so that there could be no mistaking her intent, she fired two shots as a signal for the merchantmen to heave to. Two did. The third leader, however, *Arethusa*, set every stitch of canvas she had and made off with all sails drawing. *Andromache* accepted the challenge and went off in pursuit. Noting that night wasn't far off, Talbot recorded that he felt certain *Arethusa* could outsail *Andromache* and make good her escape, while her prompt action made it impossible for the Briton to regain an advantageous position on the convoy. The commodore subsequently wrote that that "in fact was the Case." *Constitution* returned to her patrol station off Cape Francois, following fifteen days of battling adverse winds, and remained there for the next six weeks.

In the meantime, the treaty had had rough sledding in the Senate, but with Thomas Jefferson having narrowly won the presidential election, it was ratified as the Adams Administration closed its books. All during February, the secretary of the navy quietly had put the brakes on fitting out ships for further deployments to the West Indies, for the end was in sight. On 3 March, the day after the treaty ratification and the last day in office for the Federalists, the Congress had passed the navy's Peace Establishment Act. It was almost exactly what Stoddert had recommended to the Naval Affairs Committee in January. Only thirteen built-for-the-purpose frigates were to be retained by the service, six of them on active duty, the remainder laid up, each with a caretaker group consisting of a sailing master, three warrant officers, a Marine guard of nine, twelve seamen, and a cook. The navy's officer corps was to be reduced to about 150, of whom only nine would be captains. Talbot's name was not on the list as first drawn up.

On 4 April 1801, the ship *Herald* sailed from Boston for the West Indies to tell everyone to go home. She arrived at St. Nicholas Mole near the middle of May and found *Constitution* in port. Talbot's orders were to take her to Boston, pay off the crew, report which of his junior officers merited and desired further service, and keep the ship otherwise ready for duty. He sailed on 17 May, apparently after getting off a letter to the secretary expressing his views on the retention list. Following two days off Cape Francois, concluding affairs there, the big frigate left West Indian waters. She anchored once more off Boston Light in Nantasket Roads on 11 June, and moved to the inner harbor three days later.

By this time, Stoddert, who had worked hard to create the navy, had tired of waiting for the new administration to appoint a successor and resigned the office. Jefferson named Henry Dearborn acting secretary until the right man could be found. On 19 June, Dearborn wrote to Talbot personally to advise him he *would* be kept on. Talbot then seems to have reopened the entire seniority argument he had had with Stoddert with the new secretary of the navy, Robert Smith, who assumed office on 27 July. Smith's first response, naturally, was that he would familiarize himself with the situation and all that had gone before, and would get back to Talbot.

TIME FOR OVERHAUL

Although his own future was uncertain, Talbot continued to take steps to ensure *Constitution*'s renewed readiness for service. July was when he reported to the secretary the material condition of the ship, including "insufficient Beams and plank," "a subject of great distress," and when worn, equipment was sent ashore for repair and replacement parts ordered. Much of August was spent offloading the ship completely in preparation for the expected repairs to be accomplished under the guidance of Master Carpenter Hartt, one of the ship's builders.

September arrived without any decision from the secretary concerning Talbot's situation. Perhaps recognizing he no longer had the advocacy of a president, Talbot decided to conclude the matter and submitted his resignation on the 8th. Smith accepted it on the 21st, informing the commodore that because he had resigned voluntarily, he was not entitled to the four months' extra pay provided for those discharged as a result of the force reduction. That same day, Secretary Smith issued orders for Hull to take charge of the frigate and ensure her thorough overhaul.

Constitution was moved to Union (May's) Wharf on 15 October for repairs, the "navy yard" being little more than a designated plot of land. Hull's crew was reduced to that stipulated for a ship in ordinary, the overhaul to be done largely by hired civilian labor. While the major work consisted of the renewal of decks and some outer hull planking, other contractors repaired the chain and fire pumps, mended the stern lantern, made new sails and hammocks, repaired the camboose, rehung the bell, and made new main and fore yards, main and foretopsail yards, and fore and mizzen topmast crosstrees.

Hull was detached for new duties on 15 April 1802. Nicholson, now navy yard commandant, assumed responsibilities for the conclusion of the ship's overhaul. During May, quarter galleries were repaired and new rigging put in hand. Early in June, a new flagstone platform was laid for the camboose, tin was received for tinning the sail room, and sheathing paper was ordered for the expected recoppering. Sailing Master Haraden assumed charge of the ship on 18 June, however, with orders to place her in ordinary even as she was being completely painted, inside and out. Carver Simeon Skillen completed his repair work to the stern, quarter galleries, and head decorations, and submitted his bill for $369, an amount more than half the size of his bill four years earlier for the figurehead. Ephraim Thayer and two men spent eight days repairing twenty-five gun carriages.

Haraden moved *Constitution* from the wharf to an anchorage off the navy yard on 2 July, as all work gradually tapered off and came to an end. Hartt was released on the 31st. The frigate swung quietly at her moorings as events went on without her.

CHAPTER FOUR

The Ship and Life Aboard Her

With *Constitution* inactivated for the first time, it seems to be the right moment to pause in the narrative and consider what she looked like in those early days, the makeup and organization of her crew, and the routine of daily life aboard.

WHAT DID SHE LOOK LIKE?

The truth is we really don't know exactly how *Constitution* looked when first she saw service. While the designer's original draught still exists, there is much evidence that the builders did not follow the plans with exactitude. The earliest known artist's rendering was done about 1803 by Michel Felice Cornè; the earliest model dates from 1812. But if we cannot see her directly, we can construct a reasonably good image of her first appearance by extrapolation from the draught, from diary and journal entries, and from newspaper articles of the period.

Constitution's hull originally bore a broad yellow ocher band from the vicinity of the hawse pipes to the quarter galleries, the outer surfaces of the gun port lids being the same color. This band extended approximately from the level of the channels down to the top of the main wales. Below, in the "bends," the ship was tarred; above, including the quarterdeck bulwarks, she was painted black. Whether or not there was decorative painting other than this on her sides is unknown, but Cornè shows a yellow ocher "pin stripe" on the mouldings at the spar deck sill level.

The bow head area of the frigate originally was constructed with only tail and foot rails, completely free of any weather bulwarks, gratings, or privies. The bowsprit was lashed with nine-inch hempen gammoning passing through a slot in the cutwater. Topping the cutwater was a figurehead of "an Herculean figure standing on the firm rock of Independence resting one hand on the fasces, which was bound by the Genius of America and the other hand presenting a scroll of paper supposed to be the Constitution of America with proper appendages, the foundation of Legislation." Cornè shows the figure's left hand atop the fasces and his right extending the scroll. As completed, it also included "his battoon lying beneath him." It may have been painted all white. Below and aft of the figurehead on either side were the trailboards. These had carved upon them a curling vine or leaf pattern with no apparent eye-catching feature. Indeed, they even may have been unaccented with color to make them stand out.

The appearance of the stern is even more dimly seen. Modern students generally feel there were six windows in the transom, with pilasters separating them, but Cornè, in an 1805 painting of the ship, shows eight, including one located in the after bulkhead of each quarter gallery. Be that as it may, the decorations were quite resplendent. High up near the taffrail in the center was a spread eagle. Immediately below was the familiar shield of the United States being "presented" by two Nereids, who, in turn, were flanked by pairs of unmounted cannon, one resting partially atop the other. Above each outer window was another Nereid, facing the center grouping and holding a wreath in extended hands. On each quarter gallery's after outer section were the classical figures of Liberty and Justice. Framing the whole was an entwinement of carved rope. The name was borne below the windows, as it still is, but probably done in Roman intaglio rather than the modern block letters. All of this decoration undoubtedly was picked out in a distinctive color, probably the yellow ocher, but perhaps white, or, much less likely, gilt.

The quarter galleries, those "green houses" on either side of the stern, also carried the pilaster theme adjacent to their three windows. Likewise, carved bas relief thematically akin to that on the trailboards decorated the panels immediately beneath the windows, with other work forming a radial pattern on the undersides of the overhang and also "capping" the upper (horizontal) roof line.

The ship was built without bulwarks surrounding the forecastle and waist. A simple double line of hammock netting, supported by crane irons, extended aft to the entry port on either side. There were no anchor ports or billboards, nor were bridle ports present at the gun-deck level originally.

The frigate's guns probably were painted black. Their carriages also may have been black, although red, brown, and green were in common use at the time, as well. Likewise, these colors were equally popular for the deck fittings (coamings, etc.).

The earliest known portrait of USS *Constitution*, a gouache by Michel Felice Cornè, and the only contemporary representation of the Hercules figurehead. Details apparent in the picture point to its having been painted between June and August 1803 at Boston. Careful comparison with documentary evidence of the day indicates that it is one of the most accurate paintings of the ship ever done. Note particularly the absence of any bulwarks forward of the mainmast. *Courtesy of the USS* Constitution *Museum*

The Navy Department had no established painting regulations at the time, nor would it for decades.

No records have been found concerning the appearance of *Constitution*'s spars and yards. The Cornè painting, once again, is the most nearly contemporary. In it, the inner and outer thirds of the bowsprit are black or brown, while the middle third, together with the jib and flying jib booms, are yellow ocher. The masts—lower, top, and topgallant sections—are yellow ocher all the way to the trucks, with blackened doublings. The bands on the fore and main masts also are blackened. The yards are brown or black.

Furled on the yards were some of her suit of about three dozen sail comprising an acre of canvas. When set and seen close aboard they showed streaky, mottled brown characteristic of woven flax, but at a distance took on the storied whiteness and cloudlike appearance under a bright sun. The fighting tops, those perches for Marine snipers, were left "natural." Mounted on either side of each was a brass swivel "howitzer" of about three-inch bore to be used against the mass of humanity to be found above decks on enemy ships.

A number of boats were carried, but exactly how many is not known; six to eight is the likely range. Typically, one was carried in davits astern, one in davits on either quarter, and perhaps five nested in two groups in chocks on the skid beams spanning the main hatch. While most were painted white (without a different color below the waterline), it was not uncommon to use several colors to ease identification of otherwise identical boats at fair distances. One of the frigate's cutters is believed to have been blue at this time.

The Crew: Its Organization and Duties

The organization of *Constitution*'s crew was a highly structured yet flexible one that sought to assign each person specific duties in a wide range of foreseeable activities, many of which would have to be accomplished during periods of high stress. It was a system that had evolved in the seagoing community largely exclusive of national boundaries through centuries of painful trial and tragic error.

In the young United States Navy, the most senior man aboard might be an officer of the *rank* of captain, but who, because he was in charge of a number of ships, was known as the "commodore." He shared the great cabin with the ship's captain and took precedence over him in the matters of honors and ceremonies, but left the running of this, his flagship, to the captain. It frequently was the case early in the nineteenth century that *Constitution*'s captain also bore the responsibilities of being the squadron commander, as we have seen with both Nicholson and Talbot.

The senior officer directly responsible for the ship was the captain (which was both his rank and title). Generally in his late thirties or forties and with fifteen or more years of sea experience behind him, in the Continental Navy and/or merchant service, he was totally responsible for everything relating to the ship and had powers very nearly as unlimited: leave and liberty, promotion and demotion—life and death. The unforgiving nature of the sea made such authority necessary.

Next in line was the first lieutenant, the senior of the four to six lieutenants assigned. The billet today is called the executive officer. His duty was to carry out the policies of the captain, and, like the captain, he stood no watches, but nearly always was "available." He saw to the proper standing of watches and the organization and implementation of daily or periodic routines, and ensured the cleanliness of the ship and oversaw its maintenance, reporting his activities and findings regularly to the captain. All others in the ship reported to him, or through him to the captain. On special evolutions, such as coming to anchor or getting under way, the first lieutenant "took the deck"—he was in charge of the event. In battle, he maneuvered the ship in accordance with the captain's orders. In sum, the comfort and well-being of everyone on board, together with their duty assignments for a wide variety of evolutions, were his responsibility. He was a very busy man and generally very demanding of his subordinates. Normally, he never left the ship if the captain was absent, and when he did, rarely remained away overnight.

The other lieutenants were the watch standers, relieving one another in an endless rotation at sea and in port, ensuring that the captain's orders and ship's routine were carried out precisely and punctiliously. The lieutenants also were division officers, responsible for the activities and welfare of the crew and for their direction in battle, as well as for the maintenance of particular sections of the ship and at least one of the ship's boats. Prior to their entry into the young navy, these men almost invariably had been merchant captains or senior mates. The second lieutenant could not leave the ship if the first lieutenant was absent, and never could more than half the lieutenants be away at the same time. They, too, rarely were absent overnight.

The sailing master was the next in rank, and, in the early navy, generally had seen previous service as a mate. He was the navigator, keeping track of where the ship was and the course necessary to get her where she was going. It wasn't the precise science it is today: The sailing master would keep a reasonably careful plot of the courses steered and the distances made good, and at noon on clear days, determine the sun's highest azimuth at local apparent noon with a quadrant to confirm his estimate of latitude. Because he had no accurate timepiece, longitude could only be guessed at. Nevertheless, the sailing master taught the art of navigation, as he practiced it, to the midshipmen. And because he was responsible for the ship's trim (her attitude in the water), he had charge of the stowage of stores in the hold, as well as the water and spirits, and of the anchors and cables.

Because they did not stand watches, the purser, the surgeon and his mates, the chaplain, and the one or two Marine officers aboard were known as "idlers."

The purser had charge of the ship's monies and accounts. He purchased and dispensed provisions and other stores, "slops" (clothing), and small stores (sundries). Unlike earlier days when pursers made most of their money by selling their wares at usurious prices, the American purser bore the heavy responsibility for every penny and every item in the ship's account. It behooved him to keep a tight rein on the receipts and disbursements. The surgeon and his mates held daily "sick calls" for minor complaints, tended the sick and injured, and advised the captain and first lieutenant of measures to maintain a healthy crew. The surgeon himself lived in the wardroom with the lieutenants, while his mates occupied quarters in the cockpit, where the wounded were tended in battle. The chaplain attended to the spiritual needs of the crew, often as he or the captain saw them. But besides the Sunday services when operations permitted, and burials, the chaplain (especially before the 1820s, when schoolmasters were entered upon the navy's rolls) frequently taught the three Rs to the ship's boys, and perhaps the classics, a language, and sometimes mathematics to the midshipmen. The Marine officer(s), of course, had charge of the functioning of the Marine Guard, which made up about 10 percent of the total crew. The Marines were the ship's police force in peace and snipers and assault force in battle.

The idlers came from sources as varied as their callings. Pursers, as often as not, were men who had had a taste of business life ashore, although some were men of some education attracted to the naval life but whose ambitions did not extend to the handling of a ship. Navy medical men most frequently were what we today would call "interns," doctors by schooling but lacking practical experience. Chaplains may or may not have been men of the cloth. There is many an instance where the individual filling the position in fact was the captain's clerk, but being assigned to the pastoral position meant he could be paid more.

Junior to the "idlers" (and often cited as being senior only to the "ship's cat") were the midshipmen. Eight to twelve of these teenage student officers were the usual complement for *Constitution*, but in the days following the War of 1812 and prior to the foundation of the Naval Academy at Annapolis in 1845, at times there were as many as two dozen of the "young gentlemen" aboard. Generally, they came from the "better" families and had a smattering of education. They stood watches, practiced navigation with the sailing master, relayed orders from the quarterdeck to their assigned stations, and presumably prepared themselves for qualification as lieutenants. They were required to keep journals akin to the ship's log, which the captain regularly reviewed. Likewise, the sailing master, chaplain, and/or schoolmaster would report on the progress of their young charges in the subjects under their cognizance. In port, midshipmen oftentimes were employed as boat officers, supervisors of watering parties, etc.

Next in the ship's hierarchy were the warrant officers—the technical specialists: boatswain, gunner, sailmaker, and carpenter. Each ship's captain was authorized to appoint his warrant officers from among those men who demonstrated their talents in the several fields needed. The boatswain was responsible for the rigging and seeing to it that everything aloft was properly maintained; he traditionally carried a silver call (or "pipe") on a lanyard around his neck as his badge of office and, in battle, took station on the forecastle. The gunner had the job of keeping all weapons battle ready, as well as safeguarding the powder magazines. In battle, he was in the main magazine overseeing the issuance of powder charges to the long guns. The sailmaker, in addition to caring for several suits of sails, also made the hammocks, sickbay cots, awnings, and wind funnels. The carpenter, besides making repairs to the ship's structure, was responsible for the building of boats and construction of chests and barrels. In battle, he headed up what today is called the damage control party, with plugs to jam in shot holes, etc. The boatswain, sailmaker, and carpenter together made an aloft inspection daily to ensure the ship's readiness to maneuver and respond to any and every sailing condition.

Senior among the enlisted crew were the petty officers, men of demonstrated nautical talent and relatively good deportment. Principal among these was the master-at-arms, who oversaw discipline, commanded prisoners, took charge of clothing and personnel items found adrift, ensured the decorum of the berth deck, and guarded against liquor smuggling by boat crews and shore parties. The quartermasters were among the most experienced seamen aboard and had charge of signals, keeping a lookout, and steering the ship. Boatswain's mates, quarter gunners and gunner's mates, carpenter's mates, and sailmaker's mates assisted their respective warrant officers in the accomplishment of their duties. The boatswain's mates, like their leader, all wore silver calls, which were used to signal particular orders throughout the ship. Quarter gunners assisted the gunner's mates in maintaining a division of guns.

Beneath this lordly group was the great mass of the crew: armorer, tinker, cordwainer, yeoman of the gunroom, stewards, loblolly boys, cook and assistants, able seamen, ordinary seamen, landsmen, and boys. All told, there were some 22 officers and warrant officers and 378 enlisted men, according to original manning requirements. *Constitution*'s crew, after her initial service, was increased to 450 or more.

The members of the enlisted segment of the crew came from many sources and countries. The seafaring community had been a cosmopolitan one for centuries, sailors interested only in their shipmates' skills and reliability, not their races, places of origin, or past histories. At the outset of the navy, there was an official prohibition against blacks being signed on, but it generally was observed in the breach. An occasional Native American likewise found his way on board.

Pay in the early years generally was considered adequate, although not always competitive with the merchant service. The captain, combining his monthly pay and allowance for rations, drew slightly over $2,000 annually. Midshipmen, at the lower end of the officer scale, were paid about $430. Among the enlisted men, petty officers earned around $19 monthly, while boys received from $5 to $8 for the same period.

Pay could be augmented by "prize money." In a system that dated back at least seven hundred years, a victorious crew profited from the capture of enemy ships subsequently brought safely into a friendly port and adjudged a bona fide enemy. In the United States, the federal government was allocated one-half of the assessed value, and the crew divided up the remainder on a twenty-share system. The captain received three shares (one of which went to the embarked commodore, should there have been one at the time the capture was made). The commissioned officers as a body received two shares; warrant officers, two; the various petty officers, six; and the remaining crew, seven. Thus, the ship's portion of a $200,000 prize would result in $15,000 for the captain, and, at the other end of the scale, about $100 each for the seamen, boys, landsmen, and private Marines in the crew. No matter an individual's station in life, the prospect of prize money in wartime was a strong inducement to "signing on."

WATCHES

The officers and petty officers designated to stand watches normally did so on the basis of four hours on (i.e., 8:00–12:00, 12:00–4:00, 4:00–8:00) and eight or twelve hours off, depending on the number qualified and available for duty. The remainder of the crew, other than "idlers," was divided into larboard and starboard watches, working "four and four." In order to prevent the same people from having to stand the same watches *ad infinitum*, the period from 4:00 to 8:00

P.M. daily was divided further into two 2-hour periods, the "dogwatches." Further variety was provided by dividing each watch section into "quarter watches," which alternated standing their duty in the fighting tops and on the spar deck.

In making watch assignments, the most experienced group as a whole was that assigned to the forecastle, for they were responsible for not only the foremast sails and the jibs, but the anchors as well. They were known collectively as the "forecastle" or "sheet anchor" men. The similar group on the quarterdeck was the "afterguard." Individually, the most knowledgeable and agile men were assigned as fore-, main-, or mizzentopmen. It was they who worked at the dizzying heights above ship and sea, out on yardarms whose great lengths magnified the ship's every move so that they were forever in danger of being whipped off to their deaths. Here the rule was "one hand for the ship, and one for self."

BATTLE STATIONS

The crew also was organized into five or six divisions, based principally upon the gun batteries. On the gun deck were the First, Second, and Third Divisions, each assigned ten of the 24-pounder long guns (five on either side). The Fourth Division handled the forecastle guns; the Fifth, those on the quarterdeck.[1] Some captains preferred to reduce the sizes of gun crews and form a Sixth Division whose muscle power could be put to good use in bucket brigades and handling fire pumps and hoses. When formed, this division was commanded by the first lieutenant; the others, by the remaining lieutenants (the second lieutenant commanded the First Division, etc.). At least one midshipman also was assigned to each division, and sometimes, one to each long gun, to ensure the prompt and correct fulfillment of orders.

The gun crew of a 24-pounder varied from nine to fourteen men, depending upon the size of the ship's crew and how the divisions were organized. A "gun crew" actually was responsible for *two* guns: those in the same relative position on either side of the ship. Thus, several members of the gun crew were supernumeraries assigned to begin to ready the gun on the unengaged side at such time as the captain might so order; to assist in damage control if required; to participate in boarding parties; or to replace men killed, wounded, or otherwise unavailable for duty. The crew typically consisted of first and second captains, first and second spongers, first and second loaders, train tackle men, shot passers, and powder passers (the "monkeys"). The lighter carronades, carried subsequent to this time on the spar deck, required only six to nine men in each crew, even though they fired a 32-pound shot.

Operating a 24-pounder weighing about 6,500 pounds was backbreaking labor. First, the tackle securing it tight against the ship's side was cast loose and the gun hauled inboard by means of a tackle affixed to the inner end of its carriage; then the gun port lid halves were removed and stowed. The loader placed a 6-pound powder charge in the muzzle and rammed it all the way down the bore, to be followed by a wad, the shot, and another wad (to keep the shot from rolling out). A gun captain then primed the piece by inserting a quill of fine grain powder in the touch hole leading from the upper rear surface of the gun down into the bore just above the powder bag. The tip of the quill pierced the bag, making the "connection" with the outside world. The gun was hauled back into the gun port by brute force on the side tackles, then aimed by using hand-spikes to force it left or right and a "quoin" to adjust the elevation. More fine grain powder was spread around the upper end of the touch hole in the area called the "apron," all hands got clear, and the first captain stood by with a glowing slow match, awaiting the order to apply it to fire the gun. When fired, the explosion caused the gun to recoil to the limit of its breeching tackle, ready to be swabbed out and the cycle repeated. A good crew could sustain fire at the rate of a shot every two or three minutes. Carronades, being smaller and lighter, were easier to handle, even with smaller crews. Exercising the crew at the great guns occurred at the captain's pleasure, and not unusually occupied an hour or two.

There were myriad operations that had to be attended to by the crew over and beyond those associated with battle: weighing and coming to anchor, watering, sailing evolutions, man overboard rescue, etc., etc. All these assignments were made by name on the ship's watch, quarter, and station bill. Maintained by the first lieutenant, with the assistance of the division officers, it specifically told each sailor what he was to do in each evolution. The crewman, on pain of the "cat," was expected to have his part memorized thoroughly and to perform the required duty flawlessly under any conditions. Thus, the watch, quarter, and station bill completely encompassed a man's life so long as he was assigned to the ship.

At-Sea Routine

The routine aboard *Constitution* at sea logically revolved about her safe navigation through the water. The watch was set on the spar deck and fighting tops, and almost nothing was permitted in those areas that would interfere. The warrant officers' daily inspection and repairs that could occur nowhere else nor be delayed were the limit. The watch was to be quiet and alert, and if the ship was sailing in good weather and alone, a part of the watch was allowed to catnap on station.

Reveille was held at daylight (i.e., about thirty minutes prior to sunrise) and the hammocks rolled, tied, and stowed in the nettings surrounding the spar deck in less than fifteen minutes. Until breakfast, timed to feed the offgoing morning and oncoming forenoon watches sequentially, cleaning the ship and readying her for another day was the order of business. The breakfast of tea and bread or hard-tack required almost an hour to serve, consume, and clean up after. (During the latter part of this and all mealtimes, the "smoking lamp" was lighted: Those who wished to do so could smoke in the vicinity of the camboose.)

With breakfast over, the cook and his helpers began readying the noon meal—the one hot meal of the day. And elsewhere on the gun deck, the other trades began their work, which continued until 4:00 P.M., with the noon hour reserved for dinner. Forward to starboard, the area typically was reserved as a classroom for midshipmen or the ship's boys; often canvas screens were tacked up to eliminate distractive sights. In the large open deck space beneath the boat skids in the waist, the sailmaker and his mates might be making and mending sails, or the cooper refurbishing barrels. Elsewhere on the starboard side of the gun deck, between the guns, skilled craftsmen, such as the cordwainer and a tinker, plied their trades. The port side of the gun deck from the main hatch aft was reserved as an officers' promenade, where those worthies, when off duty, might bring folding stools and find relaxation in a brighter and better ventilated area than their wardroom.

Punishment most often was carried out before noon. In the United States Navy of the early years, flogging was most frequently imposed, although it was closely limited in comparison with the Royal Navy. By the Naval Act of 1799, ships' captains could award no more than twelve lashes for a single offense; courts-martial, one hundred. The limits of an offense, however, were not defined. If a man were to get drunk, pick a fight with his petty officer, then desert (the three commonest disciplinary problems), he clearly had committed an offense; but his captain legally could count *three* offenses and award him thirty-six lashes.

The flogging was done with the guilty party trussed barebacked to a hatch grating upended for the purpose. It was accomplished by one or more boat-swain's mates using the cat-o'-nine-tails—a whip with nine strands, each knotted or weighted at the free end. To ensure a proper "laying on of the lash," the mates would trade off after twelve, or perhaps only six, strokes. The decreed number of lashes applied, the poor wretch was cut down, his back tended to, and he was returned to duty as soon as possible. His shipmates, who had been required to witness his punishment, returned immediately to the day's routine. A court-martial's award of a hundred lashes per offense might result in "flogging through the squadron," where the victim was lashed to a grating in a boat and rowed from ship to ship in harbor, a boatswain's mate from each vessel laying on his command's share of the whole sentence. When the felon showed signs of succumbing to the ordeal, it would be suspended for however long it took him to recover—days, weeks—then pick up where left off and carried on either to another recovery phase or completion.

Three other forms of punishment were hanging (for capital crimes like murder and treason), "running the gauntlet," and "starting." Thieves often were made to run the gauntlet, i.e., made to crawl on all fours through a double line of shipmates equipped with knotted ropes who lashed away merrily at this most reprehensible form of seagoing criminal. "Starting" was the use by petty officers of short lengths of knotted rope, called a "starter" or "knout," to encourage alacrity in their less-than-eager subordinates. Such use might, or might not, have been specifically directed by one of the officers.

To return to the routine: Noontime saw the feeding of the oncoming and offgoing watches their principal meal of the day. A major feature of this meal was the first issue of the day of the sailor's favorite elixir, grog. With that under his belt, and a warm glow suffusing his being, "Jack" was ready for an afternoon's labors. At about 4:00 P.M., after a final titivation, it was time for the supper hour. This meal usually was composed of "leftovers" from dinner, together with bread, perhaps some cheese, and tea—and the second issuance of grog.

Each officer took his meals in his respective cabin, wardroom, steerage, or warrant officers' "mess." Each group ate at a slightly later time than the more junior one, thereby ensuring a significant number of the hierarchy would be available to respond instantly to any emergency, internal or external.

The crew similarly was organized into messes of six to ten men each and ate picnic-style seated around communal pots brought down to the berth deck. The senior member of each mess was its "president," with absolute powers concerning mess operation and etiquette. He took the first choice from the pot, and he decreed the order of serving thereafter. Customarily, one member of the mess was "elected" on a weekly basis to serve as "mess cook." He would have the responsibility for setting out the utensils from the mess chest at each meal, for delivering the meal from the camboose, and for cleaning up afterward, carefully stowing any remains, as they would constitute a portion of the subsequent meal.

It was at eight bells of the afternoon watch, too, that the purser and the stewards would go below to break out the foodstuffs for the next day's meals. The ten-pound chunks of salted meat or fish from the casks were placed in a "harness cask" near the camboose and soaked in several changes of fresh water through the night to help reduce their saltiness. What food was broken out on which day was a matter of Navy Department regulation, which could be varied only on the specific orders of the captain. Any spoilage found upon breakout was "surveyed" formally by the first lieutenant and sailing master, reported in writing to the captain, and thence to the Navy Department, which oversaw the victualing contracts.

Nothing was wasted unless it was unbelievably foul. The bread (or, more properly, biscuit) oftentimes was weevil filled. Similarly, the cheese, with age, would become alive with long yellow worms. On "fish" and "butter" days, the ship might smell like an ancient whaler.

With a diet such as this, the advent of fresh foods was of great moment. No opportunity was lost by good commanders to provide such benefits to their men. A ship newly to sea from a well-stocked port might present a startling sight (and a barnyard aroma): bullocks penned in the manger area of the gun deck; freshly slaughtered halves and quarters hanging from adjacent beams; perhaps pigs and sheep restrained in some of the nested boats, and crated chickens in others; and in the vicinity, the baled hay and bagged corn with which to sustain them for the three or four weeks the luckiest would live.

Besides the official efforts to provide fresh food, all hands could avail themselves of the opportunity to purchase "stores" ashore or from bumboats. The officers, with storerooms set aside for them, could stock up for the next at-sea period to whatever extent the mess exchequer permitted. The enlisted men, with no such luxury, oftentimes went on eating "orgies," spending their last penny on fruits and vegetables and gorging themselves until their systems revolted.

With the completion of the evening meal and the final sweepdown of the ship, the crew usually was at liberty to relax. Gathering in little groups, endless sea stories would be spun off by the older tars to awe and edify their callow compatriots. "Hammocks" were piped down at sunset, and the ship largely settled in for the night when the darkness was complete. All lights were extinguished, but for those in "officers' country," where those in steerage and the cockpit might be permitted an additional half hour and those in the wardroom until 10:00 P.M. The only people allowed to be moving about below decks after hours were the midshipman of the watch and the master-at-arms and his corporals, who routinely patrolled to ensure the ship's security against fire and flooding, and to discover "skulkers," whose presence might indicate attempted unnatural acts or impending desertion, or be the harbingers of mutiny.

In-Port Routine

When the ship was in port, a similar routine was in effect. In lieu of the many men engaged in watch standing, however, there was increased emphasis on, and allocations of manpower for, maintenance and cleanliness, as well as the need to assign working parties and boat crews to resupply and rewater the ship.

The day formally began at 8:00 A.M., after reveille, sweepdown, and breakfast, with the firing of the morning gun, which announced that *Constitution* was "open for business." On watch on the quarterdeck were a lieutenant, one or more midshipmen, a quartermaster, a boatswain's mate, and one or two boys. This group would monitor the ship's safety, both as to her own anchorage and the activities of other ships in the harbor. They would render or return the "honors" due passing ships and craft, depending on their relative seniorities. For the arrival and departure of boats, the lieutenant would ensure the timely mustering of the Marine Guard and side boys, and the observance of the correct protocol. His was a heavy responsibility, for a ship's (and thereby her captain's) reputation was made or broken as a result of the promptitude and smartness of such evolutions.

The firing of the evening gun at sunset indicated the end of the public day. Any boats away from the ship began their return trip as soon as it was heard in order to be back before dark or shortly thereafter. The Marine sentries were stationed with loaded muskets on the forecastle, quarterdeck, and both gangways. They were to ensure that no small craft came alongside the ship unheralded and that no one attempted desertion. At regular intervals throughout the night, their calls of "all's well" carried around the spar deck, while the master-at-arms and his mates maintained their vigil below.

Such was the life at sea and in harbor in *Constitution:* damp, noisy, dangerous, crowded, smelly, too hot or too cold, and in constant motion. Why did anyone ever enlist? To get away from someone or something that, at the time, seemed more disagreeable: professional failure, creditor, orphanage, irate husband or brother, fervent female, lack of food. Some did it for a place to sleep. Some even did it for patriotism or a belief that they *wanted* to go to sea. Why did any ever go back? Many never got clear of creditors or irate males wherever they went. Others went back because, like the astronauts of the twentieth century looking back at the "big blue marble," out on the expanse of the world's ocean they found themselves inexplicably close to understanding their minuscule place in the vastness that is the universe and, at the same time, their oneness with it. They respected the awesome forces of nature, and the fortunate ones survived them. It is a feeling, a sense, a landsman can never know.

The Ship and
Life Aboard Her

CHAPTER FIVE

The Barbary War

SEPTEMBER 1795–JULY 1804

BACKGROUND

The treaty with Algiers—and it had been only with Algiers, which held nominal sway over Tunis and Tripoli under the Ottoman Turk—committed the United States to paying a lump sum of $642,500 to free captive Americans and make a "down payment" for free trade; to an annual tribute in naval stores amounting to $21,600; and to making semi-annual deliveries of "presents" on the same scale as Holland, Sweden, and Denmark. Unavoidable delays in getting the money together led the acting American consul, Joel Barlow, to promise the dey, Hassan Pasha, to build him a 32-gun frigate in the United States and also to deliver some "unscheduled," better-than-average "presents." Barlow's promise of a warship, although not a part of the original deal, was accepted in Washington, and the frigate, subsequently named *Crescent*, was built in Portsmouth, New Hampshire. Designed by Fox, she was launched, ironically, on 4 July 1797—before either *Constellation* or *Constitution.*

Following the Algerine treaty in September 1795, another was signed with Tripoli in November 1796 (for $58,000) and a third with Tunis in August 1797 (for about $107,000, all told). In the great disparity of sums, as regards Tripoli, lay the germ of renewed trouble. The Bey of Tunis, Hamouda Pasha, was cautious in his reaction, because the Americans and the Algerines had become "friends," and he had a common border with the latter. Yusuf Karamanli, the bashaw of Tripoli, at a distance from his more powerful Moslem brothers, tended to be feistier. The arrival at Algiers, in the spring of 1798, of *Crescent*, the schooners *Lelah Eisha* and *Hamdullah* (part of the "naval stores"), and the brig

Hassan Bashaw and schooner *Skjoldebrand* (which had been bought by the dey), convinced Karamanli that he had been snookered.

When James Leander Cathcart, the first American consul following the treaty, arrived in Tripoli in April 1799, he immediately was berated by the bashaw, who claimed he had been promised all sorts of goodies (including a brig) by the American negotiators, none of which had been delivered. He would have them or—by Allah!—there would be war. Working through the British consul (because the bashaw at first refused to see him directly), in four days Cathcart gained a settlement of all grievances, real or imagined, for $22,500, and no brig. With eighty American merchantmen in and about the Mediterranean at this time, and only the government's chartered dispatch brig *Sophia* present, it was well to have the pirates mollified.

Threats and peevishness aside, the United States enjoyed about fifteen months without incident in the Mediterranean. Then, in July 1800, a Tripoline polacre captured the New York brig *Catherine*, bound for Leghorn. Cathcart managed to get the bashaw to disavow the act and release the merchantman, but only after three months of tough arguing—and with a threat that there would be war if Bashaw Yusuf wasn't made to feel as "loved" as his piratical associates.

Just as this latest problem with Tripoli was being resolved, the Dey of Algiers decided to flex his muscles by forcing an American warship, the 24-gun light frigate *George Washington*, under Captain Bainbridge, to transport his annual tribute to Constantinople. Bainbridge carried out the onerous task with considerable credit to himself, but it was, nonetheless, an unmitigated affront to American sovereignty and could not be ignored.

THE FIRST MEDITERRANEAN SQUADRON

Thomas Jefferson became president on 4 March 1801. When he learned of the Tripoline and Algerine attitudes and actions, he decided to send a "squadron of observation" to the Mediterranean whose purpose, as he wrote in a letter to the bashaw, was "to superintend the safety of our commerce, and to exercise our seamen in nautical duties," and, furthermore, "we mean to rest the safety of our commerce on the resources of our own strength and bravery in every sea." The squadron consisted of frigates *President*, 44, *Philadelphia*, 38, and *Essex*, 32, and the sloop of war *Enterprize*, 12. The squadron units, under Commodore Dale, were to fight if attacked, but not to seek action. As in the Quasi-War, they also were to defend any American cargo ship being attacked. These elements were to be found in the directives of the earlier war, but there was a surprising new one: Should an attacking ship be defeated, it was *not* to be taken prize. Such a ship was to be disarmed and reduced to the barest essentials necessary to make shore safely; if it sank in the engagement, then the crew was to be put ashore "on some part of the Barbary shore most convenient to you." With these orders, Dale sailed on 2 June 1801. The bashaw of Tripoli had cut down the flagpole outside the American consulate on 14 May, his way of declaring war.

As Dale's units rendezvoused at Gibraltar following a stormy crossing, they found there the two largest vessels of the Tripoline fleet, the 28-gun *Meshuda* (one-time American ship *Betsey*) and a 14-gun brig, preparing to enter the Atlantic against American shipping. Murad Rais, the Moslem admiral, denied that there existed a state of war with the United States, but Dale had heard enough in diplomatic circles at the Rock to make him suspicious. Upon sailing east, he left *Philadelphia* (Bainbridge) to keep an eye on them and to "take him when he goes out."

Through the summer and fall, Dale kept an intermittent blockade of Tripoli, causing some hardships but lacking sufficient force or logistic support to make it complete. On 1 August, *Enterprize* (Lt. Cmdg. Andrew Sterett) encountered the fourteen-gun Tripoline brig *Tripoli* while en route to Malta. For three hours, these two small vessels lay within pistol shot of one another, blazing away with all guns. Sterett hammered away until the Moslem hurled his colors into the sea, then boarded to find a shambles with sixty of the eighty-man crew either dead or wounded. Not one American even had been scratched. In keeping with orders, Sterett directed his men to "heave all his Guns Over board Cut away his Masts, & leave him In a situation, that he can Just get into some Port." The bashaw thus received a clear message as to the merits of the Americans as sea fighters.

Back in Gibraltar, Murad Rais gave up waiting for *Philadelphia* to leave. With local help, he and his crews acquired small craft and slipped across the Straits to Morocco, thence to Tripoli. *Meshuda* and her consort were left at Gibraltar, but will be heard from again.

With the coming of winter, blockading operations off Tripoli had to be abandoned because of prevailing bad weather. Too, the navy still was using one-year enlistments, which meant some sort of rotation had to be established and most ships had to return to the United States. *Philadelphia* and *Essex* stayed in the Mediterranean through the winter. *President* and *Enterprize* came home.

The Second Mediterranean Squadron

In January 1802, Secretary Smith began issuing orders to organize and dispatch a replacement squadron to the Mediterranean. *Enterprize*, the one non-frigate in the navy—and, in many ways, the type best suited for blockading Tripoli's spitkit port—was to return. The other units were *Constellation*, 38, *Chesapeake*, 36, *New York*, 36, and *Adams*, 28. To command the squadron was Capt. Richard Valentine Morris, who was given permission to take his wife with him. Morris' orders had none of the restrictions in them that had prevented Dale from making a bigger impression.

The ships sailed separately this time, little *Enterprize* returning to the scene of her earlier triumph first. Morris arrived at Gibraltar in *Chesapeake* at the end of May. It was seven weeks before his final ship, *Adams*, put in an appearance. In the meantime, he had gotten on famously with the British and had denied a move by the emperor of Morocco to secure the release of *Meshuda* and the Tripoline brig. He also sent *Constellation* (Captain Murray) to blockade Tripoli. *Essex* left for the United States in June. When Morris at last sailed from Gibraltar on 22 July, *Adams* (Capt. Hugh G. Campbell) remained to watch *Meshuda* and the emperor.

If ever there was a relaxing way to go to war, Morris found it. Proceeding at a leisurely pace, he visited ports in Spain, France, Italy, and Sicily before making Malta at year's end. Along the way, his wife announced that there would be a blessed event. Malta was as close as he had come to Tripoli in seven months. On 30 January 1803, he got his squadron under way with the intention of making for Tripoli. A gale, however, caused damage to some of the ships, and all returned to Malta. (Mrs. Morris had taken up residence there, anyway.)

On 19 February, Morris sailed again, this time for Tunis at the request of Consul William Eaton, whose machinations had gotten him in trouble with the bey. Although he had been warned that trouble was brewing, on arrival Morris blithely went ashore as if he were going on liberty—and found himself arrested pending payment of $34,000, which amount the bey felt Eaton owed him. Furthermore, the bey wanted no more of Eaton. Negotiations ultimately were successful, and Morris sailed (with Eaton) for Algiers on 13 March. Once again, he found conflict. Consul Richard O'Brien was retiring, and the dey refused to receive Cathcart as his successor. No arrests this time, just hard words, and the squadron went on to Gibraltar.

Morris returned to Malta, by way of Leghorn, on 1 May, ready once more to try for Tripoli. *John Adams*, 28, which had arrived in January as a replacement for

Constellation, was sent ahead on the 8th, and on the 12th, off Tripoli, encountered an old acquaintance: *Meshuda*, by means not now evident a Moroccan vessel carrying an American safe-passage passport. That passport, however, specified that she could not enter any port being blockaded by American forces. Because she was attempting to run the blockade, Capt. John Rodgers made her prize and towed her back to Malta.

Morris took his squadron out of Malta again on the 20th and *finally* appeared off Tripoli. There were alarums and excursions, and fruitless peace "negotiations," but Morris showed himself slothful and uncertain in everything he did. He was back in Valletta, Malta, again on 14 June, having missed the birth of a son by five days. *John Adams* and *Enterprize*, which had been left off Tripoli, came in per orders on the 30th. Tripoli was wide open.

The squadron resumed touring the Mediterranean on 11 July, heading *away* from Tripoli, northward to Naples (where *Meshuda* created considerable interest) and Leghorn, then westward to Malaga and Gibraltar.

On 21 June, Secretary Smith had signed orders to Morris directing him to turn over command temporarily to Rodgers and return to the United States, where a court of inquiry would look into his performance. End of the line for Morris. The next squadron commander would have both the resources and the will to take the war to Tripoli.

PREBLE GETS HIS CHANCE

Edward Preble was a "downeaster," the fifth child of militia Gen. Jedidiah Preble by his second wife. A person of strong feelings and an expert marksman, after three years of formal schooling and two years doing hated farm work, Edward first went to sea in a privateer shortly after his seventeenth birthday. The next year, 1779, he became an acting midshipman in the Massachusetts frigate *Protector*, 26. He was a prisoner of war briefly in 1781 when that ship was taken by two British frigates, but influential friends arranged his exchange in little more than two months. Six months later, he was a lieutenant in the Massachusetts sloop *Winthrop*, 12, and served in her on several successful cruises until she was sold out of service in June 1783. For the next fifteen years, he is known to have gone to sea regularly in the merchant service, rather quickly attaining the position of master.

In November 1798, Preble returned from a merchant voyage of some eight months' duration to find that he had been appointed first lieutenant of *Constitution*

Edward Preble was an acerbic, intense naval officer determined that his country be respected among nations and that his younger officers be imbued with his sense of service. It would be from this group, termed by a later author "Preble's Boys," that the heroes of the War of 1812 came. This portrait was done by Rembrandt Peale at Philadelphia in 1805. *Official U.S. Navy photo*

six months earlier. Because there were many loose ends from his latest voyage, he got permission to delay a further six weeks in executing the orders. As things turned out, events caused the secretary to make further changes, and Preble soon found himself beginning his naval career in command of the brig *Pickering*, 14. A four-month cruise in the West Indies netted him two prizes, and when he returned to Boston in June 1799, he found he had been promoted to the rank of captain the preceding month.

After several months of waiting, he was ordered to command the brand-new frigate *Essex*, which had been launched at Salem, Massachusetts, in September. In January 1800, he sailed from Newport on what proved to be a solo deployment to the Dutch East Indies to protect American merchantmen from the depredations of French privateersmen in the Indian Ocean. Little of note occurred; it was, however, the first time a warship of the United States had operated in those waters.

Preble brought *Essex* back to New York in November 1800. His subordinates recalled that his waspishness to some of them was an unpleasant aspect of the voyage. He had been unmercifully blunt and critical of any performance that did not meet his expectations, and ultimately caused the abrupt end of several budding careers upon their return home.

What was apparently the onset of ulcers kept Preble from active duty through 1801 and 1802. On a trip to Washington in November of that year, Preble met with the president, Secretary of State James Madison, and Secretary of the Navy Smith. It appears that he was given every reason to believe he soon would be ordered to command a frigate, and he seems to have known it would be *Constitution*.

READYING CONSTITUTION

Preble was in Boston on 19 May 1803 when he received orders from Secretary Smith to "assume command of the frigate Constitution and have her put in a condition to sail at the shortest possible period." Characteristic of the man, the very next day he came aboard, took command, and immediately inspected the ship inside and out. Sailing Master Haraden, who had been the ship's caretaker for her "10 months, 14 days" in ordinary, was impressed by this human dynamo who had read himself in as Haraden's superior. On the 21st, a Saturday, a floating stage was in place and Preble and Haraden, using hooks and rakes, conducted a visual and tactile inspection of the frigate's underwater body. From this, Preble decided that recoppering was mandatory—a killing job in the absence of a dry dock.

On Sunday, the 22nd, Preble wrote to Secretary Smith that orders already had been issued to return the frigate's guns from Castle Island so their weight could be used to help in the heaving down. By Tuesday, the 24th, Haraden was recording the work regimen for the hired laborers: Basically, they worked from 5:15 A.M. until 7:00 P.M., with an hour off each for breakfast and dinner, and "At 11 A.M. and 4 P.M. They are allowed 15 minutes to Grog."

The tide being at maximum high, on the 28th Pilot Thomas Knox kedged *Constitution* cautiously through a narrow channel to a position off May's (Union) Wharf, where she was anchored fore and aft. All the lower gun ports were planked up and caulked to ensure the hull's water-tight integrity while careened. Guns and ballast—and filled water casks—had to be distributed to assist in the evolution. Gigantic blocks about five feet tall had to be attached individually to the heads of the main and fore masts, and their mates to positions on the adjacent wharf. A 140-fathom purchase fall of 10-inch rope was rove through each

This is A. Lassell Ripley's impression (circa 1965) of *Constitution* being hove down at Boston in June 1803. Note Preble in the foreground. *Courtesy The Paul Revere Life Insurance Company, Worcester, Massachusetts*

pair of ship and shore blocks, and led to its own capstan, called a "crab." These would be used to heave her over when the time came. The rudder was unshipped and secured to the wharf. Braces were rigged against the fore and main masts on the side toward which the ship would be careened and complementary stays rigged to 18-inch-square wooden outriggers on the outboard side. Relieving tackles also were rigged *under* the hull to prevent her from capsizing, and also to be used if necessary in righting her.

The stage was set by 10 June, when all hands heaved 'round and the heavy frigate was made slowly to roll her port side out of the water. The carpenters then manned their stages and began stripping off the old copper sheets. With them off, seams were caulked with oakum and paid over with a mixture of tallow, tar, and turpentine, then sheathing paper was laid on and new sheets of copper tacked on. At the end of each day, the ship was righted.

By Friday, the 17th, this daily routine had gotten the entire port side of the hull resheathed. Preble and his toilers spent the weekend winding ship and rerigging her in order to do the starboard side. This time, the process went more quickly: At 5:00 P.M. on the 25th, the last sheet was tacked home, the carpenters hauled off their stages, giving nine cheers, and the caulkers and seamen responded in kind.

About the time Preble was ready to move *Constitution* to May's Wharf, he received the news that he would command the new squadron, not just one frigate. It would be composed of frigates *Constitution* and *Philadelphia* (still in the Mediterranean), the 16-gun brigs *Argus* and *Siren,* the 12-gun schooners *Vixen* and *Nautilus* (these four had been built recently as a result of Dale's recommendations), and that old reliable, *Enterprize.* For the first time, the Americans would have a reasonable balance of heavy gun power and swift, light craft to meet similar craft on equal terms.

Early in June, Preble had received orders to begin recruiting a crew, even as the ship was being rerigged and the jumble of her previously landed stores sorted out and brought aboard. Two of *Constitution's* lieutenants were dispatched to New York early in July and in short order filled their quotas. But, Preble lamented on 21 July, "I do not believe that I have twenty native American sailors on board" in the 165 or so then present.

Preble also had two problems relating to *Constitution's* gun batteries, only one of which was readily resolved. The "easy" one had to do with the gun ports once occupied by the 18-pounders borrowed from Massachusetts and no longer available. It seems that the 12-pounder gun carriages were incompatible with the quarterdeck gun port dimensions: They had to be landed and altered to fit. The other problem had to do with the availability of carronades as replacements for the twelves on the forecastle. The ship had been designed with them in mind, but American industry had not been up to the task. Secretary Smith questioned Preble about putting eight 42-pounder carronades aboard. Preble looked around and answered that none were available, but he thought he might be able to get some in Europe. Smith agreed. That, effectively, closed the subject for the moment. *Constitution's* batteries would remain all long guns as they had been during the Quasi-War, although considerably reduced in number.

Preble wanted to get *Constitution* to sea very much, but she had been allowed to deteriorate quite badly since Isaac Hull left her in April 1802. Preble knew, too, that if he left with a healthy ship he would be that much better able to accomplish his mission. All masts and spars above the lower sections, together with all spars outboard of the bowsprit, were newly made. The critical whispers he began hearing in mid-July did nothing to ameliorate the pace at which he drove himself and all those associated with him. He had his orders to get to the Mediterranean and take whatever action the situation there demanded to ensure American shipping, and was eager to be off. Finally, everything was "go" on 9 August—except a fair wind. Preble had to chafe and fret for five more days before heading east.

PREBLE SHOWS THE CUT OF HIS JIB

The trans-Atlantic voyage was made quickly until the frigate arrived in European waters, when she slowed to a crawl in light and variable winds. Off Cape St. Vincent on 6 September, Preble met and sent a boarding officer to the 30-gun Moroccan frigate *Maimona*, whose presence in the Atlantic caused him concern about the status of relations between the emperor and the Americans. At Preble's request, Tobias Lear, our consul-designate to Algiers who was going out to his new post with the commodore, looked over the Moroccan's papers and reported he had seen what he considered a valid signature of James Simpson, his counterpart in Tangier. No one, however, could read the Arabic documents and know precisely what they said. *Maimona* went on her way, but Preble held his suspicions.

Constitution still was struggling against fickle winds four days later when she had a nighttime encounter with what was believed to be a man-of-war. Thinking she might be *Maimona*, Preble beat to quarters, then hailed the stranger through the darkness. The stranger echoed the query. Twice Preble responded without learning the other's identity. When Preble, losing patience, threatened to shoot, his contact threatened a broadside in return, identified himself as a British 84-gunner, and ordered Preble to send a boat on board. Preble was almost apoplectic. "This is United States Ship *Constitution*, 44 guns, Edward Preble, an American commodore, who will be damned before he sends his boat on board of *any* vessel!" And to his gun crews: "Blow your matches, boys!"

Silence followed. Then a boat came out of the darkness and a British lieutenant came aboard and presented his captain's compliments. The stranger was HMS *Maidstone*, Comdr. George Elliot, a 32-gun frigate. Elliot had been taken by surprise when *Constitution* appeared so close to him; the exchange took place as a stall while he manned his guns. It was a gutty thing to do, as was Preble's willingness to defy a ship of the line. Preble's young officers thereby discovered that the commodore's terrible temper had its merits. This, perhaps, was the beginning of the deep allegiance that formed about Preble during the coming year, an allegiance of aspiring young officers who one day would be known as "Preble's Boys."

MOROCCAN MATTERS

Constitution arrived at Gibraltar on the afternoon of 12 September to find *Philadelphia*, the Moroccan ship *Mirboha* (or *Meshboha*, 22), and the American brig *Celia* in port. Bainbridge informed Preble that on 26 August he had met the other two vessels off Cabo de Gata, Spain, and that the Moroccan's responses to his questions were evasive. Further investigation proved that *Celia* had been captured by the alcaide of Tangier. Bainbridge reported, too, that he had just spent ten days to the west of the strait looking for *Maimona*, and was told of *Constitution*'s meeting with her.

Over the next few days, American warships gathered at the Rock. *Vixen* from the west and *New York* from the east came in on 13 September. Discredited Commodore Morris was in the latter. Commodore *pro tem* Rodgers arrived in *John Adams* on the 14th, together with *Nautilus* and *Meshuda*. During this period, Preble spent much time with Bainbridge and American consul John Gavino "coming up to speed" on the political tides and currents.

Morris and Rodgers both were senior to Preble. Morris, however, was under a cloud and not inclined to worry about protocol. Rodgers, who was sensitive to such matters as precedence, and told Preble so, magnanimously agreed to cooperate under Preble's leadership in gaining a resolution with the Moroccans. Both recognized that nothing could be done farther east until the intervening line of communication with America was secured. As soon as the matter was settled, Rodgers would go home.

Constitution and *John Adams* got under way on the afternoon of the 16th and were anchored in Tangier Bay before the morning gun the next day. There was no sign of the Stars and Stripes flying over the consulate—something definitely was going on. Eventually, a boat manned by Spaniards came alongside with a note from Consul Simpson saying only that the boat would bring him any message the commodore might have. Preble sent one advising of the experiences of the squadron, and that the captains and officers of *Meshuda* and *Mirboha* were in the frigates. At 4:00 that afternoon, several letters came back from Simpson. One reported that neither the emperor nor the alcaide were in town, and so there would be no negotiation until possibly the 23rd. A second missive gave the news that the American brig *Hannah* had been detained at Mogador, down on Morocco's Atlantic coast. Preble and Rodgers decided that the latter would proceed off Mogador and the ports of Larache and Sale, and warn off any American shipping. Preble would return to Gibraltar and issue fresh orders to other units of the squadron. He intended to be back at Tangier on the 19th or 20th.

Adverse winds prevented Preble from getting back to Tangier until the 25th, which did nothing to improve his temper. The news from Simpson wasn't too bad. According to the consul, it had been the alcaide who had sent out *Mirboha*, not the emperor. The taking of *Celia* and *Hannah* had been intended to force the release of *Meshuda*, not declare war, according to the emperor's minister, Mohammed Selawy. The emperor, in fact, was more interested in getting *Mirboha* back than he was *Meshuda*. Simpson suggested that Preble depart for a week, by which time some sort of schedule might be known. The consul thought the emperor ought to reach Tangier from Fez on 3 October.

Constitution left the same afternoon (25 September) and patrolled between Larache and Cape Spartel without sighting a single Moroccan. Bad weather precluded a return to Tangier, so, low on water and provisions, she put in at Gibraltar shortly before midnight, the 29th. Preble had spent the past several

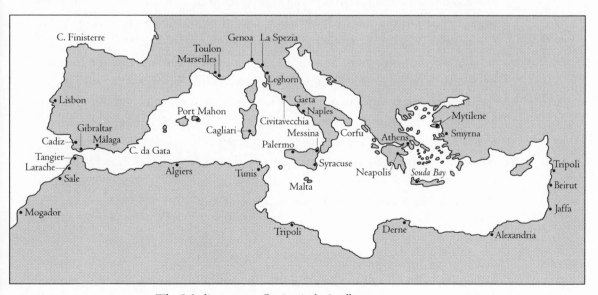

The Mediterranean Basin *Author's collection*

days confined to his cabin: Frustrations with Mohammedans and meteorology weren't good for a man prone to ulcers. Since he had last been in Gibraltar, Campbell had arrived in *Adams*, exchanged ships with Morris, and had sailed for a patrol station off Larache in *New York*. Morris had headed *Adams* for Washington, D.C., on the 26th.

Preble sailed for Tangier once more late in the evening of 3 October, having in the meantime witnessed the arrival of the last of his squadron (*Siren*, Lt. Cmdg. Charles Stewart), and sent her out on convoy duty with orders to rejoin him at Tangier.

Constitution and *Nautilus* arrived after noon the next day and found the American flag flying once more. Simpson reported that the emperor was expected on the 5th and suggested Preble ought to fire an appropriate salute as soon as he was in the castle. Preble's response was characteristic of the man: "As you think it will gratify His Imperial Majesty, I shall salute him and dress ship; and, if he is not disposed to be pacific, *I will salute him again.*" And he meant it: *Constitution* was at battle stations with guns primed and matches lighted, and would stay that way until the matter was settled.

After a day of rest, the emperor looked out of his window on the morning of the 6th to see *New York* and *John Adams* enter port and take anchorages south of *Constitution*'s. *Four* American warships were now in view. Simpson came out to the commodore with a message that only the absence of Minister Selawy was holding up negotiations, and that he was expected momentarily from Tetuan. The *Constitution*'s crew remained living at their guns.

Various delays prevented the negotiations from occurring until the 10th, but the emperor had sent out fresh meat and fowl to the Americans to make it clear that he was operating in good faith. The largely amicable talks on the 10th were followed by the return of *Mirboha* and later *Meshuda* on the 11th, and the delivery to the commodore on the 12th of the emperor's personal letter to President Jefferson reaffirming the friendship treaty his father had signed in 1786. Firing a final 13-gun salute, *Constitution* sailed for Gibraltar on the 14th. Preble had gained the security he wanted at the Pillars of Hercules.

A FALLING OUT

When Preble got back to Gibraltar, he learned of an unpleasant situation that boded ill for the future. It seems that six seamen left as prize crew in *Mirboha* had deserted before the Moroccan vessel made for Tangier. At least three of the deserters were known to be in the British frigate *Medusa*, whose captain, John Gore, had refused earlier American requests for their return. Preble wrote to the senior British officer afloat at Gibraltar about the matter. After stating the circumstances, he requested the men's return, just as he certainly would do if positions were reversed. The reply was that the men concerned were all, in fact, British citizens who since had entered His Majesty's service. Had they, in fact, been Americans, they would, of course, have been promptly returned. This "tit-for-tat" response completely infuriated the commodore, and he immediately made arrangements to shift American supplies to Syracuse or Malta, where he expected better cooperation.

Preble spent the next three weeks at Gibraltar assessing the strategic situation and making plans accordingly. *Enterprize* would escort the stores ship *Traveler* to Syracuse with the first supplies for the new base, and then overhaul her rigging. *Philadelphia* and *Vixen* were off Tripoli. *Siren* was sent to Leghorn to bring some consular presents for Lear's use at Algiers. Lear and family came back aboard from Gibraltar once the Moroccan affair was settled, and the commodore would drop them off at their new post en route to his first look-see at Tripoli, *Nautilus* in company. Preble also fired off several letters to Secretary Smith apprising him of the favorable turn of events, and repeatedly citing the need for additional units to guard his long Mediterranean line of communication while operating off Tripoli. He was, in fact, leaving *Argus*, now under Hull, in the Strait through the winter for that purpose. *Constitution* sailed for Algiers on 13 November.

Shortly after leaving the Rock, Preble sought to make an impression on his crew about the rewards of desertion. On the 15th, "We punished Edward Madden Marine with 48 lashes for refusing duty, contempt of a Commissioned Officer, Insolence to a non-commissioned Officer & attempting to desert. This Marine is a very Notorious character." Two others received thirty-six and twenty-four lashes each for drinking, insolence, and neglect of duty. When we recall that no punishments exceeding twelve lashes at a time were awarded under Nicholson and Talbot, it is apparent the severity with which Preble disciplined his crew.

A New Problem

In Algiers on the 19th, Lear and his family were landed amid gun salutes from the big frigate and batteries ashore. With the dey absent at his country seat, no diplomacy could be conducted; Preble took advantage of the serenity for a couple of days' relaxation and sightseeing. *Constitution* and *Nautilus* were under way once more on the evening of the 21st.

They were south of Sardinia three days later when contact was made with HMS *Amazon*, 38, and she had some terrible news: It was rumored that *Philadelphia* had been taken by the Tripolines! If true, it meant that Tripoline naval power was about to take a quantum jump. Preble's first concern became preventing *that* so he could get on with inducing the bashaw to sign a peace treaty. The Moslem certainly never would so long as he had a weapon like that in his hands. Putting aside his anger at the British, Preble headed for Malta, where he felt he could gain further intelligence.

Constitution lay off Valletta, Malta, on the 26th as First Lt. John Dent was rowed ashore to learn all he could about *Philadelphia*. He returned with letters from Bainbridge himself, detailing the disaster. It seems that Bainbridge had sent *Vixen* off to the neighborhood of Lampedusa on 22 October to look for two Tripoline cruisers said to be at large, leaving only the deep-draft *Philadelphia* to blockade Tripoli, a port largely supplied by coasting craft. On the last day of October, in mid-morning, Bainbridge had seen a Tripoline xebec attempting to make port from the eastward, in shoaling and reef-filled waters. He pursued until only about three miles from the city, when he realized that he was standing into imminent danger in just seven fathoms of water. It was too late; as the big frigate turned to seaward, she struck a sloping rock reef and slid up four or five feet while making eight knots. She was *hard* aground. Bainbridge tried shifting guns and ballast. He tried jettisoning most of the guns and starting the fresh water from the casks. She wouldn't budge. Nine light-draft Tripoline gunboats closed in cautiously, gradually increasing the tempo of their attack as it became apparent that the badly listing frigate could do little in her own defense. In consultation with his officers, Bainbridge determined to scuttle his ship and surrender to avoid unnecessary bloodshed. As soon as this was made known to the Tripolines, they swarmed aboard, pillaging and abusing. The Americans were led into captivity. And in just forty hours, aided by a storm that raised the water level, the pirates had *Philadelphia* afloat—the carpenter had botched the scuttling. In a few more days, they had stopped the leaks, moved her in harbor, and salvaged the jettisoned cannon, as well. Come spring, the bashaw would have a bigger frigate than the one the dey received from the Americans, and that pleased him mightily.

It was a black, black moment for Edward Preble; a time to think and regroup. *Constitution* filled away from Malta and arrived at Syracuse (Saragosa in Preble's letters) on the 28th. There, he received a warm welcome from the governor, Marcello de Gregorio, and ready assistance in establishing a supply depot ashore in government buildings at no charge. Three weeks were spent in landing stores, spare spars and boats, and other gear, and in overhauling the flagship. Preble busied himself with these things and with sending detailed reports to Washington concerning the disaster and the increased need for reinforcements. *Nautilus* was sent with two sets of letters to Gibraltar and Cadiz for forwarding. *Constitution* and *Enterprize* sailed on 17 December for Tripoli, to reconnoiter the territory and determine the location and condition of *Philadelphia*. The commodore intended to remain in blockade just as long as the winter was mild and permitted the Tripolines to operate.

There was "instant excitement" on the morning of the 23rd, just as the Tripoline coastline was sighted. *Constitution* raised a sail on the horizon to the southwest and signaled *Enterprize*, which was closer, into chase. Flying British colors, a common ruse of the day, the Americans easily closed in on their prey until *Enterprize* escorted her alongside the frigate. The capture was the fifty-ton ketch *Mastico*, which was found to have on board side arms and property known to have belonged to the *Philadelphia*. Preble ordered a prize crew aboard and sent her to Syracuse. Winter weather soon forced *Constitution* and *Enterprize* off the Tripoline coast. They too were back in Syracuse on the 29th.

Preble was anxious to know what information the papers captured in *Mastico* contained, but he could find no one locally to translate them for him. As a result, he left *Constitution* in the charge of Dent and sailed for Malta in *Vixen* on 13 January 1804. Arrival the next day was the beginning of a very profitable and pleasant nine-day stay. First, Preble discovered that the British at Malta were far friendlier than those at Gibraltar, and readily offered him the use of the port's facilities in maintaining his vessels, as well as the privilege of enlisting local males to fill out his depleted crews. Second, he was contacted by Richard Farquhar and Salvatore Busuttil, representatives of Hamet (Ahmed) Karamanli, Bashaw Yusuf's disgruntled, throne-seeking brother, who sought aid and cooperation against a common foe. Preble encouraged their proposals and forwarded them to Washington without making any specific commitments. Third, the commodore also heard from the "other side": The bashaw's representatives made peace proposals that were totally unacceptable to Preble, who intended that America never again would pay tribute to the Barbary pirates.

Problem "Solved"

Returning to Syracuse and *Constitution* on the 25th, Preble was ready to take steps to neutralize *Philadelphia.* Her quarantine period over, *Mastico* was overhauled, with Lt. Stephen Decatur, Jr., skipper of *Enterprize,* in charge. When properly outfitted, Decatur would sail *Mastico,* renamed *Intrepid* by Preble, into Tripoli harbor in company with his senior, Lieutenant Stewart in *Vixen,* and destroy Bainbridge's former command. The raid would be assisted by Maltese Salvatore Catalano, a pilot very familiar with Tripoli. The ketch's crew was made up of sixty-two volunteers from Decatur's command, together with some "gentlemen volunteers" from *Constitution:* Midshipmen Ralph Izard, Jr., Charles Morris, Jr., Alexander Laws, John Davis, and John Rowe. *Intrepid* and *Vixen* set sail from Syracuse at 5:00 P.M. on 2 February.

There was little for Preble to do until he knew the outcome of Stewart's attack. Anxiety played hell with him. On the 12th, when they had been gone ten days, he ordered a watch set at the masthead of his flagship so that he might have the earliest notice of a sail on the horizon.

The long wait ended on the morning of the 19th, when *Intrepid* and *Siren* were sighted making for the harbor entrance. Anxiously, Preble signaled *Siren* about the mission and received the welcome news that the objective had been achieved. Leaving anchoring to his first lieutenant, Stewart quickly boarded the flagship to submit his report and tell the commodore how, after a gale had delayed them for a week, the two ships again closed Tripoli, where Decatur took advantage of his closer position in a dying wind to penetrate the port on the 15th and successfully fire *Philadelphia.*

The good news was a tonic to Preble. In his letter to the Secretary Smith, he said of Decatur and company: "Their conduct in the performance of the dangerous service assigned them, cannot be sufficiently estimated—it is beyond all praise." Later in the day, he wrote again to Smith about Decatur: "The important service he has rendered . . . would in any Navy in Europe insure him instantaneous promotion to the rank of post Captain. . . . I most earnestly recommend him to the President, that he may be rewarded according to his merits." (Decatur was so promoted the following May.)

FINAL PREPARATIONS

With the naval balance restored in America's favor—indeed, with the enemy's morale having been delivered a smashing blow—Preble took time to reassess the strategic situation and redeploy his forces. For the nonce, Tripoli was left alone. By 22 February, *Intrepid* was placed in reserve in order that her personnel could be more profitably employed. *Vixen* sailed for Gibraltar with dispatches that day, and *Enterprize* went to Messina for repairs on the next. In *Constitution*, Preble had his carpenters improve the protection for his gunners by planking up the waist of the ship from "fore chains to the main mast"; henceforth, no one need be exposed on much of the spar deck. Gun ports were cut in the new bulwarks. Hanging shot lockers were installed for the guns on both decks. *Siren* was sent to Malta and then to resume the station off Tripoli.

Constitution began a busy round of port visits when she sailed from Syracuse on 2 March. She arrived in Malta the next day only to find *Siren* still there, forced back by adverse winds. *Nautilus* came in from Syracuse on the 4th. While there, Preble was apprised of rumors that the Bey of Tunis was again making threats—nothing new there, but a worry nonetheless. *Siren* and *Nautilus* sailed in company for Tripoli on the 8th with very specific orders from the commodore to stay together.

Preble wrote a long letter to Secretary Smith on the 11th. He hoped to bring the bashaw to his knees before the sailing season was out. In particular, "I expect to spend a large quantity of Powder in Fire Ships, and Infernals to blow up the Bashaw's Works." Further, he reported that several months of effort seemed about to bear fruit in his quest for the acquisition, by loan, of gun and mortar boats with which to augment the forthcoming assault. The commodore closed with the oft-repeated plea for reinforcement—"three frigates" he said this time. The day would come when these requests would bear bitter fruit.

Constitution returned to Syracuse on the 17th to provision for five months. While there, Preble received a letter from the minister to France, Robert Livingston, informing him that the diplomat, on his own recognizance, had succeeded in getting the French to agree to mediate a treaty between the Tripolines and Americans. Stores aboard, the big frigate headed once more for Tripoli four days later.

Only *Siren* was off the enemy town when *Constitution* arrived on the 26th. She had struck *Nautilus* three days earlier, necessitating the latter's return to Syracuse for repairs. Preble got the French consul, Bonaventure Beaussier, on board the day after his arrival. That one meeting convinced the commodore that the Frenchman was so biased in favor of the bashaw as to preclude his employment as an intermediary. It was obvious to Preble that the moment for negotiation was not at hand, and he could see that port activity was nil, so he sailed with *Siren* on 1 April for Tunis, where two American warships might have a salutary effect on the blustering bey.

Each night during the three-day stay at Tunis, Preble kept his crew at their guns as a guard against ugly surprises. There weren't any, however, as the bey was doing no more than making the same sort of disgruntled noises he had made for many years. The Americans sailed on the 6th for Malta and Syracuse. Haraden noted in his journal that the commodore was bedded by a fever at this time, a condition made no more comfortable by an ugly gale that slowed their progress for a couple of days.

At Syracuse, when he arrived on the 14th, Preble found the damaged *Nautilus*, *Argus* (newly relieved of her duties off Gibraltar), and the armed brig *Transfer*, a prize taken by *Siren* off Tripoli prior to the commodore's arrival. Preble seized this opportunity to augment his forces by outfitting her with sixteen 6-pounder long guns and commissioning her as *Scourge* under the command of his first lieutenant, Dent, on the 17th. *Vixen* came back from Gibraltar the next day and *Enterprize* from Messina, her repairs completed. Four days later, *Siren* was sent back to Tripoli, *Nautilus* to Messina for further repair, and *Enterprize* to Tunis bearing long-time Barbary negotiator O'Brien. *Scourge*, soon to be known as a dull sailer, made her way to Tripoli.

Constitution was under way on the 25th. She paid quick calls at Malta and Tunis, then headed north around the west end of Sicily, touching Palermo before anchoring at Naples on 8 May. Knowing from Cathcart that the King of Two Sicilies had indicated a willingness to assist the commodore in augmenting his forces, Preble on the 10th sent a letter to Gen. Sir John Acton, the British prime minister of the Two Sicilies, formally requesting the loan of eight gun boats, two mortar boats, and eight heavy long guns for "floating batteries," together with all appurtenances. Acton responded three days later, saying His Majesty would be pleased to make six gunboats, two mortar boats (or bomb ketches), and six 24-pounders available—powder, shot, and all. He also would permit the enlistment of his subjects to help man them. The long guns were brought aboard on the 16th, together with 624 shot and 4,406 pounds (79 barrels) of powder.

The flagship headed for Messina on the 19th, but adverse winds made it a six-day voyage. During the trip, Preble had the six new long guns scaled (cleaned), mounted, and installed in quarterdeck gun ports. The displaced 12-pounders were relocated in the new waist ports. The total battery thus consisted of thirty-six 24-pounders and fourteen 12-pounders—fifty long guns.

The commodore inspected the gunboats at Messina on the 26th and found them ready to be manned and sailed. He did this, enlisting ninety-six Sicilians and using most of the crew of the repairing *Nautilus.* An overnight voyage through the Strait of Messina with Lt. Richard Somers, temporarily detached captain of *Nautilus,* in command, got them to Syracuse on the last day of the month.

Preble decided to make another swing to the south while waiting for the mortar boats to be overhauled. *Constitution* spent three days at Malta and sailed for Tripoli with the peripatetic O'Brien aboard once more. *Argus, Vixen, Enterprize,* and *Scourge* all were there, working in pairs off the eastern and western entrances to the port. The first order of business was to pass supplies to the "small boys" and get an update on the local situation. This was done on 12 June. Looking into the harbor, Preble saw that the bashaw's gunboat fleet had risen to seventeen units. O'Brien went ashore on the 13th to test the diplomatic waters, but found the Moslem still unready for genuine negotiation. Preble had no doubts now that it would be necessary to thrash him into the proper frame of mind. Departing the blockade with *Argus* and *Enterprize,* he was back at Syracuse on the 25th after having "shown the flag" once more at Tunis.

The commodore moved northward to Messina on the last day of June to press for completion of the mortar boats. It required another week for him to get them clear of the yard. *Constitution* shepherded the two units to Syracuse on 9 July for three days of provisioning. On 12 July 1804, *Constitution* sailed for Tripoli at the head of a column that included *Nautilus, Enterprize,* six gunboats, and two mortar boats. The largest naval force yet seen under the Stars and Stripes was assembling off Tripoli. Edward Preble, as a latter-day captain of *Constitution* often told school children, was ready to "bash the Bashaw."

CHAPTER SIX

The Barbary War, Climax and Aftermath

JULY 1804–OCTOBER 1807

THE APPROACH

Commodore Preble soon found that getting the gunboats and mortar boats from Syracuse to Tripoli was going to be a trying experience. After thirteen hours under way, the squadron had covered barely more than half the fifty miles to Cape Passaro, the southernmost point of Sicily. There, Preble thought it best to anchor through the night so that all units would be together when morning came. As they got under way again on 14 July, *Constitution* passed towlines to four of the gunboats and both bomb ketches; *Enterprize* and *Nautilus* took the remaining units.

The Americans went first to Malta, where Preble wanted to load some stores he previously had stocked there, as well as get some boatswain's, gunner's, and carpenter's stores from the British. With only one large ship in his force, she had to do double duty as heavy bombardment ship and supply ship. Piled in the gun room and between decks were ten tons of cannister shot and about twelve tons of mortar shells. Taken on board at Malta were 92 barrels of bread, 7 of pork, 3 of suet, 6 of flour; 20 kegs of cheese; 11 casks of pease; a puncheon (122 gallons) of molasses and a pipe (130 gallons) of vinegar; as well as 57 gang casks of water. Sailing Master Haraden had his hands full stowing all these additional items and getting a decent trim on the heavily laden frigate.

The voyage to Tripoli was resumed on 22 July, after a two-day wait for a fair wind. As they proceeded to the southeast, Preble had his carpenters mounting 4- and 1.5-pounder carriage guns in five of *Constitution*'s boats. On the 24th, he spent much of the day replenishing the water casks on the small boys because they had but a six-day capacity and could be in jeopardy if weather separated them from the flagship.

Preble finally had his force assembled off the enemy's capital on the morning of the 25th. It consisted of *Constitution*, 44, *Siren*, 16, *Argus*, 16, *Scourge*, 14, *Vixen*, 12, *Nautilus*, 12, and *Enterprize*, 12, together with the six gunboats and two bomb ketches. It was not an ideal force for the job at hand. Having only one frigate with heavy long guns limited the bombardment capability, as the remaining units were armed with short-range carronades or light long guns. The small craft were heavy and unwieldy, intended for operations in calm harbor waters, while their opponents (of whom there were now nineteen) were built to work both in harbor and along the coastline. As to manpower, there may have been as many as 25,000 Tripolines in and around the city, while just 1,060 opponents floated offshore.

Weather conditions prevented the Americans from anchoring until the 28th, and shortly after they did that day a gale came up to drive them offshore and endanger the whole enterprise. After three days of battling to keep the boats afloat and together, skies cleared and the commodore was able to move in once again, arriving on station on 3 August.

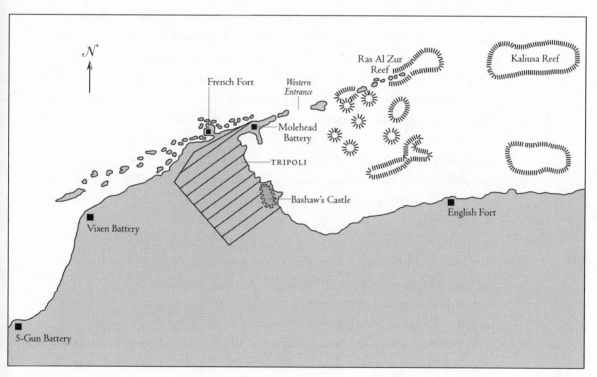

Tripoli Harbor *Author's collection*

Wasting no time, Preble rounded to about three miles north of the town shortly after noon and called each ship within hailing distance. Noting that two divisions of Tripoline gunboats had taken station at the east and west entrances to the harbor, and outside the rocks, he ordered immediate preparations made to attack the warcraft and harbor installations. The gunboats and bomb ketches were manned, and in an hour they were ready to go. Conforming to the situation, Preble divided his gunboats into two divisions, under Lieutenants Somers (Gunboats 1, 2, and 3) and Decatur (4, 5, and 6). While they engaged their opposite numbers, the bomb ketches were to take station about a half mile north of the town and lob their shells into it and the bashaw's castle. The brigs and schooners would follow the gunboats closely to give them support, while *Constitution* would remain in deep support, providing her muscle where it was most needed.

At 1:30 P.M., the American force headed shoreward, and at 2:00 the gunboats and bomb ketches dropped their tows to proceed on their own. Preble gave the signal to attack—signal "179"—at 2:30, which the bombards promptly opened. The Tripolines just as promptly returned the fire, as the shoreline and warcraft came ablaze with gunfire. Soon, black powder smoke was drifting on the easterly breeze, obscuring all but the easternmost division of enemy craft. It was this division of nine vessels that the Americans had selected as the prime target because it was the least supported by shore batteries. Decatur, whose division was the easternmost of the Americans, headed for them, but Somers, who was to support him, found it difficult to maneuver his scow upwind, and finally headed for the western Tripoline division—one against five, as one of his other two units managed to close with Decatur. The second (Gunboat 3) milled around confusedly well astern of her advancing sisters and never became engaged.

In Decatur's division, Gunboat 5 (Lt. Joseph Bainbridge) had her lateen yard shot away and lost much of whatever maneuverability she had, and although she kept advancing, she ended up having to be pulled off the rocks. As a result of these mischances, Decatur engaged with Gunboats 2, 4, and 6 (commanded by Lt. James Decatur, Stephen Decatur, and Lt. John Trippe, respectively).

Advancing into the smoke, Decatur's division attacked with round shot, grape, and cannister, as well as muskets. To the surprise of the much more heavily manned enemy boats, the order went out to close and board. Decatur was in

This painting by Michel Felice Cornè, commissioned by Commodore Preble upon his return to the United States in 1805, shows the larger units of his squadron firing in support of Stephen Decatur's gunboat division sent in to attack their Tripoline counterparts. From left to right in the foreground are *Enterprize, Nautilus, Argus, Siren, Vixen, Constitution,* the two bomb ketches, and two of the gunboats. *Official U.S. Navy photo*

the forefront of the action, quickly taking one enemy craft, then making for the next downwind. This one proved to be a tougher nut to crack, but eventually surrendered when Decatur won his duel with his opposite number. Wounded, and now having two enemy craft in tow, Decatur hauled out and headed to seaward. His slashing attack had cost the enemy two gunboats, fifty-two known killed and wounded, and eight prisoners.

While Stephen Decatur was adding to his laurels, his brother James sought to repeat the pattern. However, as he was driving Gunboat 2 against an enemy, he was struck in the forehead by a musket ball and died a short while later. The enemy gunboat withdrew behind the rocks.

Gunboat 6, under Trippe, also delivered a withering fire at close range and sought to board an enemy craft. Trippe soon found himself in personal combat with the enemy commander and received nine scalp wounds and two in the chest before getting in a fatal pike thrust. Once again, the remaining enemy surrendered with the fall of their leader. There were twenty-one killed and wounded counted, in addition to fifteen prisoners. Trippe's prize was one of the bashaw's largest galleys.

While the second division was decimating the enemy to the east, we left Somers in Gunboat 1 advancing against five to the west. His cannonade battered them unmercifully, driving them back through the western entrance to the port. His advance, however, brought him under the fire of the twelve-gun "molehead" battery. It appeared for a time as if he would be destroyed before he could maneuver his clumsy craft clear, but, luckily, a shell from one of the bomb ketches exploded in the battery, wrecking the gun platform, and allowing Somers to come off in safety.

While all this fighting had been going on, an enemy reserve division of two row galleys and five gunboats had been standing by just inside the harbor. When their mates began falling back under the American onslaught, these units sought to advance and turn the tide. *Constitution* and her consorts, however, caught sight of their movement and kept them bottled up with a withering barrage. At 4:30 P.M., the wind veered on shore and caused Preble to signal the withdrawal. The brigs and schooners moved in smartly to get the gunboats and their prizes under tow and out of range, while the big frigate laid down a heavy covering fire on the enemy's batteries. As long as she was firing at them, they remained silent. By 4:45, all were safely to seaward.

Thus ended Preble's first attack on Tripoli. In the main, he had accomplished all he had set out to do. The Tripolines, already impressed with American naval gunnery by the loss of *Tripoli* to *Experiment* three years earlier, now knew that the Americans were their betters in hand-to-hand fighting, a form they themselves had favored for centuries. Three enemy gunboats had been captured and another three sunk in harbor by the bombardment. Only fourteen Americans had been killed or wounded in the fray, while the Tripolines had suffered more than a hundred casualties. Except for the lucky shot at the molehead battery, most of the mortar shells fired landed in the town without exploding.

Constitution herself, although under fire for two hours, suffered very little. The Tripolines had not been prepared for large warships coming in so close, and as a result spent most of the afternoon firing too high. Thus, the frigate's main royal yard was shot away and a 24-pounder shot was lodged in the mainmast. Another shot, thought to have been a 32-pounder, shattered itself on one of the quarterdeck 24-pounders. A fragment smashed Marine Pvt. Charles Young's elbow, but the commodore escaped unscathed. Haraden estimated that he saw some two hundred shell splashes around the flagship, but he could find evidence of only nine having done any damage, however minor.

The squadron lay to two or three miles north of Tripoli until about 10:00 that evening, transferring prisoners and wounded to *Constitution*, restocking supplies, and making repairs. The Americans then bore off to the northeast under easy sail through the night.

At 9:00 the next morning, when twelve miles or so off the city, a lookout spotted a sail coming from the port. Preble ordered *Argus* in chase, and at 1:00 in the afternoon she returned with the French privateer *Le Rusé* under escort. Providing the Frenchman with a generous supply of stores, Preble prevailed upon him to return to port with the fourteen most severely wounded prisoners and with a letter for the bashaw. In the letter, Preble said his offer of $50,000 would remain valid until such time as more American frigates arrived, and when that happened the bashaw no longer would be offered anything but shot and shell.

Le Rusé stood in for Tripoli on the morning of the 5th, while the squadron rested and made repairs. Preble hoped to renew his attack the next day. In the afternoon, *Vixen* was sent in to reconnoiter, which caused several gunboats to move toward the rocks, but no shots were exchanged and little of note could be seen. As the sun was setting, the French vessel was seen pulling out of harbor against an onshore breeze. The message, which she delivered the next morning, was that the return of his losing crewmen had angered the bashaw, and that he saw in Preble's offer not a threat but perhaps a sign of weakness.

As he waited for this response, and for a favorable wind from the east, Preble took time to repair and outfit the three captured Tripoline gunboats for service in the United States Navy. The larger two, named Gunboats 7 and 8, were fifty-one feet long and carried a long 28-pounder in the bow. Preble had them sloop rigged using spare main and fore topgallant masts from *Constitution*. Gunboat 9, somewhat smaller, carried a long brass 18-pounder and was rerigged using *Constitution*'s spare mizzen topgallant mast.

THE SECOND ATTACK

Preble's next attack, at the urging of Lieutenant Commandant Stewart and others, was to be a bombardment of the city from a shallow bay to the southwest about 1.5 miles. With an easterly wind, the bashaw either would have to endure the bombardment or risk sending his gunboats out of the harbor to leeward, where the larger American units might cut off their line of retreat. Although there were those who preferred another frontal assault, Preble decided to give it a try.

At midmorning on the 7th, the gunboats began rowing for their assigned stations in the bay. The bomb ketches moved behind them to anchorages northwest of the city, while the brigs and schooners maneuvered to the northeast. *Constitution* remained at anchor farther offshore awaiting a favorable wind (she alone could not be rowed). The first shell was fired by Bomb Ketch 1 at 1:00 P.M. At 1:30, a breeze sprang up and *Constitution* was able to weigh anchor and move in support.

The gunboats finally attained the eastern end of the bay at about 2:00 and ran right into a fierce cannonade from two new batteries that apparently the Tripolines had erected since Preble's first attack. Although the gunboats were disordered, they returned fire and soon silenced the five-gun battery. But the eight-gun battery, which the Americans nicknamed the "*Vixen* Battery," kept up a steady fire. The nine gunboats slowly worked their way in until they were just two hundred yards off, and gradually they shot its walls away and pounded its guns until only one remained active. They also sent their shot into Tripoli itself, but little damage resulted. Each boat fired about fifty rounds during the course of the afternoon.

Around 3:00, fifteen Tripoline gunboats and galleys were seen sortiing from the western entrance to the harbor and maneuvering as if to attack the American gunboats. Preble signaled for the brigs and schooners to move to the south and east, as if scared off by the few shots the Moslems were sending their way, hoping thereby to encourage the enemy to get farther away from the entrance and then cut them off. Unfortunately, *Argus* and *Vixen* erred and stood instead to the northwest, a position from which the danger of a cutoff clearly was apparent. The pirates kept their boats behind the offshore rocks and worked westward via this "inside passage." Suddenly they charged out to the northwest, seeking to take Bomb Ketch 1 in its unsupported anchorage. Lt. Thomas Robinson of *Constitution*, who was her acting skipper, saw the danger and made for the company of the American gunboats, firing his mortar as he went. Preble brought *Constitution* down with all sails spread, an avenging eagle bent on catching the pirates before they could get back to sanctuary. But she was noticed before the range had shortened sufficiently, and the Tripolines beat the water to a froth rowing back behind the rocks.

As this was transpiring, and as Preble received a lookout's report of a strange sail to the northeast, everyone's attention was arrested by a thunderous explosion in the bay where the gunboats were. There was a stunned silence on both sides as bodies and parts flew up through a roiling, rising pall of smoke: Gunboat 9, the small Tripoline prize, had been destroyed by a hit in her ammunition.

The Americans reopened fire at a greater rate than before in revenge of their lost comrades. Gunboat 6 had her lateen yard shot away; 4 and 8 both took hits in their hulls, the latter very nearly being holed. As the wind began its diurnal shift on shore, Preble signaled cease fire and withdraw at 5:30. *Vixen, Enterprize,* and *Nautilus* were there to give them a hand getting clear. By 6:45, the entire squadron was standing once more to the northeast to spend the night.

As disengagement was going on, *Argus,* which had been sent to check up on the sail to the northeast, signaled it was friendly. Between 8:00 and 9:00 that evening, *John Adams* joined the squadron at anchor, her men giving the hard-fighting old hands three cheers. *John Adams,* 28, we've met before, but this time she arrived armed *en flute;* that is, most of her guns had been dismantled and stowed below so that more deck space was available for the supplies she had carried out to the Mediterranean. The orders given her commander, M.Cmdt. Isaac Chauncey, were to deliver the supplies, dispatches, and mail, and, if the commodore didn't otherwise direct, return immediately for another load. Preble sent a boat to bring Chauncey to the flagship, so eager was he for news.

One of the letters Preble received from Secretary Smith would have been hard to swallow at any time, but arrival just as his program of reducing the bashaw was having an effect must have made it doubly hard. It was dated 22 May 1804. After noting the bad news of *Philadelphia's* loss, the secretary reported that four frigates were being readied for deployment. Unfortunately for Preble, however, two of the captains were senior to him, and so his term as squadron commander would end. The secretary hastened to add that "The President has . . . the highest Confidence in your Activity, Judgment and Valour." Preble has left a single sentence to describe the impact of this news upon him: "[H]ow much my feelings are lacerated by this supercedure at the moment of Vicotry [*sic*] cannot be described and can be felt only by an Officer placed in my mortifying situation." This, the commodore wrote in his journal; not a word of protest appeared in any of his subsequent correspondence with the secretary.

Preble ordered Chauncey to remain with the squadron and to place his ship in as ready a state as possible. If nothing else, the frigate offered a pool of additional personnel for his depleted force.

Now that he knew he was to be superseded by Como. Samuel Barron, who sailed from America only a few days after Chauncey, Preble's ambition became the settlement of the dispute by negotiation before Barron arrived. On 8 August, he took O'Brien with him in *Argus* and reconnoitered the city to see if there were any signals flying indicating a desire to negotiate. He soon had his answer, for the Tripolines opened up on the lone American and hit her not far from where the commodore was standing. Fortunately, he wasn't hurt, and the shot failed to penetrate.

Preble and O'Brien tried again the next day, with *Vixen* accompanying *Argus*. This time, there was no gunfire. After an exchange of signals, a boat came out from shore to receive the commodore's message. The letter sent in said nothing about Preble's imminent relief (which might have given the bashaw hope) and reported the arrival of another frigate (which might discourage him). Wanting to conclude the affair, Preble upped his monetary offer to $90,000.

On the 10th, flags were seen flying in several parts of Tripoli, but it wasn't until nearly noon that the appropriate signal for parlay was seen. Once again, *Argus* and *Vixen* closed the shore with Preble and O'Brien aboard. O'Brien went himself to get the message being relayed via the French consul. The Frenchman proposed that the Americans offer $150,000 to the bashaw for the release of the *Philadelphia*'s crew—a figure half of what the Moslem previously had demanded, but one which Beaussier thought he would be in a frame of mind to accept. Preble very much wanted to bring the bashaw to peace, but the price was too high. By way of keeping up the charade, but knowing the outcome, he countered with a "final offer" amounting to $120,000. There were no signals to parlay on the 11th.

THE THIRD ATTACK

After some days of waiting for Barron's arrival, Preble began once more to plan and prepare further attacks on Tripoli. On the 16th, he sent *Enterprize* to Malta to order supplies and charter shipping to bring them out to the squadron that already was on water rationing. The next night, Preble sent now Captain Stephen Decatur and Chauncey in a small boat to learn what was happening in the port. They returned with the information that all the enemy gunboats had been moored in a line across the entrance to the inner harbor with their guns facing east, like a last line of defense. Before Preble could act upon this information, a gale came up that blew the Americans offshore until the 22nd, when Preble's favorite gentle east wind returned. While at sea, the squadron had been joined by *Intrepid* from Syracuse and a charter vessel from Malta, both with welcome supplies and water. *Enterprize* also returned, but had no word on the expected four frigates.

On the night of the 22nd, Preble tried to maneuver for another bombardment of the town, but an adverse current and fickle winds aborted the attempt. Two nights later, he tried again. This time, although conditions were poor, the bomb ketches were able to row themselves into range and begin shooting about 2:00 A.M. Only fifteen or twenty shells had been fired by the time dawn began to break, and Preble ordered them out. It had been a poor performance. Perhaps more disturbing than this to the commodore were the natural signs the old sailor could sense that the season for such operations rapidly was coming to a close. Before long, the winds and waters would make life hazardous for the Neapolitan gunboats and less livable for the brigs and schooners.

The weather frustrated another daylight attack on the 25th.

THE FOURTH ATTACK

Monday the 27th dawned cloudy and overcast with an onshore wind, dead wrong for any attack. By noon, Preble had a feeling that it was going to change for the better and ordered all hands to prepare once more for the fray. Three hours later, his hunch proved to be correct and the squadron got under way for the town on a strong northeasterly wind. As they stood in, the commodore assembled his captains in *Constitution* to discuss his plans. The frigate anchored some 2.5 miles north of the castle at 5:30, and the lesser units remained under way around her making final preparations. (The bomb ketches remained in the outer anchorage with *John Adams* and the supply ships because both had been rendered *hors de combat* by their earlier efforts.)

At 1:15 A.M. on the 28th, the wind finally abated enough to permit the gunboats to operate independently. Preble signaled them into the attack, and they proceeded to positions near the western entrance to the port from whence they could bombard, but where nearby rocks offered them some protection from return fire. Shortly before 3:00, all were anchored with springs on their anchor cables so that they could keep the guns pointed on target. A rocket skyward, a gun fired, and a false fire ignited—all in *Constitution*—was the order to commence firing. At first, the Tripolines did not respond, but then every gun that possibly could bear opened up. The enemy's gunboats fired from their anchored positions off the inner water gate, but made no attempt to close. American fire destroyed a portion of the molehead battery and sank a galliot and a galley in the harbor as well. Torn canvas and cut rigging were the worst the attackers suffered. As the dawn broke, the Tripoline gunboats began to move. One, apparently on picket duty, thrust its bow through the entrance between the rocks to attack the easternmost U.S. boat, only to have its target put two quick loads of shot and grape into it, causing six casualties and a hasty retreat. Thirteen other Tripolines came on to engage the Yankees.

Preble had been watching events carefully. When he saw the enemy gunboats become active, he got *Constitution* under way and began moving in. As she swept in, the friendly gunboats were ordered out. Said one observer, "She had her tompions out, matches lit, and batteries lighted up, all hands at quarters, standing right in under the fort." The gunboat sailors cheered. At four hundred yards from the rocks, the heavy frigate let go her lethal load at the enemy, driving them back, one sinking and two more forced to beach. Then broadside after broadside—over three hundred rounds—she bored into the fortifications, silencing them. It was a magnificent demonstration of her power. Rigging damage was all she suffered in return, although a fair number of grape shot were found embedded in her stout sides.

As she hauled out of range after her small charges, the Tripolines came to life and fired a final blast of harassing fire for morale purposes.

The Fifth Attack

Negotiations had proved futile. Barron and his four frigates still had not appeared. The fighting season rapidly was ending. Preble decided on a dramatic act to try and bring things to a head. It was time for something spectacular.

Little *Intrepid*, once *Mastico*, was about to perform her last service to her country of capture. Preble ordered his carpenters to make her over into an "infernal," a gigantic floating bomb filled with explosives and combustibles. *Intrepid* was to be run in amongst the bashaw's fleet, or even against his castle wall, the combustibles having been lighted to give her the appearance of a fire ship. The powder train would carry the fire along to the magazine, which, if the timing was right, would go off as planned, causing much destruction in its vicinity. A small crew would be necessary to guide her in under cover of darkness until she was headed fair for her target, when the combustibles would be lighted, the helm lashed, and the crew depart in attending launches.

Preparations in *Intrepid* were completed by 1 September. Now-Master Commandant Somers of *Nautilus* claimed her command as his chance for glory. Preble granted him his wish, displacing Acting Lt. Joseph Israel, who had overseen the ship's preparation, for the duration of the operation. Newly promoted Lt. Henry Wadsworth of *Constitution* was the third officer, while four seamen from *Nautilus* and six from *Constitution* completed her complement. All were volunteers.

Everything seemed right that evening for the operation, but, with *Intrepid* just four hundred yards off the western entrance, the wind turned foul and she had to haul off. Nobody in the port seems to have been the wiser.

The next dawning, as was their custom, the Tripoline gunboats left their defensive line deep in the harbor and began moving as if to take up their usual daytime positions inside the rocks adjacent to the western entrance. Soon, however, they moved to new positions under the protection of the English fort and to windward of the normal operating area of the Americans. Preble appreciated the move, seeing that it gave the pirates the weather gauge in the event the Americans deployed as they had previously. The commodore adjusted his plan accordingly, sending his gunboats to duel with their opposite numbers while bomb ketches and the frigate worked over the castle and fortifications.

It required the rest of the morning and a part of the afternoon for the brigs and schooners to tow their charges to a position from which they could descend upon the Tripoline flotilla at the eastern end of the harbor. At 2:30 P.M., the flagship signaled the attack and the two divisions went forward, one paying particular attention to the gunboats and the other to the English fort and a new fortification slightly to its west, nicknamed by some the "American fort." For the next two hours, the sides flailed away at one another without material result.

To the west, Preble had sent in the bomb ketches to bombard the city. Taking positions more than a mile off, the two craft had their best day since the attack of 7 August. Thirty-three out of forty-one shells fired actually exploded in the town. Although both units suffered rigging damage from the Tripoline return fire, it was self-inflicted damage that put Gunboat 1 out of action. Repeated firing of the massive mortar resulted in the mortar bed giving way and hull timbers starting. She broke off firing with two feet of water in her hold.

The ever-watchful Preble saw what was happening to the bomb ketches. Once more *Constitution* spread her canvas high and wide and bore down on the offending batteries. Some eighty cannon opened at her as she came, raising spouts of water all around her and sometimes throwing the spray even on the glistening canvas. At 3:30 she came to, her port broadside fair on the town, and there she lay at three cables length for forty minutes, crashing shot after shot into the pirate stronghold—over two hundred rounds this time. As on earlier occasions, the shifting wind necessitated the signal to haul off shore, which all units did without incident.

Following a day of repair and resupply, Preble found the evening of 3 September right for the infernal, *Intrepid*. A light haze covered the surface of the sea, making visibility difficult beyond a couple of hundred yards, although the stars clearly were seen overhead. At 8:00 P.M., *Intrepid* slipped her cable and headed for the port's western entrance, just inside of which three Tripoline gunboats were known to have taken their regular night stations.

Slowly, *Intrepid* moved forward and disappeared into the haze. After some moments, the Tripoline batteries were seen and heard to open fire, a fire that seemed aimed at nothing in particular. About ten minutes after the shore batteries opened up, at about 9:47 according to Haraden, there was a tremendous explosion and a burst of light. In an instant a fiery column flashed skyward. Some saw *Intrepid*'s mast rising straight up, trailing its rigging. So swiftly did the fire flash and die that none saw the mast come down. From the point of explosion fountained burning shells, arcing across the sky in all directions and raining down on sea and shore alike. And then there was deafening silence, as both sides stopped in awe of what they had seen.

Clearly, something had gone wrong. There hadn't been time for Somers to reach his target before the explosion. The haze had prevented a sure knowledge of where *Intrepid* was when she blew up. Still the American units waited off the rocks through the night with waning hope that their shipmates would come rowing out of the gloom as Decatur had done the preceding February.

Intrepid's mast could be seen resting on the rocks just to the west of the entrance the next morning, along with what appeared to be a portion of her keel or bottom. Coincidentally, three of the enemy gunboats seemed to be missing. Preble, with so few clues, concluded that Somers had been boarded, or at least cornered, by the picket boats and that, true to his word, he fired the charge so that the Tripolines couldn't get the powder. However, given the location of the wreckage at or outside the entrance, it does not seem likely that Somers got far enough to engage the gunboats. He probably missed the entrance in the poor visibility and went gently aground on the rocks on the west side of the entrance. In that vulnerable position, he may have been hit by a stray shot from one of the Tripoline guns; or perhaps the jar of grounding set off the powder; or perhaps, in the confusion that must have occurred when she struck, someone aboard had an accident or panicked. All thirteen aboard subsequently were accounted for:

two bodies still in the wreck, ten floating in various parts of the harbor or washed ashore, and one in a boat that drifted ashore farther down the coast to the west.

Preble's infernal had done absolutely no damage to the Tripolines. The loss of personnel in this bizarre mode of attack stunned the squadron. The commodore himself deeply felt the loss.

BARRON SUCCEEDS PREBLE AS COMMODORE

Preparations began the next morning for yet another attack, but without the drive that had characterized Preble's earlier efforts. The loss of Somers and company and the frustration of his inability to bring the bashaw to terms, combined with a spate of bad weather on the 5th, led the commodore to call off preparations and to make ready the bomb ketches and gunboats for return to Naples. The season, he decided, was too far advanced to risk keeping the unwieldy craft on the open sea any longer. Late on the 6th, *John Adams, Siren, Enterprize,* and *Nautilus* towed them offshore, on their way home.

Barron and two frigates, *President* and *Constellation,* were sighted at noon on Sunday, the 9th, and when they joined later that afternoon, Preble hauled down his broad command pennant. He surely didn't feel it at the moment, but the months to come would prove how very successful he really had been. (The Congress would vote him a gold medal in March 1805, the first *Constitution* captain to be decorated for his performance.)

Several days were required to effect a proper transfer of information and orders. On the 11th, Barron wrote to Preble to take *Constitution* to Malta for repairs, turn her over to Decatur, and proceed home in *John Adams.* That very afternoon, Preble chased and captured two small armed vessels flying the Greek flag attempting to run wheat into Tripoli.

The blockaders were milling about some twelve miles northeast of the city as morning twilight was breaking on the 12th. Fitful breezes veered back and forth between the northeast and northwest. *President* was standing to westward under full sail, while *Constitution,* off her port bow, was struggling north-north-eastward. Suddenly, the latter was taken aback by a wind shift and left unmanageable in the other frigate's path. *Constitution*'s stem struck *President*'s larboard bow, and then she was swung parallel and alongside by *President*'s continued forward motion as anchor fouled anchor and locked both ships together. Quickly, a spring hawser was run from *President*'s lee bow to *Constitution*'s quarterdeck capstan and a strain taken while others carefully disengaged the tangled lower yards. That done, *Constitution* set sails, and once she had speed enough to relieve the tension on the spring hawser and clear the anchors, cast off and came clear without further incident. *President*, having taken the blow on her bluff bows, suffered no notable damage. But *Constitution* had made contact with one of her most vulnerable parts: Flying jib boom, jib boom, and spritsail yard had been carried away; the Hercules figurehead and the upper cutwater and trailboards were a mass of splintered remains; and the bow head area was a shambles. Lt. Charles Gordon, the watch officer at the time, was absolved of any dereliction of duty, the vagaries of the wind being acts of God.

  Constitution departed the blockade late the next afternoon with her two prizes and arrived at Malta on the 16th, where Preble left Gordon in charge of the overhaul and repair program and moved ashore, awaiting transportation to Sicily and Naples in order to settle the squadron's accounts for his time in command.

Repairs at Malta

Work began almost immediately to ready the frigate for further service. The six Neapolitan cannon were landed and returned. The crew was busy taking down and repairing rigging while thirty-seven carpenters and twenty caulkers hired for the purpose began making her a tight ship once more and removing the mass of damaged timbers forward. On the 26th, what was left of Hercules and the trailboards was taken off, the pattern for the new billet head set up, and the timber for the cutwater started fitting. The 27th found the head remnants being dismantled and a sixty-six-foot spar brought aboard to be shaped into a new spritsail yard. Rot was found in the damaged mainmast about eighteen feet above the spar deck. In the week that followed, the yard was finished, guns and carriages overhauled, some boats repaired, and painting begun. By 2 October, the hired labor force had been reduced to twelve carpenters and eight caulkers.

  So much painting was going on at this time that it was considered dangerous to light a fire in the camboose. The crew subsisted on cold "salt provisions" for two days until the quantities of paint in the ship were reduced. The paint scheme in use at this time was a black hull above a yellow gun streak, with the hull below that tarred to the water line. The inner planking of the spar deck bulwarks and the guns were painted a *light yellow!*

In the ship, the bow head area was completed and the upper portion planked in to afford more protection to those using the facilities located there. Long oaken fishes for the mainmast arrived from Syracuse, and the tedious work of fitting and woulding them in place began. The new billet head was bolted in place on the 11th, a very simple affair almost totally devoid of the sculptor's art, as were the new trailboards. All the officers and crew were herded into the berth deck that same day and "smoked" before the local authorities released the ship from quarantine. The carpenters and caulkers were released a week later, when all boats had been completed and the taffrail (the last piece of light, decorative woodwork remaining topside) removed from atop the transom.

The long-awaited supply ship *Alfred* arrived in Malta from America on the 23rd, bringing *Constitution* eight 32-pounder carronades. The two 12-pounders that had been loaned to *Siren* while off Tripoli were not remounted, but stowed in the hold. Preble returned aboard on the 24th. Stephen Decatur relieved him without fanfare on the 28th, not knowing *his* relief's orders had been dispatched by Barron two days earlier. He would be John Rodgers, then in command of *Congress*, 36. Decatur's sole action with *Constitution* was to sail her to Syracuse, where he arrived on 4 November, and where Rodgers succeeded him on the 9th, bringing with him the entire *Congress* officer complement.

JOHN RODGERS COMMANDS CONSTITUTION

John Rodgers of Maryland was the first *Constitution* skipper not to have served in the Revolution. Born in July 1773, he entered the new navy as second lieutenant of *Constellation*, where he gained fame in her victory over the French frigate *L'Insurgente* and his subsequent performance as prize master. He was promoted to captain a month later, in March 1799, and had commanded both *Maryland*, 20, and *John Adams*, 28, before commissioning *Congress* for current service.

At the time Rodgers took command of *Constitution* at Syracuse, Barron had taken up residence ashore there, his health having deteriorated in the two months since he relieved Preble. His problem was diagnosed as "a complaint of the liver." In a letter on the 13th, he requested Rodgers to take charge and act as commodore with regard to operating the ships at sea. He retained primacy and authority for the day-to-day functions in the diplomatic and political arena involving much correspondence and little physical activity. Rodgers hoisted the broad blue pennant to *Constitution*'s main truck at 1:00 P.M. on the 14th.

Barron ordered Rodgers to take his frigate to Lisbon, departing on the 28th, where he was to recruit to make up his eighty-man deficiency. It was a bad trip. The presence of yellow fever at Gibraltar precluded a call there (and, unbeknownst to Rodgers, the supply ship *William And Mary* recently had deposited there the powder and shot for the new carronades, together with a new bowsprit specifically sent out for *Constitution*). And after "touching base" with our consul at Tangier, he ran right into a fierce Atlantic gale that sprung the bowsprit and delayed his arrival at Lisbon until 28 December. In reporting his arrival, he wrote to Secretary Smith that "The Constitution is the most laboursome & uneasy Ship I have ever commanded." He blamed it, in part, on the way her kentledge was stowed.

Immediately upon his arrival, he wrote to Consul William Jarvis informing him of his needs for recruits and bowsprit repair. Rodgers, who failed to understand the poor communications between the distant quarantine anchorage he occupied and the city, became incensed when a response was not forthcoming in what he considered to be a reasonable time. He then fired off a very harsh letter, taking Jarvis to task for sloth and indifference, and set the stage for six weeks of exchanged invective between the Marylander and the Bostonian. Despite this, the recruits were found—mostly Danes, Frenchmen, and Swedes—and a new bowsprit fashioned ashore and installed.

Rodgers headed back into the Mediterranean on 9 February 1805, making the usual calls at Tangier and Gibraltar, which was now reopened. A brief storm off Algeria on the 20th washed the gig right off the quarter, but didn't delay the ship's arrival at Malta on the 23rd, where Barron was again ashore and ailing. His hoped-for recovery had not occurred; indeed, if anything, he was failing.

At Barron's order, *Constitution* made a brief trip to the blockade on 2 March and arrived three days later. Rodgers startled the Moslems at 4:00 in the morning on the 10th by firing a single broadside into the town. He returned to Malta on the 19th and remained through the rest of the month.

Constitution made a two-day trip to Tripoli and relieved *Constellation* there on 5 April. *Vixen* remained her consort until the 17th, when *President* took her place. The blockade had resumed the rather lackadaisical, informal character it had had under Dale and Morris. The blockaders generally remained more than ten miles to seaward. There was a brief flurry of activity on the 24th when *Constitution* chased down a Tripoline xebec armed with eight guns and her two Neapolitan prizes.

Pausing in the flow of our narrative for a moment, it is time to take notice of two events that occurred during the winter and spring seasons that shortly would make themselves felt on the course of the war. The first of these was the French offensive that swept down from northern Italy and threatened to engulf the Kingdom of Two Sicilies on the mainland. It had the effect of denying the Americans the loan of Neapolitan gunboats for another season off Tripoli. The second event had begun in 1804 when William Eaton, entitled our "Naval Agent for the Barbary Regencies," was sent by Barron to Egypt with *Argus, Nautilus,* and *Hornet,* and a nucleus force of Marines under Lt. Presley N. O'Bannon, to cooperate with the bashaw's deposed brother, Hamet, in an overland attempt to overthrow Yusuf. This ragtag band of American Marines, Greek mercenaries, and Arab tribesmen made an epic march across the desert sands to Derne, capitol of Tripoli's easternmost province, which they captured from numerically superior forces in a single assault on 27 April. (From this episode comes the line "To the shores of Tripoli" in the Marine Corps Hymn. The modern Marine officer's sword is copied from that acquired by O'Bannon at the time.)

To return to our narrative. On 5 May, *President* joined Rodgers off Tripoli, bearing a letter from Consul General Lear, who remained with Barron. In it, Lear apprised Rodgers that he had received a letter from the Spanish consul at Tripoli, written at the behest of the bashaw, indicating the latter's willingness to negotiate, with $200,000 ransom as a starting point. This, of course, was totally unacceptable to Lear. The consul general also informed Rodgers that, because other squadron units were busy guarding American interests at key points along the Italian boot and pursuing other missions, it was doubtful that any offensive action could be taken before the middle of June.

RODGERS BECOMES SQUADRON COMMANDER

Essex joined the blockaders on 26 May and brought with it Lear and a surprising letter: Barron was resigning his command to Rodgers because of his continuing bad health. However, he reserved the right to resume the command if his health improved, and further restricted Rodgers's freedom of action by charging him to begin negotiations for peace without delay. Perhaps it was his poor condition that led him to this position. Or perhaps it was the fact that the Neapolitan gunboats would not be available, and also that the Eaton-Karamanli expedition had failed to rally a significant portion of the local populace to the latter's banner despite the Derne victory. Whatever the exact motivation, Hamet was to be abandoned and negotiations pressed. (Happily for us, Bashaw Yusuf was in an equally conciliatory mood, brought to that state of mind by the prospect of a renewed onslaught on his capital by what one of his spies falsely reported was a greatly augmented American force and the loss of Derne to his brother.)

Peace with Tripoli

Essex moved in closer to the city that same afternoon and hoisted the signal for parley, which was immediately answered. From that point on, the diplomats and naval officers-cum-negotiators moved at an accelerating pace. The bashaw rejected Lear's first offer, made through the Spanish consul, on the 30th. On the 31st, Lear offered $60,000 and the return of the Tripoline prisoners in exchange for the American sailors and peace. Captain Bainbridge was released from prison on parole to help work out details. On 1 June, Danish Consul Nicholas C. Nissen replaced the Spaniard as mediator, as it was recognized that both sides had a greater confidence in his fairness to the parties concerned. The draft treaty was completed and initialed on board *Constitution* by Lear and Nissen, representing the bashaw, on the 3rd. Topside, the ship's carpenters were fashioning a new flagpole for the consulate from a spare spar. It was sent ashore and erected that afternoon, while an ensign for it was furnished by *Essex*. At 10:30 the next morning, the Stars and Stripes once more was hoisted over Tripoli, saluted with twenty-one guns from the castle and from *Constitution*. The treaty was signed in the castle at noon with an American delegation led by Lear.

On the 5th, *Constitution, Essex, Vixen,* and the newly arrived *Constellation* all moved in to anchor in Tripoli harbor, the remains of *Philadelphia* still visible on the shore as a reminder of all that had transpired in and around that small body of water during the preceding four years. Bainbridge and some three hundred of his crewmen were returned that afternoon to the cheers of the squadron.

Rodgers spent the 6th redeploying his forces in light of the changed political situation. *Vixen* would remain at Tripoli for the time being to support the diplomatic mission. *Constellation* was ordered to Derne to direct the withdrawal of the Eaton force, including Hamet and the mercenaries, and the return of the city to a representative of the bashaw. *Constitution* and *Essex* sailed that evening for Malta to join *President* (which had been sent thither on 31 May) and the rest of the squadron prior to making for Tunis, where the bey for some time had been threatening war over *Constitution*'s capture of the wheat ships the preceding September.

The two-day stop at Malta informed Rodgers that thus far the bey still was merely making noises, and so he decided to wrap up the Tripoline matter himself. Sailing to Syracuse, he offloaded the *Philadelphia*'s crewmen on 11 June and then loaded aboard nearly a hundred Tripolines for repatriation. A boat from Malta delivered eight boxes of money (the ransom payment) to the passing frigates on the 13th. Rodgers was back at Tripoli on the 17th, offloaded, paid two official calls ashore, and returned to Syracuse via Malta ten days later.

Rodgers ordered the Fourth of July celebrated with all due ceremony. All ships present that morning dressed ship with every flag possessed being flown from some vantage point. At high noon, all fired sixteen-gun salutes, and that night a "gala" was held aboard the flagship, including many notables from the local area in attendance. A journal entry for the day recorded, "they (the "respectable" people) took with them 6 silver spoons a number of Glasses and Many other articles too tedious to Mention." Souvenirs, it seems, always have been prized.

At the request of Samuel Barron, Rodgers made *President* (now commanded by James Barron) available to take the ailing sailor home. *President*'s crew was exchanged with that of *Constitution*, whose enlistments were expiring, on the 5th. The Barrons headed for America the next day, the first of many reductions in force to be effected in the Mediterranean Squadron in the coming months.

Peace with Tunis

The squadron, consisting of *Constitution, Constellation, Essex, John Adams, Enterprize,* and eight gunboats recently arrived from the United States (the latter built as a result of Preble's experience), sailed for Malta on the 13th and spent eight days at that island provisioning. When Rodgers next sailed, the squadron was increased further by the presence of *Siren, Nautilus,* and stores ship *Franklin.*

This imposing force arrived off Tunis on the 30th, finding sloop *Hornet* already there. Rodgers did not miss the opportunity to make the sort of impression on a landlubber that only the massed presence of warships can. He organized his units into two columns and sailed them into the bay *in formation*, coming to anchor smartly on signal at intervals calculated to span the width of the entire harbor. It must have been a magnificent and awesome sight to have seen those seventeen white-winged beauties sweep in together, drop their anchors, and furl their sails in unison. And below the graceful canvas was the presence of all those gun ports to remind the observer of the power of these vessels. Frigate *Congress* added emphasis by its arrival on the first day of the new month.

After meeting with American Consul George Davis on 2 August, Rodgers sent a letter to the bey demanding an answer within thirty-six hours as to whether or not a state of war existed between Tunis and the United States. Legitimate problems with getting an adequate translation into Arabic led to the commodore waiving the time limit. The bey's response avoided a direct answer, pointing out that what he really wanted was the return of what he considered to be Tunisian ships wrongly captured by the Americans nearly a year before.

Rodgers held a council of war on the 4th, with Davis and Lear in attendance. His decision was to send Davis once more to the bey requiring a guarantee of peace before any negotiations were begun. He accompanied this with a guarantee of his own not to begin any offensive operations unless initiated first by the Tunisians. There followed diplomatic maneuvering involving translations, designation of representatives, and the like, until Rodgers' patience wore thin on the 8th, when he ordered Davis to move himself out to the squadron at 4:00 the next afternoon if there still wasn't any definite movement in the exchanges of notes. When this was made known to the bey, he refused to provide the required written guarantee of peace, and Davis went aboard *Constellation* as ordered, lock, stock, and barrel. The commodore made his next move on the 9th, when he ordered units of the squadron out to the mouth of the bay. They were to prevent any Tunisian shipping from leaving harbor and to force into harbor any Tunisian vessels seen in the offing. Perhaps the threat of a blockade would bring the bey to negotiate. It did.

Lear went ashore on the 12th with Chaplain Cruize of *Constellation* to meet with the bey. In two days, the two sides agreed to maintain peace. Rodgers would make available one of his ships to take an appointed Tunisian ambassador to Washington, where a resolution of the prize question would be worked out. *Congress* was assigned this mission. And finally, Surgeon James Dodge of *Constitution* was appointed to new consul for Tunis, so that the bey would not be embarrassed by the continued presence of Davis, who had represented the uncommonly hard-nosed commodore in recent parleys.

Squadron Cutbacks

Peace had come to the Americans sailing the waters off Barbary. Rodgers spent the next three weeks at anchor, reorganizing his forces and making new officer assignments so that those who had been involved longest could return to the United States. *Constellation* departed for Syracuse and home on the 23rd. *Nautilus* and *Franklin* followed; *Essex* and *Vixen* were sent to Gibraltar, and *Enterprize* to Tripoli. On 1 September, *Siren, Hornet, Argus,* and the gunboats headed for Syracuse. *Constitution* made for the same port on the 4th—as soon as *Congress* and the Tunisian ambassador had cleared port for Washington.

After nine days in port, Rodgers got *Constitution* under way for a tour of a number of Italian ports to assess the fortunes of Americans in the midst of the continental war. From Syracuse, he proceeded to Messina, then Naples and Leghorn, arriving in the latter port on 10 October. He spent a month there awaiting Lear and his wife, who had been traveling overland from Syracuse, buying the biennial gifts due the Dey of Algiers. A two-day gale delayed landing the Lears at Algiers until 19 November. A second gale made the return to Syracuse a miserable six-day trip, ending on the 27th.

On 28 December, Rodgers received Secretary Smith's directive of the preceding 5 August to reduce the size of the squadron "after peace with Tripoli shall have been affected." Three days later, he reported that it had been too late to send the gunboats back across the Atlantic safely, and that he had retained the other units until the Tunisian ambassador returned from the United States with peace assured, a situation about which the commodore knew the secretary was unaware when he wrote, but felt the secretary would approve his course of action when it became known to him. When the Tunisian returned, Rodgers thought the squadron might be reduced to one frigate, two brigs, and a schooner.

Constitution took the commodore on a brief visit to Malta late in January 1806. While there, he received the secretary's letter of 12 October 1805, wherein that gentleman ordered home all units except *Constitution* and any two of the "small vessels of war." Rodgers' response reiterated his earlier position and added that the turmoil created by the French invasion down the Italian peninsula also warranted the presence of American warships in those places where our interests might be jeopardized.

CAMPBELL RELIEVES RODGERS

Rodgers spent the entire months of February and March in Syracuse, and got under way once more on 3 April with the squadron, leaving a few people behind to close down the hospital and others to mind the naval stores. After nearly a month at Malta, he got under way on 5 May, paid a brief call at Algiers, and arrived at Gibraltar on the 21st. There, among the dispatches awaiting him, Rodgers found Secretary Smith's letter of 22 March directing him to turn over command of the frigate and the station to Captain Campbell and to return home. The change of command and exchange of crews was effected on 29 May. (One of Rodgers' last comments concerning *Constitution*, in marked contrast to that made shortly after he assumed command, was that "I have had a fair Trial of the Constitution, since the Stowage of her Ballast has been altered. . . . She sails much better, and from one of the most uneasy Ships I ever was in, is now among the most easy.") *Hornet* and *Enterprize* were left to make up the rest of the squadron.

Little is known of Hugh George Campbell; indeed, less than is the case with any of *Constitution*'s captains until her fourth decade. He is known to have been born in South Carolina, and was in command of the revenue cutter *Eagle* when that ship and he were taken into naval service during the Quasi-War. With a number of prizes to his credit, Campbell must be considered one of the more successful commanders of that conflict. Subsequently he had commanded the frigate *Adams* in Morris' squadron, and had commanded *Constellation* and *Essex* since returning to the Mediterranean with Barron.

Constitution's service in the Mediterranean largely was a peaceful routine of port visits, mostly in the western Mediterranean: Malaga, Cadiz, and Algiers during Campbell's first four months in command. In September, he took her to Lisbon, where fine naval facilities afforded him the opportunity for a badly needed refit. For three months, the frigate lay there recuperating.

The wandering life was resumed on 9 December. Subsequent port calls included Gibraltar, Algiers, Tunis, Algiers again, Cagliari (Sardinia), Malta, and, finally, Syracuse early in May 1807. The call at Cagliari was to make temporary repairs to damages suffered in a vicious gale. The rails and boomkins in the bow head area had been carried away, and the cabin windows stove in.

Constitution had been gone from the United States for over three and a half years at this point, and her crew was a collection of men drawn from ships ordered home. Enlistments for many had run out, but, by custom, they were expected to serve until the ship returned home. With no certain word of when that would happen, tempers and frustrations mounted. Incidents of desertion, drunkenness, and insubordination increased. On one occasion, all officers and Marines were placed under arms when crewmen voiced objections to the confinement of miscreants.

CHESAPEAKE AND LEOPARD

Secretary Smith had issued orders on 15 May 1807 directing James Barron to prepare to sail in *Chesapeake* as relief for *Constitution* and Campbell. Outfitting of his
flagship at Norfolk was done in a lackadaisical manner. She sailed on 22 June
with her decks littered with supplies and her crew not properly assigned stations.
As ill luck would have it, there were two British men-of-war at anchor at
Lynnhaven. One of them, *Leopard*, 50, got under way as *Chesapeake* stood out of
Chesapeake Bay. Shortly thereafter, the Briton brought Barron to with a hail that
she was carrying dispatches for Barron. The British lieutenant who came aboard
showed the captain orders from his flag officer to all subordinate units to stop
and board *Chesapeake* when found in order to retrieve a number of British deserters said to be on board the American ship. Barron rightly refused to allow his
crew to be mustered and inspected by the British. The lieutenant returned to
Leopard, which in the meantime had cleared for action, and after a few moments
of exchanged hails, the British frigate opened fire on the disorganized, unpre-
pared Americans. It was perfect carnage. In a few minutes, three Americans were
dead and twenty wounded. *Chesapeake* fired just one harmless shot before hauling
down her flag. The British subsequently took out four men and refused to accept
Barron's surrender—after all, there wasn't a state of war. All that was left for
Barron to do was to crawl painfully back to port where *Chesapeake* would have to
be repaired and where his career would be put in limbo, never to recover entirely.

Unaware that her relief thus had been delayed, *Constitution* during this period
once more was making port calls. Under way from Syracuse on 12 June, she
called at Messina, Palermo, and Leghorn, in succession. At the last port, she
loaded the fifteen-ton monument to Somers and other heroes of Tripoli subscribed to earlier by officers of the squadron to the tune of $1,240. The fifty-one
numbered cases were stowed away below for delivery home and assembly at a
place to be designated by the secretary of the navy.

THE SMELL OF MUTINY

Heading west ("below" in the jargon of the day), *Constitution* met *Hornet* at Alicante
and together sailed to Malaga. There, Campbell read an old Boston newspaper
and learned for the first time of the *Chesapeake-Leopard* affair. His first reaction
was concerned with the readiness of his frigate and *Hornet* to fight the British,

should there exist a state of war. To improve *Hornet*'s defenses, he had four of his 32-pounder carronades transferred to and mounted in the smaller unit, leaving *Constitution* with two each on her forecastle and quarterdeck, in addition to the long twelves.

News of the delay of *Chesapeake* also spread through the crew like wildfire. Already disaffected, this latest development moved some to make their discontent known. It began by a veteran petty officer requesting permission to come to the main mast to state the views of his mates. Lt. Charles Ludlow granted permission and heard them out. Respected by ship's company, Ludlow sought to smooth the troubled waters with statements of understanding and appeals to patriotism. But when he reported to Campbell a short time later, he knew the ugly mood prevailed. Campbell thought it might help to get to sea and keep the men occupied.

At eight bells of the morning watch next day, 15 August, the boatswain's mates piped all hands to quarters for leaving port, but no one moved. Campbell ordered all officers to the quarterdeck under arms and for the Marine Guard to be assembled there as well. Two long twelves were loaded with grape and cannister by midshipmen and aimed at the larboard gangway. At that point, all hands were piped aft for muster—right where the cannon were aimed—and, surprisingly, the crew responded. Campbell had the midshipmen remove the cannons' apron covers and blow on their matches. The moment of truth had arrived: The mates were ordered to repeat the call to unmoor. Given the choice, the crew manned their stations with alacrity, and the crisis had been weathered.

HOME

On the 18th, Campbell received the secretary's orders to shut down all American naval activity in the Mediterranean and return home. The threat of war with Great Britain was immediate and grave. Campbell ordered *Hornet* to Malta and Syracuse to arrange for the shipment home of stores remaining at those ports, and to Leghorn to pick up the public monies held there for the squadron. At Algeciras on the 29th, he met the new sloop *Wasp*, 18, just arriving to join the squadron. Keeping her in company, Campbell sailed *Constitution* for Boston on 8 September. They arrived on 14 October; *Constitution* had been gone for four years and two months, the longest time she ever would be absent from the United States.

CHAPTER SEVEN

Prelude to Glory

After an absence of more than four years, *Constitution* spent only a few days in Boston in November 1807. Captain Campbell had her off Sandy Hook on the 18th and at a berth at the New York Navy Yard shortly thereafter. His orders were to pay off all of his crew except a ship-keeping cadre and turn her over to the yard.

REPAIRS

On the 30th, he made the customary report of his ship's condition and repairs needed to Secretary Smith: new main and mizzen masts, new boats, replacement of one set of sails and most water casks—things one would expect after four busy years—and, most importantly, replacement of the long twelves with "heavy Carronades."

The marble monument to those lost off Tripoli was offloaded, and arrangements were made to ship it to Washington for assembly. That done, the officers were furloughed, the crew discharged, and the rheumatic Campbell turned *Constitution* over to Captain Chauncey's ship keepers on 8 December to be placed in ordinary.

By the time Commodore Rodgers resumed the New York station command from Chauncey (Rodgers had been absent on special duty as president of the James Barron court-martial resulting from the *Chesapeake* affair), President Jefferson had embarked on his ill-fated attempt to make England and France cease their spoliation of neutral (i.e., American) shipping by means of commercial restrictions. Hoping to bring them to terms by refusing to trade, he got from Congress an embargo prohibiting the departure of American ships from American ports. The navy and the revenue service were to be the enforcers. The

Jefferson-inspired gunboats bore the brunt of this police work, and those under Rodgers' cognizance cruised the coastal waters between the Passamaquoddy and Delaware Bays—some of the busiest in the country.

At the same time he was directing embargo operations, Rodgers also began the overhaul and refit on *Constitution*, largely in accordance with Campbell's report. Between 1 February 1808 and 3 March 1809 (when Jefferson's final term ended), he spent $99,967.76 readying her for further service. The gun deck now carried thirty new model (longer) 24-pounder long guns from the Cecil Iron Works, and twenty-four 32-pounder carronades from the Columbia Iron Works were installed on the spar deck. Both types were fitted with firing locks for more efficient operation. Now her battery clearly was heavier than any British frigate extant. Additionally, a new billet head and trailboards were installed at a cost of $690, replacing the "temporary" Maltese work. In February 1809, Rodgers received orders to place *Constitution* in commission as his squadron flagship. He did so on the 20th.

Preparations for sea were made slowly. The incoming Madison administration quickly substituted a non-importation policy for Jefferson's embargo, resulting in an upsurge of activity in commercial shipping that attracted idle seamen. Additionally, since shortly after the *Chesapeake-Leopard* affair, the navy had a policy of not enlisting anyone other than native-born or formally naturalized citizens. On 24 May *Constitution* and the squadron consisting of brigs *Siren, Vixen, Argus,* and *Wasp* was formed under Rodgers' command (*Siren* actually was absent on a voyage to France) with orders to patrol the coast from Cape Henry north to the Passamaquoddy. During this same period, Rodgers had the additional duty of laying up fifty-two of the Jeffersonian gunboats, which duty he performed with pleasure. *Constitution*'s crew was completed in August by a draft of men from the newly decommissioned *Chesapeake* at Boston.

"Make Work" Activity

The commodore finally got his flagship under way on 15 August on a short cruise of "instruction and observation" to Newport, Rhode Island, and New London, Connecticut, before returning to New York. On 10 September, two days after sailing again with frigate *Essex* and *Argus, Constitution* Seaman John Cochrane was lost when the main and mizzen top and topgallant masts and all royal yards collapsed in light winds. The poor quality of wood used in the recent refit was blamed. At sea repairs were completed in four days. Rodgers returned

Como. John Rodgers commanded *Constitution* for a little more than eighteen months during the Barbary War and again for sixteen months during 1809–1810. Never particularly fond of the ship, he arranged in 1810 to exchange commands with Capt. Isaac Hull in order to get *President,* a ship he considered more desirable. The portrait is by Gilbert Stuart. *Official U.S. Navy photo*

to New York briefly, and then took the frigate south to Hampton Roads, Virginia, for permanent repairs. By the middle of November *Constitution* was back in New York, where she remained moored through the winter.

On 6 February 1810, Robert Thompson, the only chaplain continuously in service since 1800, received orders from the secretary of the navy to "repair to N. York and report yourself to Comm. Rodgers. You are to remain on board the Frigate Constitution for three months for the purpose of instructing the Young Officers in the theory of navigation and lunar observations. You are thence to proceed to the Frigate President—thence to the Frigate U. States—thence to the Frigate Essex, remaining on board each, for the same purpose, three months."

In May, Rodgers took *Constitution* to sea again, and off Sandy Hook she captured the ships *Golconda* of New York and *Rose* of Philadelphia. Both had violated the Nonintercourse Act by sailing from Liverpool laden with British goods. Late in the month, he brought *Constitution, Argus,* and *Wasp* to Annapolis, whence he proceeded to Washington overland to confer with the secretary about fleet reorganization and a more aggressive naval policy.

Rodgers was given the principal command under the reorganization, that of "the northern division of ships for the protection of the American coast." Permitted to select his own flagship, he chose *President*, 44, a "follow-on" to *Constitution*'s design, said to be faster and handier than her older sister. (Rodgers had been quite dissatisfied with *Constitution* while he had her. Why he failed to perceive the reasons for her mediocre performance, as his successor would, is unfathomable now.) Thus it was that the man who would lead *Constitution* to her destiny came into command. On 17 June 1810, in Hampton Roads, John Rodgers and Isaac Hull exchanged ship commands, each taking his officers and crew with him. (Chaplain Thompson went with Rodgers from *Constitution* to *President* and died there later in the summer, his teaching tour unfulfilled.)

HULL IN COMMAND

Isaac Hull was no stranger to *Constitution*, as has been related. During the Barbary War, he first served as first lieutenant of the frigate *Adams*, 28, then commanded the schooner *Enterprize*, 12, and the brig *Argus*, 14. In these ships he served with increasing distinction. Indeed, his *Argus* was the principal naval support for the Arab-U.S. Marine assault on the Libyan city of Derne in 1805.

When he took command of *Constitution* in June 1810, he was thirty-seven years old and had been a captain for four years. A serious, thoroughgoing seaman, the short, rotund bachelor skipper was not much concerned with the perquisites of rank as with the readiness of his command and the welfare of his crew.

Hull lost no time in coming to grips with his new command. The very next day, he had the crew drilled at the guns and in the rigging. His carpenters reported finding the caulking very rotten, and on the 19th commenced recaulking. More than a month was spent by Hull in beginning to get the ship to his liking. Shortly thereafter, *Constitution* sailed for Boston to take on stores and water. Her sailing qualities proved so poor, however, that Hull was forced to write the secretary that he would be unable to rejoin Rodgers as expected. He finally sailed south on 14 July, informing the secretary, "I have no hopes of her sailing any better than she did coming here. I shall now attend to that particular but I fear she will never sail as she has done until she goes into fresh water."

In Hampton Roads once more, Hull sent divers down on the 26th to check

This watercolor sketch is said to have come from "Commodore John Rodgers' sketch-book, courtesy of the Smithsonian Institution," but neither that institution nor the Naval Historical Foundation whence it allegedly was received know of the sketchbook. The sketch is of interest because it shows the ship now (presumably 1809–1810) fitted with forecastle bulwarks, as well as triangular skysails (sometimes called "skyscrapers"). *Official U.S. Navy photo*

the bottom (which had last been coppered in 1803). They found the hull fes-tooned with marine growth: mussels, barnacles, oysters and seaweed by the basketful. As Hull put it to Secretary Paul Hamilton: "After seeing them and being assured that she has, speaking within bounds, ten waggon loads of them on her bottom you can have no doubts as to the cause of her not sailing." To emphasize his point, samples were sent along as well.

Knowing now the source of his troubles, Hull went round to Delaware Bay to get into fresh water, where saltwater marine life would die. The frigate arrived at Wilmington, Delaware, on 11 August. Using an iron drag scraper, Hull sought to remove the moribund sea life, but still they hung on. After three days in fresh water, the mussels began to fall away of their own accord. Hull hoped the oys-ters soon would follow.

The 22nd found *Constitution*, in Hull's estimation, ready for sea. Soon under way, he was off Sandy Hook by 4 September. But Hull still was not satisfied with the way the ship sailed, improved as it was. Further examination disclosed that masses of defunct barnacle shells remained firmly affixed to the copper sheathing. Only heaving down and a thorough scraping, or total replacement of the copper, could correct the situation. Nonetheless, it must have been a relief for Hull to get to sea and be active again. During the long inport periods, the crew naturally grew restive and got into trouble. The ship's log records the results of boredom and frustration: three men flogged for drunkenness and fighting on 20 July; one man flogged for drunkenness and another for desertion on 8 August; eight midshipmen reported for neglect of duty; and three seamen punished for drunkenness on 1 September.

In mid-September, after two weeks on patrol, Hull anchored in Nantasket Roads off Boston, his program of ship improvement continuing unabated. Carpenters caulked the gun deck and, on 17–18 September, some were employed cutting air ports for the berthing deck to improve ventilation. Toward the end of the month, crewmen were busy blackening the bends and whitewashing the berth deck and steerage bulkheads, and the spar deck ceiling planking had been painted green, as had one boat.

Hull resumed patrolling between Boston and Hampton Roads on the last day of September, occasionally anchoring off Sandy Hook. While there on 17 October, Midshipmen Richard Rodgers (one of those on report in August), Charles W. Morgan, and Archibald Hamilton (son of the secretary of the navy), and Dr. Samuel Gilliland received permission to go ashore near the lighthouse "to shoot." The shooting turned out to be a duel between Rodgers and Morgan over an unrecorded slight. In the exchange, Rodgers was killed and Morgan wounded. Morgan was arrested and Hamilton and Gilliland suspended from duty in an effort to "discourage a practice so much at variance with morality and common law of the country." But abhorrence of a practice did not constitute the law, any more than it does now, and all three offenders soon were restored to duty. Hamilton was transferred shortly thereafter.

Constitution next spent nearly four weeks at Newcastle, Delaware, then patrolled north to the squadron's winter rendezvous. On 21 November, Seaman Samuel Francis fell from the mizzen rigging and was drowned; the next day, Seaman Caleb Martin likewise fell overboard and was lost. When it was learned that the former had been the sole support of a widowed mother, a subscription suggested by Hull netted a surprising $1,000: three dollars per man from a crew whose per capita income averaged only ten dollars a month. New London, Connecticut, which Hull had suggested to Rodgers as a good rendezvous, was reached on the 28th. By mid-December, the entire squadron had snugged down for the winter.

The next three months, not atypically, were ones wherein the commodore, his captains, and their officers expended much of their effort in keeping the seamen gainfully employed and out of trouble. *Constitution*'s log clearly shows that the gainful employment was achieved, but that sailors inevitably would get into trouble. On 11 December, three Marines were punished for drunkenness and a sailor for theft, while the sailmakers made deck awnings, the carpenters more air ports, and the armorers a new Charlie Noble (galley smokestack). A week later, the armorers made a smokestack for the wardroom and the carpenters overhauled the chain pumps. A court-martial was held on board on 20–21 December to try several men belonging "to the U.S. Brig Argus & schooner Revenge." In January, another court-martial was convened (in the case of a man who had objected to being ordered to remove his shoes and stockings when washing decks in cold weather), and in February, a third. Two men were drummed out of service. On the positive side, the installation of air ports was completed and Midshipmen Alcott and Ambrose Fields joined the ship.

Another duel between midshipmen occurred shortly before the winter rendezvous disbanded. Charles W. Fowle allegedly made a remark to Volunteer Midshipman Joseph Brailsford that smacked of disrespect of the latter's partner at a ball. Brailsford, of course, challenged Fowle to "protect" his lady's honor. To conceal the fact that they were to duel, the two hotheads and their seconds left the ships on 15 March in a sleigh that took them to Pawcatuck, Rhode Island. There, the entire party took dinner together at a local hotel before setting out for an isolated field. Once at the site, details quickly were arranged and Brailsford put a ball in his larger opponent's thigh. Fowle lived in agony for a week before the ball chafed through the artery and killed him. He was buried in Groton Heights. Brailsford and one of the seconds, Midshipman John Packett, soon were transferred to *Argus* as a mark of official displeasure.

As if to write "finis" to the long winter, all hands were mustered to witness punishment on the 20th. Commencing at 10:30 A.M., floggings were carried out on fourteen crewmen. Most of these were for relatively minor offenses, like being drunk and disorderly (nine to twelve lashes), but Seaman Lanson Marks received twenty-four for twice deserting and writing a disrespectful, seditious letter to the secretary of the navy "calculated to excite mutiny in the rest of the crew." Marks, one must observe, was fortunate to have been serving under a humane commander. The rendezvous was broken up on 25 March 1811, with Rodgers taking *President* to New York and Hull heading for Boston.

Early in April, Hull had the gun streak along the length of the hull painted white. This is the first recorded occasion when *Constitution* did not have the dull yellow streak she bore when commissioned. The use of white paint for this purpose did not become standard practice until after the War of 1812; in fact, *Constitution* reverted to the yellow streak twice more before that war was over.

On 11 April, a court-martial sat in the case of Boatswain's Mate John Niese and Seaman John Read, charged with seditious conduct and disrespect. The two had written a letter to the secretary of the navy on 14 February demanding their immediate discharge from the service. They had informed the secretary that they had not been aware, when they enlisted under Captain Hull (then in *President*), that their term of enlistment did not begin until the ship got under way for the first time *after* they signed on. *President* had remained at anchor for seven months subsequent to their shipping. Clearly, it was a case of Niese and Read not having read the fine print, nor asking the right question. M.Cmdt. James Lawrence and his fellow court members found the two guilty of having written the letter and apprising their fellow inhabitants of the berth deck of its contents. The court awarded Niese demotion, a fine equal to his pay from the date of the letter to the date of the court, and two hundred lashes; and Read, a similar fine and fifty lashes. Then, in a move unusual in those days, the court recommended that the floggings be remitted for these first offenders who were victims of their own carelessness. Secretary Hamilton approved.

Trip to Northern Europe

Hull had *Constitution* at Annapolis on 24 May, under orders to prepare for foreign service. Secretary Hamilton told him he would be sailing to France, Holland, and England, transporting our new minister to France, Joel Barlow, to his post and delivering $220,000 in specie to Holland as interest on our Revolutionary War debt to that country. As it turned out, *Constitution* idled at Annapolis for more than two months awaiting her passenger. Hull used the time to ensure the ship was ready to voyage into potentially hostile waters. Close attention was paid to overhauling the guns, cleaning carriages and slides, repairing elevating screws on the carronades, and filling shot boxes.

Hull's crew, in the main, had been shipped nearly two years before, and soon would be eligible for discharge. On 19 July, Secretary Hamilton asked Hull just how many might be involved and urged him to do his utmost to get them to extend for the voyage. He wrote Hull again two days later, authorizing him to exchange these men for up to 149 men from other ships. After hearing from Hull, he authorized the exchange of an additional ten. Ultimately, the captain got 186 men drafted from *Essex, Hornet,* and *Nautilus,* as few of the old timers would extend.

Barlow received his instructions from the State Department on 26 July and arrived on board *Constitution* with family and suite on 1 August, whereupon Hull got under way. (Unbeknownst to the distinguished passenger, in these last few days, amidst the flurry of preparation, Hull had had to deal with an outbreak of smallpox. Reacting decisively, he had had the infected Marine moved ashore and the entire crew vaccinated. His action was timely; no further cases developed and the Barlows never given cause for concern.)

The frigate took its departure for France on the 5th. The first days at sea were pleasant ones, during which time the passengers were able to acclimatize themselves somewhat to the alien environment. Things changed shortly, however, for barely a week out the ship was beset by a gale that lasted for three days and drove the women out of sight for its duration. The passage, which had remained rough following the gale, ended with *Constitution's* arrival in the English Channel on 1 September. On the 5th, as Hull worked his way to Cherbourg, he encountered the blockading British squadron. He beat to quarters to be ready for any eventuality, and at 5:30 in the afternoon he checked his way and spoke a British frigate and then the liner *Royal Oak,* 74, the flagship of the blockaders.

With the recent *President-Lille Belt* episode in their minds, when Rodgers in *President* mistakenly had fired into HMS *Lille Belt* in a chance night encounter, the Americans were tense and expecting the worst. A lieutenant from the Briton came aboard with a message that the American captain was to repair on board. Hull's response was to identify the character of his principal passenger and indicate his intention to land Barlow at Cherbourg as directed by his government. He would take orders from no other source.

The lieutenant took Hull's message to his commodore, and soon returned with a demand that *Constitution* delay her entry into Cherbourg until a specific hour the following day. Predictably, the American captain replied that he would enter as soon as the weather permitted. The British officer left and the tension continued, but the calm remained unbroken.

Constitution anchored in Cherbourg harbor the next morning, having exchanged a salute of fifteen guns with the French batteries. Barlow and his suite were put ashore with full ceremony, the yards manned and a salute of seventeen guns.

Later, when French Rear Adm. Aimable-Gilles Troude called upon Hull, a nine-gun salute thundered out across the waters and was returned by *Courageux, 84.*

Hull sailed from Cherbourg on the 11th for Texel to deliver the specie payment. Adverse winds caused him to put into Deal, England, where he was windbound for two days. When he finally cleared Deal for Texel, he got another glimpse of the British naval effort against Napoleon: Off Flushing, he passed thirteen ships of the line on blockade duty.

Constitution arrived off Texel early in the morning of the 20th and found there a British blockading squadron of seven ships of the line and a number of smaller units. In the port could be seen several Dutch men-of-war flying French flags. On that busy morning, Hull sent a report of his mission to the British admiral commanding the local blockade, sent Purser Isaac Garretson ashore to coordinate delivery of the specie, and received from Den Helder a local pilot, a Mr. Hooglant. He continued under way offshore throughout the day. The pilot confirmed what Hull had suspected: The frigate's draft of 23 feet, 6 inches was too deep to pass over the bar into Texel.

After a day of waiting, Hull received a letter from the Dutch agents that the French intendant general and the director of douanes (customs) would not permit the landing of the specie without authorization to do so from Paris. That could take two weeks. Hull fired off three letters on the 21st—to our consul at Den Helder, the agents in Amsterdam, and Purser Garretson—voicing his concern over the diplomatic complications such a delay could cause with the British blockaders, and stating that bad weather might force him to abandon the area.

On the 22nd, Hull wrote Sylvanus Bourne, consul at Amsterdam, that "I have determined to leave the Coast immediately." The cause of that decision—weather, the British, the uncertainty of events ashore—is not known. But Hull evidently had second thoughts about the matter, for after a week of cruising offshore he was once more at Texel. There, he found that authorization had been received from Paris to land the specie, and he did so.

The American frigate returned to Deal, where Hull requisitioned winter clothing for his crew, their usual garb proving inadequate for the Channel weather they were experiencing. On 3 October, Judge Thompson of New York, a bearer of official U.S. dispatches, and Sir James Jay came aboard for passage to Cherbourg, as requested by the local American vice consul, Edward Iggulden.

Constitution sailed for Cherbourg on the 8th, and shortly after midnight on the 9th, a ship was sighted off the weather bow. Without warning, the stranger "fired two Shott at us, one struck under the Quarter and the other under the Weather Beam." Hull cleared for action, then bore up and spoke the other ship. It proved to be HMS *Redpole,* 16, a brig whose captain quickly "sent an officer on board to Apologize for firing at us." There had been no casualties and the brig soon cleared the area.

Off Cherbourg on the 12th, there was another incident. As Hull flew the appropriate signal for the French to allow him to enter port unmolested, one of the British blockaders sailed close aboard him in such a way as to obscure French observance of the flags. Apparently, the British were attempting to create an incident between France and the United States. The French batteries opened up on what appeared to them to be two enemy warships attacking the harbor. The true enemy ship turned away at the first shots, but Hull held steady. His ship was struck twice, one round taking the stern off the second cutter. Once the British ship was clear, the French saw the prearranged signal and ceased fire.

Once anchored and the misunderstanding resolved, Hull learned that he would be required to wait an indefinite time for Barlow's dispatches. Thinking he might facilitate things, Hull paid a short visit to Paris, where he took in a number of the famous buildings in the French capital and was very impressed. Jonathan Russell, Barlow's predecessor in Paris, accompanied the good captain on his return to Cherbourg.

Constitution sailed for Portsmouth, England, the afternoon of 9 November. In addition to delivering Russell to his new post at the American Legation in London, Hull was returning Judge Thompson from his mission to France. Arriving on the 11th, the passengers were landed the next day. Hull went with them to London, leaving his first lieutenant, Charles Morris, in charge.

On the evening of the 13th, Seaman Thomas Holland slipped overboard from *Constitution,* perhaps under cover of a passing rain shower, with the intention to desert. At about 8:30, a boat from HMS *Havannah,* 36, notified Morris that a man, too exhausted to say more than that he was from *Constitution,* had been taken aboard. Morris acknowledged the report and indicated the man would be reclaimed in the morning, presumably when he was somewhat recovered from his exertions.

An officer from *Constitution* appeared as indicated on the 14th to take custody of Holland, but was told that the sailor would not be returned without orders from the flag officer, Spithead, as the man had claimed protection as a British subject. Morris, upon hearing this, gained an interview with Adm. Sir Roger

Curtis. The meeting was formal and correct, but the admiral stood firm in protecting the man as an Englishman. He asked Morris if the Americans would return a deserter from one of His Majesty's ships, should such an event occur. The first lieutenant responded with the belief that Captain Hull probably would accede to any mutually advantageous agreement.

Hull returned aboard on the 17th. His humor, already soured by the discovery that two members of his gig's crew had deserted ashore, was not improved one whit by Morris's report of the Holland affair. He immediately penned a letter to Sir Roger, reviewing the case as reported by his first lieutenant, and making a formal demand for Holland's return. Curtis refused.

At this point, the incident took a new twist. That same night, Hull ordered additional Marine sentries posted to prevent further desertions. They were ordered to shoot anything seen floating near the ship. Around midnight, two or three shots awoke Hull, and there soon appeared on deck a dripping figure who told the captain, "I'm an American, your honor." John Burne (some report him as William Wallace) was sent below for a tot of rum and a warm hammock. Notification immediately was sent to HMS *Havannah*, and the next morning Hull had the pleasure of refusing to deliver him up, reversing the nationality claim.

It wasn't long before rumors abounded concerning punitive action by the British. Hull sounded out his crew and found that they were ready to a man—even those in irons, whom he ordered released—to take on a British frigate. Matters grew more tense when two British frigates shifted berths and anchored close to the American, so close that skilled seamanship would be required to get under way without fouling them. Hull, whose gunners already were overhauling their guns and "sending up Grape and Round Shott," displayed his skill by shifting his berth a mile closer to open waters smartly and without mishap. One of the British frigates followed.

The two antagonists eyed each other all day on the 20th. That night, the battle lanterns were hung and lighted, and the ship made essentially ready for action. Then, at 3:30 A.M. on the 21st: "Hove Short on the Larboard Cable, beat to Quarters and cleared away the Guns, got everything ready for Action. ½ before 4 Hove up the anchor, Made Sail and stood out into the Channell." The British frigate soon was under way, accompanying *Constitution*. She maintained a respectful distance, however, and once it was clear the American frigate had no belligerent intention, she returned to port. *Constitution* arrived in Cherbourg once more on the 23rd and remained there into the new year.

Three hours after the arrival, Morris was on his way to Paris to wait upon Barlow and bring his Washington dispatches back to the ship. He remained in the French capital for six weeks, where he saw Napoleon, and met the aging Lafayette, Tadeusz Kosciusko, and others remembered for their roles in the American Revolution.

At Cherbourg, the Americans witnessed the ceremonies attendant upon Napoleon's coronation as emperor on 1 December when "The French, Ships Dressed and fired a 21 Guns." Later that month, the French, who had been most impressed by *Constitution*, were allowed "to take her dimension."

The long wait, with the boredom, the bad weather, and the desire to be homeward bound, was typically difficult for the crew. Acting Carpenter Lewis Crofford died on the 14th and was buried ashore the next morning. Seamen Daniel Bliss and William Cooper were flogged on the 19th for "smuggling rum on board." Midshipman William C. Pierpont and Boy Abraham Harding both died the next day of influenza and were taken ashore on the 21st. The dolorous task was performed again on the 27th, in falling snow, for James Lornson.

Morris returned on 6 January 1812, and Hull sailed for home on the 9th. On this voyage, he carried some fifty out-of-work American merchant seamen who had been burdening the local consulate. And in the hold were cases of china being sent to Baltimore by Mrs. Jerome Bonaparte, the former Elizabeth Patterson of that city and now sister-in-law to the emperor, as well as goods for Dolly Madison and several others.

Two hours out, two ships were sighted making for *Constitution*. Hull, as was his custom, cleared for action. HMS *Hotspur*, 36, was permitted to send an emissary on board. After the merest formalities, the boat left and the ships parted company. The final (peaceful) encounter with the British occurred on the 15th, when Hull spoke HMS *Mars*, 74, and passed on. The stormy passage ended at anchor in Chesapeake Bay off Old Point Comfort on 19 February. Hull shifted to an anchorage nearer to Norfolk the next day. A seventeen-gun salute was fired on the 22nd in memory of George Washington.

WAR PREPARATIONS

Hull soon realized that the temper of the government was moving toward war. That, coupled with his recent experiences with the Royal Navy, brought home to him the need to be prepared *soon*, and the importance of taking full advantage of a yard overhaul. His orders to Morris were to begin overhauling rigging, recaulking the hull, washing ballast, and cleaning out the hold—all this at a time when many of the crew were being paid off and officers were taking leaves of absence.

At 4:00 A.M. on the 25th, *Constitution* got under way for the nation's capital. Entering the Potomac two days later, she paused for several days to offload a number of her guns, carriages, and shot into attendant Gunboat 61 to reduce her draft for passage upriver. Under way again on 2 April, she paused once more off Quantico the next day for further offloading, and on the 4th off Fort Washington, where Hull left the ship and went on ahead. Despite the lightening efforts, the big frigate grounded on the bar near Alexandria for 4.5 hours before finally being warped to a wharf at the Washington Navy Yard at 2:00 P.M. on the 5th.

Rodgers had been totally dissatisfied with *Constitution*'s sailing abilities, as was noted earlier. Hull, upon assuming command, had discovered at least a part of the problem and had done what he could to alleviate it. He knew heaving down and at least bottom cleaning were required, if not an entire recoppering of the underwater body, and he had secured permission to do so during the course of the European trip. Other areas to be addressed in solving the problem were her rigging and ballasting. With the many critical matters to be corrected, it was a happy circumstance that the officer assigned by the yard to assist Hull was none other than Lieutenant Nathaniel "Jumping Billy" Haraden, who had served in her under Nicholson, Talbot, and Preble, and had himself briefly been in charge of the frigate in 1802–1803.

Little time was lost in getting the overhaul under way. On Monday the 7th, the magazines were emptied and the water casks unloaded—this, despite the fact that Secretary Hamilton paid a three-hour visit to the ship, complete with seventeen-gun salute and attendant protocol. He was back again the next day for another two hours, but still the remaining long guns were landed after he left. Wednesday found the hardworking crew laboriously removing the shingle ballast; the rest of the week was occupied with stripping the masts.

As the unrigging resumed on Monday the 14th, carpenters came aboard and began "ripping up planking adjoining the [water]ways:" *Constitution* would have new decking. "Time out" was taken on Tuesday: "At 4 P.M. removed the Ship's Company on board the Gen. Greene, Rec[eivin]g Ship."

Overhauling all the rigging in a loft ashore began with the yard period's third week. Back at the ship, preparations were begun on the 23rd to heave her down.

All the spars and upper masts and fighting tops had been landed. Gun ports were hammered and caulked shut. Everything loose was put ashore. Lower masts were rigged to take the tremendous stresses of physically pulling the ship over on her side. Huge, four-sheave blocks were attached to the mast tops, with the falls run to similar blocks secured ashore, ready to be hauled by teams of oxen. The hard work and lure of the "beach" led to six desertions.

Early on 2 May began the process of heaving the heavy frigate down for inspection, first to port and then to starboard. A journal entry reports they found her "bottom better than was Expected." She was hove down "keel out" to port on the 5th and necessary patching done along her very centerline. Early the next morning she was allowed to right to the "2nd course" while the remaining copper patching was accomplished on the starboard side. She was righted on the 8th, turned end-for-end ("winded"), and hove down to starboard for the rest of the job. At day's end on the 12th, they were finished; unrigging the heavy tackle required all the next day.

The gathering war clouds continued to give impetus to the work. The foremast was unshipped on the 4th and the bowsprit on the 16th; both were condemned as unfit for further service. New spars began coming back aboard on the 22nd, the new foremast was stepped on the 25th, and the main top emplaced the next day and the foretop on the 28th. On 1 June, a trysail mast was installed to render handling of the spanker more efficient. When all done, *Constitution* would be newly rigged with sky poles (as was Hull's previous command). She would carry more and higher canvas than ever before. And what many today consider her "trademark"—the "split" dolphin striker—was installed. Haraden gave his particular attention to the ship's ballast, reducing it by a third.

The month of May had seen more than forty new hands and a number of midshipmen join the ship, the former produced by ship's officers recruiting in Baltimore, Philadelphia, and Boston. Offsetting these gains, Seamen John Jeffries and Patrick McDonald died, and William Coombs, Peter Jones, William Weri(?), James Barret, and William Kinney deserted. For Kinney, it was a second try.

Early June found the remaining yards being swayed up and installed, while below stores, water casks, and guns—all in limited quantities—were brought aboard. On the 7th, all spars were in place; on the 8th, "got 3d cutter, green boat, and gig" from the boat shed; and on the 9th, at the end of the forenoon watch, the crew was returned from *General Greene.*

Wednesday the 10th found *Constitution* under way in tow at 8:00 A.M. She was towed to a position off Greenleaf Point, where she remained at anchor until hove over the bar at 11:00 the next morning. Anchored once more off Alexandria, she spent the next week taking on stores and water, and having her new gun deck capstan installed. Secretary Hamilton visited her once more on the 13th (for 2.5 hours), but conditions permitted the firing of only fifteen guns in salute. Thus, as the war in which she was to win undying fame was about to break out, the frigate was newly rigged and trimmed and freshly cleaned; but her gun batteries were wanting and her crew far from complete.

A Most
Fortunate Ship

CHAPTER EIGHT

The Great Chase

War with Great Britain, it seemed, was inevitable. Before that nation could get accustomed to American sovereignty, she became embroiled in the waves of political instability resulting from the outbreak of the French Revolution. And with that involvement came a vastly increased need for seamen. This problem, in the "good old days" when American ships and sailors represented a third of the Crown's maritime strength, had been solved by pressing the colonials into Royal Navy service. Expediency and habit, together with a low regard for the new nation's ability to do anything to prevent it, led to the practice being continued for nearly two decades before relations ruptured. It wasn't until more than 6,000 American sailors had been impressed on grounds of "once an Englishman, always an Englishman," and some 917 American merchant ships had been condemned in British Admiralty courts for alleged neutrality violations, that a sufficient number of people in Congress could be mustered to pass a declaration of war. As it was, the decision came on a narrow margin. President James Madison declared the state of war on 18 June 1812.

Until that very day, *Constitution* had been at Alexandria, loading stores. Before the news was received, she was gotten under way by her senior officer present, Lt. George C. Read, for Annapolis, there to take on her guns and complete her manning. Captain Hull, living ashore in Washington for the past three months, remained there a few more days. The next senior officer, Lieutenant Morris, likewise was absent from the ship and remained so until the 25th, attempting unsuccessfully to get a new assignment. Thus it was Read who received, shortly before midnight on the 18th, this letter from the secretary of the navy:

Navy Department
June 18th 1812
Sir,

This day war has been declared between the United Empire of Great Britain
. . . and the United States of America . . . and you are . . . entitled to every
belligerent right to attack and capture, and to defend—you will on the
utmost dispatch to reach New York after you have made up your complement
of men at Annapolis. In your way from there you will not fail to notice the
British flag should it present itself . . . , but you are not to understand me as
impelling you to battle.

The letter is curiously cautious and timid for one announcing the outbreak of
war, and reflects the attitude then prevailing among many in high government
positions that preserving the small navy as a "fleet in being" was more important
to the successful prosecution of the war than fighting. It was a position that
naval officers themselves fought and, to the everlasting glory of the service, got
changed. But that was in the future.

At 5:00 P.M. on the 19th, Read read the crew the declaration of war. In response
they requested permission to give three cheers. It was granted. *Constitution* subsequently arrived at Annapolis about the 27th, after pausing off Thomas Creek to
backload additional guns and ammunition.

Preparations for sea were pressed. Men were shipped daily and supplies
arrived in a steady stream. Time was found for drilling the crew even as it was
being assembled; Hull wasted not a moment. While twenty-four carronades for
the spar deck were being swayed aboard, far below other crewmen were busy filling hundreds of thin, sheet lead cylinders with black powder. Stowed thus far in
the forward magazine for the carronades were 648 charges of varying weights. In
the main magazine aft were 585 loads for the long guns. And for small arms, over
7,000 musket and pistol cartridges had been prepared.

Secretary Hamilton wrote to Hull again on 3 July, again emphasizing the
"fleet in being" mentality, and ordering him to remain at New York for further
orders if Commodore Rodgers was absent. The thought that refusing to fight
was condoned must have been repugnant to the likes of the captain, a veteran of
the Barbary War under Preble.

Hull sailed from Annapolis on Sunday the 5th and eased his way down
Chesapeake Bay, constantly training his crew and continuing to gather supplies

along the way. He cleared Virginia Capes and stood northward on the 12th. On the same day *Constitution* departed Annapolis, a British squadron under Capt. Sir Philip Bowes Vere Broke, consisting of frigate *Shannon* (flagship, 38), liner *Africa* (Capt. John Bastard), 64, and frigates *Belvidera* (Capt. Richard Byron), 36, and *Aeolus* (Capt. Lord James Townsend), 32, sailed from Halifax to intercept Rodgers's squadron, notice of whose sailing on 22 June had been brought to Vice Adm. Herbert Sawyer by *Belvidera*. Four days later, off Nantucket, the squadron was augmented by the addition of the frigate *Guerriere* (Capt. James Richard Dacres, Jr.), 38, diverted from a planned repair period in Halifax. The squadron arrived off New York on the 14th.

As Hull later reported, "For several days after we got out the wind was light and ahead which with a strong southerly current prevented our making much way to the Northward." On the 15th, one of the carronades to be proofed was fired five times with double charges and double shot and "Found . . . to stand very well." "On the 16th, at 2 P.M. being in 22 fathoms of water off Egg Harbour four sail . . . were discovered from the MastHead to the northward and in shore of us; apparently Ships of War. The wind being very light all sail was made in chase . . . to ascertain whether they were Enemy . . . or our Squadron . . . which . . . I had reason to believe was the case."

"At 4 in the afternoon," the captain reported, "a ship was seen from the Masthead bearing about NE. Standing for us under all sail, which she continued to do until Sunset at which time she was too far off to distinguish signals and the Ships in Shore, only to be seen from the Tops, they were standing off to the Southward and Eastward. As we could not ascertain before dark what the Ship in the offing was, I determined to stand for him and get near enough to make the night signal."

Ever prudent, Captain Hull beat to quarters and cleared the ship for action at 7:30 P.M. With the continuing light airs, the ships closed one another at a crawl as suspense began to mount. At 10:00, the staysails were hauled down and the spanker up. Shortly thereafter, with the lone ship six or eight miles distant, Hull made the private signal of the day. This, he "kept up nearly one hour, but finding she would not answer it, I concluded she and the Ships in shore were Enemy. I immediately hauled off the to Southward and Eastward, and made all sail having determined to lay off till day light, to see what they were. The Ship that we had been chasing hauled off after us showing a light, and occasionally making Signals, supposed to be for the Ships inshore."

The chase was on! It was about 11:00 P.M.

Throughout the midwatch of the 17th, the solitary pursuer (it was HMS *Guerriere*) closed until she was within gunshot range to leeward, i.e., to seaward, the minuscule wind during the watch having shifted to south and west. Approaching 4:00 A.M., *Guerriere* launched a signal rocket and fired two guns, then hauled off to a position northward of *Constitution*. The signal was intended to inform the others that Dacres was satisfied he had fallen in with an American, but the absence of a response from those he believed to be his squadron mates caused him some confusion and led to his drawing off until the approaching dawn could clarify the situation.

The picture became all too clear with the rising sun. Hull later wrote:

> At day light, or a little before . . . , saw two sail under our Lee, which proved to be Frigates of the Enemies [*sic*; these were *Belvidera* and *Aeolus*]. One frigate astern within about five or six miles [*Guerriere*], and a Line of Battle Ship, A Frigate, a Brig, and Schooner, about ten or twelve miles directly astern all in chase of us it being nearly calm where we were.[1] Soon after Sunrise the wind entirely left us, and the Ship would not steer it fell round off with her head towards the two Ships under our lee.

What a position to be in! The wind failed and even steerageway lost. In sailor's parlance, the ship was "not under command"—and an overwhelming enemy force still having the wind was closing in. Hull took the most obvious action:

> At ¼ past 5 A.M. , . . . the ship having no steerageway, hoisted out the 1st cutter and . . . the 2nd ahead to tow ship. . . . Got a 24 pounder up off the gundeck for a stern gun and the forecastle gun aft, cut away the taffrail to give them room and run two guns out the cabin windows. At 6 A.M. got the ship head round to the Southward and set the top gallant studding sails, one of the frigates firing at us [*Shannon*].

This last circumstance only added emphasis to the desperation of the moment. Because she lacked stern ports at the spar deck level, a portion of the transom had to be cut away so that more guns could fire aft (the space of the captain's cabin, already routinely dismantled when the ship beat to quarters, was occupied by two 24-pounders run aft through the cabin windows from their normal broadside positions in the forward cabin area). The gun brought up from the gun deck was the hefty (6,900 pounds) Number One (port) 24-pounder; the "forecastle gun," an 18-pounder.

This painting, attributed to F. Muller, of the July 1812 chase, has compressed the action and rearranged ships in order to show the force in pursuit of *Constitution.* The degradation of the image in the lower right is due to improperly placed lighting when photographing. *Official U.S. Navy photo*

It was a half hour before any of the pursuers realized what Hull was doing, and he had *Constitution* swung southward again as Byron of *Belvidera* had boats in the water preparing to tow. Others followed suit. At 6:30 A.M., a sounding of twenty-one fathoms was reported routinely to the officers on *Constitution*'s quarterdeck. The situation looked grim. With a wind, there was every possibility that the American frigate could elude her pursuers, or at least outdistance enough of them to improve the fighting odds in her favor. In the present situation, even though all were equally dependent upon the wind, the greater number of enemy units, with more men and boats, held most of the trump cards. It was in this period of great tension that Hull's next senior, "that most valuable officer" Morris, his memory jiggled by the leadsman's call, suggested the possibility of kedging ship. Hull, ready to try anything, instantly saw the possibilities and ordered it done. The launch and the first cutter were assigned.

("Kedging" involves hauling an anchor out forward of a ship to the limit of its cable with a long boat, dropping it, and then, by means of the ship's anchor capstan, hauling the ship up to a position over the anchor. While this is being done, a second anchor is taken out and dropped, to repeat the process as the original anchor is weighed and again taken forward by a ship's boat. By stages, a sailing ship could be moved in a given direction despite adverse winds and currents, or in the absence of wind. It was a procedure more commonly used in harbor or other confined area.)

By 7:00, the first kedge was out and the laborious process begun. Inching across the oily swells as the sun rose in the sky (fortunately cloudy) and the summer temperature climbed apace, they finally came to the end of the tether and cut the anchor free. Then back it was the two hundred yards or so to the ship's bows, passing other shipmates taking out the second anchor, to await the next cycle. These efforts notwithstanding, the Americans continued slowly to lose ground. At 7:30, Hull hoisted his colors and tried a shot at his closest pursuer. It fell "a little short."

"At 8," Hull wrote, "four of the Enemy's Ships nearly within GunShot, some of them having six or eight boats ahead towing . . . them up with us, which they were fast doing. It now appeared that we must be taken . . . , four heavy ships nearly within Gun Shot, and coming up fast, and not the least hope of a breeze to give us a chance of getting off by out sailing them."

The British response to the kedging effort was to concentrate all their boats on the two closest pursuers, with the result that they again gained on their quarry. At 9:00, "the Ship nearest us [*Belvidera*] began firing his bow guns, which we instantly returned by our stern guns in the cabbin [*sic*], and on the Quarter Deck; All the Shot from the Enemy fell short, but we have reason to believe that some of ours went on board her, as we could not see them strike the water.[2] Soon after 9 a second Frigate [*Guerriere*] passed under our lee, and opened her Broadside, but finding her shot fall short, discontinued her fire, but continued as did all . . . of them to . . . get up with us." Shortly thereafter, with the coming of a light breeze, two boats were got in.

Through the forenoon watch the contest continued, neither side gaining an advantage. At four bells, Hull ordered drinking water to be pumped overboard to lighten ship. Over 2,300 gallons were discharged—enough to bring the frigate up about one inch. By this time, the British had concentrated all their boats on moving one frigate, *Shannon. Constitution* held her narrow margin of safety, thanks to the superb efforts of all hands. By 11:00, the breeze was sufficiently great that the big frigate overtook her remaining boats and brought them smartly aboard without delay.

A much more dramatic picture, this painting by Anton Otto Fisher not only shows the disposition of ships more accurately but also correctly adds the studdingsails, which increases the sense of urgency in the scene. *Official U.S. Navy photo*

As the new watch began, the enemy units were ranged inshore of *Constitution*, from starboard beam to quarter. With the breeze dying, the first and green cutters were put over to tow once more. Gunfire was exchanged again at about 2:00 P.M. without apparent result. The hours went by in relentless succession, each side straining for advantage: At 3:30, one of the enemy got dangerously close and then the gap widened again; at 7:00, all eight of *Constitution*'s boats were straining at tow lines. Men not actively engaged dropped and napped where they could, rotating from boat crew to shipboard duty and back again, as if on some sort of diabolical treadmill. It was a performance worthy of a seasoned crew, and exceptional for one so green. Hull's leadership must have been exemplary.

The end of the first twenty-four hours of the chase—11:00 P.M.—was marked by the springing up of a welcome breeze; "boats came alongside, hoisted up the gig and green cutter, and set the fore topmast staysail and main topgallant studdingsail." She was moving on her own, and well. Relief from the physical stress was welcomed, but the tension of the chase remained. Advantage was sought from every breath of air.

At dawn on the 18th, fortune was seen to be smiling on the American frigate. The night-long exertions had gained for her a two- to three-mile lead on her pursuers. Although the breezes remained light, Hull determined to make a break for it, and tacked eastward early in the morning watch. At 5:00 A.M., he passed close to HMS *Aeolus* without drawing fire; apparently Townsend feared the concussion of his guns would becalm the Briton and cost him his close-in position. Instead, he tacked and stood after Hull, the others following suit.

At 9:00, there was much activity in *Constitution.* The log recorded: "[F]itted and set Fore and Main skysails saw a ship to windward, supposed to be an American Merchantman standing toward us, the frigates astern hoisted American colors as a decoy, we immediately hoisted English colors, got Royal studding sails and mounts fitted, and shifted the starboard foretopmast studding sail boom which was sprung."

A full dimension of activity as anyone could expect, and with a crew that had been taxed for thirty-four hours, and yet were setting sail, effecting repairs, seeking (successfully, as it turned out) to protect a countryman, and trying to elude the enemy—all at once. But the worst was over, and they must have sensed it. By noon, the situation was beginning to be comfortable. The British hadn't given up, but it was clear that *Constitution* was outsailing them as she headed eastsoutheast. Dead astern at 3.5 miles was *Belvidera, Shannon* was on the port quarter at 4–5 miles, and *Africa* could be seen between the two, back on the horizon. Out abaft the port beam at about five miles were *Aeolus* and *Guerriere,* with *Emulous* (ex-*Nautilus*) astern of them. If they could do nothing else, they could prevent *Constitution* from getting to New York.

The gap continued to widen as the afternoon wore on. At 4:00 P.M., the closest pursuer was six miles off and still dropping astern. Hull continued to set and reset sails to gain every advantage. Carefully, he watched wind and sea for clues as to what to expect, minute by minute. This sensitivity and alertness paid him a big dividend at about 6:30 in the evening, when he saw a squall ahead. Taking in first his stunsails and royals, he had his men ready as it came down upon him. Quickly, the topgallant sails and flying jib were taken in, and the mizzen topsail and spanker reefed. And just as quickly, as soon as the squall cleared the ship (and obscured him to the British), Hull set topgallants and the main topsail staysail. He was off and running. By 7:30, two Britons were hull down—and more sail was set. In another fifteen minutes, she was drawing everything but skysails. For the next hour, the Americans were busy setting all studding sails. At

10:30 P.M., they heard two guns fired from the unseen British pursuers on the port quarter. At 11:00, as the second full day of the chase ended, only one enemy could be made out, dead astern in *Constitution*'s wake.

The Americans began to breathe a little easier, but continued to seek every advantage. "At midnight moderate breeze and pleasant took in the Royal Studding sails. . . . At 1 A.M. set the skysails. At ½ before 2 A.M. got a pull of the weather brace and set the lower steering sail. At 3 A.M. set the main topmast studding sail. At ¼ past 4 A.M. hauled up to SE by S."

First light on the 19th showed four pursuers still in sight, but all hull down, the nearest about twelve miles distant. It was Sunday, but Hull wasn't ready for a day of rest. He wanted to sail his enemy out of sight, and so, "All hands were set to work wetting the Sails, from the Royals down, with the [fire] Engine, and Fire buckets, and we soon found that we left the Enemy very fast. At ¼ past 8 the Enemy finding that they were fast dropping astern, gave over the chase, and hauled their wind to the Northward, probably for the station at New York."

Hull and his crew, who had been together at sea for just five days, had outsailed a superior (in numbers) British squadron in a fifty-seven-hour demonstration of endurance, teamwork, and skilled seamanship. It would not be the last time that this combination would embarrass their British cousins.

Two American merchantmen were spoke later that morning, and the 24-pounder at the taffrail was returned below to its normal site. Then Hull, who had been on deck continuously throughout the chase, and his officers and crew stood down as they headed for Boston. On the 20th, life returned to normal. The next day, he penned his report of the affair to Secretary Hamilton as the ship crossed the latitude of Nantucket. A brief flurry of concern occurred during the afternoon watch on the 22nd, when first two, and then three more, sail were sighted toward the northwest. Five sail together most likely were the British pursuers again; Hull hauled by the wind and sailed below the horizon unseen.

Constitution arrived in President Roads off Boston on the morning of 27 July 1812, three weeks after clearing the Virginia Capes. Hull was anxious to get supplies in lieu of those planned for in New York and learn the latest orders from Washington. Dispatches had been sent ashore even before the ship reached the Roads, to alert the local naval agent of her unexpected arrival, and to Washington with the captain's report. The frigate's arrival also quashed rumors that had been bruited about for three days that she had been ordered to sea with her magazines empty, a chicken ripe for plucking.

CHAPTER NINE

"The Americans Were Our Masters"

PREPARATIONS

When Isaac Hull brought *Constitution* into Nantasket Roads, Boston, on Sunday, 26 July 1812, he had no intention of remaining long in port. He wanted water, food, men, and news, and having satisfied those needs, he intended to be at sea again where he couldn't be trapped by the British squadron he had so narrowly eluded.

By the following Saturday, *Constitution* was ready to sail. No orders had come from Washington, but Hull learned that Commodore Rodgers was not at New York. (He also learned from that city that his younger brother, William, was critically ill.) Locally, it was said the British frigate *Maidstone*, 32, was lurking off Cape Cod and that two others were "in the bay." Being one of those naval officers who believed our few warships could accomplish more at sea than blockaded in port, Hull decided to sail without orders and almost certainly contrary to the orders he was likely to receive from Washington. So, at 5:30 A.M. on Sunday, 2 August, in clearing weather, Hull gave his fateful order to weigh anchor and get under way on a southwest-by-south wind. Hull would attack British shipping in the Halifax–Gulf of Saint Lawrence area, with the possibility of proceeding toward Bermuda, the Bahamas, and the West Indies thereafter. He hoped to hit hard in one place and then move to another before superior British numbers could be brought against him.

SEARCH

Life aboard quickly settled down into wartime routine. In the afternoon, Hull exercised his crew at quarters; having been together but six weeks, there was much to learn if they were to be a battle-ready team.

Fortunately for him, rotund Capt. Isaac Hull was well acquainted with *Constitution,* having been among her original officers and her first lieutenant. It was fortunate for him because in the summer of 1812 his crew had been newly recruited and only minimally trained. His compressed, condensed report of the defeat of *Guerriere* made it appear that it had been a neat, easy affair and sent national spirits soaring. For Hull, it brought all the "glory" he had longed for. This portrait was painted by John Wesley Jarvis at New York in the winter of 1813. *Official U.S. Navy photo*

Working slowly northeastward, Hull checked out every sail sighted and continued his intensive training program. Furthermore, the captain had his men making preparations for battle's many eventualities. Two days were spent by the sailmakers and armorers making and fitting protective iron-strapped canvas caps for the boarding party. The carpenter's and gunner's mates busied themselves making wads and sponges for the guns, while more of the former gang completed repairs to the taffrail where it had been cut away during the escape from the British. Cutlasses, boarding axes, muskets, and pistols were cleaned and readied. The boatswain and his people fitted luff tackles to the fore, main, and mizzen runners to ameliorate any damage suffered to that rigging.

At noon on the 10th, in clear, pleasant weather, a sail was sighted to the northwest. Hull turned the third reef out of the main topsail, set the fore and main topgallants, jib, and spanker, and set off after her. At 5:00 that afternoon, he fired a gun to bring the chase to, but it was ignored. At 6:15, Hull hoisted a British jack and she came to. The fifth and green cutters were lowered from the *Constitution*'s quarter and stern, and Lieutenant Morris was sent aboard. At 7:00, the green cutter returned with the information that the prize was the British brig *Lady Warren*, bound from St. John's, Newfoundland, to St. John's Island. She had been in convoy escorted by at least a frigate (HMS *Jason*, 32) and an armed brig, but had become separated from them in thick fog two days earlier. At 7:30, the other cutter returned with Morris, the merchant captain, his supercargo, mate, six crewmen, and their private property, after having fired her hold.

The *Lady Warren*'s captain informed Hull that Joshua Barney, an American privateersman, recently had taken several vessels off Newfoundland and had burned some fishing boats, as had the frigate *Essex*, 32, under Capt. David Porter. He also said that, in St. John's, it was thought that *Constitution* was with Rodgers' squadron off the English Channel.

After an uneventful and "uncomfortably cold" night, *Constitution* again went in chase at four bells of the forenoon watch. Shortly after noon, Hull sent a party aboard a brig, the British *Adiona*, bound from Shediac Harbor, New Brunswick, to Newcastle, England, with "Squar'd Pine Timber." Taking aboard her captain, mate, and nine crewmen and boys, Hull fired her at 2:00 P.M. and stood westward.

The 15th dawned with pleasant weather and light winds. Five sail were seen off the starboard bow to the southeast, and sails set in chase. By 5:30 A.M., it was apparent that one of the contacts was a British sloop of war: *Constitution* had come upon a fox in the chicken coop. The Briton soon was seen to be in the act of firing a merchant brig. As the big American frigate came up, the Briton headed first as if to board another of the merchantmen, a Dutch-built barque, but then hauled close to the wind and made all sail westward.

Hull set about determining the identities of the barque, schooner, and two brigs (one afire) he had rescued from the enemy. Sending a party to the barque, he found her to be the prize of the privateer *Dolphin* of Salem, which was the schooner to the southeast. The barque had been retaken by HMS *Avenger*, 16, the previous evening, but when *Constitution* appeared she had been left with but three Englishmen aboard. The two brigs were other prizes to *Avenger*. One they had fired and abandoned, but the second attempted escape. Hull went after her and brought her to by 2:00 P.M.; she was the *Adelina* of Bath, Maine. A British midshipman and five sailors came aboard as prisoners. Midshipman John R.

Madison and five American sailors took over with orders to proceed to any U.S. port. By this time—about 3:00 P.M.—*Avenger* was out of sight and Cape Race could be seen to the northeast.

Interrogation of the prisoners gave Hull reason to believe that he soon would be in action again. According to the captive Britons, Royal Navy frigates *Belvidera*, 36, *Guerriere*, 38, *Shannon*, 38, *Spartan*, 38, *Pomone*, 38, and *Aeolus*, 32, generally were in the area to defend against American depredations. Four of these units will be recognized as having been among *Constitution*'s pursuers a month earlier.

Sunday, the 16th, was rainy and foggy—and except for Hull's usual evening exercises, quiet. Most of Monday passed the same way, although that morning the magazines and filling rooms were inspected for readiness. After the evening gun drill, a sail was discovered ahead, despite "thick & hazey" weather. The chase continued until 11:15, when the brig shortened sail. She was the privateer *Decatur*, 14, with Captain Nichols and a hundred men from Salem. Nichols had jettisoned all but two of his guns in attempting to outrun the big frigate. It was the culmination of a totally disastrous cruise: Out just twelve days, the privateer had taken nothing, lost her fore topmast, and been chased by a British man-of-war, reportedly HMS *Guerriere*, the previous evening. Nichols told Hull that HMS *Africa*, 64, and a war brig were known to be in the area. As for him, he wasn't giving up: Two 6-pounders were enough to bring a merchant to heel. The two ships kept company through the night, then *Decatur* headed for Cape Race.

CONTACT

Hull steered in a generally southwesterly direction throughout the 18th and 19th, occasionally encountering fog and rain, but experiencing fresh breezes from the north and west and cloudiness at noon of that fateful Wednesday. At 2:00 P.M., a sail was spied to the southward and *Constitution* went in chase. At 3:00, it could be seen to be a full-rigged ship on a starboard tack. Thirty minutes later, Hull knew he had come upon a frigate.

At 3:45, the chase lay her main topsail to the mast, a clear invitation to duel. But Hull was not one to rush into things. He ordered the topgallant sails, stay sails, and flying jib taken in, the courses hauled up, a second reef taken in the topsails, and the royal yards sent down. Upon beating to quarters, his crew gave three cheers. According to Seaman Moses Smith, the legend "NOT THE LITTLE BELT" could be seen painted on one of the enemy's topsails, a reference to the British war brig that had been shattered by *Constitution*'s near-sister *President* in a night encounter the year *before* the war broke out.

A half hour later, at 4:10, when about one mile separated the opposing frigates, the enemy hoisted three blue British ensigns and "discharged her Starboard Broadside at us without effect. She immediately wore round, and discharged her Larboard Broadside two shot of which rubbed us and the remainder flying over and through our rigging, we then hoisted our Ensigns and Jack, at the Fore and Main Top Gallant Mastheads." Each time the enemy fired, Hull altered course to disturb her gunners' aim, first to larboard and then to starboard.[1] A British ball struck abaft the larboard knighthead at one point, showering splinters without effect. The American crew fired it back. Another struck the foremast, cutting a hoop in two. The American fired only when and as individual guns could be brought to bear.

After some forty-five minutes of inconclusive maneuvering, the Briton, impatient at Hull's reticence to close from his upwind position, bore up with the wind "rather on his Lab'd Quarter," a maneuver calculated to be seen as an invitation to close for a toe-to-toe slugfest, one Hull accepted. Setting his main topgallant sail, he moved in, his gun crews standing alert, double-shotting their guns with solid and grape shot for a full broadside. Another British ball came aboard, the concussion from which knocked Seaman Isaac Kingman down, but not out.

Slugfest

Hull was where he wanted to be at about 5:00. He hauled down his jib and laid the main topsail shivering to slow down as he ranged up alongside. Reportedly at his command, "Now, boys, hull her!" the first double-shotted broadside crashed out at the Briton half a pistol shot distance to larboard. Blast followed blast. The captain is said to have split his breeches, jumping up and down in the excitement. Approximately fifteen minutes later, the Briton's mizzenmast crashed over the starboard side; her main yard was shot from its slings. "Huzza boys! We've made a brig of her! Next time we'll make her a sloop!" The American crew gave three cheers and went on firing.

The return fire from the British frigate had been high. Some of *Constitution*'s braces were slashed and her fore royal truck was shot away, together with two halyards—one bearing one of the flags Hull had hoisted. Amidst the cannonade, Seaman Daniel Hogan climbed the rigging and made it fast to the topmast.

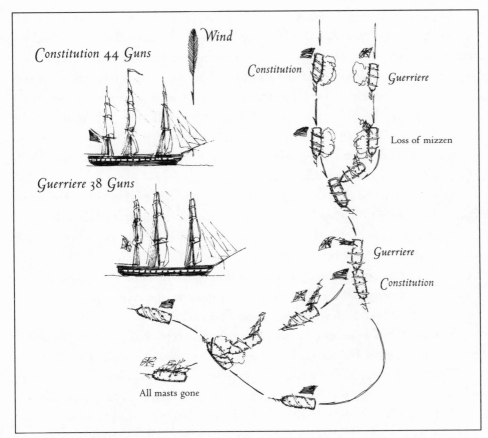

Constitution 44 Guns

Wind

Constitution

Guerriere

Loss of mizzen

Guerriere 38 Guns

Guerriere

Constitution

All masts gone

Battle diagram *Author's collection; created by John Charles Roach*

British shot hitting the hull made little impression. Someone saw a ball hit, make a dent, then fall into the sea, and he cried out, "Huzza! Her sides are made of iron!" And so the famed nickname "Old Ironsides" was born.

The dragging wreckage, jammed as it was up under his starboard counter, slowed the Briton, pulled his head to starboard, and allowed *Constitution* to begin drawing ahead. The British captain tried in vain to regain control of his ship's head. At the same time, Hull attempted to luff up across his bow and rake, "but our braces being shot away and Jib haulyards [*sic*], we could not effect it." The British frigate, swinging rapidly to starboard, crashed into *Constitution*'s quarter, smashing the boat in the davits and snagging his bowsprit in the larboard mizzen shrouds. Hitting and recoiling as the American slid forward, before breaking clear astern the Briton's bowsprit wreaked havoc with Hull's gig in the stern davits.

The record goes momentarily blank at this point. Given the fact that Hull had never before been in a ship-to-ship battle in any capacity, let alone command, and suddenly faced with a crippled enemy and finding his own maneuvering capability impaired, it is fair to assume that there was some confusion and momentary indecision. How long it took Hull to regain control of the situation and exactly what he did was not recorded either by Hull or his subordinates. His enemies, busy with their own problems, stated merely that he took up a position their larboard bow from whence he fired several broadsides into them to which they could respond but weakly.

Satisfied that the British frigate still was not under control, Hull moved to take a raking position ahead of her. For some reason—miscalculation, bungled sail handling, or unexpected movement of the enemy ship—instead of passing clear ahead, the antagonists collided, *Constitution* taking her enemy's jib boom in her starboard mizzen shrouds. The crash destroyed the American's spanker gaff and boom, and snapped off the starboard half of the crossjack yard, as she unleashed two broadsides into his bow. The Briton's flying jib boom and jib boom were carried away, and his two ragged shots in reply killed two and wounded one at gun Number Fifteen starboard in Hull's cabin, and started a brief blaze.

This unexpected and unplanned opportunity to board the enemy left both opponents scrambling for the advantage. First Lt. William S. Bush, commanding the American Marines, leaped to the taffrail to lead the charge and was killed instantly by a musket ball in the face. He was the first U.S. Marine officer ever to die in combat. Morris, Hull's second in command, sought to replace him but was downed, shot through the abdomen. The even heavier American musketry killed the British second lieutenant and wounded the captain, first lieutenant, and sailing master. Before a further attempt could be made, *Constitution*'s forward motion exerted sufficient force to pull the ships apart. The resultant whipping action in the Briton's bowsprit was transmitted through the stays to a weakened foremast, which crashed down to starboard, its plunging weight causing the tottering mainmast to follow it.

VICTORY

Hull, seeing his enemy thus completely immobilized, stood eastward with fore and main courses and a reef in his topsails, keeping his target silhouetted against the lowering sun. The crew set busily to reeving new braces and halyards, and

The Americans
Were Our Masters

This painting, one of a series of four by Michel Felice Cornè that depict the battle, shows *Guerriere's* mizzen going by the board shortly after *Constitution* opened her cannonade. The positions of the two ships are reversed from those they had in the actual battle in accordance with Captain Hull's directions. Exactly what his intent was is unknown, but it is known it was no accident of memory. *Official U.S. Navy photo*

readying the ship to resume the action. When these immediate repairs were done, he returned to find the shattered Briton had but the bedraggled remnants of the spritsail yard remaining. Unseen by Hull were the 18-pounder long guns on the enemy's gun deck that had been torn loose from their tackles and were running amok as the ship rolled her ports under in the heavy swells. The British captain wisely fired a gun to leeward in token of submission as the Yankee frigate came within a mile. Hull made the appropriate response—one gun—and this most decisive ship action was over. It was shortly before 7:00 P.M.

Third Lieutenant Read was sent to take possession of the vanquished. At 7:30, all boats were hoisted out to bring prisoners aboard, to take aid to the wounded, and to pass a towing hawser. Twenty-two-year-old Midshipman Henry Gilliam was among those with Read, and he later wrote to his uncle that he had found the decks with "pieces of skulls, brains, legs, arms & blood . . . in every directions and groanes of the wounded were almost enough to make me curse the war." Adding a bizarre note to this gory scene was the presence of molasses splattered on everything, the surviving reminder of a cask of the stuff ordered up beforehand by the British captain in preparation for taunting the defeated Yankees with switchel, a rum concoction favored by them. At 8:00, a boat returned to *Constitution* with the first of the prisoners. Principal among them was Capt. James Richard Dacres, Royal Navy, late commander of His British Majesty's frigate *Guerriere.*

The Loser

James Dacres came from a navy family (his father had commanded HMS *Carleton* in the Battle of Valcour Island against Americans in 1776) and had entered the service at an early age, attaining his lieutenancy in 1804. In 1805, he was posted to command of the sloop of war *Elk* and the following year to command of the frigate *Bacchante,* 24, on the Jamaica Station. In this post, he served with distinction. He took command of *Guerriere* about April 1811.

Dacres' ship was French-built and had been rated by them at 50 guns. She had been taken by the British off Norway in 1806, and after a two-year refit was commissioned by them as "5th rate, large 38." On 19 August 1812, she was armed with thirty 18-pounders on the gun deck, fourteen 32-pounder carronades and one 12-pounder howitzer on her quarterdeck, and two 12-pounders and two 32-pounder carronades on the forecastle—forty-nine guns in all. At the time of the engagement she was due for refit in Halifax. Her hull was fouled and there was rot in her masts; her rigging was badly worn.

Assessment

Constitution's battery at this time consisted of thirty 24-pounders on the gun deck, sixteen 32-pounder carronades on the quarterdeck, and one 18-pounder and eight 32-pounder carronades on the forecastle—a total of 55 guns. She had completed a refit only two months earlier.

The *Constitution-Guerriere* fight was a straightforward, toe-to-toe battle between two adversaries each confident in his abilities. *Constitution* was the bigger, heavier, and, because of her recent yard period, the faster. But as this fight was a slugfest, this last advantage was not a factor. Indeed, with his green crew, Hull may have decided on the direct approach, hoping to minimize having to maneuver and fight simultaneously. He fought a graceless fight, relying on his size advantage to compensate for his inexperience and that of his crew.

In terms of gun power, there was less disparity in the respective broadsides than the simple number of guns and their calibers would indicate. The French-made shot used by *Guerriere* generally was somewhat heavier than its stated size—about 8 percent, on the average. American shot, on the other hand, ran about 7 percent light. Taking this into account, and without considering *Guerriere*'s howitzer (of little moment), the resultant broadside weights were 581 pounds (British) and 692 pounds (American). But the greater result stemmed from the Americans' lower aim and the *Guerriere*'s lighter construction. *Guerriere*'s wreckage topside was more visible and of consequence in the short term, but the damage below was irreparable: About thirty American shot had hulled her below the waterline, according to Dacres. By contrast, *Constitution*'s hull damage largely was limited to the mess created in the starboard portion of Hull's cabin when the two ships entangled the second time. Dacres' guns, however, *had* done considerable damage to Hull's standing and running rigging, and spars. In addition to shot-away braces and halyards, both fore and main masts had been shot through, as was the heel of the foretopgallant mast; and the band for the main slings had been broken. Clearly, the larger dimensions of the masts contributed to their survival. In addition, the crossjack had been snapped and the gaff, spanker boom, and gig smashed, as had the larboard quarter boat.

Constitution carried a much larger crew than did *Guerriere*—about 450 versus 275–300—which rendered the superb service of her guns possible. Moreover, as we have seen, Hull had trained his men daily in the aiming and loading of their guns. Their rate of fire was abetted by the use, in part, of lead foil powder cylinders, which reduced the need to swab guns out after each shot. The British, on the other hand, were handicapped by the fact that their twenty-year-old war with France had put such a premium on their powder supply so as largely to preclude the use of powder merely for training purposes in their vastly expanded navy. Even so, this was the first frigate duel they had lost since 1803. The morale of the American crew, as well, was superior: The Britons in it, too, were willing to fight. The Americans in *Guerriere*'s crew, on the other hand, protested having to do so, and Dacres gallantly sent them below as noncombatants. Twenty-three Britons died as a result of the action, and another fifty-six were wounded; Hull had had seven killed and a like number wounded. (Eight surviving British crew members subsequently claimed political asylum when landed in Boston, and two signed on board "Old Ironsides.")

Before resuming our narrative, at this point it seems proper to ponder the effect of Fortune in this affair. What would have been the outcome if Dacres had succeeded in raking *Constitution* from astern instead of suffering the first collision? Might not he have downed one or both of the masts already damaged? Might not have *Constitution*'s steering gear been destroyed? And might not Hull then have been in the position, in a largely immobilized ship, of making the difficult decision as to whether or not more blood gainfully could be shed? John Paul Jones abandoned his sinking *Bon Homme Richard* for the newly surrendered *Serapis* in 1779. Dacres might have stepped from a dying *Guerriere* to *Constitution* if Fortune had been his that day in 1812. The British captain himself was sensitive to this, for he subsequently stated: "I am so aware that the success of my opponent was owing to fortune, that it is my earnest wish . . . to be once more opposed to the Constitution . . . in a frigate of similar force to the Guerriere," with the same crew.

To return to our narrative.

GUERRIERE'S END

For three hours, the Americans attempted to take their prize in tow. By 11:00 P.M., however, it was evident that the differing drift rates of the two ships and the difficulties of working in darkness made it an almost impossible task. The hawser was cast off. Hull kept *Constitution* "at a convenient distance" from *Guerriere* through the night, while Read and his prize crew struggled to keep her afloat. In the American frigate, repairs were begun. Both surgeons, Evans and Irvine (of *Guerriere*), worked to save the wounded. Evans himself did four amputations.

At 7:00 on the morning of the 20th, *Constitution's* foretopgallant yard and the damaged foretopgallant mast were sent down, and a new mast stepped. Elsewhere, the carpenters were preparing fishes (splints) for the damaged fore and main masts.

As the foretopgallant yard was being sent up at 7:30, Read hailed from *Guerriere* that she had five feet of water in the hold and that it was gaining on them. Hull decided to withdraw his men and destroy the hulk. By 1:30 P.M., everyone was off except for Read and his demolition party. They left for *Constitution* at 3:00.

Moses Smith has described *Guerriere's* last moments: "Presently there was a dead silence; then followed a vibratory, shuddering motion, and streams of light, like streaks of lightning running along the sides; and the grand crash came! The quarter deck, which was immediately over the magazine, lifted in a mass, broke into fragments, and flew in every direction. The hull, parted in the center by the shock, and loaded with such masses of iron and spars, reeled, staggered, plunged forward a few feet, and sank out of sight."

It was 3:15 P.M., 20 August 1812, and Hull was eager to broadcast news of his triumph. At 6:00, he beat to quarters and mustered his crew. Bush and one of the British seamen who had failed to survive his wounds were buried with proper ceremony.

This woodcut from an early nineteenth-century book represents *Guerriere*'s end. The artist, who may have been someone named "Roberts," for that name is visible on the larboard side of the transom beneath the windows, knew enough about ship construction to show individual timbers spewing out in the explosion. *Original in author's collection*

BACK TO BOSTON

At daylight on the 21st, Hull had his crew back at work repairing battle damage. Rigging was repaired or replaced, new sails bent on, and fishes applied to the fore and main masts. In the afternoon, a new gaff and a new spanker boom were fitted. Rain began to fall after 6:00, but the work wasn't done until 9:00. As the day ended, *Constitution* once again was her old self, bowling along on a north-westerly course at eleven knots.

Saturday the 22nd found the ship a beehive of activity again. The sailmakers were busy repairing sails as the boatswain's mates were fitting up two preventer shrouds. And should another engagement be in the offing, the gunner had his mates making up the thin sheet lead cylinders to hold powder charges and recovering the sponge heads with fresh sheepskin.

Early on Sunday, the 23rd, *Constitution* came up with the brig *Rebecca* after a three-hour chase. The merchant ship was bound from London to Boston under British license. Several days earlier, she had been boarded by *Guerriere*, but Dacres had only put some prisoners on her and had permitted her to continue her voyage. Subsequently, she had been made prize by privateer Joshua Barney, whose prizemaster now sailed her. After exchanging information, the two ships parted company.

The following week passed in relative quiet. Hull exercised his crew at quarters four times in six days. On the 25th, funeral services were held for the second British seaman to die of his wounds. At 6:00 P.M. on Saturday, the 29th, Boston lighthouse was sighted four leagues SW by W. At 7:30 on the morning of the 30th, Hull anchored southeast of the light—very nearly the same spot he had left exactly four weeks (to the moment) earlier. An hour later, Lt. John T. Shubrick was on his way ashore in the third cutter, bound for Washington with Hull's dispatches.

With the battle done and *Constitution* safely in home port, it is an appropriate moment to consider the background of the adulation that shortly was to engulf Hull and his men, and the effect their victory was to have on future events. As has been stated previously, the declaration of war was unpopular in several regions of the country, but particularly so in New England. It was thought that nothing good would come of it. Trade would be interrupted or destroyed, insurance rates would rise, and ships lost through destruction or capture. At sea, the Royal Navy had been well nigh invincible in nearly two decades of warfare against the might of Napoleon. The minuscule United States Navy would be swallowed whole—almost without notice.

The nautical negativism was reinforced by a disaster on land: On 16 August, after some indecisive maneuvering, the American forces at Detroit had surrendered without a fight to an inferior force of British and Indian allies. This news only recently had become known in Boston, just long enough to depress morale further.

Thus, the stage was set and the nation ready—craving—for good news. *Constitution*'s victory over *Guerriere* was all that. The fight had been decisive. *Guerriere* apparently had been destroyed with expedition and with minimum loss of life and ship damage. The mighty Royal Navy had been humbled by an upstart. A Son of Liberty again had tweaked George's royal nose.

Hull, hungry himself for "glory" and public recognition, did all he could to ensure full mileage out of this success. He wrote *two* reports of the engagement to Secretary Hamilton, on 28 and 30 August. Neither said anything about the relative positions of the antagonists as they began their slugfest or of the two collisions. The second one was shorter and more ambiguous than the first, and Hull appended a note to it suggesting that the less said about "a brilliant victory such as this" the better. Thus, this abbreviated report was made public and became the basis for most subsequent descriptions of the event. Furthermore, he commissioned Michel Felice Cornè to paint a series of four paintings depicting moments in the battle under his detailed direction. In these, the ships' relative positions were *reversed*, apparently to avoid any criticism of his having taken the (barely) downwind position and forestall queries about how close *Guerriere* may have come when dragged off course by her downed mizzenmast.

Hull got all the adulation and celebration he wanted in response to giving the nation the victory for which it hungered. The secretary responded to the news on 9 September, saying, "we know not which most to applaud, Your gallantry or Your skill—You, Your officers & Crew are entitled to & will receive the applause & the gratitude of Your gratefull country." Numerous lithographs based on the Cornè paintings were reproduced and snapped up by an eager public. Plays were written and songs sung. Congress voted Hull a gold medal, his officers silver ones, and $50,000 for all hands to share in lieu of prize money. Lieutenant Morris was meritoriously promoted to captain. New York, Philadelphia, Charleston, and Hull's home state of Connecticut vied with each other in presenting him with rich tokens of their esteem. Above all, the victory became a benchmark, a touchstone, the symbol of all that was good and right with the American way.

Perhaps the most perceptive evaluation ever written appeared in the London *Times* when the bad news reached England:

"It is not merely that an English frigate has been taken, after, what we are free to confess, may be called a brave resistance, but that it has been taken by a new enemy, an enemy unaccustomed to such triumphs, and likely to be rendered insolent and confident by them. He must be a weak politician who does not see how important the first triumph is in giving a tone and character to the war. Never before in the history of the world did an English frigate strike to an American."

In Boston town, the evaluation made up in verve what it lacked in polish:

The Constitution long shall be
  The glory of our Navy,
For when she grapples with a foe,
  She sends him to old Davy.
Yankee doodle keep it up,
  Yankee doodle dandy,
We'll let the British know that we
  At fighting are quite handy.

CHAPTER TEN

Lightning Strikes Twice

CHANGE OF COMMAND

On 31 August, the morning after his arrival in Boston's outer harbor, Captain Hull was awakened rudely by the peremptory rapping on his cabin door by one of his lieutenants. Four ships and a brig, apparently warships, had been sighted standing toward the frigate from the northeast. It was 6:30. Hull was on the quarterdeck in short order to see for himself. Warships, they were—but whose? With strong breezes from the east-northeast, he was cornered, unable to get to the open sea. Discretion ever being the better part of valor, at 6:45 the anchor cable was axed and sail set for the inner harbor before that course, too, was closed to him. Just as *Constitution* swept in through the narrows, the incoming units were recognized as Commodore Rodgers's squadron, returning from their fruitless sweep that had taken them all the way to the English Channel. This was the squadron that *Constitution* was to have joined at New York two long months ago— *President, United States, Congress, Hornet,* and *Argus.* They came to anchor in President Roads, off Castle Island, but Hull continued on up the harbor to anchor.

The next few days were distracted by the general euphoria resulting from Hull's victory, but some work was begun to ready the ship for another trip. *Guerrière's* crew members were landed, as had been the wounded. Painting was begun, covering the scars on the hull, and a party was sent back to the outer harbor to retrieve the abandoned anchor. When he went ashore for the first time at 11:00 A.M. on 1 September, Hull was met at Long Wharf by the Ancient and Honorable Company of Artillery with a salute, which was answered from "Old Ironsides." The Company then escorted him, amidst hordes of cheering Bostonians, to the Exchange Coffee House, a popular rendezvous of the day.

Six-footer William Bainbridge's career, but for the victory reported in this chapter, was a series of defeats and frustrations, and he was a man who held grudges for decades. One result was his efforts to destroy, at least professionally, the careers of those more fortunate than himself during the Barbary War. The courts of inquiry he instigated against Capts. Charles Stewart (1814) and Isaac Hull (1822) failed to recommend the desired courts-martial; he was more successful in bringing about the James Barron–Stephen Decatur duel, which resulted in the latter's death (1820). The portrait was painted by John Wesley Jarvis. *Official U.S. Navy photo*

A sad note was Hull's in this moment of triumph when he learned that his brother in New York had died during his absence, leaving a widow and children. Hull confided in Commodore Bainbridge, commandant of the navy yard, that he intended that very day to request a shore assignment in order to settle his brother's affairs and provide for his family. Bainbridge, who had been seeking a combat command, and had expected to relieve Hull in early August, promptly wrote to Secretary Hamilton suggesting that he and Hull exchange commands.

On the 7th, overhaul work began in earnest. The running rigging was unreeved and sent ashore, together with sails, yards, and water casks. On the 9th, the crosstrees were removed from the topmasts, and by the next afternoon, rigging was being removed from the lower masts preparatory to their being lifted. On the 14th, Bainbridge received the Secretary's affirmative response to his request to succeed Hull. Bainbridge took command at 4:00 the next afternoon, hoisting his broad blue pennant as a squadron commander.

A Poor Beginning

William Bainbridge, it will be recalled, had been in command of *Philadelphia* when she grounded and was lost to the Tripoline pirates in October 1803. A native of New Jersey, he had entered merchant marine service in 1789, at the age of fifteen, and had earned his first command only four years later. With the reestablishment of navy in 1798, he was commissioned a lieutenant commanding and given the schooner *Retaliation*, the former French privateer *Le Croyable*. He shortly was captured, without firing a shot, by a superior French force, the first officer in the United States Navy to surrender his command to an enemy. Bainbridge was absolved of any blame, promoted to master commandant, and given command of the brig *Norfolk*, wherein he had some success in the West Indies. In 1800, then commanding the light frigate *George Washington*, he was finessed by the Dey of Algiers into making a trip to Constantinople for him in his ship but *under the Algerine flag*. This was the first time an American warship was seen at the Porte, and Bainbridge made a very favorable impression despite the circumstance that had brought him there. He subsequently commanded frigate *Essex*, 32, in Commodore Dale's squadron before returning to the Mediterranean in *Philadelphia*.

Following his release from Tripoli in 1805, he again was cleared of any negligence, but requested and received permission to leave service temporarily to return to the merchant marine. In 1808, believing, as a result of the *Chesapeake-Leopard* affair, that war was imminent with Britain, Bainbridge voluntarily returned to active duty in command of *President*. When war didn't come right away, he again became a merchant captain. In February 1812, he had once more presented himself for service to Secretary Hamilton and, in accordance with his wishes, was given a shore command until such time as war broke out, when he would be given a ship. This was *Constitution*'s new captain: A man who had somehow survived three incidents that would have written "finis" to many a naval officer's career and whose tremendous ambition was overpowering the weak secretary of the navy into giving him precisely what he wanted.

The victorious crew viewed Bainbridge as a three-time loser and wanted no part of him. Hull was cheered off the ship, and those who openly expressed their opinion of the new captain were confined in a gunboat. Bainbridge, inwardly shaken by his reception, unsuccessfully offered Rodgers $5,000 to exchange his flagship *President* for *Constitution*.

Bainbridge's main concern in readying the ship for sea was, of course, ensuring that all spar and rigging damage suffered in the recent engagement was repaired or replaced. For the next month, the log records the tedious labor of erecting the shears alongside the main mast and removing it, and of stepping a new one. Then the process was repeated for the foremast. That done, the fighting tops had to be set back atop these lower masts, the topmasts fidded home, the trestletrees installed, the topgallant masts stepped, and all the rigging rereeved. Of course, a new gaff and spanker boom and crossjack yard also were put aboard.

One new feature was added to *Constitution*'s appearance at this time: Beginning on 21 September, the carpenters cut bridle ports into the hull about midway between the number one gun ports and the stem on either side. These ports would make it easier to moor and unmoor, and to take a towing bridle if that became necessary. In time of need, it would be possible to move guns into them to fire directly forward. Another change on the gun deck by Bainbridge was his decision to raise the level of it by five inches between the fore and main masts. This altered the sheer of the deck, essentially eliminating it and leveling the surface. Why he thought this necessary is unrecorded.

Third Lieutenant Shubrick returned to the ship during this period, having delivered Hull's victory report to Washington, and bringing with him a chronometer for Bainbridge. This is the first record of such a precision timepiece, so essential to the precise determination of longitude, being available on board.

Stores began to come back aboard on 4 October, as the crew was busy laying in the ground tier of water casks. There followed quantities of beef and pork, rum, firewood, sauerkraut, bread, cheese, cranberries, horseradish (eight barrels!), new sails, warrant officers' stores, etc., etc.

On the 16th, Bainbridge moved *Constitution* from the navy yard to a position off Long Wharf to complete loading. Five days later, he moved again to an anchorage in President Roads, from whence he could take advantage of a fair wind. *Hornet*, the second unit of his squadron, moved to the same locale on the 24th. Both wind and tide came fair on the 27th, and the two ships stood for the open sea. Bainbridge's orders were to take frigate *Essex* (Captain Porter), 32, and brig *Hornet* (Master Commandant Lawrence), 18, "to annoy the enemy and to afford protection to our commerce, pursuing that course, which to your best judgment may . . . appear to be best." The commodore already had considered this aspect of his orders and had decided to proceed first to waters off the Cape Verde Islands, then in a southwesterly direction, touching on many of the principal sea lanes used by both sides, and then farther south to the waters off Brazil, where the British at that time had considerable commerce. After two months on that coast, he intended then to proceed to the vicinity of St. Helena Island, which was frequented by British East Indiamen returning home. (*Essex*, which was in the Delaware when Bainbridge sailed, ultimately never rendezvoused with him, Porter pursuing instead an option in his orders to disrupt British maritime activities in the Pacific. This he accomplished with legendary success before finally being trapped and captured in Valparaíso, Chile.)

South Away

The first days at sea were miserable ones in strong gales and rain, but then the weather settled down and the commodore began in earnest his training program for the crew. He had them exercised at general quarters about every three days, on the average. The log through the period is replete with such entries as "The Sharp Shooters Exercising at a Mark"; "Exercised the Marines & Riflemen at a Mark"; "exercised the Boarders with Small Arms"; "Beat to Quarters Exercised the Great Guns & manovered with the Hornet."

As the newness of the current voyage wore off, and routine and boredom set in, instances of drunkenness, insolence, and fighting appeared. On 26 November, Lawrence and two of his officers were ordered to the flagship to be a court martial in the case of Marine Pvt. James Penshaw, accused of threatening the life of Midshipman James Delancy. He was found guilty and sentenced to receive fifty lashes. Five others received from six to a dozen lashes for lesser, unrelated infractions.

Landfall was made on the island of Fernando de Noronha, a penal colony for Portugal, on the morning of 2 December. Under the guise of being British, Bainbridge spent two days in the vicinity taking aboard a little water and a few supplies, and hoping to rendezvous with Porter. Failing that, Bainbridge left a letter for Porter, who had been code-named "Sir James Yeo" for the purpose of keeping the American presence a secret, and sailed for the Brazilian coast two hundred miles distant. Landfall was made on the 6th.

Constitution and *Hornet* proceeded southward along the coast. A few native craft were seen, and one Portuguese brig involved in local trade was boarded, before they arrived in the area of São Salvador (Bahia, today). Not wishing to reveal his whole strength, on the evening of the 13th Bainbridge ordered Lawrence in to the port to contact the American consul and gain the latest intelligence.

Hornet returned in the midafternoon of the 18th. Lawrence reported he had found HMS *Bonne Citoyenne*, 18, a war sloop repairing a leak caused by a grounding. The sleek, red-sided vessel was said to be carrying $1,600,000 in specie to England. From Consul Henry Hill he had learned that there was a British ship of the line, *Montague*, 74, at Rio, and two other lesser units farther south. Only one man-of-war was said to be near St. Helena. Unfortunately, at the moment *Bonne Citoyenne* was the only Briton in the harbor.

After receiving the stores brought out by Lawrence, *Constitution* and *Hornet* spent the next few days patrolling to the north and south of the port looking for prizes without success. On the 23rd, a sail was sighted close inshore making for the port, but Bainbridge's meticulous orders respecting Portuguese sovereignty precluded her capture by Lawrence, who nonetheless followed her in. While there, he issued a challenge to Capt. Pitt Barnaby Greene of *Bonne Citoyenne* to fight him, ship to ship, with *Constitution* pledged to remain aloof regardless of the outcome. Greene steadfastly refused—and rightly so, with all that gold aboard—despite acrimonious assaults on his character by the challenger and Bainbridge. Bainbridge further was angered by a hard-line letter from the governor of São Salvador complaining about the repeated entries into port by *Hornet*. The Portuguese clearly was showing his British bias. Bainbridge ordered *Hornet* to remain guarding *Bonne Citoyenne* and to take her the minute she left port and cleared territorial waters. He took *Constitution* offshore to cruise for prizes.

ENEMY MET AND CONQUERED

Between 8:00 and 9:00 in the morning of the 29th, a Tuesday, while some thirty miles off the coast, two strange sails were made out, one inshore (to the northwest) and the other to windward (to the northeast). The former was seen to continue her course along the coast while the other, the larger one, altered course toward *Constitution*. Bainbridge already had tacked in their direction. The day was pleasant and the sea nearly calm; the wind was light from the east-northeast.

By 11:00 A.M., Bainbridge and his officers believed that the windward contact was a British ship of the line. He tacked *Constitution* to the southeast to avoid being pinned into pro-British Brazilian territorial waters by a larger adversary.[1]

At noon, *Constitution* showed her colors, and the opponent shortly thereafter set a red British ensign. The enemy then flew a series of signals, the appropriate recognition signals for British, Spanish, and Portuguese warships, but of course got no response from the American.

Bainbridge realized that the contact was but a frigate at about 1:20, when it was certain she was closing, something no liner could do on his frigate in those conditions. He tacked toward the enemy, taking in his mainsail and royals. When slightly more than a mile separated them, he tacked again. Both ships now were heading southeast, with the Briton to windward on Bainbridge's larboard quarter and coming up.

At this point, the enemy hauled down his ensign, although his jack remained aloft. The commodore ordered his 24-pounders to commence broadside firing aimed at the target's rigging when the range had decreased to about a thousand yards—at nearly the maximum effective range of those guns and beyond that of anything the enemy had. Apparently, his intention was to try and at least slow her down, if not stop her, before she could outspeed him and bring her guns to bear. In this he was not successful. The enemy held fire until within range, at about 2:00, and the battle was joined, both sides firing furiously. The Briton's first salvos were the most damaging, *Constitution*'s spars and rigging being well chewed and Bainbridge wounded in the thigh. Amidst the hail of iron, Seaman Asa Curtis slid down the American's foretopgallant stay to "rebend the Flying Jib Halyards which had been shot away," thereby preventing the loss of an important head sail. The enemy frigate forged ahead and appeared to be about to cross *Constitution*'s bow for a devastating rake when Bainbridge loosed a broadside, then masterfully wore around in the smoke. It was 2:10. The enemy followed suit, but was once again left on the windward quarter—this time, to starboard. Again the enemy drew alongside and then ahead, seeking to achieve a raking position. And yet again, at 2:25, Bainbridge fired and wore in the smoke, denying the advantage. The ships once more were heading generally southeastward.

The faster frigate a third time came up on *Constitution*'s quarter and appeared to be drawing ahead when, suddenly, she wore and cut under the American's stern, unleashing a killing raking broadside at 2:35. *Constitution*'s wheel disappeared in a cloud of splinters, all four helmsmen down.[2] Eleven members of carronade crews were dropped. And the commodore again had been hit in the thigh.[3] It must have been a desperate moment for him, in pain and shocky, the remembrance of his three former failures in mind. He steeled himself and, using a midshipman aide for support, began issuing orders setting up a jury-rigged steering system down below with several midshipmen to relay orders.

While the Americans were thus engaged, the bemused enemy, unaware of the damage done, expected the American to turn to starboard and parallel his course. When, instead, *Constitution* was seen sailing steadily off, it was assumed she had had enough. The British frigate was tacked back across her wake and another raking broadside fired at rather long range. Then she tacked again and again took the weather gauge, hauling forward to larboard. Bainbridge set fore and main courses and steered still closer to the wind, now hoping to bring his carronades with their smashing power into play and inflict some crippling damage before his own situation worsened. His gamble paid off, for at about 2:40 his foe's bowsprit cap, jib boom, and headsails were shot away. Seeing *Constitution* beginning to wear again, the British captain, denied the use of his headsails to drive his bow off the wind, decided instead to tack across the wind using his spanker to drive the stern into the turn. It didn't work, and, like an airplane stalling at the top of a climb, his ship hung up heading into the wind, temporarily "in irons"—unable

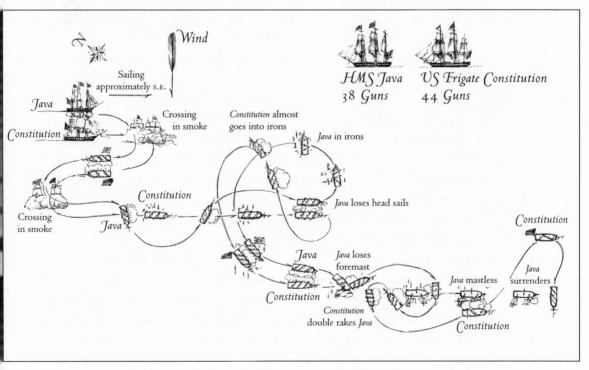

Battle diagram *Author's collection; created by John Charles Roach*

to maneuver. Seeing this, Bainbridge continued to wear his ship through nearly three-quarters of a circle to starboard, picking up enough speed to close his enemy's larboard quarter and get in a murderous rake himself at 2:50 before he had to wear to larboard to keep *his* ship under control. *Constitution* swung back to the original heading, the enemy following once he had forced his bow around.

The two frigates now ran off to the southeast, the Briton still having the weather gauge. But the advantage was seen by both sides to be shifting to the Americans. British gunfire was becoming less accurate than it had been during those first broadsides. Her loss of headsails with the destruction of the jib boom made the British frigate less maneuverable, offsetting in part *Constitution*'s lack of a wheel and slower speed. The British captain decided his best tactic was to close and take his adversary by boarding before even that opportunity was lost. Accordingly, at 3:35 he sought to run down on *Constitution*'s larboard main chains. A misjudgment on his part resulted in the remains of his bowsprit running into the American's mizzen rigging and momentarily hanging him up. There, with only one of his guns able to bear, he had to suffer the full weight of *Constitution*'s metal and the hail of musketry from her well-trained Marines. The enemy's foremast was severed just below its fighting top and plunged through two decks; then his main topmast went, cut off slightly above the cap. The resultant tangle of wreckage further disorganized his gun crews. The enemy captain was dropped by an American sharpshooter.

As they separated, both ships brought their heads eastward once more. *Constitution*, now having the weather gauge, began forereaching her battered antagonist. Bainbridge wore yet again at 3:50 and brought his ship across the opponent's bow, where he loosed a blazing raking fire. Crossing southward, he continued to wear until he crossed astern on a northerly heading at 4:13 and raked again with his starboard batteries before falling off to larboard and coming back around to take up a position on his opponent's starboard quarter, where he kept station and banged away while the enemy was unable to bring guns to bear on him. When the Briton's main yard was shot in the slings and her spanker shot away, she slowed down and Bainbridge slid forward to an abeam position. Before the Americans could set more sail, the Britons were able to shoot back with the three to five guns still operational on that side. The enemy's remaining section of foremast just above the spar deck was shot away, and at about 4:55, "Shott Away his Mizen Mast Nearly to the Deck." All this time the enemy had attempted to return *Constitution*'s devastating fire, but the tangled wreckage encumbering his

This recent painting by British artist Ken Grant shows *Constitution* blasting a smolder-ing, largely dismasted HMS *Java* at approximately 4:00 P.M. Returning about an hour later, after making some rigging repairs, she saw the British colors hauled down just in time to prevent another onslaught. This engagement on 29 December 1812 in the south Atlantic marked the third consecutive frigate victory for the minuscule U.S. Navy against a Royal Navy whose frigates had not lost a duel in nearly a decade. *Photo in author's collection; reproduced by permission of the artist*

starboard side flamed each time he shot. His cannons went still one by one until, shortly after 5:00 P.M., silence reigned. Bainbridge assumed his opponent had surrendered, since his colors had disappeared from the main rigging, and he took his ship off to windward a short distance to effect necessary repairs before clos-ing and taking possession. The time was 5:10.

But the fact was the Briton had not surrendered. First Lt. Henry Ducie Chads had assumed command upon the wounding of his captain, and strove mightily to prepare for further fighting. A staysail was rigged between a topmast jury rigged to replace the foremast and the bowsprit in an effort to bring the ship under some control. When he tried to rig a sail of sorts on the half of the main yard still aloft, the damaged mainmast— at least, the remaining lower mast— tottered and had to be dropped to keep it from doing worse damage. When *Con-stitution* began to close once more, a half hour later, the British had rehoisted an ensign to the mizzen stump and were trying to set more sail. Seeing that the

American was taking an unassailable raking position across his bow, the lieutenant wisely hauled down his flag, only just barely in time to prevent another broadside. It was 5:50. In *Constitution*, recalling the fight against *Guerriere*, the "crew gave 3 cheers, as they had done when we first beat to quarters & several times during the action." Bainbridge had his victory at last.

AFTERMATH

At 6:00, George Parker, who had succeeded the recuperating Charles Morris as first lieutenant, boarded the defeated enemy from one of *Constitution*'s two remaining undamaged boats (out of *eight*) to find a shambles. Four forecastle guns were upended, as were six more on the quarterdeck. Tangled rigging was everywhere. The wounded and dying made it a grisly scene, which was repeated on the gun deck below. The defeated frigate was HMS *Java*, 38, the former French *Renomée*, commissioned in the Royal Navy only the previous August. She had sailed from England for India on 12 November and had detoured to São Salvador because of a shortage of water. Quite similar to *Guerriere*, she carried twenty-eight 18-pounder long guns below, and two long 9-pounders, sixteen 32-pounders, and one 18-pounder carronades on her forecastle and quarterdeck, for a total of forty-seven guns. (Bainbridge had made a small change in his ship's armament since her last fight, removing the 18-pounder chase gun—leaving fifty-four guns in all.) *Java*'s gunfire, devastating in its opening broadsides, had diminished steadily in accuracy and volume as the fight progressed, symptomatic not only of damage received but of the presence of a new crew that had been allowed to fire but six blank cartridges in practice.

Constitution suffered 9 killed and 25 wounded (five mortally) out of her crew of 480.[4] Conflicting reports by several present make it impossible to be precise concerning *Java*. She had somewhere between 373 and 426 people on board at the time of the fight. Deaths were reported as totaling between 22 and 60, while the wounded were numbered at either 101 or 102. In any event, the disparate ratio of 4 or 5 to 1 in casualties between the two ships is indicative of the volume and power of the American fire compared to her enemy's.

The unusually large number of people in *Java* stems from the fact that she was carrying nearly a hundred passengers out to their new duty assignments in and around India, including the governor general-designate of Bombay, Lt. Gen. Sir Thomas Hislop.

This lithograph of *Java*'s last moments, by Nicholas Pocock, is the final scene in his series depicting various stages of the engagement, all based on sketches by Lt. George Buchanan of *Java*. Although done by different artists an ocean apart, the explosion does appear less violent than that of *Guerriere*, as noted by Surgeon Amos Evans of *Constitution*. *Author's collection*

The wrecked condition of *Java* already has been noted. On the American side, *Constitution* once again had come through without crippling damage but not entirely unscathed, Bainbridge's report notwithstanding. Careful scrutiny of the ship's log for the succeeding days discloses that both fore and mizzen masts were "wounded" severely enough to warrant fishes, as did certain of the yards. Additionally, the maintopmast had to be taken down and replaced. Thus, it would seem that the slightly larger dimensions of the masts of "Old Ironsides" had saved her—narrowly—from the fate suffered by her two opponents to date.

Considering his own "damaged" condition, the weakened state of his ship's spars and rigging, and the fact that he was thousands of miles from home in waters infested with the enemy, Bainbridge reluctantly determined to destroy *Java* rather than attempt to tow her home. Slowly—very slowly, with only two boats available—the prisoners were brought aboard and distributed about the spar and gun decks of *Constitution* under guard of American Marines, the enlisted men manacled to preclude an uprising. Last to be transferred was *Java's* mortally wounded captain, Henry Lambert, one of England's finest frigate captains, whose green, nondescript crew had not been equal to his tactical skill. It was a terribly painful move across choppy waters, but it was made with all the care and tenderness possible. By noon on the final day of 1812, all people and personal gear were clear and the demolition fires set. At 3:00, she blew up. Noted Surgeon Evans: "The explosion was not so grand as that of the Guerriere, as her small Magazine only took fire." Bainbridge made sail for São Salvador.

At 8:30 on New Year's morning, land and a sail were sighted ahead. On the chance it might be *Montague* or another enemy warship, the prisoners were herded below and confined in the hold, and the ship beat to quarters. In the heat and closeness of their confinement, the British suffered considerable discomfort—particularly the wounded. This act was to bring the wrath of some British observers down on Bainbridge's head, with charges of cruelty and malice, despite the obvious military requirement to ready his ship for battle that the situation generated.

The number of contacts grew from one to three as the distance between them closed. Soon, it was seen to be *Hornet* with two prizes: the salt-laden American merchant ship *William.* once prize to *Java*, and the British schooner *Eleanor* (or *Ellen*), which was carrying a cargo valued at $150,000. Lawrence had come out of port when *Java* and *William* first were sighted on the 29 December, and had remained hovering off the entrance ever since, keeping *Bonne Citoyenne* covered and yet being in a position to evade should *Constitution* be defeated or additional enemy units appear. Bainbridge came to anchor offshore and *Hornet* ran alongside, her tops manned and the crew bellowing out three lusty cheers. Lawrence came aboard and updated the commodore concerning events in the port, then the frigate got underway and entered São Salvador at 1:00 P.M. on 1 January 1813. *Hornet* remained offshore to nab *Bonne Citoyenne* should the Briton choose to leave while *Constitution* was busy offloading prisoners and making repairs.

Prisoner offloading began at 2:00 P.M. on the 2nd. The commodore had arranged a parole for all of them with Hislop and Chads whereby they would return to England, not to fight in this war again prior to formal exchange. Among the last to leave was poor Lambert, in dreadful pain from the musket ball that had broken a rib, punctured a lung, and come to rest near his spine. As he waited on a couch under an awning on the quarterdeck, a limping Bainbridge, suffering himself and supported by two of his officers, came to Lambert and returned his sword, saying, "I return your sword, my dear sir, with the sincere wish that you will recover, and wear it as you have hitherto done, with honour to yourself and your country." Lambert died on the evening of the 3rd, but this one act of Bainbridge's ameliorated any animosities existing between victors and vanquished and, in fact, Hislop and the commodore remained corresponding friends to the ends of their days. Chads, in his initial report of *Java*'s loss to the Admiralty, expressed his "grateful acknowledgements, this publically, for the generous treatment Captain Lambert and his officers experienced from our gallant enemy, Commodore Bainbridge and his officers."

Ten carpenters were hired in São Salvador to assist ship's company in repairing *Constitution*'s battle damage. Fishes were got out for the masts and spars. Bulwarks were repaired. Water and stores were shipped. Seaman Stephen Welsh died of his wounds and was buried.

Bainbridge now had to consider his next course of action. There still was no sign of *Essex.* (She already was farther south at the rendezvous off Cabo Frio at this time.) *Constitution* had been mauled in the fight and really wasn't fit for extended cruising far from home. British forces in the area would be rallying to his presence soon, and would be bent on revenge. And there was *Bonne Citoyenne*. Weighing all these factors, the commodore decided to head back home, taking with him *Hornet*'s two prizes. *Hornet*, he ordered to remain off São Salvador until *Bonne Citoyenne* sailed, or superior British forces appeared, or until about the 25th of the month, when she was to head for home, reconnoitering Dutch Surinam and British Guiana along the way. All four ships departed São Salvador on the afternoon of the 5th. Ordinary Seaman Reuben Sanderline died of his wounds on the 6th and was buried at sea.

Home to Boston

The trip northward was uneventful and, in the main, pleasant. Ordinary Seaman John Cheevers, whose brother James had been killed outright in the fight, died of his wounds, and Lt. John Aylwin followed him on the 29th. (Aylwin had been *Constitution*'s sailing master during the engagement with *Guerriere* and had been wounded in the same manner on that occasion. His lieutenancy had come as a reward for his gallantry.)

During this homeward trip, Bainbridge wrote his report of the engagement and many letters to friends. One of these that has come down to us indicates that even before receiving the news of Decatur's victory, the commodore was not a totally happy man. In a letter to John Bullus, then naval agent at New York, he made the surprising statement that, "My Crew owing to the constant Exercise we give them, are very active & clever at their Guns. But in all other respects they are inferior to any Crew I ever had." Was it the crew that had steered the wheel-less ship and handled its sails in a brilliant maneuvering contest with a faster-sailing enemy that he was criticizing? Did he really mean it? Was he laying the groundwork for defending himself against criticisms of the casualties incurred or the damage received? Or unfavorable comparison with Hull's and Decatur's achievements? There seems to have been an abiding negative streak in Bainbridge.

When *Constitution* appeared off Boston Light on 15 February, the city had been aware of Bainbridge's victory for six days. First public notice of it had been given during a performance of "Hamlet" at the Boston Theatre. In the audience that night were Rodgers, Hull, and some other officers.

Adverse winds prevented the ship from entering the harbor immediately. When Bainbridge finally was able to come ashore at Long Wharf on the 18th, the city was ready for him. The route to the Exchange Coffee House was decorated with flags and streamers. A procession was formed at Faneuil Hall that included the Ancient and Honorable Artillery Company, the Boston Light Infantry, and the Wilson Blues. The tall commodore was escorted by Rodgers and the stumpy Hull, as well as other notables. Two bands played. And for the next two months Boston and the country gave themselves up to honoring the latest naval heroes. Congress again voted a gold medal to a skipper of *Constitution* and silver medals for the junior officers, and also voted $50,000 in lieu of prize money to reward the *Constitution*'s crew for *Java*. Bainbridge realized $7,500 from this largesse; the average seaman or ship's boy received about $60.

The loss of *Java*, their third frigate to be defeated in four and a half months, led the Admiralty to take action. Gunnery training was revitalized. Small ships of the line were converted into razees and larger frigates built to counter these American champions. And, effective immediately, no frigate of the Royal Navy was to engage an American 44 one-to-one; only when in squadron strength was the Royal Navy to take on an American heavy frigate. Thus, fifteen years after she was launched, *Constitution* had proved conclusively the correctness of her designer's work.

CHAPTER ELEVEN

Stewart's Trials and Triumph

OVERHAUL

Constitution began her overhaul a few days after her return to the navy yard. Because of limited facilities and ongoing work, much of the frigate's work was contracted out to civilian concerns. Wharfage for her had to be rented, as did storage space for her rigging and sails. Commodore Bainbridge's first report to the new secretary of the navy, William Jones, in office since January, indicated his command would require new beams, waterways, decks, ceilings, and knees. Her copper, although patched by Captain Hull, ought to be completely replaced. He believed her frame and planking to be sound. Also required were a new set of sails, some spars, and considerable rigging.

Ripping into the decks showed Bainbridge's estimate to have been quite accurate. By 14 March, he could report that two-thirds of the beams needed to be replaced, saying some were so rotten he was surprised they hadn't given way. Poor weather was slowing the course of the overhaul, but the commodore, who, shortly after writing this letter resumed the duties of yard commandant as well, was optimistic that it could be done in a reasonable time.

Progress also was slowed by demands being made by the forces growing on the Great Lakes. Hull's defeat at Detroit the previous summer made it obvious that the United States was in great danger of invasion from Canada, and that control of Lakes Ontario and Erie, in particular, was vital to the country's security. The British recognized the situation as well. Thus, there evolved a naval building race on these freshwater lakes hundreds of miles from the sea. For the Americans, it meant transshipment of naval stores over incredibly difficult trails to Sackett's Harbor, New York, and Presque Isle (Erie), Pennsylvania, for these forces. Only the timber was available in the immediate neighborhood. Because the navy suffered from a shortage of men and materials throughout the war, stringent measures had to be taken to provide the needed resources. Men and materials were diverted from the saltwater units to do the job. Frigate *John Adams*, being rebuilt in New York, was laid up and her entire crew and allocated stocks sent thither. "Ninety-four men from Boston," mostly *Constitution*'s crew, were ordered west in April. (Ultimately, about 150 of her crew trekked first to Sackett's Harbor, then some went on to Erie where they fought to victory at the Battle of Lake Erie the subsequent September.)

Constitution waited until the third week of May before suitable deck timbers arrived. By the middle of June, much had been accomplished. Some joiner work remained, but the one big job left was recoppering. In rebuilding the upper bulwarks, Bainbridge reportedly caused three gun ports to be built into the stern at the spar deck level, possibly as a result of Hull's experience when chased the previous summer.

So matters stood when Capt. Charles Stewart arrived from Norfolk on 22 June 1813. He formally took command of *Constitution* on 18 July.

A NEW CAPTAIN

Charles Stewart came of Irish stock, was red-headed, and a couple of inches above average height. Born in Philadelphia, he was the youngest of eight children of a merchant captain who died when Charles was two. His stepfather arranged a billet as cabin boy for him at the age of thirteen, when his limited formal education ended. Nearing his twentieth birthday, and already a qualified skipper, Stewart accepted a lieutenancy in the new navy in March 1798. He served in *United States*, 44, and commanded *Enterprize*, 12, and emerged from the Quasi-War as the senior lieutenant in the navy. Stewart was the first commander of *Siren*, 16, and was second in command to Preble in the Mediterranean Squadron (1803–1804), participating in all the major actions during these years and earning a congressional sword. He achieved his captaincy in 1806, but, like Bainbridge, obtained leave to reenter the merchant service. Again like Bainbridge, he was back in Washington late in 1811 to pursue a combat command in the imminent war. Not until December 1812 did he get one: *Constellation*. Unfortunately, before he could get his frigate to sea, a large British blockading force, including four ships of the line, trapped him in Norfolk. He eagerly accepted

Red-headed Charles Stewart was a close friend of Stephen Decatur and Richard Somers, both of whom achieved "glory" in the Barbary War. Unlike his friends, who suffered early deaths, Stewart served for decades, being made the navy's first "Flag Officer" in the late 1850s and not crossing the bar until after the Civil War. His double victory, coming as it did when the war was ending in 1815, never achieved the notoriety his superb tactics and ship handling merited. The portrait is by Thomas Sully. *Official U.S. Navy photograph*

orders to *Constitution* five months later. Stewart was literate, just, and a thorough-going professional.

The new captain was immediately faced with an unusual problem in *Constitution:* In the month of July, nearly two dozen men deserted. Correspondence is silent on why this happened, but it may have been that it was in reaction to the shocking loss of *Chesapeake* right off Boston Light on 1 June. Not only did that event signal dramatically the end of the American series of naval victories, but as defeated *Chesapeake* crewmen were repatriated from Halifax—at least one eventually was reassigned to *Constitution*—vivid tales of the swift, savage fight may have led some men to decide to escape the possibility of such British retribution. The desertion rate continued high, with another forty-four running before the end of the year.

Secretary Jones issued Stewart's sailing orders on 19 September. He was to take *Constitution*, when ready for sea, out across the Gulf Stream, then southeastward to the South American coast at Cayenne. Disrupting British commerce as he might, he was to work his way northward through the Windward and Leeward Islands. After clearing Mona Passage, he was to proceed to the English Channel, diverting to Savannah or Charleston "for refreshment and intelligence" if he thought it prudent, and resume his assault on British bottoms. He then was to prowl the French and Iberian coasts, look in at Madeira, and make a second pass at Cayenne and the islands before returning home "in the spring." A tall order and a favorite among Navy Secretaries: Benjamin Stoddert had had similar plans for *Constitution* and *United States* in 1799.

Stewart got the ship rerigged and pressed recruiting. He returned her guns aboard, mounting twenty-two 32-pounder carronades on the spar deck and thirty 24-pounder long guns below. His own unique contribution to *Constitution's* capabilities was the construction of "a portable sheet iron furnace for heating *red hot shot,*" which fitted into the back of the camboose and which, Stewart noted, could heat twenty-one 24-pounder shot "in 22 minutes with a pine wood fire." The impetus for building the furnace came from the captain's concern about winning free from an encounter with superior forces and the expectation that use of hot shot would surprise and confuse the opposition at a critical moment. By 8 December, when *Constitution* was manned fully and ready to go, the British blockade of Boston was in place with six to seven warships operating between Capes Ann and Cod. In addition to requiring a fair wind and tide to get to sea, Stewart had now to watch for an absent or distracted enemy.

To Sea, At Last

Stewart finally got the opportunity on the 31st when, at 3:00 in the afternoon, and with no enemy in the offing, he weighed anchor and cleared Boston Light on his first war cruise. Striking out to the south and southeastward, he sought out British merchantmen engaged in the West Indies trade, heavily laden, home-ward-bound cargo ships lightly convoyed by escorts rarely amounting to more than one frigate per group.

The first action to occur was when *Constitution* went in chase shortly after dawn on 13 January 1814. After firing three warning shots, she brought to a schooner, which proved to be an American, the *Regulator.* A few hours later, she was in chase again; but both foretopmast stunsail booms sprung at about 4:00 and the chase was lost with the coming of night.

Uneventful days followed as Stewart directed his command out into the central Atlantic at the latitude of Cuba, then slanted back down to the southwest toward the South American continent. Except for overhauling the Portuguese *Adrianna*, 20, on the 15th, the sea was bare.

On the 30th, Stewart held only his third practice at general quarters, and during it there occurred a bizarre incident: "Boatswain's mate Richard Ormerod's pistol going off half cocked in his belt wounded him severely in the thigh." Ormerod survived. They then were about three hundred miles due north of the mouths of the Amazon River.

As Silas Talbot had done nearly fifteen years earlier, Stewart slipped westward, just barely maintaining contact with the shore. A chase eluded him in the shoal waters close to the Guiana beach on 1 February. In chase again at dawn on the 3rd, Stewart soon identified his quarry as a Royal Navy war brig. Harassed by the big frigate all day long, HMS *Mosquito*, 18, finally was seen to go aground amidst the shoals, her masts shivering at the shock of contact. Knowing that he could not get at her, Stewart hauled off.

All was quiet until the 8th, when, in the afternoon, *Constitution* went in chase of what was identified as a British packet. Unfortunately, she was lost in the darkness. (She was the war brig *Columbine*, 20, and she shortly alerted Rear Admiral Durham's squadron off Barbados to the big American's presence.) Stewart must have been thinking about being reported, for on the 11th he made his identity less clear by repainting the gun streak yellow, in the British style.

The captain had been observing his crew for about six weeks at sea at this point, and had come to some definite conclusions about their skills. When recruiting during the nearly nine months in port, his lieutenants had had to make their assessments of the mens' skills based on the spoken answers to a few questions. On the 12th, the captain made his evaluations known: He demoted thirty-four "able" seamen to "ordinary" seamen.

The heavy frigate again went in chase during the waning moments of the evening watch on the 13th. This time, there were two contacts. The first she overhauled at 2:00 A.M. It proved to be the British armed merchant ship *Lovely Ann*, 10, laden with lumber, fish, and flour. Taking out the Britons and putting aboard a prize crew, Stewart resumed the chase of the second contact at 3:00. Nearly six hours later, a shot through her sails brought His Majesty's Schooner *Pictou*, 14, to a halt. *Pictou* had been convoying *Lovely Ann* from Bermuda to Surinam. Placing a prize crew aboard, Stewart returned with his prize to the *Lovely Ann*. There, he

185

*Stewart's Trials
and Triumph*

caused the merchantman to be emptied of her cargo (most of it into the sea) and readied it to carry the Britons to Barbados under a flag of truce. Midshipman Pardon M. Whipple was placed in charge, and, *Pictou*'s Captain Stevens having given his parole for his crew, the sixty-odd prisoners (including one woman) were placed aboard and *Lovely Ann* sent on her way.[1] *Pictou* was scuttled.

Moving west toward Tobago, Stewart came across another British merchant on the 17th, and in a chase lasting little more than an hour had the schooner *Phoenix* in his bag. Loaded with lumber and official dispatches, she had been enroute from Demerara to Barbados. After taking out the crew and passengers, Stewart scuttled her. Among the dispatches, Stewart found a petition from the merchants of Demerara pleading for escort ships to convoy fifty-one cargomen that had been waiting there for many weeks. This paralysis of British shipping by the mere threat of American activity was, certainly, every bit as important in the war at sea as the captures themselves.

Passing into the Caribbean between Tobago and Grenada, Stewart then turned northward. An hour's chase after first light on the 19th rewarded him with the capture of the brig *Catharine*, bound from Grenada to St. Thomas. As before, the prize was scuttled after removal of all persons. Moving westward, he encountered a Swedish brig southeast of Puerto Rico, bound for St. Barthélemy, and passed all of his British prisoners to her for setting ashore.

A chase early in the morning of the 23rd proved to be another Swede. As her identity was being established, another contact was sighted heading northward into the Mona Passage just east of Puerto Rico. Off in pursuit at 10:30, *Constitution* "gained slowly" on her quarry through the day as they beat against headwinds. By 4:00 that afternoon, it was clear the contact was a frigate. At least fourteen gun ports could be made out in the gun streak. Thinking it might be *President* (which actually had arrived in New York from the West Indies on the 18th), at 5:30 Stewart had the appropriate day signal displayed. In response, the stranger hoisted a British ensign and fired a gun to windward, a recognized signal of challenge. Stewart shaped his course for his adversary's larboard quarter, setting the foresail in the prevailing light wind, while sending down the royals and clearing for action. At 5:45, *Constitution* lost the wind and went dead in the water. Shortly thereafter, a fickle breeze allowed the quarry to set all sail and move away. She was hull down on the horizon by 7:30, when *Constitution* finally moved again. Nightfall, and gusty weather that tore three sails of "Old Ironsides," permitted the enemy to escape.

Back in the Atlantic once more, *Constitution* headed northwest to pass along the Bahamas and have a look at traffic in the Gulf Stream. On the 24th, an American privateer was spoke. On 1 March, she overhauled a Swedish ship and a Spanish brig, and on the 7th, she spoke the Russian ship *Independence* in the Gulf Stream at the latitude of today's Daytona Beach. For two days Stewart attempted to make contact at Charleston, but bad weather kept the pilot boats in port, and low visibility denied him a landfall. Amid growing signs of a southeasterly (onshore) gale, he hauled back out to seaward.

Stewart worked his way eastward to a position southeast of Bermuda where "The Mainmast appeared to work in the neck rather too much." He continued on a course counterclockwise around Bermuda until the 26th, when he realized the mainmast was cracked nearly from fighting top to fife rail. Clearly, it was time to seek refuge in a friendly port. Stewart opted for Boston, which deep water port alone had not yet felt the full brunt of the British blockade and where, the winter only beginning to wane, they would not yet be present in numbers, in any event. A heavy squall on the 27th gave the crew fits as the mainmast persisted in bending forward despite the slack in the stays.

Constitution made landfall in the vicinity of Cape Ann and turned southwestward for Boston. At 8:00 that morning, 3 April, two ships were sighted to the east-southeast standing toward her on a fresh breeze from the east. In a half hour, it was clear they were warships, and by 9:15 there was no mistaking the fact that they were gaining with every possibility of being able to cut off *Constitution* from her home port. Stewart set skysails and royal stunsails in the near calm, trusting that the mainmast would not fail him. At 10:00, the Americans began pumping fresh water overboard to lighten ship. Spare spars and provisions followed, and then the "spirits." The breeze came steady at about this time, so that by 10:30 it was apparent she was opening the range on her pursuers. Stewart was too much a seaman to trust to the momentary good wind, and when he came abeam of Halfway Rock at noon, he rounded to the north and entered Marblehead harbor, dropping anchor at 12:30. The two British frigates, *Junon* and *Tenedos*, both 38s, rounded to about six miles offshore, unwilling to chance the unknown waters leading to the port. A few hours later, when he was satisfied that an attack was not in the offing, Stewart shifted his berth to an anchorage abreast the fort in the adjacent town of Salem. The two Britons began their blockade patrol, hoping to catch this most famous of the American frigates when next she sortied.

Constitution sweeps confidently into safe haven at Marblehead, Massachusetts, on 2 April 1814 while her British pursuers follow more cautiously. Her second escape of the war was cause for the publication of yet another broadside song when she regained Boston two weeks later. *Author's collection*

Two weeks later, in the absence of the lurking British, Stewart brought his ship back to Boston for a new mainmast and new sails. He was hopeful still of making his mark in a memorable way.

COURT OF INQUIRY

As he struggled to ready his forces on the Great Lakes in response to growing signs of a major British effort, Secretary Jones, at the instigation of Bainbridge, was casting a critical eye on Stewart's report of his curtailed cruise.[2] On 19 April, he wrote to Stewart of his disappointment and advised him that a court of inquiry would be ordered to satisfy certain questions he had regarding the rectitude of Stewart's decision. Two days later, Jones told Bainbridge to open a court of inquiry with Como. Oliver Hazard Perry. Jones wrote that *Constitution* had "undergone a thorough repair and reequipment of the most ample kind." Why, he wanted to know, had the cruise lasted only ninety-two days? Was the ship, in fact, materially deficient in any way? How serious was the reported outbreak of scurvy? Had consumables been prudently managed? Was the crew of proper size? How serious was the problem with the mainmast? In lightening ship when being chased on 3 April, was there any reason to believe the items jettisoned had been selected to make the provisions situation look sufficiently serious?

Perry arrived on 2 May from Newport, and the inquiry commenced the following day. Stewart's prepared statement was straightforward, cogent, and, at times, directly at odds with some points made by Secretary Jones in his letters of 19 and 21 April. He began by pointing out that he had carried out his orders to the letter until, after being prevented by weather from contacting Charleston and heading for the English Channel, in the vicinity of Bermuda he became aware of a weakness in the mainmast. In deciding on a course of action, he took several other factors into account: (1) both suits of sails, which he and Bainbridge had evaluated during the overhaul as serviceable, had proven nearly worn out; (2) some thirty of the crew were incapacitated by typhus, and a few cases of scurvy, which, on occasion, had been known to multiply rapidly, had surfaced; and (3) the crew, in the main, had refused to go on reduced rations, making provisions less plentiful than they might otherwise have been. Stewart finally decided to go to Boston because he thought it was less heavily blockaded than more southerly ports; that he could get in, repair, and continue on his cruise before the season of fair winds for the blockaders was upon them; and because going to Boston was least off the track to the Channel. *Constitution*'s captain concluded his statement with the observation that his shortened cruise of ninety-two days without a port call was, nonetheless, the longest made by any unit of the navy in the war to date.[3]

Testimony by the lieutenants, the sailing master, and the surgeon supported their captain's statements. Sailing Master Eames added that the ship was "leaking more than Ships of War generally" through her decks and near the stem. Purser Pottinger provided statistics on provisioning and consumption, the muster roll, and an inventory of items jettisoned on 3 April.

The taking of testimony and subsequent deliberations required nearly a week. The report, which Bainbridge signed on 9 May, offered the following opinions: (1) that Stewart had not been negligent in preparing for the cruise; (2) that he and his officers had been attentive to the well-being of the crew; (3) that the crew was of authorized size; (4) that the ship had sufficient provisions for three months still on board, but water for only two; (5) that the jettisoned items had been appropriate to the purpose; and (6) that Stewart had exhibited doubtful judgment in putting in to port when he did. Noticeably absent are any opinions concerning the condition of leaks, the mainmast, or the sails, the three items that could have reflected adversely on Bainbridge as the navy yard commandant who had initiated and overseen the "thorough repair and reequipment of the most ample kind." No court-martial.

BLOCKADED

As Stewart defended himself and got his ship back in condition, *Junon* and *Tenedos* continued their vigil, watching not only *Constitution* but frigate *Congress*, 36, in Portsmouth, New Hampshire, as well. On 7 May, HMS *Nymphe*, 38, arrived on the scene and replaced *Tenedos*. On the 9th, *Nymphe* "made all sail towards Boston to make a reconnaissance" while *Junon* did the same toward Portsmouth. The next day, "The ship within one mile of Boston Lighthouse . . . saw the constitution [*sic*] nearly unrigged. No other man-of-war in the harbour." Unchallenged, *Nymphe* moved offshore once more to prey on shipping rounding the head of Cape Cod while *Junon* took station off Cape Ann, unconcerned about a serious reaction.

On the 22nd, the Boston blockaders were strengthened by the arrival of HMS *Ramillies*, 74, wearing the flag of Rear Adm. Thomas Masterman Hardy, who had been Lord Horatio Nelson's flag captain at the Battle of Trafalgar in 1805. The augmentation of the British squadron only served to increase tensions in and around Boston. For Stewart, it was frustrating to find himself once more trapped in harbor just when he had hoped to resume the cruise. *Nymphe* came back off Boston Light on 4 June to check on *Constitution* "who, we heard, was ready to sail." Not so, although Stewart had received his sailing orders. HMS *Bulwark*, another 74, arrived on the scene on the 7th.

As July opened, the inshore blockaders again included *Bulwark*. She and *Nymphe* closed on Boston Light to check up on the two American men of war. "Observed United States ship Constitution . . . ready for her." *Nymphe* checked in again on the 19th and "observed the Constitution ready for sea. There are various reports concerning her and none to be depended upon." Still another 74 joined the British the next day, the *Spencer*; on the 23rd, HMS *Leander*, 50, reported for duty. According to a squadron officer, "She is one of the large new fir frigates, mounting fifty guns, twenty-four pounders and forty-two pounders, 500 men. I think her a great deal more than a match for the Constitution." At this point, there were three third-rates, three frigates, and several lesser craft in the British squadron all massed to capture an as-yet incomplete third-rate (Bainbridge had launched *Independence*, 74, on the 22nd) and, more particularly, a hated frigate.

So passed summer into fall. The British squadron was augmented further by the arrival of *Newcastle*, a sister to *Leander*, and *Acasta*, a new 44-gun frigate also built in response to the successful American design. As the weeks went by, Stewart, knowing that the normally worsening weather conditions on the New England coast would make life more difficult for the British, enlisted additional seamen to bring his crew up to full strength and waited for his opportunity.

OFF AND AWAY

By mid-December, the blockaders had been reduced to the frigates *Newcastle* and *Acasta* and the brig-sloop *Arab*, 18. All of the others had been reassigned or were, as in the case of *Leander* at Halifax, in upkeep. Sunday, the 18th, dawned fair and clear, with a fresh breeze from the west-northwest. To seaward, there was no enemy in sight. At 2:00 that afternoon, Stewart set sail, and his longed-for moment was at hand. Cheered by people massed on Long Wharf and by the privateer *Prince de Neufchatel*, 18, "Old Ironsides" glided swiftly down the harbor and out to the open sea, the only American frigate running free. Wrote Chaplain A. Y. Humphreys in his journal: "We felt that the eyes of the country were upon us and that everything within the bounds of possibility was expected from us. . . . [T]he fact was to present itself, that whatever might be our success there was little chance of being able to realize a safe arrival to port, should we be in anywise crippled by an equal force or by disaster of the ocean."

Arab returned the next day to find the quarry had escaped and promptly sailed for Provincetown, off which *Newcastle* and *Acasta* were anchored in protected waters. She reported the news on the 19th, the same day *Leander* sailed from Halifax for Boston. The three frigates were united once more on Christmas Eve, and the senior officer, Capt. Sir George Collier of *Leander*, had to decide their course of action. Learning from the other two skippers' stories, all fallacious, that *Constitution* was joining up with *Congress* from Portsmouth and *President* from the Delaware for a major strike against British shipping in home waters, Sir George got under way in pursuit of the imagined squadron toward the English Channel, leaving *Arab* as the sole blockader. On the 28th, they captured *Prince de Neufchatel*, which had sailed three days after *Constitution*.

In the meantime, Stewart looked for stragglers from the British blockading squadron off the Delaware and Chesapeake Bay and, finding none, headed for a position on shipping lanes west of Bermuda. By dawn on the first day at sea, the clear skies had given way to a gray overcast and the seas were making up. Soon, *Constitution* was buffeting into a head sea and shipping water through leaky gun port lids. Life became a wet misery for the crew, compounded by the fact that the fast getaway had left the ship short of fresh provisions. Within four days, such fresh meat as there was had been expended. Tea and sugar were gone, as well. The wardroom mess had been poorly stocked because paper money was being discounted thirty percent in Boston and the officers would not ask for credit.

The officer of the deck reported hearing a gun as dawn broke on Christmas Eve, surmising that it might be a signal gun of a convoy or a man-of-war. In a couple of hours, a sail was sighted. At 10:00, Stewart came upon a schooner showing the Union Jack upside down, a signal of distress. The American warship hoisted a British ensign. A ship's boat soon arrived with papers identifying the vessel as the *Lord Nelson*, which had been in convoy from St. Johns, Newfoundland, to Bermuda and the Windward Islands until parted from it by the same gale that had bedeviled "Old Ironsides." The smaller ship had been much damaged. Stewart placed a prize crew aboard, which promptly hoisted the Stars and Stripes. At first, the British skipper thought it was a joke because he had been told that the entire U.S. Navy had been bottled up. As he already had told Stewart the convoy had been escorted only by a frigate and a sloop, and that a second storm rendezvous had been arranged to the *east* of Bermuda, the "joke" was on him. Both ships headed thence.

The next morning, Stewart took *Lord Nelson* in tow and sent working parties aboard to avail himself of her cargo as the two continued on under easy sail. She proved to be a "perfect slop ship and grocery store, very opportunely sent to furnish a good rig and bountiful cheer for Christmas." There soon was flowing aboard the frigate generous quantities of tongues, corned beef, smoked salmon, dried beef, codfish, pineapple, cheeses, barrels of loaf sugar, brandy, gin, port wine, tea, flour, and hams "inferior not even to Smithfield Virginia." The chaplain termed the bounty "more precious than the diamonds of Golconda." That afternoon, before sunset, *Lord Nelson* was scuttled, all her bounty safely struck below in the American frigate.

At the rendezvous, there was no sign of the convoy. A Spanish brig met on the last day of the year offered no clues to its whereabouts. Moving to the southeast,

Stewart continued hopeful. At nightfall on 3 January 1815, having passed south of the Tropic of Cancer, he gave over the chase, deciding to remain in the area in hopes of intercepting Europe-bound Britons entering the Atlantic via the Windward or Mona Passages from the Caribbean. He was about 150 miles north-northeast of Puerto Rico. The American privateer schooner *Anaconda* of New York, met as she was heading north, reported no sign of a British convoy. With that, the captain headed east to get into the shipping lanes from the Southern Hemisphere.

On the 9th, he ran into another gale that had *Constitution* rolling heavily in the trough, shipping water through every opening and wetting even the berth deck. To help her ride better and to preclude their loss, Stewart had the topgallant yards sent down and unshipped. Life got no better until the storm finally passed them by on the 14th. Inspection of the ship found that some guns had had their tompions washed out of their muzzles and the shot rolled out of them into the sea. On the 18th, Seaman William Harrison fell overboard from the fore channels. Despite the fact that they then were in chase, Stewart paused to rescue him. He was picked up by the boat in just eight minutes, "a degree of despatch seldom surpassed," but it took another thirty for the boat to return to the ship and be hoisted aboard. The chase, a brig, could not be come up with before sunset and was given over. Stewart turned northeastward.

By the 20th, *Constitution* was in the sea lanes some three hundred miles west-northwest of the Canary Islands. On the 21st, she chased and spoke a Portuguese ship and a French brig. She brought to the French brig *Cassimere* three days later, and placed the crew of the *Lord Nelson* aboard her for delivery ashore. A Portuguese brig was stopped on the 25th. Another storm from the 29th to the 31st made life a misery once more. Stewart shaped his course northward on the latter date, and on 6 February turned eastward for the waters off Cape Finisterre.

On the 8th, Stewart spoke and boarded the Hamburg barque *Julia*, bound from Cork to Lisbon, which gave him news of a rumored peace. And at 4:00 that afternoon, an officer boarded a Russian brig from Kinsale and received confirmation of the rumor. Thus did Stewart learn that peace was imminent. The initialing of the treaty at Ghent, which had taken place on 24 December, only made peace likely; until ratified by Parliament and Congress, the state of war continued to exist.

Constitution patrolled an area off Cape Finisterre for the next several days, sometimes coming within fifteen miles of the shore. The winds were blustery and the air chill, so much so that Stewart had occasion to punish masthead lookouts for being more concerned about their comfort than catching sight of potentially enemy ships.

Chaplain Humphreys and First Lieutenant Ballard were taking their "constitutional" on the quarterdeck when Ballard was attracted by the actions of "Guerriere," a terrier belonging to 2d Lt. Beekman V. Hoffman. The dog had scrambled up atop a carronade and onto the hammock cloths, come to a point, and begun barking. Looking to see, Ballard was startled to find a frigate bearing down on them from windward under "a press of sail." The lookouts once again had been inattentive, and this time the consequences might be fatal. As *Constitution* beat to quarters, the stranger swept across under her stern and Stewart, now on deck, slewed his ship around to parallel the other's course, setting sail as he did so.

Constitution soon was abeam, from whence it appeared the other frigate was at battle stations. Both ships were rolling heavily, their gun deck ports shipping water. At 8:00 P.M., Stewart hailed, and again, and again. No response. Ordering the gun deck to hold their fire unless fired upon, he had the three forward quarterdeck carronades fire at the stranger. Now there came a response: She was the Portuguese frigate *La Amazonas*, 44. Stewart ordered her to heave to, which order was obeyed, but heavy seas made boarding impossible, and the two went their separate ways. Securing his guns, the American tended slowly southward while the captain further disciplined his lookouts, and all agreed a certain canine had earned his keep.

Dawn of the 16th found *Constitution* within sight of the Rock of Lisbon at the mouth of the Tagus River. She was looking for HMS *Volontaire*, 38, earlier reported by a merchant ship as shortly to be bearing the Duke of Beresford and his family to England from Portugal. In sight were a sail dead ahead and another on his starboard quarter; Stewart chose to chase the latter, again flying the British ensign to confuse his quarry. At 7:30, the chase was seen to be Portuguese, so Stewart came about and made for the other contact, which, at long range, was thought to be a privateer. (This ship was, in fact, HMS *Elizabeth*, 74, which shortly thereafter went into Lisbon, learned that "Old Ironsides" was in the area, and promptly got under way again in pursuit. Unbeknownst to Stewart, also in the area was *Tiger*, 38, commanded by one James Richard Dacres, who had lost *Guerriere* to *Constitution* two and a half years earlier and wanted another chance. He, too, became a hunter when he learned of his old adversary's presence.) At 9:00, before he could come up with the imagined privateer, Stewart spotted a fat merchantman ripe for the plucking and shifted the chase to what promised greater profit. A few hours in chase and use of the Union Jack brought into his bag the British *Susanna*, bound from Buenos Aires for Liverpool with a cargo of hides, tallow, vicuña wool, and nutria pelts valued at $75,000. She also carried two "tiger" cubs (probably jaguars), which Stewart had chained in one of *Constitution*'s boats stowed amidships.

Continuing to move southward for the next two days, Stewart prepared to defy the odds and get *Susanna* back to an American port. At daylight on the 19th, *Constitution* went in chase for the first time since taking the Briton, but it proved to be a Russian ship, *Josef*. The ruse of flying the British colors and pretending to be HMS *Endymion* failed, however. The master of the Russian ship knew the American boarding officer *by name* and reminded him that the two ships had been moored within two hundred yards of one another throughout the summer of 1814 in Boston. This incident would place *Constitution* in great peril. A second chase that day turned out to be another Portuguese, *Fama*, homeward bound from the Brazils, on board of which Stewart placed *Susanna*'s crew. Late that afternoon, he ordered *Susanna*'s prize crew to head across the Atlantic. (They made it.)

A Tactical Triumph

The 20th of February dawned cloudy and hazy with a cold, damp east-north-east wind propelling *Constitution* in a southwesterly direction under short canvas. Madeira was about 180 miles to the west-southwest. All was quiet, but Stewart was keeping an alert watch because his activities of the preceding ten days certainly must have stirred up a hornet's nest off Gibraltar, a major Royal Navy base. At about 1:00 that afternoon, a ship was spied on the larboard bow, heading toward the American. In half an hour, a second contact was sighted beyond the first and somewhat to westward, "both standing close hauled towards us under a press of sail." It was clear that the first unit was a full-rigged ship, probably a combatant. So matters stood until near 3:00, when the nearest contact signaled to the other and turned southward, apparently so the two could join company. Stewart crowded on sail in pursuit, setting his stunsails as the big frigate gathered way. He was certain he had two Britons before him and thought their maneuvering meant they intended to keep away from him until nightfall, when they might elude him. Every stitch of canvas was set in *Constitution*, alow and aloft. At about 3:45 a sickening cracking sound gave warning that the main royal mast was giving way. Slowing his pursuit, Stewart quickly sent men aloft to cut away the wreckage while others prepared a spare spar. In an hour, it was aloft and the main royal drawing smartly once more. With the range closing again, *Constitution* "fired on the chase from the first gun 1st division and the chase gun on the forecastle." The range was too great.

It was apparent that the enemy would be able to combine forces before Stewart could come up on the nearest one, so he cleared for action and made deliberate preparations for battle. Shot was gotten up and powder charges made ready. The decks were sanded. Gun crews were divided to man the guns, port and starboard, simultaneously. Personal weapons for the boarders were broken out and positioned in tubs about the decks, ready to hand.

About the time *Constitution* resumed the chase, the enemy "passed within hail of each other, shortened sail, hauled up their courses, and appeared to be making preparations to receive us." Stewart knew now he had his sought-after fight before him. After briefly trying to get the weather gauge, the Britons formed a column heading westward with the wind coming over their starboard quarters and with about one hundred yards between them. The smaller of the two was in the lead.

A little after 5:00, *Constitution* broke the Stars and Stripes as she came ranging up on the windward side of the enemy column. They responded by hoisting red ensigns. At about 5:20, "Old Ironsides" was alongside the aftermost ship at about six hundred yards with her sails lifting gently, her momentum carrying her forward until she was in a position at the apex of an isosceles triangle, her opponents' column forming the baseline. From this ideal position, Stewart, standing near the larboard entry port for a better view, "invited the action by firing a shot between the two ships which immediately commenced with an exchange of broadsides."

A British ball killed two men nearby in the waist and continued its way to smash one of the ship's boats, putting an end to the "tigers." Firing continued hot and heavy for about fifteen or twenty minutes, when enemy fire slackened markedly, his shot falling short. By this time, the sea and the combatants were smothered in smoke, and the sun was lowering across the western horizon. (Sunset came at 5:48.) In the smoke and dimming light, the aftermost Briton altered course to starboard to close the distance and get his guns into more effective range. Stewart ordered a cease-fire to allow the smoke time to drift clear ahead and to determine the condition of his opponents. It took a few minutes before the aftermost of his opponents came into view, and appeared to be luffing to cross under his stern and rake. Blasting a final broadside into the smoke where

A moment early in the battle between *Constitution (center)* and *Levant (left)* and *Cyane (right)*. The latter is seen attempting to close on the big American frigate as the smoke rolls away ahead of her consort. *Constitution* appears to have backed her main topsail and top-gallant and is about to give the *coup de grace* to *Cyane*. *Artist unknown; photo in author's collection*

he assumed the leading enemy was, Stewart threw his main and mizzen topsails flat aback, with topgallants still set, shook all forward, let fly his jib, braked his ship, and unleashed a heavy fire.[4] The rear enemy attempted unsuccessfully to wear away, receiving much damage to his sails and rigging and a hail of musketry in the process. He fell out of control, coming to his bow in a southeasterly direction, sails flat aback and headsails and spanker either ruined or snarled in wreckage. As this was happening, the leading enemy appeared out of the smoke, seemingly trying to get across *Constitution's* bow and rake *her* from ahead; but Stewart once again filled his sails, boarded his foretack, and shot forward. When the enemy wore to larboard, Stewart rewarded him with two raking broadsides in the stern from a hundred yards, at which time the Briton ran off to leeward and darkness to escape the heavy fire and to restore order to gun crews that twice had attempted to desert their posts.

Looking east, Stewart saw that the larger of his opponents was attempting to get under way again. He wore short and slid into position on his larboard quarter. Just as he was about to give the starboard battery an opportunity from a range of only fifty yards, the enemy struck his colors, showed a single light, and fired a gun to leeward. The time was 6:45. In short order, Second Lieutenant

Hoffman was aboard with fifteen Marines to take possession of HMS *Cyane*, 24, a light frigate under the command of Capt. Gordon Thomas Falcon.

At 7:45, having taken the enemy officers into *Constitution* and assuring himself that his prize crew could control *Cyane*, Stewart set off after the other enemy. That ship had not, in fact, run away, but had, instead, drawn off to effect repairs to her sails and rigging, and was returning to the fray. Thus it was that, within fifteen minutes of setting sail, Stewart found himself bearing down on an enemy that, in turn, was heading for him. At 8:40 the two passed each other at fifty yards going in opposite directions and exchanged starboard broadsides. The enemy then wore to run with the wind. Stewart adroitly wore short and got in a stern rake before he was out of range. Realizing how unequal the contest was, the latter made all sail, seeking escape. Stewart quickly was in chase, and at 9:30 began picking away at him with two bow guns, every shot being carefully sighted and few missing. The range steadily decreased until the American seamen could hear planking being ripped up as their shots told. Some of these sounds were those of the tiller being shot away. A few minutes after 10:00, as *Constitution* was ranging up on the larboard quarter and recognizing there could be no escape, he

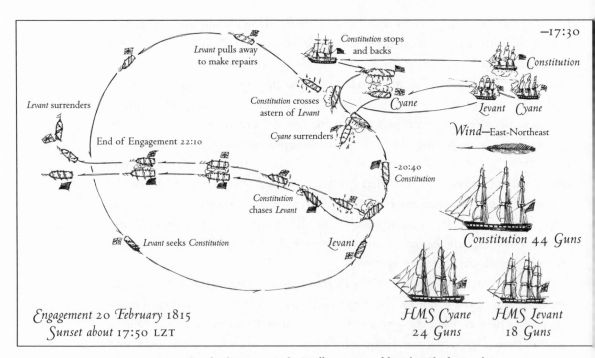

Battle diagram *Author's collection; created by John Charles Roach*

came by the wind and also fired a leeward gun. 3d Lt. William B. Shubrick went over to accept the surrender of HMS *Levant,* a new 18-gun corvette commanded by Capt. George Douglas, the senior of the two British captains. A midshipman accompanying Shubrick has left this record of his first sight of *Levant's* quarter-deck area: "The mizen [*sic*] mast for several feet was covered with brains and blood; teeth, pieces of bones, fingers and large pieces of flesh were picked up from off the deck."

The British ships had sailed from Gibraltar on 16 February as units of a covering force spread out to protect convoys bound for England and the West Indies. After a brief stop at Tangier for provisions, they had sailed "in trail" of the West Indies convoy with a mission of preventing its being surprised from astern. *Cyane,* the larger foe, carried thirty-four guns into this fight: twenty-two 32-pounder carronades on her gun deck and ten 18-pounder carronades and two long 9-pounder chase guns above. *Levant* carried eighteen 32-pounder carronades, one 12-pounder carronade, and, again, two long 9-pounder chase guns. Whatever their aggregate weight of metal, their strength lay in weapons whose maximum effective range was on the order of four hundred yards. In contrast, *Constitution* carried the batteries that had served her so well in this war: thirty long 24-pounders, twenty 32-pounder carronades, and two 24-pounder "shifting gunades."[5] The maximum effective range of her long guns was about twelve hundred yards—three times greater than that of the carronades—and gave Stewart the option of fighting at longer ranges when it was advantageous to do so.

The absence of records makes it difficult to assess crew sizes and casualties with precision. *Constitution* appears to have had 451 officers and men aboard at the time of the engagement, while, in round numbers, *Cyane* had 180 and *Levant,* 140. *Constitution's* log states that she suffered four dead and fourteen wounded that evening, including no officers. As regards the British losses, estimates by Americans on the scene place the death toll in *Cyane* at twelve and in *Levant,* twenty-three; they counted twenty-six wounded in the former and sixteen in the latter. The bulk of these undoubtedly occurred as a result of the repeated rakes "Old Ironsides" poured into both ships; since it was a night action, Marine snipers only briefly made the sort of contribution they had in previous engagements.

British gunners in this fight appear to have concentrated more on the American frigate's hull than they had in previous encounters. Aside from a few lines cut in the opening blasts of grape shot, *Constitution* suffered only the loss of her foretopgallant yard aloft; her hull, on the other hand, was found to have about a dozen 32-pounder balls embedded in it, none of which opened a serious wound. *Constitution's* heavy batteries, though, had wreaked havoc in her opponents. All of *Cyane's* lower masts had been wounded, and the main and mizzen masts were tottering; every bowline and brace but one had been shot away; also wounded were her fore yard, maintopgallant yard, gaff, driver boom, crossjack, foretopgallant mast, and fore and mizzen top masts, the latter falling during this period. Five or six of her carronades had been dismounted as the lighter scantlings of her hull failed to stop the American's "heavy iron." She had been hit eight to ten times between wind and water. *Levant* had her tiller shot away. Her rigging, too, had been decimated, all her lower masts were wounded and the mizzen mast was threatening to fall, the maintopgallant yard had been shot away, and the hull was pierced below the waterline by several shot.

In summary, Stewart and *Constitution* had everything going for them in this fight: heavier gun batteries (although he could only suspect so beforehand); a tough hull better able to resist damage, with spars and rigging to match; and, thanks to the fact that the British blockade had put so many Americans on the beach, Stewart had been able to ship what was perhaps the most experienced crew "Old Ironsides" ever would have. Stewart himself proved to be a superb tactician and ship handler who took advantage of every break he got and acted decisively to deny the enemy any. He fought at ranges that ensured his gunners rarely would miss while his enemies were working beyond their maximum effective range. His experienced crew, in which he had the greatest confidence, was able to respond with alacrity to his demanding orders for swift and certain sail handling. If his adversaries can be said to have done anything "wrong," it would have to be having had the temerity to challenge him in the first place. On *that* day, in *those* circumstances, Stewart, *Constitution,* and the crew simply were unbeatable.

AFTERMATH

It required but three hours to put *Constitution* back in condition for further action, but the same could not be said of her prizes. After laying to through the night, the trio got under way under easy sail the next morning, heading southward to put more distance between themselves and the centers of British naval power. But there was another reason, as well: Malcolm Ross, the fat, jolly little master of *Susanna,* had told Stewart that HMS *Inconstant,* 36, was en route to England from Rio de la Plata bearing one million pounds sterling in bullion. With

Constitution (center), *Cyane (left)*, and *Levant (right)* approaching Porto Praya in the Cape Verde Islands three weeks after their battle. Note the British ensigns flying beneath the Stars and Stripes on each of the prizes. Repairs effected at sea have largely restored the ex-Britons' sailing abilities. *Artist unknown; photo in author's collection*

more than a third of *Constitution*'s crew lost through prize crews and casualties—including the first and second lieutenants, sailing master, at least four midshipmen, chaplain, and sailmaker—and numerous British prisoners aboard, another fight with any frigate would be risky, but the lure of so much potential prize money was irresistible. (If successful, the captain's personal share would be a whopping $150,000.) What a rewarding way to end a war cruise begun with so much apprehension.

Boats plied regularly back and forth between captor and captives as American working parties repaired the damage they had caused, and as prisoners, prize crews, and baggage were redistributed. On the 23rd, a gang was sent to *Levant* that took out her mizzen mast and floated it to *Constitution* for repairs; it was back in place before sunset the same day.

Constitution's log contains this entry for the 25th: "The prisoners orderly except some of the British Officers of whom this ship's ward room officers complained, that they did not conduct themselves, below, like gentlemen, being in their language indecent, vulgar, and abusive to each other." So unpleasant was their company that Chaplain Humphreys, upon learning that he was being reassigned to the prize crew in *Levant*, wrote in his journal, "A reprieve to any condemned malefactor was never hailed with sincerer gratulation."

Captains Falcon and Douglas were not above conducting themselves with similar pettishness. On one occasion, Falcon observed to Ballard that the toilet facilities in "Old Ironsides" were substandard when compared to those he had enjoyed in his ship. Ballard is reported to have responded that the Americans were not so concerned about such matters "provided our guns tell well, and you can be a competent judge of how far that end has been obtained." On another occasion, Stewart is said to have returned to his cabin from attending to some business on the quarterdeck only to find Falcon and Douglas in a heated argument. At contention was which of them had been most at fault for their collective defeat. Stewart listened to the acrimony for a few moments, then reportedly told them, "Gentlemen, there is no use in getting warm about it; it would have been all the same whatever you might have done. If you doubt that, I will put you all on board again and you can try it over." The offer was not accepted.

The ships continued slowly southward as repairs went on in *Cyane*. Stewart had decided to head for the Cape Verde Islands, where he would parole the troublesome Britons and take on fresh stores before returning across the Atlantic. Repairs to *Cyane* were completed on 4 March. Stewart promptly placed his small force in a scouting line, the ships separated at maximum signaling distance on a line perpendicular to the direction of advance. By this means, he intended to minimize being surprised by the enemy he knew must be looking for him, and perhaps yet nab *Inconstant*. When they ran into fog on the 6th, he brought them back into a tight little group. At 4:00 that afternoon, still in thick fog and with little wind, a lookout in *Levant* caught sight of land.

In another two days, the group anchored off the island of Maio, one of the smaller Cape Verdes some twenty-five miles northeast of the principal island of São Iago. Because the anchorage was very exposed, Stewart lay there for twenty-four hours waiting for the fog to lift. When it didn't, he got under way anyway at 3:00 the next afternoon, feeling he could navigate safely the short distance to Porto Praya on the big island.

Constitution and her prizes anchored in the harbor of Porto Praya at 11:00 A.M. on the 10th, after *Levant* narrowly had avoided running aground as they entered. Stewart was suspicious of Portuguese neutrality, but received assurances from the governor on that score and a promise that the countryside would provide him with the fresh provisions he desired. It was Stewart's intention to capitalize on the presence of a British brig in harbor by chartering it as a cartel to take his paroled prisoners home. He sent Douglas and Falcon ashore to make these arrangements, and when they returned to report success he permitted two of their officers and twelve seamen to go aboard the brig to ensure that it did not try to sneak away in the night.

CHASED

The next morning, Stewart began shifting prisoners to the British brig and had sent a working party of seventeen ashore to load stores. About noontime, Shubrick had just assumed the duty as officer of the deck when he was attracted by the stifled exclamation of a British midshipman and the apparent whispered reprimand he was receiving from his lieutenant. As he was trying to determine what had caused the little byplay, his quartermaster called his attention to the harbor entrance where a low, heavy fog covered the sea. Visible above it were the upper masts and sails of a ship. That must have been what had startled the midshipman. Stewart was called immediately. By the time he reached the deck, two more sets of upper sails came into view, obviously the rigs of warships; all three were bound into the harbor. No doubt recalling that the American frigate *Essex* had been taken by the British in the neutral port of Valparaíso in 1814, Stewart took instant action to get his ships to sea. Just four minutes after sighting the last two contacts, he cut his anchor cable, set topsails, and stood out of the bay on a course calculated to give him the weather gauge for whatever was to follow. Signals to *Cyane* and *Levant* ordered them to follow suit, which they did with a speed that testifies to the competence of their prize masters and small crews. Realizing what was happening, some of the British prisoners already ashore for transfer to the cartel rushed to the Portuguese fort and began firing at the escaping Americans.

Constitution and her consorts just cleared East Point, marking the northern limit of the harbor, as their pursuers came into long cannon range from the south. The enemy crowded on sail. "Old Ironsides" crossed her topgallant yards and set main and fore courses, spanker, flying jib, and her topgallants, and headed eastward, the wind coming from the north-northeast. The gig and first cutter, which had been moored astern, were cut adrift. *Cyane* and *Levant* followed the motions of their leader smartly. Now it was going to be decided on the ships' sailing abilities. Stewart thought his pursuers were two ships of the line and a frigate.

What Stewart did not learn until much later was that his pursuers were *Leander*, *Newcastle,* and *Acasta,* those three frigates especially built to counter "Old Ironsides" that had held her blockaded for eight long months in Boston. After learning of her escape, as we have seen, Collier headed for the English Channel with this group. Failing to find his quarry there, he had patrolled southward until the trail became warm off Portugal. It grew red hot when he encountered the Russian ship *Josef* on the same day *Constitution* met *Cyane* and *Levant.* The master told the Britons all they wanted to hear. After that, it became only a matter of time before the two sides would meet again.

The chase was continuing at a smart ten knots. It was observed that *Acasta* gradually was weathering on both *Cyane* and *Levant,* but not on *Constitution,* which slowly was pulling away from her consorts. Seeing that that particular enemy, whatever her specific rate, was bigger and faster than *Cyane,* whom she shortly would have under her guns, at 1:10 Stewart signaled Hoffman to tack to the northwest. This Hoffman promptly did, without drawing a single enemy after him. The British commodore evidently intended solely to "get *Constitution.*" (Hoffman subsequently idled awhile to the northwest, assuming that if he were pursued the British most likely would look for him to run with the wind. When he felt they must have passed safely ahead away from him, he shaped a course for New York, where he arrived on 10 April. *Cyane* was purchased by the U.S. Navy for $40,000 in 1815 and served actively until 1827. She finally was broken up in 1836.)

At 2:30, one of the pursuers tried firing at *Constitution,* but the range was too great. By 3:00 it was becoming apparent that *Levant* was being endangered as *Cyane* had been. Hoping to divide the enemy and thereby improve the odds for them both, at 3:12 Stewart signaled to Ballard to tack to the northwest. This time, all three pursuers tacked after the smaller vessel. *Constitution* quickly sailed over the horizon and out of danger. (Collier reportedly signaled Capt. Lord George Stewart of *Leander* to continue the pursuit of *Constitution,* but he declined on the excuse that his foretopsail yard was sprung. Ballard, seeing that he had become the center of attention, determined to run *Levant* aground on the island and burn her. He was dissuaded from this course because of the many prisoners aboard, and instead returned to Porto Praya to try Portuguese "neutrality." The British squadron, as Stewart had feared earlier, moved in without a pause and began bombarding the hapless *Levant* from a range of one hundred yards, and after enduring fifteen minutes of what must be reported as haphazard fire, Ballard had *twice* to haul down his flag before the British accepted his surrender. Collier never was able to provide a satisfactory explanation for his actions that day; the fact that he had allowed *Constitution* to escape eventually led to his suicide in 1817.)

HOMEWARD BOUND, BUT NOT DIRECTLY

Constitution stood south until she reached the latitude of Guinea, then headed southwest, still hoping that the horizon ahead would be broken by the appearance of *Inconstant*. Stewart knew that the warmer clime could have an adverse effect on the 225 prisoners confined below and, recognizing the risk arising from having a crew barely in the majority, set up a system of exercise for his involuntary dependents. Each morning, one-third of the captives was permitted on the spar deck, while a second third passed its time on the gun deck and the remainder stayed in the hold. Each noontime, the groups were rotated. At the end of the first dog-watch, all returned to the hold. On 18 March, Stewart required all prisoners to bathe in tubs set up in the channels. This was repeated on the 24th, by which time *Constitution* had passed south of the Equator.

Cabo de São Roque, the northeast corner of Brazil, was sighted on the 26th. Stewart turned northwest. When, four days later, he received the morning report noting but 6,000 gallons of "fresh" water remaining, he decided to put in at "Maranham" (Maranhão Island; the community was and is named São Luís), at the mouth of the Itapecuru River. Prior to entering port on 2 April, Stewart had all of the enlisted prisoners put in irons so there could be no "surprises" during the normal confusion attending the start of a port call.

Fourth Lt. William M. Hunter was sent ashore to make contact with local government officials and learn the latest news. He returned shortly, saying it would be all right to land the prisoners and arrange for their return to England, but that no one yet knew whether peace had become a fact. A local ship chandler of British origin refused to furnish them with supplies.

Prisoner offloading began at 8:00 on the morning of the 4th. Not for the first time, Stewart received complaints from the Britons about thievery. This time, the captain composed a search party of his officers and British officers to search the ship and crew from keelson to main truck—and even into the empty water casks—for the supposedly purloined goods. Nothing was found.

Stewart got under way for home on the 13th, but foul winds prevented him from negotiating the tortuous channel until the 15th, when he finally reached the open sea. Moving to the northwest, toward the Antilles where the British squadrons roamed, Stewart ran daily exercises at battle stations to whip his diminished crew into some fighting trim for what might lay ahead. Ten days later, *Constitution* went in chase at daylight. By 8:30, then some four miles on the contact's weather beam, Stewart saw she was a two-decker. A short while later, it was seen that *Constitution*'s foretopmast was badly sprung, so Stewart prudently kept his distance until repairs could be made. The liner, possibly HMS *Venerable*, 74, showed no curiosity in her smaller neighbor and continued on her way.

Constitution arrived off San Juan, Puerto Rico, on the morning of the 28th, and Stewart sent Hunter ashore for the latest intelligence. Late that afternoon, he returned with confirmation that the peace treaty had been ratified. (In fact, America had ratified the Treaty of Ghent on 17 February, but because there was a twelve-day "time late" clause built into it to provide time to communicate that fact to the far-flung naval units on both sides, *Constitution*'s capture of *Cyane* and *Levant* stood as valid wartime conquests. The British recapture of *Levant*, however, technically was after the fact.)

Stewart took his departure from Puerto Rico late the next morning, bound for New York, where he arrived off the Battery on the afternoon of 15 May. He marked his return with a fifteen-gun salute and went ashore to the plaudits of his fellow countrymen, enjoying much the same reception as Hull and Bainbridge had received in Boston. Even as the festivities peaked, the *National Intelligencer* made a prophetic proposal: "Let us keep 'Old Iron Sides' at home. She has, literally, become a *Nation's* Ship, and should be preserved. Not as a 'sheer hulk, in ordinary' (for she is no *ordinary* vessel); but, in honorable pomp as a glorious Monument of her own, and our other Naval Victories."

Congress could do no less than vote Stewart a gold medal for his classic action, making him the third successive skipper of "Old Ironsides" to be so recognized and his ship the only one that could boast of having had *all* her captains in that war decorated. Stewart and his crew also received prize money for *Susanna* as well as the value of *Cyane* and *Levant* (the sum for *Levant* coming from the Portuguese government, which had so supinely allowed its neutrality to be violated at Porto Praya).

Following the festivities in New York, Stewart returned *Constitution* to Boston at the end of the month, where forty-six of her crew were transferred to duty in *Congress*, 36, and another six in *Enterprize*, 12, then being readied for duty with Bainbridge's squadron in the Mediterranean. The remainder crew was paid off and Stewart departed on furlough on 16 July.

Objective analysis of the War of 1812 must conclude that the victories of *Constitution* and *United States,* together with those of *Essex* and the war brigs, had no direct effect on the course of the war. The losses suffered by the Royal Navy were no more than pinpricks to that great fleet: They neither impaired its battle readiness nor disrupted the blockade of American ports. By comparison, Perry's freshwater victory on Lake Erie in 1813 and Thomas Macdonough's on Lake Champlain a year later prevented the overland invasion of the United States and determined the course of the war. What *Constitution* and her sister *did* accomplish was to uplift American morale spectacularly and, in the process, end forever the myth that the Royal Navy was invincible. They demonstrated unmistakably that the American man-of-warsman was every bit as good as his British cousin and that his ship could stand with the best. The big frigates made Americans proud to be Americans, proven equals to any other nation in the world.

CHAPTER TWELVE

Mediterranean Sojourn

IN ORDINARY

The War of 1812 had ended. For the navy, however, there still was a problem requiring attention: the Algerines. Misjudging that their depredations would go unnoticed in the events of the larger conflict, they had resumed their piratical ways. Even as *Constitution* returned to port, other ships were being readied or had sailed to correct this error. "Old Ironsides," however, bearing the scars of her most recent victory, was given a rest. Accordingly, she was sailed north to Boston, arriving before the end of May.

Any thoughts of sending the frigate to the Mediterranean as reinforcement or relief for those units recently departed ended up being changed by what transpired there. Como. Stephen Decatur, whose squadron had sailed only five days after *Constitution*'s arrival at New York, acted so decisively in his dealing with the Dey of Algiers that the business was done by the end of June. For *Constitution*, it meant entry into the quiet and uncertain limbo of "ordinary"—"mothballs," to the modern sailor—on 25 January 1816.

A NEW ATMOSPHERE

"Old Ironsides" was moored in the backwater of naval activity for four years, years in which the United States Navy itself stood high in the esteem and pride of the young country. This pro-navy attitude was, perhaps, manifested most clearly in the "Act for the gradual increase of the navy of the United States" passed on 29 April 1816. For the first time, the country was committed, in peacetime, to a policy of fleet expansion seeking comparability with European navies.

Twenty-one new ships of the line and frigates were authorized at a cost of a million dollars a year for eight years. Existing ships were inspected and repaired or stricken, as conditions warranted. Half of this growing force generally was kept in commission at any particular time.

It was in this expansionist atmosphere, in April 1820, that navy yard commandant Isaac Hull received orders to repair *Constitution* for service. As the work began, and the decayed outer planks were ripped away, Hull was encouraged by what he found. Everything below the berth deck appeared sound, and he even had hopes of saving *it*. Spar and gun deck planking would have to be totally replaced, but many of the beams and knees "may answer again."

By early July, outer hull planking had been replaced up to the lower gun ports, and above them to the plank shear. Some of the gun deck beams were in and "kneeing off." On the 25th, the Board of Naval Commissioners, in response to an earlier query, told Hull to get *Constitution*'s guns back from *Independence* (now in ordinary), whence they had been transferred five years earlier.

In September, Hull began to fret about the board's intentions regarding *Constitution*'s future employment. Winter wasn't too far away, and she still had to be hove down, rigged, and fitted with sails. The board ignored all of his questions, except to tell him that Baker's pumps were to be installed in addition to the chain bilge pumps. October came in foul, slowing work markedly. Unfortunately, it was out in the weather where most of the work was: laying and caulking the spar deck and erecting the quarterdeck bulwarks. On the last day of the month, the board bombed Hull with orders to copper the ship and "in all respects [have her] equipped for service with all practicable dispatch." Immediately, he began preparations for heaving her down. He told Washington, however, that he expected "such severe weather before we can be ready, that we shall have a disagreeable time in doing it."

Constitution was hove down and out on Saturday, 25 November, and five strakes of copper put on before the day was out. It was seen, too, that the lowest part of the cutwater and the forwardmost section of shoe were missing; repairs were effected by the 27th. The coppering job was completed on 8 December. Despite Hull's fears about the weather, the whole operation had taken two weeks—the same time Commodore Preble needed for the same job in June 1803, and only three days longer than Hull, himself, had used in May 1812.

The coppering finished, Hull pressed on with the overhaul. During the next two weeks, he manufactured and installed a new foremast, inspected and returned the mainmast, positioned the fighting tops, and was busy setting up the lower rigging. By nightfall of the 22nd, all 150 tons of iron kentledge was aboard, and he had begun pruning back his workforce. As of Christmas Eve, 40,000 gallons of water had been sent aboard, and, Hull told the board, she could be ready for sea even before a crew could be recruited.

In summary, the following work had been accomplished: sails, bulwarks, inner and outer planking between ports, channels, ten strakes below the gun ports, most top timbers and stanchions, counter timbers, spar deck and gun deck beams, spar deck knees and planking, gun deck and spar deck waterways, quarter galleries, head, cutwater, carved work on stern, gun carriages, gun deck and berth deck spirketting, stern planking, copper, and caulking, all new; some upper futtocks were new; one-half the gun deck knees had had to be replaced; part of the berth deck planking was new, as was some of the bottom planking; and repairs had been made to the hold ceiling planking, the capstans, and the carronade beds and slides. The joiners had rebuilt the magazines and much of the cabin, wardroom, and steerage, and had repaired storerooms on the fore and after orlop. Aloft, the ship sported, in addition to a new foremast, a new bowsprit, all new topmasts and topgallant masts, and all new lower and topsail yards.

In completing the sparring and rigging of *Constitution,* Hull incorporated two developments that hitherto had not been employed in large men-of-war: spencers and sliding gunters. The former were fore-and-aft sails similar to the spanker, but lacked its boom. Provided at both the fore and main masts, they would permit "Old Ironsides" to be sailed closer to the wind than her square rig alone allowed, in effect making her somewhat like a schooner as regards that capability. The sliding gunters were "mast extenders," with an iron hoop at one end to fit over each uppermost mast section and raised into position by a halyard affixed about one-third the spar length up from the hoop passing through the truck at the top of the mast. They were handled from the fighting tops. These Hull had fitted apparently so that skysails could be employed when desired without having to carry the more conventional "sky poles" permanently in place more than two hundred feet above the water. In another "first" for the ship, he also provided a ringtail—a sort of stunsail—for the spanker. What a cloud of canvas she could put up now!

Hull regunned the ship with the usual thirty 24-pounder long guns on the gun deck. Some of these were those the ship had received in 1808, while the remainder were the slightly lighter model cast in 1816. The spar deck received

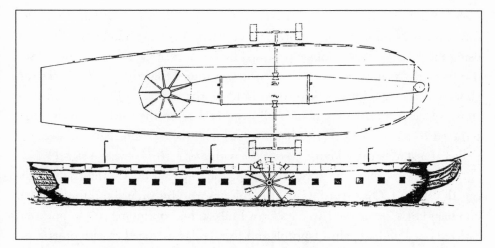

Sailing Master Briscoe Doxey's "propello marino," a set of "strap-on," man-cranked paddlewheels, successfully drove *Constitution* at three-and-a-half knots against wind and tide. The involved evolution necessary to rig and unrig them, however, doomed the idea to nothing more than a dead-end experiment. *Original plans in Rare Documents Room, National Archives*

sixteen of the lug-mounted 32-pounder carronades she first had gotten in 1808, six forward and ten aft. Additionally, the two "shifting gunades" were returned to quarterdeck gun ports.

Early in February 1821, rendezvous (that is, recruiting offices) were opened to ship a crew for "Old Ironsides." Hull set about busily ordering the necessary clothing for 430 sailors, hammocks, powder and provisions for the ship—all this without any guidance from Washington as to the locale or duration of her forthcoming employment. The naval commissioners finally wrote on the 22nd to say that the ship would be going to the Mediterranean.

An Experiment

During that same month, Secretary Smith Thompson ordered Sailing Master Briscoe S. Doxey from the Washington Navy Yard to Boston, there to conduct an experiment. Doxey was to construct and demonstrate the practicability of the "propello marino," a device "invented by him for propelling becalmed ships."

Doxey arrived early in March, and, with the assistance of Naval Constructor Josiah Barker and his men, set about erecting his machine and installing it in

Constitution. In essence, it was a "portable" set of paddle wheels installed on axles through the Number Six gun ports and cranked by a large number of the crew using the mechanical advantage provided by the anchor capstan. The first tests, during mid-April, were aborted when it was found that the paddles were too short and they couldn't "take proper hold of the water." Following modifications, successful tests were made in Boston harbor on the 23rd, when the ship, tethered to an anchor by "two hausers [*sic*] lengths" as a precaution, was propelled at a stately three knots. *Constitution* with *paddle wheels*—what a sight!

Experiment or not, the work of readying the ship for duty continued throughout this period. On 1 April, Capt. Jacob Jones read his orders and took formal command of *Constitution.* Two days later, Hull, in his continuing role as outfitter, ordered one hundred pairs of pistols and sixty cutlasses, together with other armorer's stores and a blacksmith's kit, from the Washington Navy Yard. Navigator's charts, instruments, and journals he requisitioned on the 11th, the day after *Constitution*, now fully rigged, watered, and provisioned, and needing only completion of her manning, was moved out of the yard to an anchorage off Hancock's Wharf. There she remained, but for the experiment, until 7:00 A.M. on 13 May 1821 when Jones headed her back to Mediterranean waters.

"DOCTOR" JONES

Jacob Jones was a man of somewhat above-average height, lantern jawed, and, as naval officers of the day went, of easy temperament. Born in Delaware in 1768, he truly was one of the "old men" of the navy, having been thirty-one years old before becoming a midshipman in 1799. (He had been trained in medicine, and had tried his hand at both doctoring and court clerking before turning to the sea.) He served first in *United States* under Commodore Barry and then in *Ganges*, a 24-gun converted merchantman, in the Quasi-War. It had been his misfortune to be William Bainbridge's second lieutenant in *Philadelphia* when that frigate was lost, and Jones had spent nineteen months as a prisoner of war on that occasion. Following duty in New Orleans, in 1810 he was promoted to the rank of master commandant and given command of the brig *Argus*, 18, and the following year commissioned the ship-sloop *Wasp*, 18. In that command, he earned fame and a congressional gold medal by defeating the British sloop of war *Frolic*, 18, in a vicious action that left both combatants disabled. Promoted to captain, he was given command of the captured frigate *Macedonian*, 38, but the British kept him

Jacob Jones is remembered mainly because he was one of those with Capt. William Bainbridge when that officer lost the frigate *Philadelphia* to the Tripolines in 1803 and for his defeat of HMS *Frolic* while commanding *Wasp* in 1812. One midshipman in *Constitution* under his command wrote of him "[He] is an excellent man, but he has his crotchets" and "is far from disposed to make a display." He also wrote that "the ship will not be in any kind of discipline." Jones's easygoing ways would contribute to the arrival of the senior officer of the navy, Como. John Rodgers, on scene in 1825 to redress the notorious reputation of the Mediterranean Squadron. *Official U.S. Navy photo*

bottled up in New London for the duration of the war. *Macedonian* later was a unit of Bainbridge's squadron in the Mediterranean immediately after war's end.

Jones, who seems to have made up for his late entry into service by pursuing a career with an unusually high proportion of sea time, was anxious to shake out *Constitution*'s sails. The receipt of defective supplies caused some delay. Doxey's "marvel," the test completed, was dismounted and stowed below, ostensibly to test further during the cruise.

DOLDRUM DUTY

The voyage across the Atlantic quickly was made and was one of the most peaceful the ship ever experienced. In twenty-one days she was at the Rock of

Gibraltar. There, she found *Columbus*, 74, wearing the broad pennant of Bainbridge, and the brig *Spark*, 14. The area was much different, politically speaking, since Preble's days. The Barbary pirates, insofar as the Americans were concerned, no longer were an active problem. Napoleon was out of power and coming to the end of his days on a remote island in the South Atlantic; much of Europe still was recovering from the two decades of upheaval. The American naval depot at Port Mahon, Minorca, under consideration five years before the War of 1812, had come into existence. There were no crises to make combat a possibility. Bainbridge and his two ships headed home on 6 June, three days after Jones had come in.

If the area was quiescent, Jones, in his fifty-third year, was equally willing to let things drift. Even before leaving Gibraltar, one of his midshipmen (who basically was an admirer) was writing home that "the ship is not, and will not be in any kind of discipline." Under way on the 11th, Jones wended his way to Port Mahon, arriving on the 20th, where liberty was granted to the crew by watches, a new development since the coming of peace. A three-day trip brought them to Genoa on the last day of the month. *Constitution* was the first American frigate to visit that port. The Fourth of July observance in the ship consisted of 24-gun salutes at noon and sunset, and an oration by the chaplain. Jones seems to have liked this city particularly well and spent much time ashore. His officers, too, regularly took the opportunity to ride out into the hinterlands to escape the boredom of shipboard routine.

Constitution sailed from Genoa to Leghorn between the 18th and 20th, and there found the ship-sloop *Ontario*, 18, the sole other unit of the U.S. Mediterranean Squadron. The two lay in harbor there until the 30th, when Jones got them under way for Gibraltar. Shiphandling drill was conducted for the junior officers on 2 August as the two ships lazed along under gentle breezes. On the 7th, *Constitution*'s main topgallant stunsail boom "accidentally fell from aloft" and struck Gunner's Yeoman George Willard on the head; he lingered in agony for nearly three hours. Burial was the next morning.

Strong gales buffeted the ships on the 11th and 12th, and as the storm abated on the 13th, an American ship in distress was sighted. She had lost both her main and mizzen topmasts in the storm. *Constitution* kept her in tow all that day while her carpenters manufactured new masts from the spare spars the big frigate carried. Late that evening, the ship *Hazard* was whole again and on her own. *Constitution* and *Ontario* arrived at Gibraltar on the 17th, where they lay until 5 September.

Jones brought both of his ships back to Port Mahon for nearly a month's upkeep beginning on the 12th. The day after his arrival, he offloaded Doxey's "propello marino" into a warehouse ashore, determined to have nothing further to do with that clumsy contraption. The crew enjoyed regular liberty runs ashore where the incredible poverty of most of the people made the tars' meager monies cover legendary debaucheries.

When they got under way again on 9 October, the commodore planned to survey a somewhat greater portion of his area of responsibility than heretofore, and somewhat more energetically. Proceeding first off Genoa, he detached *Ontario* to pay a call there while he continued on toward Tripoli, going the long way around the west end of Sicily rather than through the Strait of Messina. *Ontario* once again was in company when the two arrived off the bashaw's capital on the last day of the month. The American consul came out to confer and dine with the commodore, and spend the night; then the two ships turned westward once more. There was a similar touch at Algiers on 14 November before dropping the hook again at Gibraltar. They had been under way for forty-four days, shaking out a few of the cobwebs engendered by the long port visits. But after twenty-six days in Gibraltar, Jones moved the squadron back to Port Mahon for the winter. Arriving on 21 December, they found there the schooner *Nonsuch*, 6, which would serve as Jones's dispatch boat. She was welcomed most for the mail she brought with her for both ships.

Constitution was moved into the "navy yard" on 2 January 1822 for an overhaul. On the 10th, Seamen Samuel Oakly and William Taylor were punished for drunkenness, the only instance of a flogging recorded during Jones's entire tenure. On the other side of the "ledger," the chaplain christened a child on board with the name Constitution Jones Nelson on Sunday, the 13th. How this came to be is not recorded. Neither is it known whether this log entry for the 28th is somehow related: "A Carpenter employed making a Coffin for Charles Nelson, eldest son of one of the Seamen." It appears that *Constitution* was in an unaccustomed "family way" on this trip, in any event.

The curse of the early navy—dueling—once more afflicted *Constitution*'s officers on 4 February, when Midshipman John S. Paine shot Midshipman Thomas B. Worthington through the body, killing him instantly. A court-martial was convened on the 13th to try Paine for his part in the affair. It found him guilty in findings published on the 28th, and sentenced him to be suspended from service for six months. He was detached that afternoon.

Washington's birthday at Mahon was the occasion of a 22-gun salute at high noon and the day chosen by *Constitution*'s midshipmen to host a dinner for their opposite numbers in a visiting Dutch squadron, the midshipmen from *Ontario* and *Nonsuch,* and their own lieutenants. One of the "hosts" termed it "a stupid dinner that cost me four dollars" (about a week's salary).

"Making the rounds" recommenced on 12 March, when *Constitution* and *Ontario* headed southwest and *Nonsuch,* southeast. After a week at Gibraltar, Jones sailed for Cadiz for a two-week stay before returning to Gibraltar once more on 11 April. A few days later, *Nonsuch* came in, and then the whole squadron reentered the Mediterranean on the 18th. It was a difficult time for Jones, for while at Gibraltar he had received news from home that a new baby had died and his third wife, whom he had married early in 1821, was not well. And to compound his pain, he also had received official notice that it was planned to leave him on station for yet another two years.

The squadron reached Leghorn on 2 May after looking in briefly at Port Mahon in search of expected mail. The log for the 6th contains the notation, "Carpenters scaffing [*sic*] skysail mast on the royal mast." Evidently, the sliding gunters had not proven successful and Jones was having the royal masts extended to provide fixed skypoles. The last few days of the Leghorn stay was one of repeated honors and ceremonies: side boys, salutes, mock drills, and lots of spit and polish for the visiting dignitaries, including Lord George Byron, the romantic poet. The squadron cleared for Naples late on the 23rd.

Jones now was headed for the eastern Mediterranean, which area he had thus far neglected. Greece was the reason for his interest. For many years, brigands known as Klephts had roamed the Grecian mountains in Robin Hood fashion, practicing brigandage against their Turkish overlords; similarly, Grecian pirates long had infested the island-studded waters of the Aegean Sea. The example of the French Revolution had aroused these activist elements of the native Greek populace to seek their own sovereignty. During 1821, these two groups had risen up and coalesced to provide the spearhead of an independence movement against the Turks. The moribund Ottoman Empire reacted predictably but inadequately, and it appeared that the rebels would be successful. For the United States and other maritime nations trading in the area, there was concern that their neutrality be respected by both sides, both ashore and afloat. *That* is what Jones was setting out to do: ensure that American people and property were not being victimized in the ofttimes brutal actions of the conflict. After brief stops at Naples and Messina, the three Americans headed through the Strait of Messina for the hot spot.

As the squadron entered the Aegean on the night of 16 June, "heavy firing" was heard coming from the direction of Crete. The next day, pilots taken aboard from Milos told the Americans of the serious fighting between Turks and Greeks on the big island. Standing on to the northeast through the Cyclades, at 2:00 A.M. on the 19th, Third Lt. David Geisinger, on watch, was startled by the appearance of an explosion in the direction of the strait between Lesbos and Chios. At noon were sighted the thirty units of the Turkish fleet laying to in the strait, their "Red Banners" clearly visible. *Constitution* attempted to enter the narrows, but the wind prevented it and the squadron altered course to go around the island. A Greek sloop was noted heading northwest, but neither Greek nor Turk appeared to take notice of the other or the Americans. Near sunset, an Austrian frigate was met, which reported that the large explosion had been caused by one of two Greek fire ships successfully expending itself against the 74-gun flagship of the Capudan Pasha with the loss of all hands. The second fire ship had missed its target, but all the Greeks reportedly escaped . . . in the sloop? Rounding the island on a southeast heading the next morning, the Americans sailed through the wreckage of the unfortunate Turk en route to Smyrna, which port was reached the next afternoon near sunset. They were the first American warships ever to visit that port.

Jones spent only two days at Smyrna. His consultations with the U.S. consul and local American business interests indicated no problems worthy of the commodore's attention. Passing back the way he came, Jones paused off Milos to discharge pilots on 2 July, then reconnoitered the sea lanes between there and Hydra, a Greek stronghold, before returning westward once more. A two-day provisioning call at Malta and one of just twenty minutes at Malaga, where the ship was refused quarantine anchorage, broke up the run to Gibraltar, which ended on 1 August. The "round" terminated at Port Mahon once more on the 12th, where the ships spent two weeks in upkeep, overhauling boats, painting hulls, and taking on stores—and the crew had daily liberty.

The next round was more or less done "counterclockwise:" Under way on the 26th, the squadron touched at Gibraltar, Algiers, and Leghorn before *Constitution* returned alone to Port Mahon on the last day of October. (*Ontario* had been left to idle in Leghorn while *Nonsuch* was busy running errands.) Jones made still another trip to Algiers and Gibraltar beginning on 12 November. On 6

December, the day after leaving port, *Ontario* was spoke as she headed for the Rock. Late that afternoon, an American brig was sighted with its ensign flying upside down. She proved to be the *Sultana*, out of Boston. A collision the night before had cost her her bowsprit and had fouled up much of her rigging. Taken in tow like *Hazard*, she was joined by two carpenters of "Old Ironsides," David Lloyd and A. Blakesley. The two ships parted thirty-six hours later, separated by strong gales that continued for three days. The carpenters were dropped off at Gibraltar, where the frigate would pick them up at a future date. Repeated storminess caused the big frigate to beat back and forth off the entrance for two days before she finally was able to enter Port Mahon on the 20th and snug down for the winter.

As had been the case in 1822, the winter season of 1823 was spent in overhaul. New lower stunsail booms, which doubled as boat booms when in port, were made by the carpenters, the ship was scrubbed and painted inside and out, the masts and boats refinished, and the rigging worked over. A new feature of the ship's routine was a weekly exercise at general quarters, apparently in an effort to reduce a little the very great boredom of the duty. Sail drills were held late in March to get the topmen back in harness for the coming cruising season. That season began with the squadron getting under way on 9 April. On the 11th, they were heading on a southerly course in midafternoon when the frigate was struck by a merchant schooner that passed on aft. In the squally weather, contact was lost, but the American squadron kept searching until she was rediscovered at about 5:00. Jones sent a boat, but the merchantman sank as they attempted to board her. All but the captain of *Becton* (or *Pictou*), knocked overboard in the collision, were saved.

The squadron continued its voyage to Algiers, where it lay to for a day while *Nonsuch* carried in communications to the consul. *Constitution*'s rotten flying jib boom carried away in light breezes while there, and was replaced a couple of days later as the squadron was making for Gibraltar, where, on the 23rd, a 24-gun salute was fired in honor of the coronation of King George IV.

Following eighteen days in Gibraltar, Jones made for Malaga (five days), Tunis (another five-day stay), Syracuse (six days), Malta (six days), and Leghorn (fifteen days) before touching base once more at Port Mahon on 26 July. Needless to say, nothing had occurred to disturb the tranquility. The commodore moved out again with the squadron in company on 6 August, bound for Gibraltar. A heavy gale en route cost *Constitution* her crossjack yard, but the carpenters readily replaced it while at the Rock.

The new U.S. minister to Spain, Hugh Nelson, came aboard with his suite on the 20th. They had been transported from the United States in *Congress, 36,* and had arrived in Gibraltar on 15 July. Finding that the anarchical conditions then prevailing in Spain made travel from Gibraltar to Madrid exceedingly hazardous, the minister had gone in *Congress* to Cadiz, where conditions were said to be somewhat safer for travel. Being rebuffed by those in control at Cadiz, he had returned to Gibraltar, and *Congress* had proceeded under orders to Brazil. He would make "Old Ironsides" his residence until it was safe to travel to his post.

Setting sail on 8 September, *Constitution* and *Ontario* went first to Málaga, then to their base at Port Mahon. While in that port, a heavy northwest squall "blew away" *Constitution*'s main and mizzen skysail masts. She, herself, dragged her anchor and had to drop another to keep from grounding. The ever-ready carpenters had new skypoles in place within three days. And hoping that this might be his last call at Mahon, on 6 October Jones had Doxey's paddlewheel rig returned aboard and stowed below for transport to the United States.

All three units of the squadron sortied on the 10th and made Gibraltar eleven days later. Finding that King Ferdinand VII had regained control of Spain, *Constitution* and *Nonsuch* sailed on 2 November on a quick trip to Cadiz, where Minister Nelson and party debarked for Madrid. The two ships returned to Gibraltar on the 16th. Jones knew, at this point, that he was to be relieved. His had not been a successful tour. Whether because of the man or the situation, the American squadron had become something of an embarrassment to the government. The lack of discipline and many unsettling incidents ashore caused by sailors (and officers) on liberty led the Department of the Navy to take positive action. A new commodore of the right stripe soon would straighten out the disciplinary problem. And there was an additional reason for wanting a strong leader in the Mediterranean at this time: The Greek independence movement, after initial successes, was falling apart through the stresses of internal disagreement and external pressures brought on by the advent of Egyptian forces supporting the Ottoman Turks in their efforts at suppression. This, in turn, gained the attention of the nations represented in the Congress of Vienna, who were concerned that what had been a small-scale local conflict might boil over and involve them. England, France, and Russia were moving to "confine" the war. The United States, with large trading interests in the region, had to be prepared to defend those interests.

The "changing of the watch" began on 4 December with the arrival of the ship-sloop *Erie, 18. Ontario* headed back into the Mediterranean four days later, firing a parting seven-gun salute to Jones. *Erie* was sent "above" on the 13th, while *Constitution* swung at her anchor, waiting for the moment when she could head home. As it turned out, she would wait for more than *four months*. The log on 9 April 1824 says, "At 5h 20' saw a sail with American colours—& made her number which proved to be the Cyane, our RELIEF [the log keeper's emphasis]." (This was, of course, the same *Cyane* captured by "Old Ironsides" in 1815.) At 8:30 P.M., *Cyane's* skipper, Capt. John Orde Creighton, came on board *Constitution* and, after being briefed, succeeded Jones as acting commodore, awaiting the arrival of the man specifically picked for the position. Jones got *Constitution* under way at 9:20 the next morning and made a forty-day passage to New York. Her arrival at the navy yard on 20 May somehow symbolizes the entire deployment: The larboard anchor was dropped and parted its cable; the starboard anchor was dropped and likewise parted its cable; the ship drifted aground, where she remained for nine hours before floating free and being safely anchored. Jones hauled down his pennant on the 31st, leaving *Constitution* to be readied for a return to the Middle Sea under a new commander.

SAME OLD BUSINESS—BUT UNDER NEW MANAGEMENT

Thomas Macdonough was *Constitution's* next captain. Born in Delaware in 1783, he obtained his warrant as midshipman during the Quasi-War with France. He was attached to the frigate *Philadelphia* under Bainbridge, but was on detached duty when that ship was lost to the Tripolines and so escaped imprisonment. Being familiar with the ship, he was one of those in Decatur's band that destroyed her in Tripoli in February 1804. A tall, commanding figure, young Macdonough also was in the thick of it next to Decatur in the first battle of gunboats in August 1804, making a material contribution to the capture of two of them. For these deeds, he received a sword from Congress. In the War of 1812, then-Lieutenant Macdonough had been placed in charge of the naval defense of Lake Champlain. On 11 September 1814, his small squadron of locally built craft defeated a similar British force, thereby ending almost before it had begun a planned British invasion down the Hudson River valley. For this action, he was promoted to captain and awarded a gold medal by Congress. His postwar duties had included three years as commandant of the Portsmouth Navy Yard and command of the frigate *Guerriere*, 44, in the Mediterranean. Exactly when he took command of *Constitution* is uncertain, as log keeping was not resumed until

The Hero of Lake Champlain, Thomas Macdonough commanded *Constitution* for about sixteen months in his final, fatal tour of duty. He is seen here in this engraving by J. B. Forrest, based on the portrait by John Wesley Jarvis, proudly displaying the medal of the Society of the Cincinnati, which granted honorary membership to the victorious naval officers of the War of 1812. *Official U.S. Navy photo*

the date of her sailing, 29 October 1824; he was referred to as being in command as early as 23 June.

As the ship set out for familiar waters, Secretary of the Navy Samuel Southard was taking steps to better organize the administration of his department. Newly on board *Constitution* were printed forms for monthly reports to be submitted by each ship in the squadron via the commodore. Henceforth, not only would they submit muster rolls upon sailing and when paying off, now they would regularly report on the attachments and detachments of officers and men, as well as desertions, deaths, and discharges. Secretary Southard also directed that henceforth, insofar as possible, all correspondence to the Navy Department was to be written on foolscap. (Papers all the same size would be easier to file and handle.) And not long after *Constitution* reached her duty station came a directive that, commencing 1 July 1825, seniors would make out semiannual fitness reports on all officers. The navy was taking on a look all too familiar to serving officers today.

Macdonough took *Constitution* across the Atlantic in twenty-five days, a most respectable passage. Awaiting him at Gibraltar was *Cyane.* Macdonough, being senior, took over as acting squadron commander pending the arrival of Commodore Rodgers, the stern disciplinarian and respected senior officer of the navy, whom the Secretary had selected as the man to set things to rights once more. Still, Macdonough—and undoubtedly Creighton before him—knew where the winds were blowing and already was tightening up. For starters, the days of free and easy liberty parties were over.

The two warships got under way and headed into the Mediterranean, Macdonough having decided that Gibraltar was too far removed from likely areas of interest to be the proper place to winter over. On 2 December, *Ontario* joined the flag and *Cyane* was ordered elsewhere. They lay to off Algiers for two days while communicating with the shore, then proceeded to Tunis, anchoring there on the 11th. Outgoing Consul Charles D. Coxe and his family were taken aboard *Ontario* for transportation to Syracuse, whence they could continue their journey home. The two units reached the Sicilian city shortly after noon on the 21st, joined shortly thereafter by *Erie.*

A first order of business in *Constitution* was to attend to her main mast, where evidence of rot had been discovered in its head. Into the new year the carpenters worked, excising bad wood until they were sure none remained, then fashioning a replacement piece from one of the spare spars the ship carried, and finally scarphing it in place and replacing the hoops. By 13 January 1825, the mast was being rerigged. The very next day, as the two ships swung out of phase at their anchors, *Ontario* fouled *Constitution,* carrying away her jib boom. More work for the carpenters.

Constitution and *Erie* got under way on 5 February, the former having on board the American consul for Syracuse, who wished transport to Messina. The seventy-five-mile trip into the Straits of Messina required *five days* as adverse winds caused the ships to sail miles latitudinally for every mile gained to the north. Once there, the two settled down once more into the winter routine of overhaul. Midshipman Augustus Barnhouse was required to resign on 8 March for "ingentlemanly and unofficerlike conduct," a sure sign that the "good old days" were no more. He left the ship immediately.

Back in the United States, Rodgers was receiving his orders at about this time. His primary mission was to make contact with the Turkish minister of marine, the Capudan Pasha, in order that a treaty might be drawn up placing relations between the two countries on a formal basis. Naval officers had become involved in what otherwise might be expected to be the province of the Foreign Service because European diplomats in Constantinople were maneuvering actively to prevent such talks between our minister and the Turkish foreign minister. The sultan, Mahmoud II, had let it be known that his naval commander-in-chief would be an acceptable line of communication, and since the two representatives could meet without suspicion at sea, the secrecy of the proceedings could be preserved and alien meddling avoided. The commodore's second mission was to restore good order and discipline in the squadron. For his flagship, Rodgers was given the new ship of the line *North Carolina*, 74. He sailed on 27 March.

Constitution and *Erie* continued at Messina as Rodgers beat a stormy passage across the Atlantic. *Cyane* joined them there on 6 April and *Ontario* on 9 May, the latter after having gone to Gibraltar from Syracuse. Finally, no doubt wondering why he hadn't heard any more about Rodgers, Macdonough got the entire squadron under way on 29 May and headed for Gibraltar to see if there was any news there.

Rodgers and *North Carolina* arrived in Gibraltar on the 30th. The commodore was surprised and disappointed not to find his squadron waiting for him. The more he thought about it, the angrier he got—so much so that, as he wrote Secretary Southard, "I shall feel it my duty to remove him from the command of the Constitution, for not meeting me here or apprising me where I might find him." This was to cause some harsh words to be delivered to Macdonough later when he first met Rodgers, but the latter quickly changed his attitude when he learned that his junior had been operating completely in the dark, and the two subsequently were on the best of terms. While waiting for his other ships to arrive, Rodgers provisioned for five months and then left to show the flag at Málaga, Algeciras, and Tangier.

Macdonough and the squadron sailed into Gibraltar on 12 June, learning for the first time that Rodgers was in the area and that he soon would be back. The commodore came in at 2:30 in the morning of the 17th and took over the command. For nearly a month they lay there as he inspected each ship and saw to it they were brought to his standards. *North Carolina* led them eastward from the Rock on 9 July.

Stopping briefly at Tunis, the squadron proceeded directly to the Aegean and anchored off the island of Paros early on 9 August. During the voyage to Paros, *Constitution*'s log had been filled with entries like "took in sail to maintain station on the flagship" and "lay to waiting for the squadron to come up." She was like an Arabian stallion in a herd of percherons, getting ahead of them almost without effort. What a frustrating time it must have been for her watch officers, harnessed with the responsibility of staying with a plodding liner.

The squadron was under way once more on the 14th, bound for Smyrna (Izmir today), where Rodgers hoped to learn from American consul David Offley the whereabouts of the Capudan Pasha, Khosrew. They arrived on the afternoon of the 19th. Offley had no knowledge of where Khosrew might be. But if the commodore was frustrated in the pursuit of his mission, the reputation of the American squadron was raised immeasurably when many officers and men from the ships helped fight a major fire in the city and undoubtedly saved many lives. Rodgers received a testimonial letter from the merchants commending these unselfish efforts.

On the 30th, near midnight, the squadron stood out from Smyrna, making sail for Vourla, some twenty miles to the westward, to water the ships. This was the sultry month of August, when temperatures of 95 degrees in the shade were recorded, and because of it and partly as a result of their exertions in Smyrna, a considerable number of men came down sick. *Constitution* had at least 10 percent of her crew on the binnacle list. A temporary hospital was established on a small island, variously called Round or Uras Island, where it was hoped better ventilation and cooling sea breezes would correct the situation. In the week that followed, *Constitution* lost Marine Pvts. William Sawyer, David Lockhart, and James W. Swords, and Ordinary Seaman John Sloan to the malaise.

The squadron moved on shortly before noon on 8 September, Rodgers intending to make for Napoli de Romania (today Nauplia), then the capital of the Greek revolutionary government. However, in rounding north of Uras Island, *Constitution* went aground. Rodgers signaled the remaining ships to reanchor and then came on board the frigate to learn firsthand the seriousness of the accident. Happily, there was no important damage; the ship was refloated at 9:00 that evening, and all were under way once more early the following morning.

Napoli de Romania is located at the head of the Gulf of Argos on the west coast of Morea (the Peloponnisos), a craggy town of great natural defenses. It was to here the Greek revolutionaries had retreated, forced back by the unremitting pressure of the Egyptian army, which had entered the fray on the side of the Turks seven months earlier. So long as they could maintain their link with the sea, the Greeks could not be ousted from this stronghold. When the

This portrait shows Daniel Todd Patterson as a lieutenant commandant on the New Orleans Station. There, in the waning days of the War of 1812, his efforts contributed directly to Gen. Andrew Jackson's victory over the British at Chalmette, south of the city. Following his tour in command of *Constitution*, he served as a naval commissioner, commanded the Mediterranean Squadron again, and was commandant of the Washington Navy Yard. He died in 1839. *Official U.S. Navy photo*

American squadron arrived on the afternoon of the 12th, it was well received by the struggling revolutionary leadership. They could not, however, enlighten the commodore as to the current location of the Capudan Pasha. Rodgers sailed on the 18th, having decided to give over his attempt to make contact with the Turk during that sailing season, and made directly for Gibraltar. *Ontario* was left in the Aegean to represent American interests at sea during the winter.

A New Commander

By the time Gibraltar was reached on 9 October, Macdonough was in a bad way. He had been suffering for some time from consumption, and it was apparent that his condition had grown markedly worse. In response to his request, Rodgers directed Flag Capt. Daniel T. Patterson to proceed to *Constitution* and relieve the ailing hero of Lake Champlain. Patterson reported aboard on the 14th and took command without ceremony, either late on the 16th or early on the 17th. Five days later, attended by Surgeon William Turk, Macdonough left "Old Ironsides" as a passenger in the merchant brig *Edwin*, bound for Philadelphia. He died just as the capes of Delaware were sighted some three weeks later.

New Yorker Daniel Todd Patterson was a little more than two years younger than his predecessor, and like him had become a midshipman during the Quasi-War. He had been shipmates with both Macdonough and Jones in *Philadelphia* during the Barbary War and, with Jones, had gone into captivity when that unfortunate ship was lost. Subsequently, he had served on the Gulf Coast and had spent all of the War of 1812 in Louisiana, making significant contributions to the defense of New Orleans. For these actions, he was highly commended by Gen. Andrew Jackson and the Congress, and promoted to captain in February 1815. He had remained in the South until selected as flag captain by Rodgers.

While the squadron was at Gibraltar, it was joined by the frigate *Brandywine*, 44, on her maiden voyage. This "grandchild" of *Constitution* had just returned the Marquis de Lafayette to France following his memorable "reunion" tour of America, and arrived without either Como. Charles Morris or Capt. George C. Read, both of whom had escorted the marquis to Paris.

Following a stay of more than five weeks, Rodgers left Gibraltar for Port Mahon with the squadron—*North Carolina, Constitution, Brandywine,* and *Erie.* The thirteen-day voyage was completed on 29 November. *Erie* was to relieve *Ontario* in the Aegean.

Constitution, the grand old lady of the squadron, was assigned an overhaul at the navy yard in Mahon, whence she moved on 3 December. Two days later, amidst the hustle and bustle of stripping ship, Patterson was ordered by the commodore to assume command of *Brandywine*, per the desires of Secretary Southard. First Lt. Elie A. F. Vallette became the "commanding officer" of "Old Ironsides." (In those days, a full-fledged captain of a ship might also be known as its "commander," but a senior man with more restricted powers, what we might term an "officer in charge" today, was called the "commanding officer." Thus, Vallette was to be the frigate's lord and master while she was in overhaul. The problem of a "commander" would be addressed when she was ready again for sea.) Through the remainder of December 1825 and most of January 1826, *Constitution* lay pierside with her stores, ammunition, and rigging ashore. Her guns were shifted back and forth about the decks as gangs of caulkers made her tight once more. The work schedule ran dawn to dusk, with no mention of any liberty

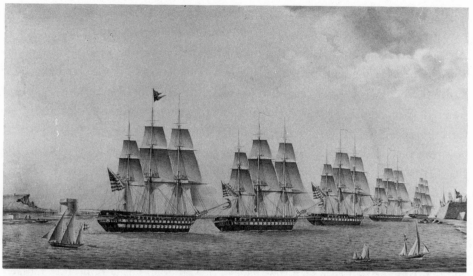

This painting by Mahonese artist A. Carlotta purports to show the U.S. Mediterranean Squadron under Commodore Rodgers as it departs Port Mahon on 26 January 1825. The first three ships, from the left, are the liner *North Carolina* and frigates *Brandywine* and *Constitution*. The last two (order unknown) are the ship-sloops (or corvettes) *Erie* and *Ontario*. The incident is fictitious: *Constitution* was at Syracuse, Sicily, the entire month of January 1825. *Official U.S. Navy photo*

parties (nor any duels). Colors were lowered to half-mast on 22 January, when the squadron learned of Macdonough's passing; *Brandywine* fired nine minute-guns. The next day, Read, newly arrived from France, relieved Vallette and became *Constitution*'s commander. Work virtually was completed by the end of the month; the frigate moved back out to anchorage on 3 February.

The schooner *Porpoise*, 12, arrived in port on the 16th bearing orders for *Brandywine* to return to the United States. Being senior to Read, and not wishing to pass up any opportunity for notable service, Patterson requested and got Rodgers's permission to exchange commands with his junior, just as Rodgers himself had done with Hull in 1810 in another swap involving *Constitution*. The actual exchange was made on the 21st, although further personnel exchanges and transfers went on for several days. Two notable additions to *Constitution*'s officer personnel were Schoolmaster George Jones, who subsequently wrote sketches of life aboard as he found it, and Midshipman David Dixon Porter, much later to be the navy's second admiral. *Brandywine* sailed on the 26th.

Rodgers got his squadron under way for the sailing season on 10 April. He paid the usual call at Gibraltar—more than three weeks—and made stops at Algiers (three days) and Tunis (another three) before setting sail for the Aegean and a hoped-for rendezvous with Capudan Pasha Khosrew. Pauses at Milos and Paros further delayed his arrival at Vourla until 19 June. There, the squadron watered; *Constitution* took on 35,150 gallons. From thence, on the 30th, the Americans proceeded to Mytilene on the island of Tenedos, arriving on 2 July. The local governor provided Rodgers with the certain information that Khosrew was at the Dardanelles with his whole fleet and offered to provide guides for an overland journey hence, should the American wish to pay him a visit. Having offered Rodgers guided access to his country, the official *then* asked what country was represented by the flag with the red and white stripes! The commodore was well aware that Bainbridge had visited Turkey a quarter century earlier, but the Turk said it was the first time he had ever seen that flag. (The Capudan Pasha himself, on a later occasion, also would express ignorance of where the United States might be.)

On the 4th, just when some of the American officers were hoping to celebrate their national birthday with excursions ashore, the calm of the morning was broken by the distant sighting of ships coming up over the northern horizon. It was a Turkish fleet of two liners, four frigates, and seventeen corvettes and brigs. Uncertain of their intentions, the Americans beat to quarters. As the Turkish flagship glided past *North Carolina*, that ship began firing the traditional 4th of July noontime salute. Thinking it was for himself, the delighted Turk, Khosrew's immediate junior, the Capudan Bey, responded in kind.

As the fleet swept into anchorage off Mytilene, one of the frigates ran aground, but came off a few hours later, much as *Constitution* herself had done at Vourla the year before. Nonetheless, the report of this grounding caused the Capudan Pasha himself to come to Tenedos to investigate the incident, thereby saving Rodgers his planned journey overland. On the 6th and 7th, the American and the Turk exchanged calls and conducted the long-awaited negotiations. Although no treaty was immediately forthcoming, the stage was set for the completion of the desired pact four years later.

On the 9th, Rodgers got his squadron under way so that he could reconnoiter the entrance to the Dardanelles. When the ships bearing the strange striped flag appeared off the forts, paroxysms of alarm shook the defenses, whose commanders sent off alerts and requests for support to repel the enemy as far as Constantinople. The Capudan Pasha, having been made the wiser by his recent meetings with Rodgers, is said merely to have laughed at the fears of his subordinates and enhanced his reputation with the depth of his knowledge. The Americans returned to their anchorage off Mytilene.

A second division of Turkish warships appeared on the 14th, this time including Khosrew in his flagship, bearing his "ensign . . . of silk; a pure red, and so long as to reach the water, when the breeze declines." The next day, the two leaders exchanged salutes and visits, followed by a further exchange of visits and gifts by ships' captains and officers. All considered it a very successful day—except, perhaps, the enlisted men who had been kept at their stations and performing, largely from dawn to dusk.

By Monday, the 17th, all were exhausted by these expressions of friendship and amity, and ready to get on to other things. Rodgers got *North Carolina* and *Constitution* under way late that afternoon. (*Ontario, Erie,* and *Porpoise* all had been sent on other duties during the preceding days.) They beat to windward (north) and then, with all sails set, came down on the Turkish fleet, running close aboard with shrouds manned with cheering sailors before going on their way.

The two big ships were back at Vourla the next morning, where they remained until 11 August, watering and doing routine maintenance. From there, they went to Athens, but remained only a few hours on the 13th because a sudden storm threatened them at anchorage. Next, at Milos, they were rejoined by *Ontario.* Sailing on the 21st, Rodgers left *Ontario* behind in her now-familiar commerce protection role and returned down the Mediterranean to Port Mahon, dropping the hook in those familiar waters on 10 September.

While the rest of the squadron continued active in representing American interests around the Middle Sea, *Constitution* remained at Port Mahon (and Patterson with his mistress) for the rest of the year and beyond. Evidently her thirty years of service were beginning to tell markedly. In November 1826, Rodgers ordered the frigate's entire crew have their terms of service extended to 31 July 1828. Thirty-two refused to accept the order and apparently were exchanged with sailors from homeward bound units. In March 1827, her decayed main mast was sent ashore for repairs that required more than two weeks of full-time effort by the carpenter's gang. On the 30th, she got under way for the east, under orders to take up duties previously assigned to *Erie,* which had returned to the United States, and *Ontario.* The repairs effected during her long stay must have been superlative, for she made the run to the vicinity of Malta in just two days—a run of some five hundred miles.

Patterson made the routine calls at Milos and Vourla before arriving at Smyrna on 25 April for briefing by the steadfast Offley. He sailed on 3 May for the short trip to Scio (Chios) where, in 1822, the Turks had massacred 80,000–90,000 Greeks and destroyed the city. Moving south and east from there, *Constitution* sailed past Samos and came to anchor not far from the ruins of the city of Ephesus, which had been founded by the Greeks in the eleventh century B.C., and once had been a Roman provincial capitol. The captain and his officers made a brief sortie ashore to see the Temple of Diana, the Arcadian Way, and the church where Saul of Tarsus had preached.

Having satisfied his curiosity, Patterson got under way again on the 7th, heading west. Passing between Tinos and Andros, then past Kea, he came to the island of Aegina on the 10th. Admiral Canaris of the Greek revolutionary navy paid a call the next day. A short sail on the 14th brought the big frigate off Athens, which city then was being besieged by the Turks.

Patterson next decided to check up on the situation at the centers of revolutionary power, so he headed south on the 17th, and, after calling at Paros for four days, went on to Napoli de Romania. On 1 June, the captain had to go ashore to settle a problem arising over the handling of some supplies brought in by the American ship *Chanticleer*, which, it appeared, were going into the wrong hands. In conjunction with the authorities, things soon were straightened out. Greek General Colocotroni paid an official call to the ship later in the day. Clearing the port the next morning, *Constitution* returned to Smyrna, where she arrived on the 8th.

Fourth of July 1827 was spent at Smyrna. *Constitution* fired a 21-gun salute at high noon, in accordance with the custom, and received in response the same salute from the men-of-war of England, France, Holland, and Austria then in port. Two days later, she shifted to Vourla for water, and then on the 12th made for Athens once more. On her arrival on the 13th, it was learned that the Turks were essentially in control of the city. The frigate moved to Salamis on the 18th, where Patterson acquired an ancient statue. The statue borne back to the United States from Psyttaleia Island was a headless one of Demeter (or the Roman Ceres), goddess of harvests. Patterson ultimately presented it to the Pennsylvania Academy of Fine Arts in Philadelphia, where it was installed over the entrance.

At Aegina on the 27th, Patterson exchanged visits with the expatriate British naval officer, Admiral Lord Cochrane, who was present in his flagship, the frigate *Hellas*, and who, with others both famous and infamous from many lands, had come to help the downtrodden Greeks throw off the oppressive yoke of the Ottoman sultan—a mixture of romantic idealism and political humbuggery in a small corner of the world.

Constitution met *Porpoise* at Milos on 2 August. The latter brought Patterson the news that he now was the commander of the American squadron in the Mediterranean, Rodgers having sailed from Gibraltar in *North Carolina* the previous 31 May. (Unbeknownst to Patterson, his tenure as commodore already had ended, for Como. William M. Crane had entered the Mediterranean early the previous month in USS *Java*. Uncertain communications would keep him in the dark for some time to come.) Knowing from Lord Cochrane and other sources that British, French, and Russian intervention in the revolution rapidly was bringing things to a climax, "Commodore" Patterson decided that the place for him to be was Smyrna where, through the consul, he could gain the most accurate information possible, and where resided the largest American business community in the region. There he anchored on 7 August to await developments.

August became September, and then October, and still nothing decisive had happened. Late in the month, as Patterson had decided to "take a turn" around the war zone and was about to weigh anchor, a French steamer came in with the stunning news that a combined British-French-Russian force had completely destroyed the Turkish fleet at a place called Navarino on 20 October. The news, of course, caused a sensation. Most feared was the reaction of the Turks, who already in this civil strife had made a reputation for awful and fearful decimation of civilian and alien populations. The extensive foreign business community at Smyrna was apprehensive about what the Turks might do for vengeance. Foreign warships then in port, other than *Constitution,* moved close inshore and began outloading their nationals. Patterson made all preparations to fight quietly and kept his ship in her normal anchorage, a gesture appreciated by the local pasha, who swore to keep any rioters out of the foreign quarter. For days, rumors ran rampant as to what was happening elsewhere, but there continued to be tranquility in Smyrna and silence from the direction of Constantinople. Only the American consulate continued to fly its flag, the sure sign that the consul still was in residence. November came, and with it a lessening of tensions and a growing confidence that the situation was as stable as could be expected. Satisfied that he had done his duty, Patterson got *Constitution* under way down the Mediterranean on the 15th and arrived back in Mahon for a reunion with his mistress exactly a month later, having stopped for two days at Tunis enroute.

As had become her routine, *Constitution* moved into the yard for winter refit on 9 January 1828, where she remained until 3 April. On the 28th of the month, fully provisioned, she turned her bow again westward, heading for home. She made the expected stop at Gibraltar, but adverse winds kept her in port much longer than any of her crew wished. *Constitution* sailed at last from Gibraltar on 23 May, after three years and eight months of humdrum duty in the Mediterranean, and arrived back in Boston on the 4th of July, just in time to fire the traditional salute at high noon. The task of preparing her for ordinary required until the 19th, when Patterson hauled down her commissioning pennant. None were sure it ever would be hoisted again.

*A Most
Fortunate Ship*

CHAPTER THIRTEEN

Rebirth and Brouhaha

A TIME OF UNCERTAINTY

When *Constitution* came back to Boston on 19 July 1828, she was a venerable thirty-one years old. There were no orders from the Board of Commissioners to ready the ship for further service so the gallant frigate was placed in ordinary. A "house" was erected to protect the spar deck from the weather.

In the fall, the ship routinely was surveyed (inspected) at the direction of the board. It was found that her frame was sound, but that she would need much new planking inside and out, as well as new coppering and total recaulking. She also would require new lower masts, new yards throughout, a new jib boom, a maintopmast, and several stunsail booms. All running rigging and two anchor cables would have to be replaced. Five boats had to be surveyed, as would many blocks and deadeyes. Sails and awnings, of course, would have to be new. Repairs could restore gun carriages to service, but all carronades needed new beds and slides. In his estimate, Naval Constructor Josiah Barker tallied all these items up and found they would require more than $112,800.

Barker revised his estimate downward in March 1829. On 1 September 1829 and again on 31 July 1830, she was end-for-end ("winded") to even the effects of sun, wind, and weather on her. On 17 August 1830, Secretary of the Navy John Branch requested that the commissioners provide him with data on "all works which are now in progress for repair of vessels, also a list of all such as are now deemed to require repairs." Statements were to be appended to this latter list detailing conditions of these vessels as disclosed by formal survey, the cost of effecting repairs, and the value of each unit when repaired.

As a result of this directive, yard commandant Charles Morris was to provide the requisite information on *Columbus, Constitution,* and *Independence,* all then in ordinary at Boston. Barker conducted the actual surveys and, in *Constitution*'s case, again noted a sound frame and keel. Beyond that, however, nearly everything was in need of replacement or very extensive repairs. And in the normal way of human events, the projected cost had risen to $157,903. If done, the resultant ship, it was thought, would "be worth about eighty percent of a new ship of the same class." By comparison, repairs to *Independence* would cost over 40 percent more while those to *Columbus* would be 35 percent less. Morris sent these estimates to the board on 28 August.

Enter Oliver Wendell Holmes, Sr.

Before these reports reached him, the Secretary was asked by the board specifically for reports on *Constitution* and *Macedonian.* The fact of this request, together with the more general one calling for information on all ships, soon became public knowledge, and, just as quickly, was misinterpreted. On 14 September, in the Boston *Advertiser* there appeared an article erroneously reporting the navy's decision condemning the frigate to the shipbreakers. It said, in part: "Such a national object of interest, so endeared to our national pride as Old Ironsides is, should never by any act of our government cease to belong to the Navy, so long as our country is to be found upon the map of nations." Two days later, again in the *Advertiser,* there appeared a poem by a young student, inspired by the article, that would preclude any course of action by the navy other than total restoration. Oliver Wendell Holmes had written the stirring stanzas of "Old Ironsides," the first of which runs

> *Ay, tear her tattered ensign down!*
> *Long has it waved on high,*
> *And many an eye has danced to see*
> *That banner in the sky;*
> *Beneath it rung the battle shout,*
> *And burst the cannon's roar;*
> *The meteor of the ocean air*
> *Shall sweep the clouds no more.*

Published by other newspapers around the country, and distributed by handbill in some cities, these lines aroused a public clamor.

Largely ignored in the "to-do" was the 18 September edition of the highly respected *Niles' Weekly Register,* which noted the alarmist report, but doubted that "those having superior authority" would ever "permit a proceeding so repugnant to the best feelings of all the people." If, indeed, wrote the editor, the *Constitution* were too far gone, "let her be hauled upon the land, and have a house built over her, to remain so long as her wood and iron will hold together."

While the noise ebbed and flowed across the land, the commissioners received the survey report and passed it to Secretary Branch on the 20th. In two days, the directive was en route to Boston to repair *Constitution* "with as little delay as practicable."

During the fall and early winter, Commodore Morris proceeded with a determination of his supply needs. He estimated that 59,000 feet of white pine was required, together with 31 yellow pine beams for the berth and orlop decks. On 24 February 1831, Morris recommended to Commodore Rodgers, who again headed the board, that repairs to the ship be delayed until the drydock then under construction in the yard was available, if there was no "urgent necessity for her services." He noted that, because of her "age and frequent repairs," she was considerably hogged; "her original lines . . . altered and injured." These defects, he felt, could best be corrected by placing her in the dock. Should they heave her down, as had been done in the past, "The defect will be still further increased, and besides the risk . . . the repairs cannot be so advantageously or so thoroughly made as in a dock."

The decision to retain "Old Ironsides" in service had been heartily endorsed by the American people. It took little consideration on the part of the commissioners to await the availability of a drydock for the best job possible. Some preparatory work was done in and for the ship as she waited. By early April, all of her bulkheads had been taken down to ease the passage of workers and materials through the ship. Later, a survey of remaining stored rigging found it unfit for further use, suitable only for "junk." By spring 1832, all articles and fittings had been removed.

Commodore Bainbridge relieved Morris in the summer of 1832. Commanding officer of *Constitution* for a short time in 1812–1813, and having attended to her material needs in a previous tour as navy yard commandant, he was well acquainted with the ship.

Construction of the dry dock proceeded without any major interruptions. The board wrote to Bainbridge on 7 November to have *Constitution* ready for docking "as early in the spring as the weather will justify." On 4 December, they

Jesse Duncan Elliott had a quixotic career in the navy, to say the least. Hero of an early minor action in the War of 1812, his subsequent conduct at the Battle of Lake Erie, when he failed to support Como. Oliver Hazard Perry, forever cast a shadow on his character. Numerous times in his later career he acted in alleged ignorance of orders, and his retrospective statements about such instances bear little relation to what was recorded officially or by contemporaries. His term of association with *Constitution*, then, is unique in her history. *Official U.S. Navy photo*

inquired when the ship could be docked and how soon she would be ready for sea. The answers, dated 28 December, were "April 1" and "four months."

By the time April came around, Bainbridge had submitted a letter resigning command of the yard because of failing health. While awaiting a successor, he was responsible for readying "Old Ironsides" for docking. Mid-month found the protective roof removed and the ballast being taken out. On 28 April 1833, Bainbridge reported the ship "in readiness to be placed in the dock." In May, Como. Jesse Duncan Elliott appeared as Bainbridge's replacement. A cantankerous and unpredictable individual amid equally feisty peers, Elliott, as will be related, was the cause of the most ludicrous episodes in the ship's history.

Late in the month, the board ordered that *Constitution*'s docking be held in readiness as President Andrew Jackson had indicated a desire to "witness the ceremony." It was expected he would be in Boston between 25 June and 1 July. On 23

June, Rodgers wrote to Elliott ordering him to let *Constitution* "stand on her blocks so as to straiten [*sic*] her." The ship was to be stripped as far as necessary to determine the extent of repairs needed, but since the board expected to be in Boston about 10 July, more "particular directions in relation to her repairs" would wait. In the meantime, Elliott could prepare materials and augment the workforce in light of obvious repairs, but, came the admonishment, "Great care must be taken to preserve the original form and dimensions" of the ship "in the course of repairs."

First Dry-docking

At 5:30 the next morning, 24 June, shorn of masts, but with Vice President Martin Van Buren, Navy Secretary Levi Woodbury, War Secretary Lewis Cass, and Massachusetts Governor Levi Lincoln in attendance, *Constitution* was dry-docked. (President Jackson was in town but "unable to be present.") In command once again, especially for the occasion, was Commodore Hull, up from his post as commandant of the Washington Navy Yard. By 1:00 P.M., she was safely "shored and secured." Scrapings from her barnacle-encrusted bottom became much sought-after mementos of the occasion.

During this month of June, Elliott began a project that would bring controversy swirling about his head. The precise reasons for his action have been clouded by the subsequent uproar and apologia, but it was at this time that he ordered from a twenty-eight-year-old local woodcarver named Laban S. Beecher a figurehead of Andrew Jackson, which he planned to install in *Constitution*. He apparently expected to curry favor with the president despite existing regulations that limited use of figureheads to ships of the line.[1]

The commissioners were more than a month late in making their inspection of the yard and the ship, not arriving until 15 August. The very next day, however, a letter was sent to Elliott, giving priority to the restoration of *Constitution* over other yard work. It further directed him to conform to "her former internal arrangements, as reflects the position of her decks—accommodation for officers—store rooms and similar objects, taking great care to preserve the original form of the bottom." (Upon docking, the keel was found not only to be badly hogged, but some thirty inches out of line, as well.)

Hull, evincing his continuing interest in the ship, wrote to Elliott at about this same time inviting him to make requisition on the Washington Navy Yard for all iron and composition castings needed for her repair. (Earlier, Elliott had been told to ship all copper sheathing to Hull for recycling. The latter subsequently had canes, snuffboxes, and many other articles made from the wood and metal removed from the ship and sent to "notable persons" around the country. The commissioners arranged to have picture frames made for their offices. President Jackson even received a small phaeton made from *Constitution* wood by the firm of Knowles and Thayer in East Amherst, Massachusetts, in which he rode during the inaugural ceremonies for his successor.)

In September, Chief Naval Constructor Samuel Humphreys, son of Joshua, arrived in Boston to review the frigate's restoration plans and settle any questions Elliott had. His guidance was given to Elliott on 16 September, in line with earlier general directives to maintain or restore original characteristics. Work proceeded apace, and by late November outside planking had been completed below the wales and the clamps were in for the berth deck. Elliott recommended to the board that No. 1 felt (of Russian manufacture) be used "before coppering her" rather than No. 2 (British made). He wished instructions as soon as practicable in order to press on with the work. The board's response was dated just three days after Elliott's request: Use English felt because it is of closer texture, more consistent thickness, and more worm resistant than the Russian.

Constitution's berth deck beams were being put in as December began, and she was planked up to her "thick-strake." Elliott noted that if the mild weather then being experienced continued through the winter, the ship repairs would be completed by early spring. Tests of the rigging removed in 1828 showed it to be useless and to require complete replacement, but the board told him not to fit her with rigging until further orders.

The weather continued unseasonably mild into the new year. On 8 January 1834, the board was advised that the berth deck had been laid, outside planking completed to the port sills, and the ports themselves were being framed. The gun deck beams would soon be in place; the ceiling planking had almost reached that level. It might even be possible to undock her by 15 March, Elliott reported.

In the next five weeks, work progressed to the point where the spar deck planking was about to be laid. Barker, in immediate charge of the restoration, recommended to the board, with Elliott's concurrence, the installation of Lester "metal (bilge) pumps" on the gun deck and hoped for a quick answer so that the spar deck work wouldn't be delayed. The response, dated 24 February, specified two chain pumps of seven-inch bore to be installed abaft the mainmast and two Baker's pumps forward "as heretofore."

The figurehead of Andrew Jackson carved by Laban S. Beecher at Boston with the replacement head by Charles J. Dodge of New York. (Note the seam at what appears as the jawline.) It was replaced by a more sophisticated version, by J. D. and W. H. Fowle at Boston, after the ship's return from her circumnavigation. *Official U.S. Navy photo*

The board, in the same letter, took up some matters concerning external decoration. When finishing the stern some "slight carved work of the scroll or wreath character may be adopted to guide the painter and relieve the flatness." The billet head and curve of the cutwater were to be restored as they had been, but the bow head area was to be protected by "close woodwork as was recently done with *United States.*"

FIGUREHEAD FUSS

From the foregoing, it would appear that the powers in Washington were unaware of Elliott's project to place a figurehead of the president on *Constitution.*

If that was the case, the cat shortly would be out of the bag, for the word was out in Boston. Because of Jackson's western background and his actions against the Second United States Bank, he was a most unpopular figure in that city. The local people assailed the planned "desecration" of "their" beloved frigate with handbills demanding action.

With such inflammatory calls in circulation, and with Beecher, the carver, telling him of being approached by irate citizens, Elliott was forced to surface the project. On 1 March, he wrote the commissioners that the figurehead nearly was finished and bore a "remarkable strong resemblance" to the president. He said he would await their decision as to what was to be done with the now-controversial piece and offered as the lame excuse for having gotten into the predicament that "on an examination of the papers on file in my office I could find nothing which had offered as a guide to my predecessors but what left the ornamentation of public vessels built or repairing at this yard entirely to their discretion."

The board responded to Elliott's surprising report by calling his attention to published regulations, which required a commandant, in making repairs, "to act in strict conformity to the instructions from the Board . . . or to the report of the officers of survey, and no additional repairs, or alterations, of any moment are to be made, without instructions from the Navy Commissioners." The board felt that this had "been averted to" with the long-established usage of substituting billets for figureheads in vessels less than "Ships of the Line," and should have led Elliott to consult with the board before giving the order. However, since the figurehead was nearly finished, Elliott either could put it aboard *Constitution*, or hold it for installation on either *Vermont* or *Virginia*, ships of the line then under construction at the yard.

Elliott also had had Beecher carve bas relief busts of Isaac Hull, William Bainbridge, and Charles Stewart, and had them installed on the stern of the ship. They outlived the original Jackson figurehead and apparently remained on board for forty years. About the 21st, Beecher came to Elliott with a report that "three highly respectable citizens had offered him $1,500 for permission to carry the image away in the night." The artist thought he might be able to realize as much as $20,000 if he chose to bargain, according to one account. The pot was beginning to boil.

Elliott's immediate response to the threat was to order a party of seamen to Beecher's studio on Commercial Street to bring the Jackson figurehead by boat to the yard and safety. The statue, roughed out only to the shoulders, was placed in the Machinery House near the dry dock (the uss *Constitution* Museum today), where Beecher subsequently worked. Later on the 21st, upon hearing of rumors that a raid might be attempted by local citizenry, the Elliott directed M.Cmdt. John Percival of the receiving ship *Columbus* to take aboard a supply of cutlasses and boarding pikes with which to arm the yard's seamen should the need arise. There was no raid.

Despite the distractions, Elliott found time to write to the board about another item of *Constitution*'s restoration. Work on the ship had progressed to the point where the joiners soon would be erecting bulkheads and otherwise rendering the ship more habitable. Elliott sought the board's guidance as to the kind of wood to be used in and whether or not "the Bulwarks and stern part of the cabin be ceiled" (i.e., sheathed), and what with. Three days later, the board directed that the after cabin be fitted with hardwood. The forward bulkhead of the main cabin, together with those for the wardroom, steerage, and all others, were to be made of pine. The stern and sides of the cabin were not to be covered, but the overhead could be ceiled with pine and painted.

This decision by the board did not satisfy Elliott. He wanted a more sumptuous cabin, and on 5 April he wrote again, pleading that "a slight ceiling be put upon the stern and sides and painted." The board, however, stood firm on the grounds that ceiling those areas would "injure the durability of the planking."

The Jackson figurehead was put firmly in place on *Constitution* during April. By the latter part of the month, all of the outer hull work was done, and the ship was ready for caulking and a first coat of paint. A proposal to relocate the channels higher on the ship's sides was being discussed between Boston and Washington, but this was relatively superficial work and had no immediate impact on the progress of work.

But at 9:00 A.M. on 1 May, the ship carpenters hired to copper the ship struck for higher pay. Those working at the local civilian shipyards were getting a dollar more a day than Barker was willing to pay. Elliott, noting that there were many other carpenters working elsewhere in the yard at the lower pay, said he wouldn't pay them even one cent more. He gave them twenty-four hours to reconsider their position. Most returned to the job that afternoon; all were back the next morning and the coppering neared completion a week later.

The board, curious to know how successful the restorers had been on straightening *Constitution* and reducing the hog, on the 7th ordered Elliott to plan on taking appropriate measurements before and after her undocking. Using the gun deck as the reference plane, two sets of sights were to be taken at points 6,

Constitution is shown moored outboard of the inactive ship of the line *Columbus,* herself alongside a quay wall at the Boston Navy Yard in this contemporary woodcut. Partially visible to the right is the razee *Independence.* Clearly evident at the frigate's bow is the offending figurehead of Andrew Jackson. *Official U.S. Navy photo*

31, 56, 81, 106, 131, and 156 feet abaft the apron (stem), and 4 feet forward of "the after end of the gun deck plank." Forty tons of ballast were to be emplaced prior to undocking.

All the while *Constitution*'s restoration progressed, the local press pursued Elliott. Some, the most kindly, referred to him as "Mr. Elliott," the others, as "an enemy to your country," a "political partizan," "sychophant," and "coward." He was threatened with tar and feathers, and assassination. The figurehead was termed "the desecration of this national ship." Through it all, Elliott stuck to his avowed purpose of honoring the president.

A PLOT IS HATCHED

Sometime during May or early June, there arrived in Boston from the West Indies a merchant skipper with a cargo of sugar. While idling in the offices of his employers, Henry and William Lincoln, the conversation turned to the fig-urehead controversy that had Boston so embroiled. The master of the ship, Samuel Worthington Dewey, later cousin to the then-unborn "Hero of Manila Bay," George Dewey, off-handedly stated he would get rid of the offending Jack-son on the smallest of wagers. The younger Lincoln jokingly offered a hundred dollars and Dewey, with a reputation for daring, quickly took it up. The conversation passed on to other topics and the Lincolns forgot about it.

On Saturday, 21 June, *Constitution* was undocked, still without channels installed, but with the stumpy figurehead of Jackson, draped in cloak and baggy trousers, and with a top hat, prominent at her bow. Elliott had her moored between *Columbus* and *Independence* (a razee in ordinary). To watch over his pride and joy, a guard was placed forward on *Columbus*, in a position from whence he could view the figure; a second was stationed on the forecastle of *Constitution;* and a third on the wharf nearby. The moorings were so arranged that, at night, a light from a forward gun port in *Columbus* would illuminate Jackson. And in the "immense crowd" watching the undocking evolution was young, observant Sam Dewey.

Two days later, Elliott submitted to the board his report on the "before and after" sights taken as the ship was undocked. Differences, he wrote, could be noted at only three of the eight stations used. These were insufficiently large (three-eighths of an inch) to be of concern. *Constitution* had, indeed, been "straightened." Rodgers directed Elliott, in a letter on 2 July, to reinstall the covering that had protected her from the elements prior to her docking. The frigate would not be needed before the following spring.

ANDREW JACKSON BEHEADED

July 2nd, however, was a day of infamy as far as Elliott was concerned. By nightfall, a thunderstorm "of unusual violence" rapidly was enveloping Boston. The thick blackness was broken intermittently by crashing lightning bolts in whose flashes might have been seen a small boat with a lone occupant pull away from Gray's Wharf and head for the navy yard on the other side of the Charles River. The occupant was twenty-eight-year-old Sam Dewey, bent on winning his bet. He soon was below the tumblehome of *Independence.* Slowly, silently, he sculled forward around her bow and slipped beneath the cutwater of "Old Ironsides."

Dewey climbed up the manropes and worked his way out to a position forward of the cutwater and slightly below the top of the figurehead, his back to the bowsprit stays. Fortuitously, the planking of the bow head area had been completed earlier that day, offering him a perfect shield from observation by the forecastle sentry. He began by starting a cut through the neck of the figurehead, but the screech of metal on metal shortly told him he had hit a bolt. Looking to see if anyone had heard the noise, he spotted the wharf sentry peering intently in his general direction. Dewey remained stock still, until the torrential rain overcame the guard's curiosity and sent him scurrying back to his shack. Young Sam began his next cut 'twixt chin and lower lip, and this time met no obstacles. In a moment or two the deed was done: "Old Hickory's" pine pate rested securely in the headsman's burlap bag.

Returning to his boat the way he came, Dewey found that it had swung in close to *Constitution* in the meantime and very nearly had been swamped by water draining from the frigate's deck. Gingerly he got aboard and carefully worked his way clear of the moored ship. He succeeded in getting his craft safely back to Boston's friendly shore. Soaking wet and triumphant, he went immediately to his mother's house on School Street and hid his trophy in the woodshed.

With the clear dawning of the 3rd, Dewey's handiwork became known to Lt. James Armstrong, whose unhappy duty it was, as an officer serving in *Columbus*, to report the decapitation to Elliott. Elliott lost little time in penning a long report to the secretary of the navy, now Mahlon Dickerson, and requesting instructions. Bostonians in the main were delighted by the big joke that had been played on the cantankerous commandant. The severed head made the rounds of a number of club meetings and parties in the area, including one at which forty-four prominent Whigs honored Nicholas Biddle, president of the United States Bank.

At the yard, Elliott promptly increased the security forces around "Old Ironsides," with a naval officer and a Marine posted at night specifically to defend the remains of the figurehead from any further depredations. A wise move. A second attempt by persons unknown was made on the evening of the 5th. Soon discovered, one of the infiltrators escaped over the yard wall. A second man was thought to have drowned. The rowboat they had used in their approach became the commandant's prize.

Some time later, Dewey took *his* prize to Washington, intending to deliver it to President Jackson himself. But the president was seriously ill when Dewey arrived and so, after apprising Vice President Van Buren of his mission, he was directed to deliver the remains to the secretary of the navy. Dickerson's first reaction to the sight was to threaten legal action; but, recognizing that the suit would have to be tried in Boston, he acknowledged Dewey's immunity and allowed him to leave after hearing his story in detail. The Secretary then wrote to Elliott and told him to do nothing further concerning the figurehead for the time being, but to cover the raw cut with a tarpaulin. The public in Boston was to be allowed to calm down and find other amusement.

OVERHAUL CONCLUDES

On 15 August, the commissioners were in Boston once again, to apprise themselves with the progress of yard development and to check on the ship work being done. Concerning *Constitution*, they directed the installation of her channels in a new fashion then being tested. They were to be so located that their undersides would be placed on "the lower part of the second strake above the spar deck sill . . . so far from the seam only as will allow for caulking." The effect of this would result in the channel being some sixteen or seventeen inches higher than the spar deck, and would require them actually to be a series of short platforms between the spar deck gun ports.

On 26 October, Elliott reported that *Constitution*'s channels had been installed in the new, higher position. At the same time, he noted that all who had seen the result agreed that she would lose "the workings of the whole of her spar deck with the exception of two guns on each side." He also felt that, without the channels to block it, the concussion of the guns on the gun deck soon would enervate spar deck crews. It was his desire that the matter be referred to a board of naval architects. (This was the second time he had made this proposal: The board had denied the earlier instance on 20 September.)

Rodgers wrote Elliott on 9 December to cover "Old Ironsides" over, as the Secretary had not issued orders for her use, but had to reverse himself six days later. The ship was to be prepared for sea with all stores except provisions.

Now the tempo picked up. On the 19th Elliott was told to embark guns from stores as follows: 24-pounders lettered "A" and numbered 33, 34, 56 through 70, and 78 through 85; twenty 32-pounder carronades lettered "O" and numbered 1 through 18, and 21 and 22; and two Congreve 24-pounders (the "gunades"). Elevating screws for the guns were taken from sloop *Boston*, then in ordinary at the yard. Three days later, Elliott wrote that the ship would need 13,000 pounds of cannon powder and 2,300 pounds of priming powder more than he had available in the yard magazine. On Christmas Eve, Barker reported to the commandant that the bowsprit was in, rigging going on, all but one sail finished, and water casks ready. These were in addition to the eighty-eight iron tanks installed when the ship still was in dry dock. This same date, Rodgers informed Elliott that the necessary powder would be shipped from Norfolk.

The new year, 1835, marked its arrival in an end to the mild weather. The mercury plunged below freezing and stayed there for twelve days. Boston Harbor became sheeted with ice as far as Fort Independence. Ship work stayed on schedule, but it looked as though she'd be icebound.

Rodgers, perhaps concerned by all the activity occurring in Boston since 15 December, wrote Elliott on 8 January cautioning him not to proceed so rapidly on *Constitution*'s outfitting that the rigging was not given "a proper stretch" and readied to withstand the North Atlantic gales prevalent at that time of year. Elliott was ahead of the board in this matter: No rigging was being installed until it had been "on the stretch with heavy weights" for forty-eight hours.

After two weeks of freezing weather, it turned unseasonably mild and Elliott moved quickly. *Constitution*'s lower rigging was "overhead" by the 13th and the topmasts up on the 15th. Rigging continued apace, and the topgallant masts were up by the 27th. By this time, too, all water and provisions had been stowed, and anchors selected (two of 55–60 hundredweight and five of 50–55 hundredweight). Elliott was hopeful that she would be ready for sea on 5 February, if the two-inch chain anchor cable from the Washington Yard arrived on time.

Constitution was ready to receive her officers and crew on 9 February. Shortly thereafter Elliott wrote Rodgers advising him that the chain pumps "gave satisfaction" but that the channels were most unsatisfactory. He enclosed some damaged chain plates, hoping they would convince the board of "the insecurity of trusting to them, or the bolts, when fitted, in that manner." In setting up the rigging, the bolts had been drawn into the wood, twisting and fracturing plates. The board wouldn't budge.

As Bainbridge had done before him, Elliott had himself relieved as navy yard commandant and assigned as commander of "Old Ironsides." On 2 March, *Constitution* sailed for New York with the Elliott family aboard, her spars once more standing tall and her black hull accented by the white gun streak now carried all the way around the enclosed bow and cutwater. Astern, the regal decorations of her youth had given way to a memorial to past glories. And up forward, just beneath the bowsprit, was the incomplete figurehead of Andrew Jackson, shrouded in canvas. Happily, Bostonians did not carry out their threats to bombard the frigate in the Narrows if the hated statue were still on board—this, despite Elliott's final gesture: painting the canvas with five stripes, recalling the five-striped flag raised in Massachusetts at the outset of the War of 1812 to protest the war and foster the embryonic (and short-lived) secessionist movement by the same parties who were, in 1835, anti-Jackson.

CHAPTER FOURTEEN

The Mediterranean, Pacific, and Home Squadrons

QUICK TRIP TO FRANCE

We have seen how Commodore Elliott left Boston the center of controversy because of the Jackson figurehead. In a small way, the problem preceded him to New York in March of 1835, for the secretary of the navy had taken the trouble to arrange for restoration of the damaged piece during his stay there, surprising the commandant of the New York Navy Yard, Como. Charles G. Ridgely, by his direct action. The latter complained about it to the secretary on 9 March, the very day *Constitution* arrived in that port. Ridgely also worried that the carvers, Dodge and Son, wanted six weeks in which to remake the entire figure. Secretary Woodbury believed it would take two or three days to replace the head only, and was "much mortified" to learn the ship was still in port on the 13th, as President Jackson wanted the ship out of the country as soon as possible. The repair was completed on the 14th.

While these repairs were being made, Elliott received on board Edward Livingston, former secretary of state and currently our minister to France. For twelve years, the two countries had been negotiating claims resulting from the American Revolution and the Napoleonic wars. We were demanding $25 million in payment for French depredations against American ships and property, and the French wanted a much smaller amount to pay for supplies provided in the 1770s. In 1831, a treaty had been ratified to settle the question, but when the first French payment fell due, their Chamber of Deputies failed to appropriate the money. The matter dragged on. In his annual message to Congress in December 1834, President Jackson recommended that the Congress pass "a law authorizing reprisals upon French property," if the debt were not paid promptly. Understandable French reaction to this resulted in the recalling of ministers, although the French legislature voted the money and authorized its payment once the Americans gave a "satisfactory explanation" of the president's remarks to King Louis Philippe. *Constitution* was assigned to hurry Livingston back to France with Jackson's response.

Under way on the 16th, the voyage ran into difficulties the first night out when the frigate slammed into a gale. Upper yards were sent down and storm sails set, and still the ship scudded along at better than ten knots. The storm worsened through the night, the masts straining and her canvas threatening to rip clear of the bolt ropes. The bow dug repeatedly into walls of rushing water; and it came by the hogshead into the wardroom past the rudder casing.

As often happens at such times, there occurred a moment of peace, long enough to let the crew think that, perhaps, the worst was over. Then came a warning cry of "Look out to windward!" as a monstrous wave was sighted rushing out of the darkness at them with the force of a careering freight train. With a sickening lurch, *Constitution* rolled into the trough ahead of the wave and then was hit by a towering wall of water. A thunderous roar blotted out all other sound as it cascaded across and into the ship. It was gone almost as quickly as it had come. In the relative silence that followed, a series of heavy, jarring thumps was felt and heard forward. Number 16 starboard gun, one of the gunades, had leapt from its carriage and been propelled through its port by water. It was dangling outside the ship by its breeching tackle, its more than two tons of cast iron threatening to beat in the bow.

The jib boom snapped off and was blown away at about this time, causing some ship control to be lost. A tremendous sea pooped her and threatened to wash everyone and everything off the spar deck. Elliott's gig was smashed to smithereens. A second wave followed, but the ship withstood it. Seizing the moment, an axman hacked at the breeching tackle and succeeded in dropping the errant 24-pounder into the sea. That danger past, and recognizing that the severity of the storm precluded his continuing to carry any press of sail, the commodore hove to until the next afternoon, when it abated.

The remainder of the voyage passed uneventfully, and the anchor was dropped at Le Havre on 10 April. Because of the uncertainty of the diplomatic situation, *Constitution* remained in France while Livingston went to Paris with the president's message. The minister informed the king that Jackson had meant no insult to the French, but he refused to "explain" his threat of reprisal. As might be expected, this was unsatisfactory to the French; Livingston returned with his retine to the frigate, expecting that war would be formally declared before he reached home. (As it turned out, the British prime minister, Lord Palmerston, stepped in as mediator and brought about a peaceful resolution of the difficulty.)

Constitution sailed from France on 16 May, and after a five-day stop in Plymouth, England, headed for home. She needed five days to beat to the western end of the channel against head winds, and then it became apparent that there was a gale somewhere to the southwest. That night, because the officer of the deck reduced sail in accordance with general orders to adjust them at his discretion that the ship might ride safely and comfortably, the high winds drove her to leeward so far that she was in danger of being wrecked on Scilly Isle. When apprised of the situation, Elliott daringly ordered all possible sail set in an attempt to drive her westward of the land before the wind could drive her north onto it. It was a chancy thing. His new rig, with the raised channels, very nearly did him in. The billowing sails placed such a strain on the shrouds that the chain bolts at their lower ends actually were being drawn out, as a claw hammer pulls a nail. Luffs were placed on the weather shrouds to help take up the strain, but still more came free. It was touch and go, the race in doubt. Rocks covered in spray were seen all around as the ship careened through a gurnet at nine knots and better. At last, she came through and was safely in the Atlantic.

New York was reached on 23 June. It had been a trip to remember.

HURRICANE

Constitution sailed once more on 19 August, to proceed to the Mediterranean as flagship of that squadron. On the 30th, Elliott saw that he was in for another bout of weather. The wind veered unexpectedly five and six points. Long, stringy cirrus clouds were followed by their lower, denser stratus cousins. The sea began to roll. And the sun, on setting, was blood red. The barometer was plunging. No doubt about it, they were in for a "blow."

As before, light spars and upper masts were sent down. Boats and other topside equipment were thoroughly lashed down. Inboard lifelines were rigged so that men might move about the spar deck in greater safety. The hatches were battened down. And relieving tackles were rigged in the wardroom so that emergency steering would be available in the event the wheel was carried away.

The sky was completely obscured by dense, black clouds when dawn came dimly, and the waves had grown huge. *Constitution* rode under close-reefed maintopsail and a storm staysail on a starboard tack as the winds came to her from the southeast. She was in the so-called "dangerous semi-circle" of a hurricane— the worst place to be. Placing his stern to the first hard blow, as the best option among no good ones, the commodore was steering for the *center* of the storm, not away from it.

In no time at all, the frigate's world became one of mountainous waves spuming great tendrils of spray ahead of them; of driving, lashing rain; of a rolling, dark cloud cover alive with Nature's energy. The maintopsail, though close-reefed, tattered with a thunderous clap. All hands were called to the spar deck with the ominous call "All hands save ship!" to be ready for any emergency. Orders were best transmitted with hand signals. For twenty-four hours, they were battered, clinging to the lifelines, and existing on cold "salt stuff."

There was a sudden silence at 7:00 the next morning. *Constitution* was in the eye of the hurricane, an area of seeming calm and silence in the midst of so much turmoil. The sailors knew it would be a short respite; none at all, in fact, for advantage was taken of these moments to check the ship's security. First, the darkness returned, and then the seas, stoving in ports and crushing boats. Finally, the winds returned in a terrible blast, threatening to take the masts right out of her. This was the worst the storm could offer, and having survived the onslaught, *Constitution* and her crew had merely to hang on as the hurricane swept on by.

But another surprise awaited them: Later that morning, as the weather improved, a huge iceberg was sighted ahead. It floated majestically in the still-stormy sea, seemingly unmoved by the forces around it. Elliott wisely gave it a wide berth, recognizing there was more of it below the surface than above. So large was it that the frigate sailed in relatively calm waters with peaceful breezes in its lee for an estimated two miles. As she passed clear, the foresail was shredded in the renewed blast of wind.

By late in the day, life was able to return more nearly to normal. Double lookouts, however, were kept because of the possibility of meeting more icebergs. That night, a thermometer was watched closely so that any sudden drop in water temperature might warn them of an icy presence.

At the start of the forenoon watch on 2 September, a lookout reported a ship, fine on the lee bow. Closer investigation showed it to be an American in distress, her foremast gone and her ensign flying upside down at half mast. She was wallowing terribly. Elliott hailed, and learned she was sinking. The seas still were heavy, so he decided to stand by until it was safe enough to launch boats. The

Constitution is shown at Port Mahon, Minorca, during 1837. Also present are, from left to right, the schooner *Shark*, the sister of "Old Ironsides" *United States*, and the corvette *John Adams*. The Andrew Jackson figurehead is clearly evident at *Constitution's* bow. *Courtesy Peabody Essex Museum, Salem, Massachusetts, neg. #20,913*

rescue began two hours later and was accomplished without injury. Saved were sixty passengers and crew, fifteen of them females. Shortly after all were aboard *Constitution* and the boats stowed, the hulk rolled over and went down. That she had managed to last long enough for the rescue was attributed to her cargo of cotton, which had helped keep her afloat.

In the Middle Sea

Constitution spent but a day at Gibraltar before proceeding to Port Mahon, the navy's long-time base on the island of Minorca. She arrived there on the 19th and remained in port making voyage repairs and reprovisioning.

On Sunday, the 27th, some of *Constitution's* officers attended a "low dance" in the city, while others went to a party at the Dutch consulate. The first group somehow got themselves into an argument with local citizens and sought to leave the place without a greater disturbance of the peace, but someone had gone for the guard. At the same time, the officers at the consulate decided to return to the ship on foot. This latter group was surprised by the sudden appearance of soldiers threatening them with fixed bayonets and assuming they were the miscreants. The ten Americans drew their swords and were well on their way to overcoming the twelve assailants when a second detachment of "guardia" arrived on the scene, accompanied by the "rabble of the city." Lts. Charles W. Chauncey and John Colhoun, Passed Midshipman Frank A. Bacon, and seven others soon were overpowered and thrown into jail. Colhoun had been bayoneted in the back, but would recover. Fortunately, the party was allowed to send word to Elliott, who got in touch with the governor. At 4:00 the next afternoon, after Elliott had threatened to land an armed force, the unfortunates were released and finally made it back to the frigate.

The fear of cholera, and perhaps incidents like the foregoing, led Elliott to decide against what had become the traditional wintering over at Mahon. On 1 November, having relieved Commodore Patterson, he got *Constitution, Potomac,* 44, *John Adams,* 28, and *Shark,* 12, under way for a tour of the eastern Mediterranean, to make diplomatic visits and check up on American interests in that region. From Mahon, they went east to Athens, where the flagship hosted the Greek king, Otho, and his queen on a day-long visit. Port calls followed at the islands of Cira and Vourla, Turkey, in November; Smyrna, Turkey, in January 1836; and Gibraltar and Tangier briefly in February. Two months were spent using the facilities at Lisbon for overhaul before returning to Mahon in the middle of April.

On 23 May, *Constitution* sailed for Toulon to pick up mail and funds from the American consul, then headed for her first visits to Italian ports on this cruise: five days in Genoa and ten in Leghorn. Stops at Civitavecchia, port of the Papal States, and at Naples followed.

Heading down Italy's boot, the squadron made calls at Palermo and Messina before crossing the Ionian Sea to Corfu on the 30th. Athens was regained on 19 August after calls at Milos and Napoli di Romano. King Otho and consort visited the ship once more. Here, *Constitution* was joined by her sister ship, *United States,* for duty in the squadron—two of the three original ships in the navy working together thirty-nine years after they were launched.

Souda Bay, Crete, and Sidon and Beirut (Lebanon) were visited before Elliott came to anchor in Tripoli (then Syria), amidst the Egyptian fleet. During an exchange of visits, the commodore was subjected to some boasting by the Capudan Pasha, who extolled the speed and handiness of his flagship. Elliott could not ignore the challenge: In the trip to Jaffa (Tel Aviv), a distance of less than a hundred miles, he sailed "Old Ironsides" completely around the Egyptian flag-ship *twice* while beating him handily. (This occurred in September 1836, and became one of Elliott's oft-told tales.)

The viceroy of Egypt paid an official visit to the ship while she was in Alexandria, and then she paid a call at Tripoli, Libya, her first since those mem-orable days more than thirty years earlier. The year was rounded out by visits to Tunis, Mahon (for stores), and Cadiz before starting the new year at Lisbon once more, on 4 January 1837. After three weeks at Lisbon, *Constitution* returned to Mahon for her annual two-month stand-down period, after a stop at Gibraltar.

COLLECTOR OF ARTIFACTS

Elliott's second "grand tour" of the Mediterranean began on 23 April, when he sailed for Marseilles, where he took aboard Gen. Lewis Cass, then minister to Paris, Mrs. Cass, Master Cass, *three* Misses Cass, and six others. The commodore was only too happy to accommodate another strong Jacksonian. Cass's mission was to observe the political situation in the eastern Mediterranean and report to the president. In the weeks to follow, the cruise took on all the appearance of an avid collector making the rounds of antique shops and flea markets. Paying calls at nearly all of the ports visited during the previous year, as well as additional ports in Cyprus and Turkey, the commodore amassed a curious collection of ancient memorabilia, which he subsequently delivered to a number of colleges on his return to the United States. Stowed away in *Constitution*'s hold—and even-tually in every safe corner—were a stuffed ibis, two marble eagles, a marble head, a limb from a cedar of Lebanon, two Roman sarcophagi, a half dozen marble columns, a set of casts of papal busts, two paintings, a dozen miscellaneous pieces of ancient worked marble, a *mummy*, myriad coins, a vase brought up from the sea bottom at the site of the Battle of Actium, and a variety of "antiquities" from Palestine, Syria, Greece, and Crete.

Midshipman Edward C. Anderson accompanied the commodore on his archaeological sweep through the Holy Land that was a part of this odyssey. Armed with a protective *firman* from Sultan Mahomet Ali acquired during a call at Constantinople in July, Elliott and the Cass party, together with Anderson, Midshipman John W. Brice, Assistant Surgeon Daniel C. McLeod, a quarter-master, and one or two servants, set off from Jaffa on 3 August. By camel and donkey they traveled to Jerusalem, the Dead Sea, the River Jordan, Jericho,

Nazareth, the Sea of Galilee, Damascus, and Baalbek, before arriving at Tripoli, where the executive officer, Comdr. William Boerum, had brought *Constitution*. At the Dead Sea, Anderson was "amused at Commodore Elliott. He was trying to dive [in the Dead Sea] & his great fat body rolled over and over like a cask, unable to sink." Cass later indicated a curiosity about dervishes to the Pasha of Damascus. As a result, the Americans were horrified as these religious fanatics demonstrated their faith, not by frenzied dancing as was expected, but by being lifted from the ground on the cutting edges of scimitars, spitting themselves on skewers through various parts of their bodies, handling white-hot horseshoes, chewing blazing charcoal, and allowing themselves to be ridden over by horses. (One, a fourteen year old, apparently was killed during this last demonstration, but witnesses couldn't be sure.) Later, at Baalbek, Elliott was frustrated in his hopes of adding a bas relief eagle he had read about to his collection: It turned out to have been done on a four-ton keystone. Anderson was delighted when they got back aboard ship.

The frigate returned to Mahon in October, transferred the Cass party to *United States* for return to Marseilles, and remained in port into the new year. Most of the month of February 1838 was spent at Malta.

Constitution began her seventh and final stay of the cruise at Mahon on 19 March. A few days later, many officers from the squadron attended the local horse races. Elliott and Lt. Charles G. Hunter of the flagship each had animals entered in one particular meet. It turned out to be a very close race, one in which the lieutenant excitedly and loudly claimed victory. Elliott, seated nearby on a mule (!), immediately charged over to Hunter and disputed the claim, ultimately asserting that the junior's refusal to change his mind was tantamount to "separating the Honor of an officer from that of a Gentleman." Hunter protested the slur, and an enraged Elliott had to be restrained from hitting him with a cane. The lieutenant was suspended from duty by the commodore and confined to quarters.

Hunter wrote to Secretary of the Navy George Badger, objecting to the treatment he had received. Elliott, upon learning of this, ordered his junior court-martialed for disrespect and contempt toward a superior officer. When the court-martial acquitted Hunter, Elliott attempted to arrange a second court, ordering his secretary and Chaplain Thomas R. Lambert to find precedents for such a proceeding, and to develop a list of "reliable" officers in the squadron. The chaplain reacted by sending an anonymous letter to the secretary describing the whole affair in detail and recommending the commodore's court-martial upon his return home. Elliott got a copy of the report and deduced its author, but his subsequent efforts to discipline the chaplain came to naught through an unrecorded course of bureaucratic and judicial noncompliance followed by those squadron officers the commodore had ordered to conduct a court of inquiry and draw up charges.

With the officers setting such poor examples, it comes as no surprise that crewmen regularly and repeatedly indulged their baser impulses ashore in Mahon. The men, however, were flogged for their intoxication and efforts to smuggle liquor into the ship—up to thirty lashes at a crack—and the cat was let out of the bag even on Sunday to accommodate the miscreants.

It also was during this final stay in Mahon that Elliott "rounded up" a second collection for return to the United States: livestock, for himself and others. Penned initially *en masse* in the ship's waist beneath the boat skids were five jack-asses, one jenny, an Arabian bay horse, five Arabian mares, three Arabian colts, an Andalusian colt, three Andalusian hogs, and two Syrian hogs. Recognizing that the livestock never would travel well in such a manner, Elliott caused seven guns on either side to be disabled by having timbers fastened from their trucks to the overhead deck beams to form stalls into which the animals then were placed. Anderson found himself designated officer in charge, but managed to get reassigned as a deck watch stander before the ship got under way. Eight or nine crewmen made up the care and feeding party.

Constitution, "Elliott's Ark," began her homeward voyage from Mahon on 15 June. With the commodore's typical luck in this regard, the heavily laden frigate ran into a gale as soon as she entered the Atlantic. Elliott headed southwest to pick up the prevailing trade winds, but before crossing paused at Madeira for a week to refresh the stock. The odyssey came to an end off Fortress Monroe, Virginia, on the last day of July.

Trouble flared almost immediately as the commodore decided to offload his livestock to the village of Hampton prior to moving the ship to Norfolk where the men, most of them long since having completed their enlistments, would be discharged. By the time the boats moving the animals ashore returned to the ship at 5:00 that afternoon, their crews found their mates running amok. Many were intoxicated. Some were chasing the musicians while others were hurling mess gear about the berthing deck. Having tried unsuccessfully to quiet the lower deck disturbance, the master-at-arms was forced to retreat before their assault to the safety of the wardroom. Another group was seen chasing a black man by the name of Ennis, whose head was bleeding from repeated blows of a tub. They were deterred by three midshipmen, who placed Ennis in protective custody.

In an effort to bring order out of chaos, all hands were piped to hammocks on schedule (about 9:00). As they streamed up to get their bedding from its stowage in the nettings, a group released three of their mates who had been confined in irons under the watch of a Marine sentry between the two forward starboard carronades. All then went to the forecastle. At this point, the commodore, accompanied by Lt. Oscar Bullus, approached the men and admonished them for having released the three prisoners. He told them the three should be returned and that discipline must be preserved. He also stated unequivocally that the ship would be moved to Norfolk in the morning and the men discharged. A number responded with "No, no!" A man named Birch, referring to Ennis, cried, "Kill the Negro!" No move was made against the officers; neither were the prisoners returned. Elliott and Bullus retired to their respective quarters and the crew continued to roam the ship without control until about 11:00, when all either were too tired or too drunk to continue. At no time had the Marines been placed under arms.

The next morning, the crew responded with alacrity when orders were piped to unmoor ship. Upon reanchoring, and while furling sail, they cheered spontaneously. That done, Boerum spoke to the men, telling them the commodore was pleased with their conduct, that they had done their duty, and were now at liberty to go on shore.

Elliott made no report of what had transpired. By the time the ship was placed out of commission on 18 August, all of his trophies had long since been offloaded, and the "thick slimy filth" covering the gun deck in way of the disassembled stalls had been laboriously removed. What had occurred became public knowledge, however, when Lts. Charles H. McBlair and Bushrod Hunter included details in the list of charges they brought against Elliott for his conduct in the Mediterranean and use of *Constitution* as an animal transport. The court, when it met in 1840, found the commodore not guilty of failing to suppress a mutiny, but guilty of enough other charges to suspend him from service for four years, the first two without pay.[1]

ON TO THE PACIFIC

Constitution was in ordinary from 18 August 1838 to 1 March 1839, when she recommissioned under Capt. Daniel Turner, who had served in the ship as a midshipman under John Rodgers in 1809 and 1810. During the War of 1812, he served on the Great Lakes under Oliver Hazard Perry, earning a congressional silver medal, and subsequently saw duty in the Mediterranean and in the West Indies.

For this cruise, *Constitution* was flagship for Como. Alexander Claxton, commander-designate of the Pacific Squadron. His orders were to protect American commerce on the west coast of South America as far as Panama, to cruise to California occasionally, and to "look in" on the Sandwich and Society Islands as conditions warranted. He would have two to four smaller units to assist him in carrying out his responsibilities.

Her first port call was New York, where she arrived on 20 April to complete her crew, and received Powhatan Ellis, minister to Mexico, and his suite for transportation south. That worthy came aboard on 19 May; Turner got under way the next day and soon had stunsails set under fair skies. As the sailors put it, "Our frigate was . . . walking off under a cloud of sail, . . . quick on the heel as ever."

Vera Cruz was reached on 16 June after twenty-seven days at sea. Minister Ellis, retinue, and baggage were landed with all due ceremony on the 19th. *Constitution* departed early the next morning, and after a brief call at Havana, was away for Rio. The thirty-three-day voyage was a pleasant one for ship's company, but showed signs of growing problems between the commodore and the captain. Claxton and Turner were longtime friends in the service, one considering the other something of a protégé. In fact, Claxton particularly requested the younger man for his flag captain. It seemed that the cruise would be made on the happiest terms for all concerned. Boredom, however, is a condition very much to be combated at sea, and the means to do so are limited. Claxton had no other ships in company; neither could he possibly spend all his days corresponding, particularly since weeks would pass before his letters could be sent. As a result, he began injecting himself into the ship's routine with every intention of being helpful to Turner and in no way meaning to imply any shortcomings on the latter's part. One day, Turner found out that the purser had issued some clothing to the crew without his permission. The purser, McKean Buchanan, reported that the commodore had ordered him to do so. When confronted by Turner, Claxton said merely that he thought it was a minor, but necessary, action and that he hadn't wanted to trouble his friend with it. Other instances where the commodore inserted himself into routine in small ways led Turner to tell his superior directly that it wasn't his place to become involved unless he felt the captain wasn't doing his job. Friendship carried the day, and all seemed settled.

Constitution spent two weeks in Rio, her sailors enjoying the sights and liberty, and then it was away for Cape Horn on 9 September. Two days out, shortly before noon, Seaman William Johnson fell overboard from the mizzen top. A boat was lowered immediately, but all it found was the man's hat.

After passing south of the Falkland Islands, another tragedy struck the ship: Through some miscalculation or other on the part of the purser, an insufficient quantity of whiskey had been shipped, and "Old Ironsides" had run dry. Not until they rounded the Horn and reached Valparaíso could any relief be expected. If ever a blow could be struck at a ship's morale, this was it. Some of the sailors turned to an expedient available to them in small stores: They bought up all the *eau de cologne* the purser had stocked and mixed it with a little hot water and sugar. These enterprising businessmen then sold it to their mates for up to a dollar a bottle. It took the officers three or four days to uncover the operation.

Constitution sighted Staten Island on the 27th and the Horn itself two days later, having up until then had remarkably pleasant weather. Her good fortune was not to last, however, for by the next morning she was laboring under almost bare poles "against the tempestuous elements." Wrote a participant later: "The gale continued without interruption for sixteen or seventeen days, buffeting which 'Old Ironsides' proved herself the sturdy and efficient seaboat she was always celebrated for: no ship was ever more comfortably secured against the bitter blasts and drenching billows than was ours on this occasion." Once clear of the gale, *Constitution* made steady progress northward. On the evening of 28 October, 3d Lt. R. R. Pinkham died of an "abscess of the left lung" that had become apparent shortly after leaving Rio. The next day, at noon, sail was shortened and the ship hove to; all hands were mustered aft to bury the dead. The band played the "Dead March" from "Saul" as the six gun captains of Pinkham's division bore his remains, covered by the Stars and Stripes, to the lee gangway. Following a reading of the burial service by the executive officer, the body was committed to the deep as the Marine Guard fired three volleys.

Sail was set and Valparaíso raised on 2 November.

ON STATION

The sloop of war *St. Louis*, 18, was found waiting in port. She had beaten the big frigate by two days from Rio. It soon was apparent, however, that only rarely did anything happen with alacrity on this station. Thirteen days were spent watering

South American ports of call *Author's collection*

and provisioning, and another eleven in a leisurely sail up the coast to Callao, Peru, the principal American rendezvous on this coast of South America. *Constitution* remained at anchor there for a full three months, while readiness was forgotten and the crew found pursuits more to their liking in runs on the beach.

During this time, too, Claxton's boredom again led him to take an increasing hand in the ship's affairs. Incident followed incident until Claxton and Turner grew increasingly frigid toward one another. The matter came to a head on 2 February 1840, when Turner sent a letter to the commodore requesting permission to return to the United States. Claxton responded that he hadn't the authority to grant the request. Turner sent a second: to be allowed to move ashore until such time as the secretary of the navy (now James K. Paulding) could make his pleasure known in the matter. Claxton again turned Turner down, this time on the grounds that there was no captain who could relieve him. (The commodore, of course, considered it beneath his station to command his own flagship.) From this time onward, the commodore and the captain apparently communicated with one another only by formal letters.

Given the fine state of affairs in the "high command," it was a good thing it was such an indolent station. Between late February and early June, *Constitution* made visits to Talcahuano, Chile, and Payta, Peru, with a month's "rest" at Callao in between. She then settled down for another three months at Callao.

Not all of the sailors' amusement came from the beach. In New York, ship's company had chipped in and purchased a library of three to four hundred volumes. This was placed under the charge of the ship's yeoman, who kept them stowed in the fore passage of the orlop deck near the armory. Time was set aside on Sundays for the exchange of books; reportedly, there were many avid readers. Authors in the collection included Scott, Marryat, Cooper, Irving, and Bulwer-Lytton.

In Rio, the crew had subscribed something on the order of $250 for the purchase of theatrical equipment: a wardrobe of varied costume parts and a full range of paints with which to make scenery on old canvas. "Damon and Pythias" was the first production attempted, at Callao, and was well received not only by ship's company, but by visiting British and French officers, as well. Something called "Ruffian Boy" and a farce entitled "Lying Valet" were two other works in the repertoire. So taken were the thespians with their success that the crew chipped in an additional two or three hundred dollars for more equipment. At least two pieces were composed on board: "Life in Peru" and, inevitably, "Old Ironsides."

Constitution sluiced the mud of Callao harbor from her anchors once more in the middle of September 1840 and proceeded north again. A quick stop was made at Payta, "celebrated for its cloudless skies, agreeable women, profusion of onions and scarcity of water," before heading to Puna, Ecuador, for a two-week stay where one could find "relentless mosquitos [*sic*], trees loaded with delicious oysters and guanas, paroquets and alligators in no small quantity." It is small wonder that the *Constitution*'s crew were happy to return to Callao on 11 October for two more months of swinging with the tide.

The seasons in the southern hemisphere are reversed from those in the northern, and so on 2 December *Constitution* left Callao for the higher, cooler latitudes farther south. She made Valparaíso nine days later and remained for most of January 1841. In February, Claxton initiated a court of inquiry into the activities of

Purser Buchanan, suspecting him not only of arranging the whiskey shortage when rounding the Horn, but also of falsifying his records, purchasing rotten tobacco, stealing clothing stocks intended for the crew, and overcharging them for small stores. The squadron commander, openly against pursers in general, attended each daily session and personally cross-examined witnesses. In the month that followed, he amassed over three hundred pages of testimony.

Talcahuano was visited from 4 February until 8 March, and was always thought of as a place of death by the crew thereafter. On 2 March, a seaman by the name of Gibbs slipped and fell into the water from the starboard boat boom and never came to the surface. Two days later, Quarter Gunner William Leeds died of dysentery, a malady that had spread to others in the ship. Dysentery also ended the adversary relationship between commodore and captain by bringing the former to his death shortly before breakfast on 7 March.[2] Turner assumed command of the squadron in accordance with navy regulations, but did not assume the title of commodore.

It was decided to inter the late commodore in Valparaíso instead of the detested Talcahuano. The frigate got under way on the 8th and arrived there three days later, her ensign at half mast. The funeral began at 11:00 A.M. the next day. In the procession, besides the officers from "Old Ironsides" and 250 crewmen, were officers from HMS *President*, the French frigate *Thetis*, the Danish frigate *Bellona*, the Chilean frigate *Chilia*, and the French war sloop *Camille*, as well as a detachment of Royal Marines, and the masters and supercargoes of every merchantman in the harbor. As they made their way to the cemetery, the mourners were accompanied by *Constitution*'s band. Minute guns were fired by the frigate. Following the graveside service, both the U.S. and Royal Marines fired three volleys.

Returning to Callao on the 26th for her final visit, *Constitution* remained at anchor for three months, preparing for the voyage home and awaiting her replacement.

The 4th of July was a memorable one during which the crew celebrated not only the nation's birthday but their imminent departure for home, as well. A double tot of grog from official sources, coupled with liberal amounts of smuggled goods, turned the frigate into a scene of drunken revels, with singing, swigging, and fighting all going on simultaneously in various parts of the ship. Twenty-six months of tedium were swilled away in herculean fashion. Fortunately, nothing worse than many bad hangovers were suffered as a result, and no enemy chose the moment to attack.

Perhaps the absence of an enemy on the 4th was fortuitous, because on the 10th both Turner and the commander of HMS *President* received official reports of an incident the preceding November, when a drunken, braggart Canadian named McLeod had been arrested for announcing publicly in New York that he had killed an American named Durfee three years earlier in an incident on the Niagara River involving Canadian dissidents. The British prime minister demanded his release and warned that if McLeod were executed there would be "war, immediate and frightful." Such was the extent of the information the captains received.

Turner ordered the ship prepared for battle, quietly, while a wary eye was kept on *President.* Bulkheads were struck and furniture sent below. Battle lanterns were hung. Extra powder cartridges were made up and distributed evenly between the magazines. Round, grape, and canister shot were broken out and placed in their ready racks and boxes. Long out of the habit, the crew took two hours to complete this task.

While these preparations were going forward, *President* and her consort, sloop *Acteon,* gave the Americans a thrill by suddenly getting under way and maneuvering about the harbor. It brought to the Yankee minds a remembrance of *Essex* being cornered and defeated in Valparaíso by a similar combination twenty-seven years earlier. They wondered if it would happen again. Eventually, the British returned to anchor. Turner stood down from battle stations. Both sides eyed each other and waited.

GOING HOME

No shooting resulted from the war scare. *Constitution* got under way the next day, 11 July, to begin her voyage home. (One result of the incident, however, burst upon the crew a few nights later when Turner beat to quarters during the midwatch to make a point about readiness.)

The depletion of the whiskey supply on the outbound voyage already has been mentioned. On the homeward trip, hot water for evening tea was stopped. Water wasn't in short supply; firewood was, and Turner, mindful of the possibility of war with Britain, was husbanding his supplies early, in case it became necessary to run all the way home without another port call. Ship's company grumbled at first, but when informed made no further complaints.

The voyage proved to be a swift one, free of head winds and ice. The big frigate flew around the Horn, passed the Falkland Islands and the Rio de la Plata as fast as anyone could hope. On 24 August, they sighted their first sail since reentering the Atlantic and from a Brazilian brig learned that war between Britain and the United States continued to be just a threat. Four days later, off Rio, they encountered our war sloop *Marion*, which confirmed the good news. *Constitution* dropped anchor in the beautiful harbor of Rio at 9:00 that evening, and the crew had their hot tea.

Turner found frigate *Potomac*, 44, bearing the broad pennant of Commodore Ridgely of the Brazil Station, and schooner *Enterprize* already in harbor. On the morning of the 29th, he saluted the commodore with thirteen guns. A few days later, Dom Pedro II, seventeen-year-old emperor of Brazil, made a grand tour of the harbor and was greeted by salutes from all the warships present. And, on another evening, the *Constitution's* crewmen again got roaring drunk.

Ridgely boarded *Constitution* on 12 September, a sick man. He, together with his clerk, a chaplain, two or three midshipmen, and about twenty seamen, all invalided or with their time expired, would ride her home. The frigate got under way on the 15th to three cheers from the other American warships. On her way down harbor, she clipped HMS *Queen Victoria*, ketch, which had failed to veer her anchor and clear the channel. The Briton lost her flying jib and jib booms for her lack of cooperation, while *Constitution* had a davit arm ripped from her larboard quarter.

The last leg of the voyage was almost perfect. Except for a brief, severe squall on 21 October, the winds were fair and fresh. Twelve knots was not uncommonly found upon tossing the log. So swiftly was *Constitution* proceeding that, on the 23rd, she overhauled the barque *Sarah*, which had left Rio eleven days ahead of her. Then the winds largely failed until the 29th, when they came fair once more. Two days later, she saluted liner *Delaware* (Commodore Morris), 74, and dropped anchor in Hampton Roads at 6:00 in the evening. A day or so later, the steam tug *Poinsett* towed her to an anchorage below the navy yard. The commission ended when Turner went ashore on 11 November, the crew was paid off, and the ship was in the custody of the yard. Four days later, she began a four-month post-cruise dry docking for repairs and recoppering.

THE HOME SQUADRON

Constitution had arrived in the United States as the new secretary of the navy, Abel P. Upshur, was working to establish a new squadron, the Home Squadron.

Como. Foxall Alexander Parker, Sr., used *Constitution* for half of 1843 as flagship of the new Home Squadron. When she was found to be in need of repairs for which money was lacking, early in the new year he and the crew transferred to USS *Brandywine*. (Three decades later, his son, Foxall Alexander, Jr., was active in founding the U.S. Naval Institute.) *Official U.S. Navy photo*

As he informed Commodore Stewart on 4 February 1842, the squadron would be composed of all active ships in local waters not either in ordinary or overhaul, or earmarked to other squadron assignments, and would be kept in readiness to respond rapidly to any crisis as it broke. Stewart, the squadron's first commander, found his ships scattered from New Hampshire to Louisiana, and numbering everything from the still-shaking-down steam frigates *Missouri* and *Mississippi* to the aging *Constitution* swinging on her hook off Norfolk Navy Yard.

On 4 March, Capt. Edward R. Shubrick, whose older brothers William and John had served in the frigate in the War of 1812, requested orders to command *Constitution*, hoping she might be ordered to the Mediterranean. The secretary earmarked him for that duty with no promises. By late April, Secretary Upshur decided that the newer frigate *Columbia* would be the next sent to the Mediterranean. Her commander, Capt. Foxall Alexander Parker, Sr., had no wish to make the cruise and so informed the secretary. On the 27th, Upshur sent letters to Parker and Shubrick offering them the opportunity to exchange commands, indicating that he intended to activate *Constitution* to succeed *Columbia* in the Home Squadron. Agreement was soon forthcoming and the exchange effected.

By the last week in May, *Constitution* had all her lieutenants and midshipmen on board, but providing the sailors was delayed by requirements to man higher priority units, and it was mid-June before she was ready to return to commission. Long-termers from the decommissioning ship-sloop *Levant* and apprentices from the receiving ship *Pennsylvania* were among those who came aboard. Even then, on 22 June, she was commissioned with only a partial crew and with First Lt. Charles W. Chauncey as "commanding officer," Parker enjoying a leisurely furlough.

On 14 July, the ship received, via the schooner *Martin Smith,* four 68-pounder Paixhans guns, weapons authorized for all liners and frigates late in 1841. These were monster shell-firers that were located in pairs in the midship ports on either side of the gun deck in place of a like number of 24s. Named for their French inventor, Gen. Henri Joseph Paixhans, these medium-range muzzle loaders could fire exploding shells and so represented a new capability for the old frigate.

Parker finally appeared on the 15th. For months, *Constitution* lay swinging at her anchors, some of her crew finding little else to do but fight, drink, or attempt desertion. A deranged Marine private jumped overboard and drowned. The carpenter's gang was kept busy for a while closing off a portion of the storeroom below the cockpit to become a shell-filling room for the new guns. The ship was not fully manned until the end of September, when men were transferred from *Macedonian,* an indication that as a "ready force" the Home Squadron was a sham. Parker finally put to sea on 10 November and spent the next three weeks in basic seamanship and gunnery exercises off the coast. He returned to Norfolk earlier than expected on 2 December, forced in by leaks so excessive that the officers were ousted from their staterooms and all the men's sea bags soaked.

Secretary Upshur's expectation shortly to use the frigate on "special service" was dashed when *Constitution* was found in need of repairs by a survey board. On the last day of December, she was shifted to a berth off the navy yard, her place in the Home Squadron to be taken by *Brandywine.* In the weeks to follow, the sails were landed, the lower and topsail yards transferred to *Brandywine* together with the gun deck battery, and then all stores were shifted to the other ship. At 9:00 A.M. on 16 February 1843, Parker placed her out of commission and immediately transferred the crew and himself to *Brandywine.*

CHAPTER FIFTEEN

Around the World

GETTING READY

Constitution had lain idle about six months when the Navy Department directed the Norfolk Navy Yard to estimate the cost of preparing her for "special service" of three years' duration. Naval Constructor Foster Rhodes responded that $70,000 would be needed, an amount that greatly exceeded the funds available. Capt. John "Mad Jack" Percival was ordered to conduct an independent inspection. He reported he could ready her for no more than $10,000. Como. Lewis Warrington, chief of the new Bureau of Construction and Repair, confirmed Percival's estimate. He got the green light.

All the familiar details of a ship's overhaul were repeated once again. Two are worthy of note. First, Percival docked the ship and completely recaulked and recoppered her (she had been taking water at a considerable rate on the last leg home from the Pacific in 1841). Second, the two chase gunades were landed.

Orders came for the ship to be completely ready for sea as of 1 April 1844. From 18 March, she loaded stores and received drafts of seamen from the receiving ship ("guardo") *Pennsylvania*, a ship of the line in reduced commission. By 11 April, however, "Old Ironsides" still was short of men and no more were to be gotten at Norfolk. Percival, who had taken command formally and placed *Constitution* back in commission on 26 March, received permission to sail for New York to complete manning. He departed the yard on 12 April and cleared the Capes on the 17th. The trip northward was a trying ten-day affair that began with a three-day gale that drove them out into the Gulf Stream before they could head for their destination. *Constitution* anchored off Castle Garden, near the Battery, on the 27th.

Capt. John Percival gained the nickname "Mad Jack" from numerous headstrong acts performed early in his career. Why this old man was assigned to lead *Constitution's* circumnavigation is unknown, but age had in no way dimmed his penchant for impulsive conduct. *Official U.S. Navy photo*

John Percival, one of the navy's genuine characters, was born at Barnstable, Massachusetts, in 1779, the same year that John Paul Jones defeated HMS *Serapis* off Flamborough Head. A midshipman during the Quasi-War with France, he spent a total of sixteen years in the merchant service both before and after that brief period as a man-o'-warsman. These commercial voyages took him to ports in Europe and Africa and on Indian Ocean shores. Percival reentered the U.S. Navy in 1808 and was assigned to *Siren.* During the War of 1812, he served with dash and daring in a gunboat that captured a British liner's tender, and then in the war brig *Peacock,* which captured fourteen British merchantmen and two men-of-war. He was promoted meritoriously to lieutenant for his exploits, and also earned his nickname. After the war, he had a series of routine assignments, including duty at the Boston Navy Yard when Commodore Elliott was commandant. He was, as one subordinate wrote, "something of a tradition of the old Navy days" and held in great reverence, especially by midshipmen and enlisted men. He had a reputation as a tough but fair commander. At sixty-five, Percival was the oldest captain *Constitution* was ever to have.

Constitution spent more than a month in New York. The cause for the long delay was not recruiting, for ninety-two men were received from the guardo *North Carolina* on the 28th: It was waiting for a diplomatic passenger, as had happened several times before. This time, the frigate would carry Henry A. Wise to his new post as minister to Brazil. He wasn't ready to sail until 27 May, when he appeared with wife, four children (one just eight months old), secretary, and seven servants. Percival turned over the entire cabin to the Wises and had an area nearby on the gun deck partitioned off with canvas as a temporary cabin for himself.[1]

Away Rio

Percival finally was able to get under way at 10:00 A.M. on the 29th, towed down to Sandy Hook by the steamer *Hercules*. En route, "huzzahs" were exchanged with the inbound ship of the line *Columbus*. Percival's orders were to check on the safety of American merchants, survey new waters, seek potential sites for future naval coaling stations, and show the flag around the world.[2]

The wind was fair and the seas calm as the ship headed east for the Azores. (Prevailing wind patterns were—and are—such that it was more efficient to sail east, then south and southwest, than it was to attempt to sail directly for the Brazilian bulge.) The balmy start to the extended voyage put Percival in a particularly light mood, and he even permitted the men "idle time . . . away from stations," a rare privilege that also accomplished the practical end of allowing them to air out the berth deck.

On Sunday, 2 June, it was so peaceful that the ship sailed with her awnings fully spread, fore and aft. Promptly at 10:00, the church call was heard throughout all decks, and crew and passengers alike went to their assigned positions. Abaft the weather gangway in order were the warrant officers, midshipmen, lieutenants, and the captain and passengers. Ship's company was mustered to leeward. After First Lt. Amasa Paine read the service, Percival read the Articles of War (they applied to the passengers, too, as long as they were aboard). Then Purser Thomas M. Taylor called the general muster, and each man passed around the capstan individually under the close scrutiny of "Mad Jack." As Fifth Lt. John B. Dale noted, "woebetide him with long hair or unshaven chin!"

Flores, westernmost of the Azores, was sighted on the 12th, but dying winds left them with another four days at sea before making the harbor of Fayal. This was the first visit by an American frigate. American vice consul Frederick

Dabney called upon Wise and Percival the next morning, and made his estate, "Bagatelle," available to the diplomat and the ship's officers. The Wise family took advantage of this opportunity to enjoy more familiar surroundings once more.

Dabney threw a ball for *Constitution* on the 18th, which was well attended by the local Portuguese gentry. It lasted until two the next morning, and all pronounced it a success despite the fact that there were few on either side who spoke the others' language. Percival reciprocated with a reception and dance on the ship the next afternoon.

Constitution was under way again on the 20th, the Wises having reoccupied the great cabin. In three days they were at anchor once more: in Funchal, Madeira. Found in the harbor were the British razee *America*, 60, as well as Portuguese frigate *Diana* and a war brig.

Madeira proved to be a pleasanter stay than the wretchedly poor Fayal. The Wises again moved ashore to the residence of our vice consul, Mr. Baynim. He, too, threw a party in honor of the ship's visit. The major attraction of Funchal for one member of the crew, at least, was the opportunity to purchase a *warm bath:* luxury for the equivalent of sixty cents.

A brief, two-day sail brought *Constitution* next to Santa Cruz on the island of Teneriffe (now Tenerife), one of the Canary Islands, on 1 July. It proved to be a decaying society with beggar women and naked children in the streets, and soldiers of the Spanish garrison very much in evidence. The 4th of July was observed by a twenty-one-gun salute at noon, an entertainment in the cabin for the officers, and the firing of some rockets in the evening.

Percival got under way on the afternoon of the 6th, followed out of the harbor by the French corvette *Berceau*, also bound for Rio. For several days the two warships kept informal company, but on the 10th the Frenchman shaped a course to pass between the Cape Verde Islands and the African mainland while the Americans took a more westerly heading. Southward they went, out of the trades and into the equatorial doldrums. There were days when not fifty miles were made good.

In the evening of the 23rd, as the ship was nearing the Equator, an old seafaring ritual was begun: the "crossing the Line" ceremonies, when those who had never before ventured beneath the Southern Cross ("polliwogs") were initiated into its mysteries by those who had ("shellbacks"), generally with high jinks and hilarity—and some discomfort for the neophytes. It was just after the setting of the evening watch when a lookout sang out, "Light ho! Dead ahead!" From the bow head area there shortly appeared the "herald" of "Neptunus Rex, Lord of the Watery Domain." An old forecastleman named Fitzgerald, wrapped in a "toga," came aft and haltingly delivered his master's greeting to Percival. With great formality, he asked for a list of those on board new to "the Line" and requested permission for King Neptune to board the next day in order to welcome his new subjects with proper ceremony. This, of course, the captain graciously accorded. Fitzgerald disappeared back into the bow head, and shortly thereafter was seen Neptune's "flaming chariot" passing down the ship's side. (It was, in fact, a half barrel of tarred rope-yarns made up for the purpose.)

At 9:00 the next morning, as *Constitution* lay hove to, King Neptune arrived in his chariot (a map chest mounted on some spare gun carriage trucks) with "Queen Amphitrite" and company. After an exchange of greetings with Percival (and a round of "Bob Smith"), the royal entourage established itself on a dais on the forecastle, and the rounding up of "polliwogs" began. For the next two hours, the initiates, some brazen, some fearful, were brought before the lord of the sea to hear their "sins" proclaimed, had their faces "shaved" with razors made from barrel hoops, had a disgusting mixture stuffed in their mouths, and were tumbled and nearly drowned in a tarpaulin filled with water. Wise managed to save himself from the ministrations by offering a keg of spirits to the monarch of the seas.

The days passed quietly as the ship moved southward. On the 27th, a strange sail was sighted astern and continued following along the same course. On the 30th, *Constitution* met and spoke the stores ship *Erie*, 4, which had been with her for a part of her tour in the Pacific Squadron and was only now returning home. The mysterious stranger first sighted on the 27th was identified the next afternoon: It was *Berceau*.

With the coming of dawn on 2 August, the famed Sugar Loaf was sighted. Percival came to anchor in Rio harbor that afternoon amid men-of-war from England, France, Genoa, Brazil, and Portugal. American frigates *Congress*, 36, and *Raritan*, 44, also were present, as well as brig *Pioneer*. A few days later, Wise and his party were put ashore with all appropriate ceremony.

Throughout the month, Percival was busy readying his ship for the long voyage ahead. This was to be the last modern metropolis they would see for many months. He sought the finest foodstuffs, recognizing their importance to the health and well-being of his crew. He also attempted to ameliorate the expected debilitating heat of the tropics with a new paint scheme: He had the hull painted with white lead to reduce absorption of the sun's rays. And he had the gun streak

Constitution (right) and *Raritan* ride at anchor at Rio de Janeiro in the summer of 1844, before Percival repainted his ship white. From this angle, the massive "broken nose" effect of the Andrew Jackson figurehead is clearly visible on "Old Ironsides." Note too the presence of spencer gaffs on the fore- and mainmasts, a change in her rigging effected in the 1820s. *Official U.S. Navy photo*

done in *red*, "somewhat to the wonderment of the Brazilians, who think we have put on *war-paint*." Passed Midshipman Isaac G. Strain joined the ship there, having had to abort an intended expedition into the interior when his civilian associates backed out. He became the ship's sailing master while Gough W. Grant, his predecessor, was promoted to acting sixth lieutenant. Naturalist J. C. Reinhart was another new face on board, replacing a botanist named Chandler, who chose to return to the United States.

ACROSS THE SOUTH ATLANTIC

Percival left Rio on 8 September, heading southeastward in fair weather. That afternoon, the captain closed the port visit with a final call of "all hands to witness punishment" as nine men got their just deserts for smuggling liquor on board, drunkenness, or getting into trouble while on liberty. The days following passed quietly, the crew sometimes diverting themselves with small amusements. On the 17th, for example, some "fished" for a trailing albatross by trolling astern a hook baited with a piece of fat pork. One finally struck and was snagged. He was hauled aboard, squawking and flapping. Tiring of the bird's efforts to rid itself of its snare, the sailors released it after one cut off one of the bird's feet for a souvenir.

Gradually, the days grew cooler and the winds fitful. Some days, they lay becalmed; on others, they moved right along at an eight-knot clip. Rough, squally weather became their lot. Percival spent two days in the vicinity of Tristan da Cunha, hoping to be able to secure water from that island, but continuing gales led him to head for the Cape of Good Hope. On the night of 3 October, the ship was struck by a ferocious gale whose winds snapped the crossjack in two places and tumbled the ship about in "hay cock seas." Swells from astern smashed through the rudder coat, inundated the wardroom pantry and ruined a night's sleep.

In the Indian Ocean

The gale abated the next day, and at noon the sailing master was able to fix their position as being on the edge of Agulhas Bank. They had rounded the Cape and entered the Indian Ocean. A new crossjack was fitted on the 6th, a Sunday. Bad weather, adverse winds, and confusing currents consumed eight days before the big frigate arrived in St. Augustine's Bay, on the southwest coast of Madagascar, a wood and watering stop for whalers.

Hardly had the anchor gotten wet before a gaggle of native canoes came out to the ship bearing a strange assortment of locals ready to do business—and steal the unwary blind. Somewhere along the line, these bandits had acquired some outlandish names: Prince Green (the head man), John Green (his "purser"), John Stouts, Captain Amber, Captain Martin, and the like. Their attire was as wild as their names, comprised as it was of cast-off items of western civilization and naval clothing. Some bore letters they supposed recommended their services to the newcomers, but which really called them out as rascals. The *Constitution*'s crew, of course, did nothing to disenchant them. The females accompanying these Malagasy "merchants" were "in the most primitive state of nudity." A lieutenant waxed eloquent in his journal entry, writing of "the women with but little more covering [than] a strip of cloth around the middle, their figure shining in voluptuous and greasy contour."

Water and wood stocks replenished, *Constitution* required five days to sail next to Mozambique, fading capital of Portuguese East Africa, anchoring there on the 25th. Her entry into port proved to be a test of seamanship, as Percival was forced to tack repeatedly into a head wind, at times coming within four hundred yards of the surf before coming about.

Percival paid an official call on the governor general, Brig. Gen. R. L. d'Abun de Luria, accompanied by his clerk. It was a friendly meeting during which the captain learned that the entire American trade with Mozambique, begun about ten years before, consisted of an annual voyage by a brig from Salem (*Emmerton*) and another (*Richmond*) from New York. Each brought in cotton and took out ivory, gums, and copal. There was an active slave trade between that coast and Brazil, but no Americans appeared to be involved. Percival sailed on the 28th.

Next port of call was back on Madagascar's west coast, to the adjacent towns of Majunga and Bembatooka, where *Constitution* arrived on 1 November. There, American trade was dominant, and predominantly from Salem. There was even a commercial agent in residence in this out-of-the-way spot. A nine-gun salute was fired to the "Queen of Madagascar" the next morning, with a plain white flag flying at the fore truck because "the Malagash flag appeared to be of this appearance."

The Americans were made to understand that thievery was considered to be the most heinous of crimes. Grisly evidence was pointed out on a nearby sand spit: a series of pointed poles, one of which carried the decaying head of a thief. The punishment for stealing was being burned alive and the corpse beheaded. Two other skulls seen lying near the poles subsequently were smuggled aboard ship by midshipmen intent on exotic souvenirs. Twenty-nine men were allowed liberty until sunset on the 3rd. The seventeen who returned on time mostly were very drunk. Percival took a party of officers and men ashore the next morning, ostensibly to visit a nearby fort (where the guns were found to be "the survivors of the original battery of Noah's ark"), but, in reality, to track down his recalcitrant sailors, who some thought were plotting a "minor mutiny." They ultimately were found, and, after a "small fight," were returned to *Constitution* that afternoon with heads throbbing both from rum and hard knocks. Most were awarded a swift twelve of the cat.

Leaving Majunga, Percival headed north at Nos Bey Island, off Passandava Bay, on the 7th. There, he filled his water tanks before getting under way for Zanzibar. En route, on the 13th, all hands were called to witness punishment in the case of Seaman Edward Brett, the leader of the Majunga "mutineers." Because he realized that Brett, though a troublemaker, was popular with the crew in general, Percival took the unusual step of reading the charges personally. Brett, he said, had sought to strike the captain, had threatened him, and had sworn at him.[3] Others present at the time of the altercation stated that, in their opinions, Brett had been at least sufficiently sober to have known to whom he was speaking and to have been responsible for his actions. With that, Brett was triced up and received twelve lashes of the cat. Justice was done, the crew satisfied that it was fair, and nothing more came of the incident.

Constitution anchored off the town of Metany on the morning of the 18th. There she found her old sailing partner, *Berceau*, busy surveying the harbor. While some of his officers were visiting the French, Percival, who wasn't feeling too well, dined with eight or ten others as guests of the sultan of Muscat, then resident in his southernmost territory. On Sunday, the 24th, he led the crew at Divine Service, delivering a sermon based upon the story of Lazarus and the rich man, one of his favorites.

His ship stocked for the first time in months with fresh meat, vegetables, and fruit, and after having stayed up until 4:00 A.M. to observe a total eclipse of the moon, Percival headed *Constitution* out across the Indian Ocean on the 26th. It was a long haul in those equatorial waters. Some days, the ship made good 240 miles; on others, a wind couldn't be found, the sails slatting against the masts as the mercury went above 100 degrees and the black hammock cloths became too hot to touch. Percival's repainting of the hull was believed to have been most beneficial. As the days went on, however, the sick list began to grow, some coming down with dysentery or a fever of some kind, others taken ill as a result of overeating unripe or unfamiliar fruits. Percival himself was forced to his cot by what was variously reported as gout or inflammatory rheumatism in one or both of his feet. At times, he was able to hobble about on crutches, but Paine had to take on more and more responsibility for the operation of the ship. There were forty-three on the sick list on 18 December, and it was growing. The first death of the voyage occurred on the 20th, when Seaman John P. Weston was found moaning unintelligibly on the berth deck near sick bay shortly before expiring. Two days later, bandsman Christian Fischer, a German in his fifties, succumbed. Burials were conducted as quickly as possible following post mortems. On the 23rd, Percival ordered his day cabin converted into a hospital ward for the sick while he, himself, largely was confined to the after cabin.

Christmas 1844 was a dolorous day, given the nearly sixty crew who were sick and the temperatures that never got below 80 degrees. The wardroom had a dinner of shoulder of pork, ducks, and preserved (canned) soup, but no one had the spirit. The wine was "passed by as so much poison." A comet was visible on the southwest horizon that evening, but aroused very little interest.

THE FAR EAST

The high land of Sumatra was a welcome sight at sunrise on New Year's Day 1845. Light and adverse winds, however, continued to frustrate the debilitated crew until the 3rd, when they arrived at notorious Kuala Batu. (In February 1831, treacherous Malay pirates temporarily captured the American merchantman *Friendship* as she lay at anchor off the town, killing a number of the crew. In response, President Jackson had ordered *Potomac*, 44, to apply suitable chastisement. One day shy of the first anniversary of the attack, retribution was delivered. It still was a vivid memory thirteen years later when another "44" appeared.) Present off the town was the Salem merchant ship *Carolina Augusta*. Po Adam, a Malay who had been an ally in the earlier fracas, paid a call on the ship and was thought to be "not very prepossessing."

Percival received Rajah Chedulah, one of the ringleaders in the *Friendship* attack, with his "ragtag and bobtail" suite abed in his cabin. His indisposition did nothing to improve his diplomacy (if any were required), and he proceeded to tell the rajah that peace between him and the Americans rested solely on the good conduct of the Malays. There were, he said, many American "big ships" ready to punish evildoers.

Midshipman Lucius M. Mason of Virginia died on the morning of the 6th of dysentery and "inflammation of the brain." *Constitution* got under way at 4:00 that afternoon with Po Adam as pilot, bound for Annalaboo and Wylah to look in on American traders in those ports. Mason was buried en route with full honors. Po Adam was put ashore at Wylah.

"Old Ironsides" departed Wylah late on the 8th, heading for Singapore and a recuperation period. It was an unbelievably difficult trip. Adverse winds and currents fought her all the way, turning each mile made good into a victory over Mother Nature. Forced northward, she first spent two days in sight of the Nicobar Islands. Then it took her until the 24th to pass Prince of Wales Island (Pulo Penang) and enter the Straits of Malacca proper. Once in that unfamiliar, relatively narrow gut, she anchored each night. On some days, only twenty to thirty miles were made good. Petty Officer Peter Wolfe died in the forward cabin on the evening of the 29th; he was buried the next morning. Singapore was sighted, at long last, on the last day of the month, but three more days were needed to reach it.

The *Constitution* that arrived in Singapore on 3 February was but a sad shadow of the smart frigate that had cleared New York so lightheartedly eight months earlier. Her spars still stood tall, all right, and her yards were squared and rigged taut. But below she looked to be the scruffiest of merchantmen. The worn lead-white had splotches of old black showing through; the ribband of bright red had grown dim and was similarly mottled by its underlying coat of white. Rust streaks streamed down and aft from the chains and the pins in the hull. President Andrew Jackson, the figurehead, was more a mendicant, a tramp dressed in a millionaire's cast-off finery. Among her people, "Mad Jack" was bedridden, and more than sixty cases, mostly of dysentery, reposed about her decks. The time had come to "get well."

First on board was the consul, Mr. Balestier. He offered quarters at his house to Percival, who, once he was satisfied that the needs of his ship and crew were being attended to, accepted the invitation. His hostess was a daughter of Paul Revere.

The day after the consul's visit, Percival received a call from the British commodore whose broad pennant flew from the frigate *Cambrian.* He was a tall, erect gentleman of an age with the captain, genial and relaxed. A curious expression was seen to cross his face as he paused on the quarterdeck, receiving the honors due his station. He seemed at once puzzled and a little surprised. Paine escorted him below to meet "Mad Jack," who managed to be up on crutches as his guest entered. The commodore was quick to offer the services of his surgeon and any other facilities the Royal Navy had that might speed Percival's command back to health. Then he asked if this was the same *Constitution* that had fought so brilliantly in the War of 1812. When told that she was, the commodore revealed his interest: He was Henry Ducie Chads, who had had to surrender *Java* to Commodore Bainbridge on these very decks, thirty-three years before and half a world away.

With the crew once more healthy and the ship overhauled and replenished, Percival sailed out for Borneo on 10 March. He was little improved, however, and had to leave the ship's operation to his "Number One."

BAD TIME IN BORNEO

Constitution needed a week, working against head winds, to raise the Borneo coast. When she dropped anchor off the Sambas River (sixty miles south of Cape

Api) on the 17th, she was believed to be the first American warship to have moored in those waters. Shortly thereafter, Sailing Master Strain was sent off in the fourth cutter to reconnoiter the immediate coast. He reported the area virtually uninhabited upon his return. Percival then ordered the first cutter and the gig launched and manned for an expedition some forty miles up the river to the town of Sambas to determine which colonial empire claimed it and what trade opportunities there might be. Placed in charge was Second Lt. William C. Chaplin, supported by Marine 2d Lt. Joseph W. Curtis, the sailing master, Midshipman Colville Terrett, Assistant Surgeon Marius Duvall, naturalist Reinhart, and twenty-three armed sailors and three Marines—armed because the area was said to be infested with murderous pirates, eager to take advantage of the unwary.

The expedition's journey up the river was accomplished uneventfully. In fact, the Americans found considerable native assistance in making their way in unfamiliar waters. They also received a warm welcome from the Dutch governor at Sambas and learned that trade would be possible at reasonable tariffs; cotton goods were particularly desired.

After two days' absence, Percival grew anxious about Chaplin's party and dispatched a second expedition to "the Chinese town" (probably Pamangket, a short distance inside the river's mouth) from whence it could respond to any hint of trouble upriver. Fourth Lt. James W. Cooke headed this detachment, assisted by Dale, Surgeon Daniel C. McLeod, Midshipman Joseph J. Cook, and Professor Estabrook, in the third cutter. The captain's concern proved unwarranted, however, and both parties returned to *Constitution* at 9:00 P.M. on the 20th.

The big frigate proceeded north slowly on the 22nd, her officers well aware that the charts they had were neither correct nor complete. Cautiously, it was under way each morning and anchor each night until the northwest corner of Borneo (Tadjung Datu) was turned. On the 29th, a fair wind gave them a few hours of real progress before it failed them; still, it was safer to anchor at night, as heavy nocturnal rains further reduced any capability they had for finding their way along.

The tension of groping through dangerous waters by day and anchoring off a hostile coast each night soon had its effect on the crew. The men grew edgy and began to grate upon one another; this was particularly true between sailor and Marine, where enmity traditionally existed. Several fights were reported to Percival, the most serious of which involved Seaman Thomas Starkey and Pvt. Arthur DeBlueg. As the instigator, Starkey was awarded twelve lashes of the cat by the captain; he gave DeBlueg nine as the willing respondent.

This concern over being attacked also was reflected in the repeated exercises of the Marines in small arms practice against various targets, and of cutter crews in "defending" their boats while making landings or withdrawals. One drill even involved suspending Marine snipers from the fore yard to provide high supporting fire to the cutters. The ship's gun crews, too, were drilled to defeat the piratical threat.

Late on 4 April *Constitution* very nearly grounded due to a twenty-mile error in the chart, and was saved only by Paine's quick action. She finally arrived safely off Brunei on the 6th, having been groping through some of the world's most hazardous waters for more than two weeks.

Chaplin again headed a boat expedition ashore to the city of Brunei (now Bandar Seri Begawan) to offer a treaty of commerce and friendship, but returned the next morning empty-handed. According to the British "white rajah," Sir James Brooke, the Americans' interpreter was so bad that the whole intent of the visit was misunderstood by the native sultan; otherwise Brooke might have had competition on his hands for dominion over the area. The Americans departed on the 10th, pausing long enough off Labuan Island for Reinhart to determine that there were no coal deposits on it.

In standing north from Labuan, "Old Ironsides" came as close to defeat as ever she would, for Paine unwittingly took her into an extensive area of reefs and shoals still known as the Dangerous Ground. The first near miss occurred at sunrise on the 12th, when she lightly scraped her keel on some coral about fourteen miles north-northwest of Labuan. A kedge anchor was lost in maneuvering her clear. Two more days were spent in looking for leads north in much the same manner as an icebreaker in pack ice before Paine headed southwest once more—until he suddenly found himself blocked by a semicircle of coral reef. In kedging her out astern, a second anchor was lost and she again "touched lightly." On the 16th, another "perfect horseshoe of coral rocks"; another effort to tow her astern through the one passage out. By that evening, it seemed as if they might have found a safe channel. On the 17th, they made five miles, and so it went. A final scare—a near-miss on Luconia Shoal—and they finally were able to turn north on the 23rd after an eleven-day ordeal.

THE FIRST TIME

Land was sighted to the northwest as early as 2 May, but contrary winds prevented the ship from even closing the coast for six days, let alone enter port.

After another two days of battling contrary winds at the entrance, the great frigate was at last able to beat into the bay. On the starboard hand, mountainous ridges, their roots in the sea, marched into the distance to the west and northwest. To port, the blunt abrupt knob that would become known to a later generation of Americans as Monkey Mountain gave way to low flat land that made up the south shore of the bay. Rounding to smartly west of the knob, *Constitution* came to anchor, two months from Singapore and three weeks shy of a year since she had sailed out of New York. The date was 10 May 1845.

"Old Ironsides" was at Tourane (now Da Nang), Cochin China (Vietnam), and the first order of business was to make arrangements for the burial of one Cooke, musician, who died that day. A plot was secured within the limits of a native burial ground at the foot of Monkey Mountain for the sum of two dollars, perpetual care included. When the burial ceremony was completed, the ship shifted berth deeper into the bay, and made preparations to water ship.

On the 13th, a recuperating Percival sent the redoubtable Chaplin ashore to visit the Mandarin of the city, taking with him a small party of junior officers, sailors, and Marines. Guided by a Chinese from the crew, the group proceeded along city streets and finally through a double line of soldiers to the courtyard of the principal mandarin's house. Each soldier was dressed in a knee-length coat of red with a circular green emblem on the chest, and wore a conical wooden helmet sheathed in metal, and each bore a tall spear with a brightly colored pennant attached just below the head.

The lieutenant, his party grouped behind him, was seated at one side of the table set up in the open. The chief mandarin, with his umbrella bearer and other attendants, appeared shortly thereafter and took the seat opposite. Despite all the ceremonial, the meeting was but a short exchange of introductions and pleasantries, with the mandarin agreeing to pay a call on board the American man-of-war.

The next day, Wednesday the 14th, the Chinese, as they were termed, called on Percival and were received with appropriate ceremony, despite the fact that the crew had begun to repaint the ship in her familiar black and white scheme. All went well, and the Chinese left after having been given a tour of the ship. During the tour, however, one of the visitors had slipped back to the cabin and delivered a letter to Percival, saying his life would be forfeit if his master found out. Opening it after the departure of his guests, Percival found it was from a French missionary, Bishop Dominique Lefevre, who stated that he was "surprised at not having heard from his former letter," and appealed again for help as his village had been "delivered over to pillage" and that he, "with twelve Cochin Chinese, were then arrested and under sentence of immediate death."

The Americans were shocked into precipitate action. "Here," wrote Dale, "was an opportunity of a rescue from this semi-barbarous nation. It was enough for us to know that a fellow Christian was in danger of his life. The strongest and most instant measures must be taken. Humanity was to be our warrant rather than the law of nations." Percival quickly called for a party of fifty sailors and thirty Marines, all "armed to the teeth," loaded them into the ship's boats, and headed for the beach. Up the streets, across the marketplace, and through the double line of soldiers went Percival. The natives acted as if nothing was going on, but the American skipper took the precaution of stationing an unbroken line of U.S. sailors and Marines in sight of one another all the way from the boats to the chief mandarin's house. Help could be called at the slightest hint of trouble.

The captain took his place at one side of the table, and the Oriental headman at the other. Some time was spent by Percival satisfying himself that he was, in fact, talking to *somebody*. That point settled, he demanded that the mandarin dispatch immediately a letter he had prepared to the Frenchman, and that an answer be returned within twenty-four hours. Furthermore, the three known local leaders would be held in *Constitution* as hostages. If the deadline was not met, Percival declared he would take possession of the three forts near the town and all the shipping he could lay his hands on. All of this he announced despite the presence of numerous armed soldiers, the fact that the causeway along which the Americans had come could be enfiladed by two of the forts, and "a fellow who stood by the big gong with uplifted hammer ready to sound the tocsin!" For reasons beyond the mystified ken of the Americans, "the tocsin did not sound," and they returned to the frigate with the three hostages and two attendant pipe bearers, no one having made a move to stop them.

Tensions mounted on board as the twenty-four hours ticked away. When the appointed time passed without result, Percival directed the cessation of the watering operation and cut all communication with the shore until the arrival of the bishop's reply. *Constitution* again shifted anchorages to a position closer to town and just a half mile from one of the forts, and fired ten ranging shells. Further to reinforce his demands, the captain then directed that three war junks seen anchored a mile and a half off be captured. The ship's three largest boats were armed and manned in short order, and quickly under way with the sailors' valor "screwed up to the highest notch."

It soon became apparent that the three targets would not get away, being both anchored and moored to the shore. The wretched, half-naked people manning them offered no resistance to the hallooing Americans who came piling aboard, and all the junks were moved and anchored off the quarters of "Old Ironsides." Strain was tasked to keep them under observation, and during the night alertly prevented one of the three from sneaking off.

The next three days passed uneventfully and then, on Monday the 19th, *Constitution* was kedged still closer to the river mouth at the town and well within range of the forts on either side, springs being used to keep her starboard battery trained shoreward. Indications from the shore were that all of Percival's threats had had no effect, except that the Cochin Chinese now were refusing even further negotiation until the hostages were released. The captain went ashore again in the same manner as before, and again largely was ignored by the populace. Returning to the ship after a long and fruitless parley, he ordered the three hostages released and hoped thereby to break the stalemate.

In the excitement of kedging in closer to town and standing at battle stations while Percival parleyed ashore, the Americans had ignored their three prize junks. When Strain inspected each of them that evening, he made an amazing discovery: With the Americans looking the other way, the hill fort commander apparently had managed to send a detachment out to the captured craft—not to retake them, but to punish the junk commanders for being prisoners. Strain reported finding all three men had been whipped with bamboo wands and each yoked with two pieces of heavy wood four to five feet long. The bindings at the ends of the yokes bore the seal of the mandarin. One of the skippers, possibly the senior of the trio, also had had his *eyes* cemented shut with a pitch-like substance likewise bearing the imprint of authority. So great was the fear of these men of the mandarin that they refused the American intention to relieve them, indicating by vivid signs that they would be beheaded. However, they willingly shifted the three junks to anchor again closer to "Old Ironsides" and farther away from the hill fort.

Tuesday dawned squally and nasty. Taking advantage of the cover provided by the wind-driven rain, the three war junks slipped their cables and ran with the wind, seeking escape from the Americans by dashing upriver. One shortly was retaken as *Constitution*'s opening broadside of nine rounds caused her crew to drop anchor and jump overboard, some probably drowning. The other two succeeded in crossing the bar and appeared to be making good their escape.

But the American boat crews sent in pursuit of them were not to be daunted by the tempestuous weather and seas, or potentially hostile Chinese. Pulling boldly, the launch and four cutters surged past six or eight armed boats loaded with native soldiers, through waters covered by the guns of the forts on either bank. The native craft scattered without a shot fired. The second junk soon was retaken without opposition and a small guard left on board.

Onward pressed the American force, leaving pacific red-coated troops to port and starboard. A mile upstream, the last escapee was found run aground and abandoned, its sails destroyed. After a quick inspection, the Americans completed preparations to refloat the junk before there appeared an "Indian file" of armed Chinese, 150 of them, who took up positions just twenty yards off. The boat crews gripped their cutlasses and leaped into the three-foot-deep water, sent up "a real Anglo-Saxon shout" and charged pell-mell at the Chinese. These "took to their heels in a most precipitate manner" and were not seen again. The Marines busied themselves gathering *coconuts* on the way back to the boats, while an old Chinese watched the whole ludicrous affair impassively from his porch nearby.

The return of all three junks under the guns of "Old Ironsides" was accomplished uneventfully, the weather even moderating temporarily to make the long pull easier. A short time later, however, it kicked up again, and one of the junks broke loose and broached. It took the Americans until late evening of their busy day to refloat her and return her to the anchorage. The Chinese ashore once again confounded their visitors by transporting a large wooden anchor a mile and a half on their backs to assist the Americans in their task.

As day dawned on the 21st, "the view was wild and grand. Heavy, lowering clouds were rushing onwards from the sea, and wreathing wildly about the mountain summits all magnified into gigantic spectres by the rainy atmosphere; while rollers were tumbling in upon the beach to leeward, and the long sand spit from the river, one drift of snowy breakers." And to the Americans' surprise, three ships wearing "the yellow flag of Cochin" were seen anchored below the hill fort on the side of Monkey Mountain. They apparently had come in quietly during the night.

The weather moderated during the night that followed, and the thermometer, which had been as low as 78 degrees during the gale, again rose to an oppressive level. Still no sign or word of the French priest. The junk that had broached was found to be leaking badly and was returned formally to the Chinese, who were perplexed that the others weren't returned also. Percival attempted to visit the three newly arrived ships, but was refused permission to go aboard, his gig being pushed off "with oars & sticks."

Credulity concerning the situation was further strained on the 23rd, when trade was reopened for provisioning the ship. The next morning, two letters were received from the mandarin and "from little officers" (whoever they were). The former said nothing was known about the Frenchman and asked for the return of the junks; the other stated that the priest would be surrendered when the junks were returned. To reinforce the demand, provisions were stopped until the junks were freed. Percival bowed to this, and food and water again came to the ship, but no Frenchman.

On the 25th, Percival made a final try for the bishop by sending a letter ashore to the effect that he would leave shortly for Canton, where he would report the incident to the French authorities, who undoubtedly would wreak swift retribution. The response indicated that the threats were considered hollow, and that unless a "good letter" was drafted, no further communications would be forwarded to the king.

Threats had failed, bribes rejected, and thus far at least, aggressive actions tolerated. But beneath the surface, the native leadership was marshalling its forces. There were the three brigs that had arrived. The junks had been refitted. And three ships that had been lying in ordinary were completing reactivation. Ashore, the forts were being refurbished and extended, their approaches being rendered more difficult. Percival recognized that the situation could only get worse and his solitary frigate, glorious record notwithstanding, insufficient to the task. After sunset on 26 May 1845, after sixteen hectic and fruitless days, *Constitution* departed, leaving things much as they were before she arrived. "Mad Jack" vented his frustrations by firing six shots from his starboard Paixhans guns at an island off the harbor entrance. Only one reached the target. Dale sums up this first U.S. Navy-Marine Corps experience in Vietnam thusly: "[I]t seems, I must say, to have shown a sad want of 'sound discretion,' in commencing an affair of this kind, without carrying it through to a successful issue."

Prophetic words.[4]

China Visit

Percival's next stop was China, but even before he arrived there he learned of what the next chapter was to be in the adventures of Lefevre. On the 30th, while some ten leagues off Hainan Island, he spoke the British ship *Duilius*, from

Singapore for Hong Kong. A French squadron had been present when she left fifteen days earlier, whose admiral was in receipt of the bishop's *first* letter. He sent a unit of his force, *Alcmene,* to get the bishop, which it did without incident, for returning him to his own people was what the locals had wanted all along and failed to make Percival understand. Subsequently, upon learning of *Constitution's* efforts in the affair, King Louis Philippe—who, it will be recalled, attended her launching—is said to have directed that Percival and his crew be rewarded for their efforts. Political turbulence in France, however, forced him from the throne in 1848. Too, Percival's impetuous actions were repudiated by his own government as being unauthorized and excessive, and relations with the Cochin king were restored only years later.

The frigate arrived at the anchorage about six miles below Macao on 5 June and received her first mail from the United States since leaving Rio nine months earlier. While Percival paid calls on the Portuguese authorities, the crew spent the day catching up with their loved ones at home. Some evidently celebrated in other ways, for on Monday, the 9th, "Punished all the first Cutters for drunkenness and smuggling liquor (except 6)."

Constitution's was only the ninth visit of an American warship to China, and it came at a time when the relationship between the Celestial Kingdom and the United States was blossoming. Como. Lawrence Kearney had arrived in China in 1842 with frigate *Constellation* and sloop *Boston* just as the First Opium War was concluding. In the Treaty of Nanking, which brought peace that summer, the British received Hong Kong and "most favored nation" trade considerations. In reporting these events to Washington and in discussions with the Chinese, Kearney had set in motion a chain of events that resulted in the completion of the Treaty of Wanghia in July 1844, which granted Americans similar commercial arrangements. In fact, Como. James Biddle in the liner *Columbus* had just gotten under way from New York for China to exchange treaty ratifications.

Having ascertained the political situation, Percival got under way and headed up the Pearl River on the 18th, just the third time an American man-of-war had done so. The trip did not begin auspiciously, for the big ship soon was on a mud bank. Floated off later in the day, she renewed the voyage the next morning. Blenheim Reach (Whampoa), some fifteen miles below Canton, was reached at noon on the 20th.

Constitution swung at her hook deep in China for the next six weeks, while Percival called on officials of the Kwantung government, dealt with complaints of

American merchants, and had his portrait painted by a Chinese artist. For the crew, it was a period of growing boredom and increasing sickness. The ship had followed the summer season northward. Day after day, they had to endure stifling heat, high humidity, swarms of mosquitoes, and nearly daily rainstorms that only made the climate more oppressive. The men were no better able to withstand the conditions than they had been in the Indian Ocean; the sick list began to grow once more. Captain of the Foretop Charles Lewis died on 17 July and Ordinary Seaman Michael Fritt at about the same time. Both were buried ashore. Percival, considering he had accomplished everything that required him to be near Canton, started downriver on the last day of the month, a favoring breeze allowing him to set the royals and starboard stunsails. The sick list again stood at sixty, most suffering from dysentery.

Percival dropped down as far as the Wantong Passage, where he anchored near the French frigate *Cleopatre* on 3 August. The new anchorage proved to be somewhat cooler, improving the health situation, although Pvt. Henry Lohman died of dysentery on the 13th. Seaman George Fuller's death was the last to occur in China, on the 24th. *Constitution* moved to her original berth below Macao on the 27th and began taking on stores in preparation for the next leg of her journey. Through all the long weeks inside China, drinking water had been secured by filtering the river water through charcoal. The result was said to be "very good," but probably was the cause of the return of dysentery.

China was left astern on 1 September, as Percival headed his frigate for Manila, capital of the Spanish Philippines. Luzon quickly was raised, but then head winds and calms left the ship drifting along at a snail's pace. At dawn one morning, the Americans awoke to find themselves nearly surrounded by a squadron of what obviously were European men-of-war, six of them. Who were they? Were they at peace or war with the United States?

A flag unfurled from what evidently was the flagship of the unknown squadron (a steamer) revealed they were British. A lieutenant from the steamer informed Percival that the squadron was commanded by Rear Adm. Sir Thomas John Cochrane. The admiral sent a request for any provisions that could be spared, because the adverse winds had extended his expected time at sea to the point where they were about to run out. Percival gladly complied, having so recently provisioned, and officer visits were exchanged while five tons of bread and four hundred gallons of whiskey were transferred. "Mad Jack" plied his guests with brandy and water and cigars, and startled them with the way he spat all about the cabin. With a final salute from the British, each side went on its own way. *Constitution* subsequently anchored near Corregidor on the 11th and finally made it to Manila on the 18th, where she spent a week.

ACROSS THE PACIFIC

Constitution paused briefly off Batan Island, one of the small specks dividing the Bashi Channel from the Balintang Passage north of Luzon, on the 26th. From the island, Percival was able to purchase a few bullocks for fresh meat, and to top off his water supply. Seaman Edward Robinson deserted there and was left behind. The Pacific Ocean was entered on the 28th, an event that seemed to the crew to mark the start of the voyage home. The custom of "splicing the main brace" was observed on the 30th to celebrate the captain's thirty-sixth wedding anniversary.

Light winds sent the frigate to the southeast for three days and then northward to the vicinity of the Ryukyu Islands. From there, she was able to head roughly northeastward, on the great circle sailing for the Hawaiian Islands. This took her somewhat to the south of the coasts of Japan, "that *terra incognita*, where no Western barbarian may dare cast anchor, except one annual Dutch ship at a single port of Nagasaka [*sic*]." Perry's opening of Japan to the West still was eight years in the future. The last piece of Asiatic territory seen by the American sailors was a solitary rock sticking out of the ocean, known as Lot's Wife.

The trans-Pacific crossing required fifty days, in all. Gales made shipboard life miserable on two occasions: 20–24 October and 3–5 November. The ship was leaking so badly that ten to eighteen inches of water were pumped from the bilges twice a day. *Constitution* arrived off Honolulu on 16 November, having come in from the *eastward*, where the winds had taken her. Because of her draft, she had to remain anchored outside the reefs.

Unwanted news awaited Percival in Hawaii. He found there Como. John D. Sloat of the Pacific Squadron in his flagship, *Savannah*, 44. Sloat, aware that trouble was brewing at home over the "Texas affair," informed "Mad Jack" that he and his ship would be detained in Sloat's command as needed reinforcement pending resolution of the difficulties with Mexico. Percival was to stock for six months and proceed to join the squadron on the West Coast while Sloat remained in Honolulu as long as necessary to settle another minor diplomatic dispute.

There transpired during this Hawaiian stay an incident pregnant with implications for the future. It seems that two years earlier, a British man-of-war had appeared and had bulldozed King Kamehameha III into ceding his kingdom to the British Empire. Shortly thereafter, Commodore Kearney of China fame showed up and, in defending American rights in the islands, ultimately caused an end to British rule after five months. Recalling that unhappy situation and the reasonable course of the U.S. Navy, on the present occasion the Hawaiian foreign minister approached *Constitution*'s lieutenant of Marines, Joseph W. Curtis, to survey the Honolulu area quietly and recommend to him where fortifications might best be placed to thwart enemy aggressors. Curtis' secret report recommended Pearl Harbor.

The Hawaiian king was entertained on board the famed frigate during her stay. "Mad Jack" saw to it Kamehameha learned the ship's winning record against the Royal Navy and gave him a thorough tour, including the magazine and shot room. His Majesty expressed a particular interest in the Paixhans guns and accordingly was given a live firing demonstration, much to the delight of his subjects on the nearby shore.

The ship's officers were treated to a genuine Hawaiian luau featuring pit-baked dog on 1 December. Although initially put off at the prospect of eating dog, a little "puppy tasting" by the more adventurous members of the wardroom had them declaring it was "very nice." Some overate dog and poi to the point where they were afflicted with "that damnedest, most filthy, disgusting, loathsome disease that God Almighty ever punished his errant mortals with": dysentery. One, at least, still would claim to feel the aftereffects eight months later.

Constitution sailed from Honolulu on the 2nd, making for the California coast. The trip was a bad one of constant storms. As they neared the coast on the 27th, the rain began coming down incessantly and heavy fogs made navigation dangerous. A break in the weather on the last day of the year showed Percival that no one was in Monterey Bay, and the next day he filled away for Mazatlán, Mexico, again in squalls and rain. In a week, the weather improved. From whalers, they learned that the squadron was, in fact, at Mazatlán. They arrived on 13 January 1846. Sloat had arrived ahead of them. Present were war sloops *Levant, Warren, Portsmouth,* and *Cyane,* schooner *Shark,* and stores ship *Erie.*

For more than three months, the big frigate idled on her hook at Mazatlán. War did not come. Morale plummeted with the continued absence from home and lack of purposeful activity; the flogging of drunken libertymen was nearly

constant. Sloat was in a difficult position. Most of the squadron was in a deteriorating condition, including both frigates. Still nothing happened, although
rumors ran rife. Finally, he bowed to Percival's repeated reports of the ship's
material problems and vermin infestation, and permitted *Constitution* to sail for
home. It was 22 April, only three days before fighting began. The crew partied
all night that first one at sea, the toast to "Sweethearts and Wives" being drunk
to exhaustion. They would have seven weeks to recover from their celebrations,
for it took *Constitution* that long to work her way south-southwestward through
the doldrums and into the prevailing westerlies of the South Pacific that would
carry her to Valparaíso, Chile.

HOMEWARD BOUND

A week was spent in Valparaíso stocking up before the ship headed south once
more, making preparation to double the Horn as they went. All guns forward of
the foremast and aft of the mizzen were moved amidships and lashed down.
Gun ports were shut and caulked. Hatches were battened down and tarpaulins
secured over them.

Cape Horn was sighted on the 4th of July in as wild a holiday as any of the
crew ever would experience. Sleet and snow squalls followed her into the
Atlantic. By the 15th, however, they were enjoying beautiful weather and relishing
every diminished mile home. An accident on the 20th caused the cruise's last
fatality when Seaman John Moore was struck in the head by a swinging block.

In Rio again on the 28th, *Constitution* was greeted by Minister Wise, participated in salutes to the birth of the emperor's second child, and began replenishing, and the crew started painting the hull for the last time. Mail and newspapers awaited them in profusion. It was learned that the war with Mexico had
begun two months earlier, and many no doubt gave thanks that they had been
able to leave the Pacific Squadron in the nick of time. Because of the war situation, when she sailed on 5 August, the big frigate had in convoy the American
coffee ships *Mazopha*, *Chenango*, *Margaret Hugg*, *Tweed*, *Fabian*, and *Abo*. Before she
cleared the Brazilian hump, ten more merchantmen had opted for her company.

The voyage to the Delaware Capes, where the convoy dispersed, was uneventful until the coast was in the offing. Somewhere off Cape Hatteras, *Constitution*
came upon a mastless hulk, all that remained of the brig *Washington*, which had
been under the command of Lt. Comdr. George M. Bache, a descendant of

Benjamin Franklin. She had been employed on coastal survey and had been cast on her beam ends by a hurricane on 8 September, rolling the masts out of her. Bache had been one of the ten to twelve swept overboard. The hulk was taken in tow and turned over to the Philadelphia pilot boat *Enoch Turley* when the convoy broke up.

In the waning days of this epic voyage, the old frigate's crew made every effort to restore her to spit and polish for her return home. Midshipman John E. Hart made his own unique contribution, donating some red paint so that the figurehead could be brightened up.

Constitution arrived home in Boston on Sunday, 27 September 1846, having sailed, by official reckoning, 52,370.5 miles, and received a twenty-eight-gun salute from the city. She was towed to the navy yard the next day by the brand-new steamer *R. B. Forbes*, first ocean-going tug in the country, and moored alongside the ship-sloop *Jamestown*. "Mad Jack" hauled down her commission pennant and went ashore on 5 October.

Hart has left his parting sentiments: "[S]he is now come home like her aged Commander to lay her old bones up 'for a full due.' She has gone about like a 'Good Samaritan' and her life has been a tissue of benevolent actions from the time she first left the land that grew her timbers, until she returned to be stripped and her old war-worn and tempest-torn frame laid by a deserted old hulk. Every old plank, bolt, spar and rope yarn in her has a share of my love. . . . I can scarcely bear the idea of leaving her, but I must."

CHAPTER SIXTEEN

Mediterranean Finale

WORK-UP

The principal reason for *Constitution*'s overhaul and recommissioning in 1848 was the widespread outbreak of revolutions in Europe. Beginning in France with the deposition of King Louis Philippe, rebellion caught on in Austria, Germany, and Hungary, and finally Italy, which was then yet a collection of petty kingdoms and city-states. Heavy American commercial interests in the Mediterranean Basin made it incumbent upon the navy to take what steps it could to protect our people and trade in the unsettled region. So "Old Ironsides" was docked and readied for one more tour of duty in those familiar waters.

An advance in technology led to the removal of the chain pumps with which the ship had been equipped for fifty years. Mechanically complex and operationally problematical, they were replaced by simpler suction pumps—operated in the manner of railroad hand cars—that have remained in the ship ever since. At the same time, the pair of equally obsolescent brake pumps forward of the mast on the gun deck, used for bringing fresh water up from the "well," was succeeded by a bronze model installed forward on the berth deck, more convenient to where the crew ate.

The most obvious change made in the old frigate was the replacement of the clumsy Jackson figurehead that Commodore Elliott had installed in 1834. A more glamorous rendering of the late president was done by the Boston carvers John D. and William H. Fowle. This new Jackson stood tall with a stern visage, clad in well-fitting attire topped by a draped cloak. He carried a scroll in his right hand and his left was tucked into the front of his tailed coat, à la Napoleon. The Fowles also carved new trailboards for the ship; these were similar to those still to be seen on her today, but with a flower reminiscent of a Tudor rose in the position currently occupied by the national shield. The Fowles were paid $330 for their work.

Noticeable to those who were familiar with the ship was the installation of a new main fife rail. The old, multilevel model gave way to one patterned on the fore fife rail, shaped like the Greek letter "pi," its cross bar abaft the main mast and arms extending forward on either side of it.

Perhaps the most important change effected during the preparation of "Old Ironsides" in 1847–1848 was the major alteration of her gun batteries. In 1845, a Navy Department Board of Standardization had recommended that henceforth 32-pounder long guns and 8-inch Paixhans guns be employed as the basic naval cannon. Approved and implemented, it was time for *Constitution* to be brought into line. To accommodate the new guns, all of her gun ports were enlarged to be three feet high and forty-two inches across. The port sills on the spar deck were raised to eighteen inches, while those below went to two feet. Twenty 32-pounder long guns were emplaced on the aging frigate's upper deck, while twenty-six of a heavier model, together with the four Paixhans, went on the gun deck.

Marylander John Gwinn, whose orders to command *Constitution* were dated 31 August 1848, had had an unusual career pattern for a naval officer of that day; one might say it was the antithesis to that of seagoing Jacob Jones. Gwinn received his warrant as a midshipman in 1809, and spent the opening months of the War of 1812 on a schooner in Chesapeake Bay. He had the misfortune to be assigned to the sloop *Frolic*, 18, the first ship to be completed at the Boston Navy Yard, which was captured by the British on her maiden voyage in 1814. He spent the rest of the war as a prisoner. In the decade that followed, he made two Mediterranean deployments and a trip to northern Europe in three different ships. Between 1828 and 1848, he spent a total of ten years at the Philadelphia Navy Yard, three on leave, and five awaiting orders. Like Commodore Preble, it appears that his physical condition was not up to his ambition and broke down at times. Before commanding *Constitution*, he had been captain of *Vandalia*, 18, and *Potomac*, 44—each for a year. He formally placed "Old Ironsides" back in commission at 2:30 P.M. on 9 October 1848. It took him exactly two months to complete her outfitting and manning. *Constitution* began what was to be her final voyage to the Mediterranean at 9:00 A.M. 9 December.

The transit to the Strait of Gibraltar was made in twenty-three days, but instead of breaking the voyage there, Captain Gwinn headed her directly for his first port of call, Tripoli, where he arrived shortly after noon on 19 January 1849. For the next two days, the crew was busy loading aboard the personal goods and household effects of Consul Daniel Smith McCauley, who was being transferred to Alexandria with his pregnant wife, six children, and a servant. Gwinn set sail on the 22nd for Malta, where he remained for a little more than two weeks before heading east. Moderate gales discommoded the travelers for two days, but the voyage was otherwise without event until, on 24 February, "At 9:30 Mrs. Frances Ann McCauley . . . gave birth to a Son, who received the name of Constitution Stewart." The poor lad came by his name rightly: He was the grand-nephew of Capt. Charles Stewart, victor in *Constitution* over HMS *Cyane* and HMS *Levant* in 1815.

Constitution idled for more than a month in Alexandria as Gwinn and his officers took advantage of the opportunity to visit the famed pyramids. The captain himself returned aboard on 23 March with McCauley's predecessor, a Mr. Wells, whom he would carry to La Spezia. He learned from mail awaiting him that Como. William Bolton had died nearly a month earlier and he was now acting squadron commander. The winds came fair on the 27th.

The trip proceeded without incident: Candia sighted on the last day of the month and Cape Spartivento five days later, they rounded the west end of Sicily on 9 April, and arrived at La Spezia on the 12th, to find the screw steam sloop-of-war *Princeton* (first propeller-driven warship in the world) and stores ship *Erie* already there. La Spezia had become the navy's principal base in the Mediterranean during the preceding year or so. The continuing notorious conditions ashore at Port Mahon had led the Spanish government, in 1846, to ask the Americans to close their base down. In the present situation, the shift to La Spezia had both good and bad points. Proximity to the scenes of rebellion in Italy meant that American interests could be readily guarded; but that very proximity also made it viable only so long as the belligerents respected American neutrality. That there was turmoil in the hinterlands became obvious to the *Constitution*'s crew after they had been in Leghorn (ten miles south of La Spezia) for ten days. The 10 May log reported the arrival of an Austrian army before the city that began a bombardment lasting into the next day, when the city capitulated. Nearly a dozen "Livornese" came aboard seeking protection during these hectic

Constitution entered Malta late in January 1849 on what would be her only call at the island during the deployment. She was then en route to Alexandria, Egypt, carrying Consul D. S. McCauley, his pregnant wife, and others from Tripoli to their new diplomatic post. Note the less intrusive new Andrew Jackson figurehead. *Courtesy Peabody Essex Museum, Salem, Massachusetts, neg. #20,916*

days. On the 13th, Gwinn transferred them to the steamer *Allegheny*, which, for nearly a week, was busy evacuating these displaced persons to refuge elsewhere on the coast. By the 21st, the city was quiet once more and liberty parties were permitted to land. *Constitution* went north again to La Spezia on the 27th.

During the eight months since Gwinn had taken command, the ship had become increasingly unhappy. Never before or since has her log been so filled with notations of punishments awarded to crew members. Whether because of his professional attitude or the physical discomfort ulcers were giving him, Gwinn caused men to be flogged at a spectacular rate: In fact, he averaged close to one flogging for every day he was in command. Punishments were laid on either with the cat-o'-nine-tails or with the "colt," nothing more than a knotted rope. Desertion and drunkenness were, of course, common offenses calling for discipline, but others noted included such acts as "carelessly leaving an iron loose in the top," "letting a heaver fall out of the Top," "throwing soapsuds in the eyes of the Capt. of the Afterguard" (a petty officer), "smoking after 10 PM," and "for filthiness in cooking" (the wardroom cook!). All of these latter offenses are examples of the sort of incidents that always occur in a command where the crew feels its leaders are treating them unfairly. They could be fiercely loyal to a bastard of a captain who was professionally competent while strictly enforcing official regulations; they found ways of demonstrating their protest of a bullying, incompetent, or erratic leader. Something definitely was wrong in *Constitution.*

Whatever the reason Gwinn had for using the cat so frequently, and however much the sailors considered it a proper punishment for genuine infractions, they were running contrary to the popular feeling back home. Since 1845, there had been a potent movement afoot to do away with the practice. In fact, while Gwinn was busily being a martinet, the House of Representatives voted to *prohibit* flogging forevermore. It became the law on 28 September 1850.

Constitution took on stores at La Spezia, then sailed south to Naples, arriving late on 7 June. Here, in the Kingdom of Two Sicilies, was more political turmoil, for King Ferdinand II was contending not only with unrest in Sicily itself, but attempting to support Pope Pius IX in his confrontation with the Austrians from the north. The big frigate spent the rest of June and all of July there, a potent reminder that American neutrals would be protected.

POPE PIUS IX ABOARD

On 25 July, Como. Charles W. Morgan arrived in the sidewheel steam frigate *Mississippi*, 10, to assume command of the squadron. Anxious to go on to Tunis with the least possible delay, and therefore wishing to avoid the required quarantine, Morgan was briefed by Gwinn as the former sat in his barge alongside the frigate. When told of a proposal Gwinn had received from our chargé d'affaires in Naples and Rome that *Constitution* proceed to Gaeta and there be visited by Pope Pius and King Ferdinand, Morgan adamantly opposed it verbally and later in writing on the grounds that both were then contesting their thrones against revolutionaries in a conflict in which the United States had avoided taking sides. Instead, the commodore ordered Gwinn to proceed "with as little delay as possible" to Messina, then to Sardinia and northern Italy to safeguard American interests in those places. Morgan sailed for Tunis later that afternoon.

Gwinn got *Constitution* under way on the afternoon of the 30th with Chargé d'Affaires (Naples) John Rowan aboard, and on his orders proceeded to Gaeta, arriving early on the morning of 1 August. Near noon that day, the king and the pope were received on board with yards manned and a 21-gun salute for each. It was the first time a pope had set foot on American territory. (A commissioned ship

Pope Pius IX at a quieter moment. The pontiff's visit to *Constitution* marked the first time one in his office had set foot on American territory. Alas, the poor man got seasick even as the ship rode at anchor! *Library of Congress LC-USZ62-73934*

in the United States Navy has the same legal status as a piece of American soil, in the same way any of our embassies around the world do.) The king visited every part of the ship. At the request of the Catholics in the crew, they were lined up on the gun deck and received the pope's benediction. Upon returning to Gwinn's cabin, the pope became ill—seasick in an anchored ship! When the dignitaries departed, nearly three hours later, yards again were manned and two 21-gun salutes fired. *Constitution* got under way late that afternoon and returned briefly to Naples to drop off Rowan (and fire a 21-gun salute in honor of the "accouchement of the Queen of Naples") before proceeding southwest to Messina.

The pope subsequently sent 150 rosaries for the eighty Catholics in *Constitution*'s crew, together with a silver medal bearing his image and coat of arms to Gwinn. The commodore, on the other hand, was outraged by what he viewed as an outright violation of America's neutrality and flagrant disobedience of orders on Gwinn's part. As a mark of his disapprobation, Morgan recommended to Secretary of the Navy William B. Preston that the offending frigate and her captain be ordered "to the Brazil Station, or some other station" and another unit sent to the Mediterranean. But an event occurred to put a more permanent "finis" to the incident.

Captain Gwinn Dies

Following a twelve-day stay at Messina, an ailing Gwinn took his command westward to Palermo. He dropped anchor there on the afternoon of the 21st, and later in the month moved ashore to the Trinacria Hotel in hopes that some time ashore would allow him to regain his health. On 1 September, in the evening, "Capt Gwinn being dangerously ill on shore assembled all the officers in the Cabin and offered up prayers for him." At 3:18 P.M. on 4 September 1849, John Gwinn died of chronic gastritis with "severe cerebral complication" (probably a small, steady hemorrhage at the base of the skull, judging by comments he had made in letters home). In memory of "our late beloved Captain, the officers of this ship will wear on the left arm for 30 days 'Crape' as a token of respect to his memory." First Lt. James H. Rowan took command in accordance with navy regulations and lowered the flag to half mast.

The ship's carpenters spent much of the 5th building a coffin for the late skipper. After placing the remains in it, it was sealed in lead so that, some day in the future, the body might be disinterred and returned to the United States.

The funeral took place on the morning of the 6th. All the ship's boats were used to take all off-duty officers, one hundred sailors, and thirty-seven Marines ashore for the procession to the Protestant burial ground near the Lazaretto and graveside ceremonies. The solemn occasion was a shambles even before the marchers reached the gravesite. Perhaps giving vent to their own bitter memories of their late captain, at least fifteen men deserted along the line of march, while others got roaring drunk on wine purchased from roadside vendors. About a quarter of the participants either were dispersed or disheveled by the time the actual burial took place at 11:30, as nine minute-guns boomed out from the frigate in the bay. Now-Captain Rowan evidently believed wholeheartedly in the policies of his predecessor, for he had thirty-four men flogged the next day for their misdeeds during the funeral. This was the saddest human experience to be found in all *Constitution*'s history.

New Captain

Rowan made the short trip from Palermo to Naples during the 8th and 9th, and there reported Gwinn's death to Morgan aboard his flagship, now the razee *Independence*, 54. Morgan drew upon the resources available to him in the larger ship and directed Capt. Thomas Conover of the flagship to take command of *Constitution*. He did on the 18th.

Thomas Conover hailed from New Jersey and had been in the navy since 1 January 1812. He had served with David Porter in *Essex* during that frigate's epic operations in the Pacific, and later had commanded the galley-gunboat *Borer* in Thomas Macdonough's victorious squadron on Lake Champlain. On the latter occasion, he was voted a letter of thanks and a sword by Congress.

Conover had little opportunity to show off his seamanship skills in command of *Constitution*, for between his arrival on board and the end of November, the ship was under way fewer than eight days—half of them spent moving northward from Naples to La Spezia late in September. Brief round trips up to Genoa and down to Leghorn were all that broke the monotony of swinging at the hook. At the end of November, "Old Ironsides" moved back to Genoa, where she wintered over. A happy fact for the crew through all these long months was that there were only half as many floggings as there had been under Gwinn.

In the afternoon of 27 January 1850, a heavy squall struck the ships at anchor in Genoa. A Grecian brig dragged her anchor at the height of the blast, coming down hard across *Constitution's* stem. The crash carried away the flying jib boom, the jib boom, and both boomkins, but Andrew Jackson apparently escaped injury. The American sailors cut away the brig's foremast back stays, by which she was hung up, and "with great difficulty" moored her alongside until the blow was over. As if this weren't problem enough, the sloop *Jamestown*, 20, also dragged her anchor, swung into *Constitution's* starboard quarter gallery, smashing some window frames and shattering the boomkin above it. When the storm was over, the old frigate's boats were used to haul off her two assailants and see to it that they were reanchored well clear of her. Repairs occupied the carpenters until the first day of the new month.

The 1850 sailing season opened for *Constitution* on 3 March as she got under way for Toulon, France, for a visit that took up the latter half of that month. It was an all too brief break in the routine, however, for she was back in La Spezia on the last day of the month to resume the tedious round of duty "go's" at Leghorn and La Spezia. In April, May, and June, she was once in Genoa, twice in Leghorn, and thrice in La Spezia.

The people of "Old Ironsides" got another break in their routine in July, when she was ordered to Marseilles, where she spent an entire month, and then to Naples for another two days. The 26th of August found her back in La Spezia for stores. She moved on to Genoa from 30 August through 17 September, then went back to La Spezia to make preparations for the voyage home. Throughout all of October, she lay in that Italian port, taking on stores, receiving personnel going back to the states, and transferring some of her people who were early in their enlistments to other units of the squadron. The last two men ever flogged in *Constitution* received their punishments on Saturday, 19 October 1850.

The anchor was weighed in La Spezia for the last time on 2 November at 1:20 in the morning. Following a farewell three-day stay in Genoa, it was westward ho! Corsica was seen on the 12th, Minorca two days later, and Cabo da Gata on the 17th. At that point, head winds began to bedevil the ship; she didn't make Gibraltar until the early evening of the 27th. There, she waited four days with more than two hundred other ships for a fair wind to carry them out into the Atlantic.

A Collision

The wind came fair on 1 December. *Constitution* and all the others swarmed out of port. With her vast cloud of canvas towering nearly two hundred feet into the sky, the old frigate showed her stuff as she overhauled slower craft and swept westward. By sunset, she had outdistanced all those who had left the Rock with her.

At one bell of the night watch, one of the cathead lookouts cried, "Light ho!" Only a brief flash, it was believed to have been about two points on the port bow. A dark object was next seen ahead, and although an attempt was made to miss it the big frigate smashed into a brig, hitting right between the masts in the starboard side; both whipped and snapped off. *Constitution* had the tip of her flying jib boom split and one half of her dolphin striker carried away. Conover was called as the officer of the deck ordered the stunsails taken in and the ship hove to. Boats were put over to search for whatever they hit, but nothing was found: no wreckage, no people. Conover got under way once more.

A few minutes after moving on, a member of the crew appeared before the officer of the deck, a bedraggled young lad in tow. Upon questioning, he turned out to be the cabin boy of the British brig *Confidence* of Cowes, which had been taking coal to Barcelona when struck. There had been eight in the crew. The boy said he had caught a cable at the bow and managed to work his way up to and in through a gun port. As the minutes passed, other crewmen from *Constitution* showed up, escorting similarly drenched and dazed Britons, each of whom had caught onto *Constitution* as she crushed her way through their ship, and who had been found wandering about the gun deck and forecastle. Soon, all but the captain and first mate were accounted for. The crewmen reported that a light from *Constitution* had been seen (her port side light, in fact), but that the officers had argued as to whether it was a light on a ship or ashore, and had done nothing to avoid the collision.

While these people were turning up at the quarterdeck, another *Constitution* sailor stepped from the forecastle into the head to relieve himself, and was startled to hear some of the most exquisite cursing ever. Peering cautiously over the bulwark, he saw below him a man clinging to the wooden legs of Andrew Jackson and swearing at the figurehead for not doing something to help him aboard. The American tar grabbed the highly vocal stranger by the collar and, calling for some of his mates to help, soon had the man aboard. He turned out to be the missing mate of *Confidence*. In his stunned state, he had mistaken the bow ornament for a real person and was understandably upset by the bloke's seeming un-Christian attitude. When he calmed down, the mate said he had seen the captain knocked overboard when *Constitution* hit them, so there would be no further discoveries that night.

The remainder of the trip home had but two further incidents to disturb the peace. On Christmas Day, Seaman Joseph Bryson got in a fight with Captain of the Mizzen Top Peter Wilson and stabbed him. Placed in double irons, Bryson was dishonorably discharged upon arrival; Wilson survived. Early in the new year, a sudden squall carried away the crossjack in the slings—a two-day repair job for the carpenters.

A lookout sighted land in the vicinity of Barnegat, New Jersey, on 10 January 1851. Shortly before noon the next day, steamer *Cinderella* took *Constitution* in tow and, aided by steamer *Wave*, brought her safely to the Brooklyn Navy Yard. The ship was in ordinary before month's end.

Even as these events were transpiring, questions were being raised as to *Constitution*'s future. In his part of the navy's 1850 report to Congress, the chief of the Bureau of Construction, Equipment, and Repair, Capt. William Skinner, was suggesting that she, together with the other two original ships, *United States* and *Constellation*, all of which he deemed more costly to repair than they were worth, be returned to the ports where they were launched to serve as memorials. As it turned out, neither of the others would see active duty again, but it would be many years before *Constitution* would become a memorial, by which time the captain's proposal long since had been forgotten.

CHAPTER SEVENTEEN

African Adventure

BACKGROUND

America's initial action to end slavery was the passage of a bill on 2 March 1807 prohibiting American participation in the African slave trade. Enforcement of the law, however, was observed in the breach. Slave trading continued, and further pressure caused Congress to pass another bill on the subject on 3 March 1819. In this one, the president was authorized to use American men-of-war to "seize, take, and bring into any port of the United States, vessels of the United States unlawfully engaged in the transportation of any negro, mulatto, or person of colour."

The sum of $100,000 also was appropriated in the same bill to assist in the establishment of a safe haven for such slaves as were rescued somewhere "on the coast of Africa." This provision resulted in the founding of a colony in the vicinity of Cape Mensurado on 15 December 1821. For more than a quarter century, it was led by a governor under the aegis of the American Society for Colonizing the Free People of Colour of the United States. On 26 July 1847, having reached an adequate level of self-sufficiency, it was declared the free and independent Republic of Liberia, and the last governor, Joseph J. Roberts, himself a colonist, became its first president.

As for its part in implementing the "police" aspect of the new law, the navy promptly sent the corvette *Cyane* as escort for the transport *Elizabeth*, carrying the first group of colonists. Thereafter, it was customary for American warships to pay periodic visits to the African coast, but what was done to suppress the slave trade was done by the West Indies Squadron, which was established in 1821 and which primarily operated against Caribbean pirates. The African Squadron finally was organized in 1843 and was supposed to be comprised of ships mounting an aggregate of eighty guns, on a par with the British, who were the most active in seeking to stop the traffic. Each party was to stop and board its own nationals.

New Leaders for "Old Ironsides"

Rhode Islander John Rudd recommissioned *Constitution* on 22 December 1852 at New York. He was the first officer of the rank of commander to be regularly ordered to command the frigate, an indication of her advancing age and diminishing position as a fighting unit in the mid-century navy that was shifting from wind to steam propulsion. Rudd had been appointed a midshipman in late 1814, just as the war was ending, and had been a commander for over twelve years. He previously had commanded the brig *Dolphin*, 10, in the Home Squadron, and the war sloop *Dale*, 14, when she had been assigned to the Pacific Squadron. His ship would wear the flag of Como. Isaac Mayo. Mayo was no stranger to West Africa, having commanded a unit of the squadron ten years earlier under Como. Matthew Calbraith Perry. (Other units on the station during 1853–1855 included the sloops-of-war *Marion*, 16, and *Dale*, 14, and the brig *Perry*, 8. As they were dispersed and never operated in company with *Constitution*, they will not appear again in this narrative.)

Mayo broke his flag aboard on 23 December, making himself at home in the newly installed flag quarters erected on the spar deck abaft the mizzen mast. This poop cabin included a central reception room, sleeping cabins for the commodore and his clerk, a clerk's "office," a pantry, a washroom, and a head. Windows were installed in the transom and in the two after gun ports on either side—gun ports that had long since ceased to be in regular use. It was a remarkably efficient use of the limited space available. Captain Rudd, of course, used the cabin on the gun deck.

Surprisingly, the commodore's presence on board did not presage an immediate departure. It wasn't until two months later that *Constitution* took aboard powder and shot from Ellis Island. Finally, at 8:20 A.M. on 2 March 1853, a steamer towed the frigate clear of New York harbor.

To Africa—The Long Way

Before taking station off the west coast of Africa, however, Mayo headed first for the Mediterranean to transport the new U.S. consul to Tunis, Col. Joseph H. Nicholson, to his post and call on the Mediterranean commander, Silas H. Stringham.

Como. Isaac Mayo had served under Como. Matthew Calbraith Perry in the African Squadron when it was organized in the early 1840s. That experience stood him in good stead as squadron commander himself a decade or so later. On 18 May 1861 he submitted his resignation in order to join the Confederacy, but was dismissed instead. He died that same day. (The painting is attributed to William E. West [circa 1838].) *Courtesy the Maryland State Archives, Commission on Artistic Property, MSA SC 1545-1196*

Pausing at Gibraltar for five days, Mayo ultimately found Stringham and his flagship *Cumberland*, 50, at La Spezia. He finished his business with Stringham in short order, then spent nearly two weeks sightseeing and rejoined *Constitution* at Leghorn on 24 April, where it had arrived late that afternoon to complete provisioning.

Mayo got under way again on the 29th, paid a three-day call at Tunis while disembarking Nicholson, and spent another three days at Algiers, considered by many on board as the finest visiting port on the entire littoral. While there, "thousands" of the local populace enjoyed touring the ship. Another leisurely sail brought the commodore back to Gibraltar once more on 2 June, where he spent a further seven days.

Constitution stood to sea on the 9th and paid a brief call at Tangier. Upon her departure the next day, adverse winds caused Rudd to return to Gibraltar, where five days passed awaiting favorable conditions. HMS *Sans Pareil* saluted the commodore's broad pennant as she stood in on the 14th. Captain Dacres, the British comman-der, was the *son* of the captain of HMS *Guerriere*, defeated by *Constitution* in 1812.

When she sailed on the 15th, "Old Ironsides" was one of 168 sail to stand out, so long had a fair wind been wanting. In five hours, she sailed them all out of sight.

ON STATION

Funchal, Madeira, was reached on 18 June—three and a half months since leav-ing New York—and the African duties finally taken up with the official act of relieving the sloop-of-war *John Adams*. But not with alacrity. *Constitution* swung at her hook while the commodore exchanged civilities and pleasantries with the local gentry. One evening, Mayo gave a gala on board, with the ship's band pro-viding music for dancing "until a late hour."

Under way from Funchal on 3 July, *Constitution* called briefly at Teneriffe before coming to in Porto Grande, São Vincente Island, for two days. British Gen. Hugh Wheeler, together with a Lord and Lady Russel, were feted at a gala on board on the evening of the 12th that included dancing and fireworks. The next morning found the ship on the move once more.

In Porto Praya, also in the Cape Verde Islands, for a week (15–21 July), Mayo encountered the steamer *John Hancock* and storeship *John P. Kennedy*, vessels assigned to Como. Cadwalader Ringgold, en route on a survey expedition to the "China Seas," the northern Pacific, and "Behrings Strait."

Just hours out of port on the 22nd, *Constitution* came upon the *George*, a British schooner in distress. To ensure the safety of the merchant's crew, Mayo directed Rudd to see the vessel into port. A slow, four-day trek got *George* snug in Porto Grande and the frigate again on her way, touching briefly a second time at Porto Praya for any late-arriving mail before sailing for Monrovia, Liberia.

PEACEMAKER

Under way from Monrovia on 25 August, *Constitution* stopped at Sinoe (Greensville today) and Cape Palmas. During the latter stop, in conversations with the governor about slaving operations in the area, that official asked Mayo to see what he could do to put an end to a tribal war that had been simmering on Liberia's southern boundary for some three years. At issue were the slave raids of the Barbo tribe against the Grebo people. Mayo consented.

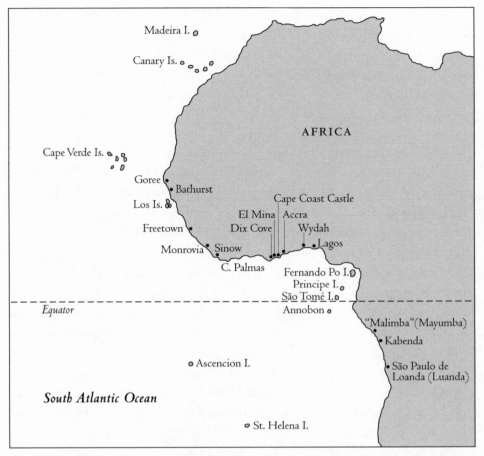

African ports of call *Author's collection*

Arriving off the mouth of the Cavally River on 4 September, Mayo sent a lieutenant ashore to scout the terrain and locate the disputants. The Grebo town was soon located and the people found ready and willing to end the unhappy situation. Across the river, however, the Barbos threatened the lieutenant with death and vowed to resist any force sent against them. Mayo reacted to his emissary's report decisively.

At 8:30 the next morning, five boats—including the barge bearing the commodore—with Rudd, two hundred men, a 12-pounder howitzer, and rockets, put off from the frigate and pulled smartly toward shore. Holding the bulk of his force off for the moment, Mayo sent in one boat under a white flag to renew the mediation offer. This again was rebuffed. Equally determined, the commodore commenced a bombardment of the Barbo town on the river's left bank with both the howitzer and the rockets. It required only the destruction of a few huts to convince the natives that negotiation was the only sensible course of action. (One Barbo had been wounded: A woman [and they "are known for their curiosity"] was singed on the arm by an exploding rocket as she peeked from behind a tree.)

Before the sun was high in the sky, deputations from both tribes were brought to the poop cabin of the frigate for a "Grand Palava" with Mayo. By hand signs and pidgin English, the savage nobility in all their animal finery conversed with the crusty old salt in his blue and gold. In the end, after "going through various frantic actions," and accompanied by the "Spewing of Water & Shaking of Hands," a peace was agreed to. (The "spewing of water"—literally, the same sort of performance required of us by a dentist—was meant to wash away the bad words and feelings; perhaps the shaking of hands was purely to satisfy the Americans.) Dinner for the deputations followed, and the former enemies returned ashore after the presentation of "dash" (trade goods gifts).

On 6 September 1853, the Barbo-Grebo Peace Treaty formally was ratified on board *Constitution.* With more dash the natives were put ashore. At that, the frigate weighed anchor for the Gulf of Guinea.

Constitution visited four ports on the Gold Coast during the subsequent two weeks: "Dix Cove," near the Pra River; Elmina, which fort had been visited by Columbus in 1482–1483 and still was in fighting trim; Cape Coast Castle; and finally, Accra. "Entertainments" often were held on board to bring some freshness into the lives of the people manning these perilous outposts and to provide an outlet for the ship's company's boredom and frustrations. The embarked band undoubtedly provided adequate music, and the crew were enthusiastic if grossly amateurish thespians.

Constitution arrived at Fernando Po (Island) on the 29th, having stopped overnight at Lagos, then still under native rule. Here, calls were made on the local Spanish authorities and the ship was watered. Leaving the volcanic island on 2 October, Mayo next ordered the frigate to the mouth of the Gaboon River (more probably, Libreville, which had been founded only four years before) to touch base with the French authorities there before moving on to the Portuguese island of São Tomé, where she anchored on the 14th in Man of War Bay.

While en route to São Tomé, a court-martial was held on 4 October in the case of Ordinary Seaman John Monohain for entering the medical storeroom and "appropriating" two bottles of wine therefrom. With two other enlisted men as witnesses against him, he declined any defense. The court awarded him loss of liberty privileges for a year and the forfeit of twenty dollars.

Constitution crossed the Equator for the first time on this cruise shortly after leaving São Tomé on the 15th. By the 26th, she had begun patrolling between "Malimba" (Mayoumba, Gabon) southward to the Angolan coast. And on that particular day, she spent six hours in a fruitless chase of a swifter, shallower-draft slaver. Not only was Mayo's "squadron" numerically insufficient for the mission, his flagship was ill-suited to it. Ex-slavers made the best anti-slavers.

SLAVER CAPTURED

Continuing south, the frigate called at Kabenda, a Portuguese enclave north of Angola, before arriving off that shore. There on 3 November, she chased and brought to (using British colors) the American schooner *H. N. Gambrill* of New York. The boarding officer found clear evidence of slaving operations, although she was empty at the time. She quickly was declared a prize and placed under the command of Lt. John DeCamp, who remained in company. This was *Constitution*'s last capture.

Two days later, another schooner was overtaken, but she proved to be a Portuguese war schooner, the *Conde de Jozal.* Later that same day, the commodore brought his two ships to anchor at Ambriz overnight before proceeding to São Paulo de Loanda (Luanda, Angola), whence they dropped their hooks on the 8th. Here, nine days were spent in rewatering (at a cost of two gallons for a penny), resupplying the ships, and making repairs. On the 13th, Mayo ordered DeCamp to return *H. N. Gambrill* to the United States for adjudication.

PATROL RESUMED

Refreshed and restored by this "break" in the voyage, "Old Ironsides" was under way once more on the 17th, headed west-southwest, bound for the British island of Saint Helena. It took twelve days to cover the roughly 1,200 miles direct distance, hardly a memorable sailing.

A leisurely five days were passed at the friendly British colony. Here, Napoleon had been exiled after Waterloo until his death in 1821. Some of the American officers took advantage of the opportunity to visit the emperor's final residence. The commodore and the ship staged one of their familiar "entertainments" on board for their British hosts on 5 December, with dancing on the quarterdeck "until a late hour." On the official side, Mayo succeeded in making arrangements to have stores for American ships on the African Station warehoused on the island at no cost. Henceforth, there would be supply bases at both extremities of the station, located in areas proximate to, but clear of, the inimical African shore.

On the 5th, the day after leaving Saint Helena, the crew was assembled to hear of the success of Commodore Perry's squadron in preparing for the opening of Japan to Western trade. Three cheers were given to honor the event. Pausing two days at Monrovia, "Old Ironsides" drove on northward for Porto Praya, dropping her anchor there on 6 January 1854.

For the next five months, *Constitution* idled among the Cape Verde and Canary Islands, in April getting as far north as Madeira. Dignitaries were received on board, entertainments held, and minor diplomats provided with interisland transportation. Late in January, she made a quick trip to the Los Islands to pick up twenty-one survivors of the wrecked American merchant ship *Sylph* and return them to Porto Grande for onward transportation. Finally, on 22 June, she weighed anchor at Porto Praya and filled away for Monrovia, beginning her second tour of the station.

More "Diplomacy"

Following eight days in port, *Constitution* proceeded to Cape Palmas, where the local governor requested the commodore to exercise his proven powers of mediation, this time in settling a territorial dispute between the Grahway and Half Cavally tribes. He agreed, and the "palava" was held that day in his cabin. The same sequence of talk, "frantic actions," the "spewing of water," and "dash" marked progress to another successful outcome. The frigate quickly was under way that evening (18 July).

The ship called again at Cape Coast Castle, and on the 23rd provided an anchor and cable to the American merchant ship *Winnegance* at Serra. Continuing eastward, she found a considerable amount of shipping off what is today the coast of Dahomey. In three days, sometimes under false colors, she stopped, inspected, and released as innocent one Spanish, one Dutch, one Hamburg, five British, and "several" Portuguese merchantmen. She anchored off the Lagos River on the 28th.

On the 31st, "King" Docimo of Lagos and his principal advisors called upon the commodore and were received on board with full honors, including a thirteen-gun salute and the king's flag being flown at the fore truck. A treaty was signed that granted "most favored nation" status to the United States in Lagos. King Docimo was given a carbine, a pistol, and ammunition. Late in the day, the frigate sailed.

Standing to the south-southeast, a five-day run was made to "Prince's Island" (Principe) where, in West Bay, the ship took on water and some provisions. On 8 August, a working party went ashore and disinterred the body of the late N. M. H. Abbott, son of Capt. Joel Abbott, U.S. Navy, and once clerk in the ship-sloop *Macedonian*, for return to his homeland. He had died as his ship was en route to join Perry's Japan expedition fifteen months earlier and been buried there by his grieving parent, an old compatriot of Mayo. The remains were encased in canvas and pitch and brought to the ship.

Southward again on the 9th, Rudd brought his ship to off "Anna Bona" (Annobon) Island in order to take on fresh fruits and vegetables before turning eastward to close the African shore once more. On the 19th, the order "splice the Main brace" was heard, and all hands celebrated the forty-second anniversary of *Constitution*'s victory over HMS *Guerriere*, perhaps the most popular of her many successes.

The coastal patrol proved to be a difficult one as calms, capricious airs, and a northward-setting current all conspired to defeat progress. In the seventy miles between Mayoumba and Luanda, during the period 24 August–5 September, the ship was forced to anchor thirty-one times in order not to lose ground. On the latter date, she arrived in Luanda, and Commodore's Clerk Edward Cobb noted in his journal that the people there were "a fine race, and seem to be much more intelligent, than any other tribes we have heretofore visited."

(An unwitting diplomatic action occurred here as a result of normal ship's routine: It seems that on the day prior to *Constitution*'s arrival, the local "king" had decoyed two British traders to his village and taken them prisoner. The subsequent arrival of the frigate and the routine firing of her morning gun led him to believe that retribution was at hand and caused him to release his prisoners! At a subsequent "palava," a friendship treaty was agreed to between the king and the local white merchants. Lt. Christopher R. P. Rodgers was the official witness to the signing.)

On 8 September, *Constitution* stood out of Luanda and turned northwestward, ending her last visit to those waters. Crossing the Equator at 6:00 A.M. on the 17th, she paused briefly at Cape Palmas before coming to anchor at Monrovia on the 22nd. A week later, Ordinary Seaman James Lee, while preparing a quarterboat for lowering, was struck in the head by a parting block, knocked into the water, and drowned. His was the first fatality from any cause in the eighteen months since the ship had left home waters, a truly remarkable accomplishment in view of the terrible conditions of the station, and a testimonial to the attention given his crew by Rudd.

While beating in to Porto Grande more than two weeks later, a rapidly freshening wind caused the splitting of the jib, mainsail, and foretopsail, and caused the crossjack to be carried away. Prudently, Rudd stood away from the land and effected necessary repairs. Porto Grande finally was entered on 19 October.

For the next five and a half months, the easy cycle of trips amongst the islands, Cape Verde to Madeira, that characterized the first quarter of the year, was repeated. Early in her stay at Porto Grande, *Constitution* was rammed by the American whaling barque *Macta*, which missed stays while standing off and on the harbor entrance and struck her amidships. Damage in the frigate was limited to the loss of an accommodation ladder, but the whaler was "much damaged in the bows." Later, again at Porto Grande, the Abbott remains were "temporarily reinterred." *Constitution* was in Madeira for Christmas and the beginning of 1855, then returned to the Cape Verde Islands.

A Reunion of Sorts

During one of her calls at Porto Grande, there was in harbor the British missionary yacht *Allen Gardiner.* The cleric embarked requested and received assistance from the Americans in repairing his vessel's pumps, and later was entertained at a gala. It was an especially emotional event for him, as his father had come aboard *Constitution* as a prisoner from *Guerriere.*

In February, she made a swing eastward, looking in at the Gambia River, stopping at Goree, Senegal, and reconnoitering the Los Islands one last time. During much of March, she sailed about the Cape Verdes until, at Porto Grande on the 31st, the crew heard the welcome word passed, "All hands up anchor for home." It was 6:30 P.M., and the main brace was "spliced."

Going Home

The voyage westward was uneventful until the twenty-third day out—and just 300–400 miles from her destination—when *Constitution* met and spoke the

American ship *Isaac Jeames*, outward bound from the Delaware Capes. The merchant captain passed on the news that a Spanish frigate, *Ferrolana*, recently had fired upon a U.S. mail steamer, the *El Dorado*, off the coast of Cuba. Mayo came to the conclusion that they might be needed in the Caribbean area and turned south accordingly. The next day, he put fifty-two crew members in double irons for twenty-eight hours for protesting his decision.

Mayo entered the Caribbean early in May, and it was while he was off the south shore of Cuba seeking to rendezvous with units of our West Indies Squadron, on the 5th, that Marine Pvt. James Sherry died of dysentery, the only man lost to illness in the entire cruise.

Still seeking other American units, Mayo circumnavigated Cuba and entered Havana on the 16th. Three days later, the screw steam sloop-of-war *San Jacinto*, 6, stood in, wearing the broad blue pennant of the commander of the U.S. Home Squadron, Como. Charles S. McCauley. Mayo, being junior to McCauley, caused appropriate honors to be rendered and substituted a red command pennant for the blue one previously flown, proclaiming his subordinate position. Having already learned that the *Ferrolana* matter was being dropped, Mayo departed for home on the 21st.

Constitution arrived at Portsmouth, New Hampshire, on 2 June 1855. Her African adventure, which had seen her at sea 430 out of 822 days and had covered 42,166 miles, was over. Mayo hauled down his flag, and the ship herself was decommissioned on the 14th. Her days of regular operational duties were over. She was almost fifty-eight years old.

CHAPTER EIGHTEEN

Second-Rate Ship

A NEW ROLE

The training of young naval officers, as we have seen, had been left largely to "on the job" training. Secretaries and senior officers of the navy repeatedly had recommended the establishment of formal schooling for these youngsters before they regularly were assigned to shipboard duties. These recommendations were not acted upon, for one reason or another, until Secretary George Bancroft was able to convince the Congress to appropriate the monies needed for the navy to acquire Fort Severn at Annapolis, Maryland, as the site for such a school. It opened its scholastic doors for the first time in October 1845, with three students under the charge of Capt. Franklin Buchanan. During 1850–1851, the school was designated the "Naval Academy" and was reorganized with a four-year curriculum.

By the middle years of the decade, it had become apparent to the staff of the academy that additional space was needed to house its students, as well as a place where the young midshipmen could begin their education in rigging and shipboard routine. What better vehicle for both purposes than one of the old sailing ships? Since 1854, "steam ships" had been joining the fleet at an accelerated rate; it was possible to retire those pure square-riggers not already in reduced status. And what better ship was there to teach and inspire the young salts than "Old Ironsides" herself, the undisputed champion of fighting sailing ships? Thus it was that *Constitution* was taken in hand on 20 July 1857 for leisurely restoration and outfitting as a school ship for the Naval Academy.

CONVERSION

The big frigate was hauled out on the ways at the Portsmouth Navy Yard for thorough overhaul of her hull. While she was high and dry, the earliest known photographs of her were taken, showing the sleek lines and great depth of her large hull dwarfing the men working around her. It is evident in these pictures that her waist had been enclosed and the bulwarks on her forecastle and quarterdeck raised by planking in the hammock stowage. It is not known whether the "boxing" was new with this overhaul. Another obvious change made at this time was the replacement of the six windows in the stern with just three, and a further one was the planking up of quarter gallery windows but for one centrally located single pane. The gun streak was extended all the way to the after edge of the now-solid galleries.

Constitution was returned to her normal element in May or June of 1858, where conversion to a school ship commenced in earnest. The poop cabin was gutted and rearranged as two recitation rooms. Forward, the main hatch area of the spar deck largely was decked over and a small house erected on it, containing two more recitation rooms. Down below, "The three study rooms were on [each side of] the gun deck, bulkheads having been run along parallel with the sides, and the gun ports serving as windows. . . . [L]ockers, one for each midshipman, were fitted up against the sides on the berth deck. Forward was the wash room, the number of basins averaging about one to five of the washers." As for armament, the batteries of "Old Ironsides" were reduced to six 32-pounders of 42 hundredweight and ten of 33 hundredweight, sixteen guns in all. Her official classification was changed to "2nd rate ship," and she was recommissioned by Lt. David Dixon Porter on the morning of 1 August 1860.

TAKING UP NEW DUTIES

After several days of sail drill, Porter got his ship under way on 5 August and made the entrance of Chesapeake Bay a little more than a week later. Several days of tacking northward in steadily more restricted waters brought him to anchor off the Annapolis Bar in the very early morning of the 18th. Her deep draft necessitated a delay of two days as she offloaded stores and equipment and pumped water tanks so that the bar could be cleared. This was accomplished in

Constitution as stationary school ship at the U.S. Naval Academy after the Civil War. Note the classroom building erected over the main hatch, the windows in the gun ports, and the fact that she has only a single dolphin striker. By this time she had been outfitted with steam heat and gaslights supplied from ashore. *Courtesy the U.S. Naval Academy Museum*

the tow of steamers *Merchant* and uss *Anacostia* late on the 20th, and she came to anchor off the Academy at 10:00 that evening. Shortly thereafter, the big ship was moved to a mooring at the end of a long narrow walkway jutting out from the shore, where she received all of the fourth classmen from the school. Lt. George W. Rodgers, nephew of the late commodore, relieved Porter as captain.

The fourth classmen were the newcomers to the academy, the neophytes. Academy commandant, Capt. George S. Baker, decided it would be best to house and train all 127 of them in isolation from the distraction of the shore and the influence of the upper classmen. So it was that these lads studied and worked all day in the frigate, and one-sixth of them were marched to the bathhouse on shore every night. The lads got into all the normal sort of high jinks one would expect of teenagers, and "authority" reacted predictably: A common punishment for a boyish prank was three days locked in a blacked-out room in the wardroom area.

CIVIL WAR

The question of slavery in the United States had galled regional politics for decades, gradually moving opposing groups into positions from which only war could move them. The slide toward this internal holocaust had been accelerating steadily during the latter part of the 1850s; the election of Abraham Lincoln to the presidency in November 1860 brought the country to the brink, and his inauguration the following March to the last, fatal step.

Before that happened, however, in February 1861 occurred the first major examinations for the new midshipmen. These resulted in the "bilging" of a considerable number of the young lads. The unfortunate shortly received letters from the secretary of the navy informing them of separation procedures and the date of their departure. When that day arrived, it was discovered that no one had made transportation arrangements, and so the newly made civilians were required to spend one more night aboard the frigate. The hammocks they were to use were slung well forward on the berth deck, away from the midshipmen. At "Taps," some secreted 32-pounder shot in their bedding, and when "Silence" was called for by the master-at-arms, they continued to jeer, laugh, and catcall. When Lt. John H. Upshur, the executive officer, was called to the scene, the miscreants tried to bowl him over with cannon balls in the semi-darkness. Soon, drums were heard "beating to quarters," and all the boys, midshipmen and civilians alike, were toeing the line at their stations. For several hours they were kept there at attention, waiting for the perpetrators to confess. Finally, the bigger, stronger midshipmen managed to pass the word around that if the civilians didn't confess they would be leaving with black eyes or worse in the morning. Once they stepped forward, the midshipmen were allowed to turn in. The civilians remained at quarters until sent ashore after daylight, bleary eyed and rumpled.

The Naval Academy was, geographically and socially, right in the middle of the confusion dividing the country. Maryland was Northern economically and Southern in sympathies. Which way the state would go was unknown. Across the Severn River from the school, what appeared to be a volunteer cavalry troop could be seen practicing formation maneuvers. The local citizenry outside the thin walls surrounding the academy hurled threats and rocks into the compound, threats that included the capture of "Old Ironsides" to be flagship of a rebel fleet.

Rumors and fears prevailing locally at Annapolis were heightened by news coming from elsewhere in the country. The miracle of the telegraph not only helped government be more responsive: It disseminated information as never before. Underscoring the concerns of those at the academy was an awareness that the Pensacola Navy Yard already was in Confederate hands, that Fort Sumter had been evacuated (14 April), and that the moment of crisis was nearing at Norfolk. Secretary of the Navy Gideon Welles telegraphed on 20 April orders to defend *Constitution* "at all hazards. If it can not be done, destroy her." Similar orders went to Como. Charles S. McCauley, commandant of the Norfolk Navy Yard, relative to his yard and the ships there. Shortly after 4:00 the next morning, McCauley directed the destruction of his command. One of the ships present was "Old Waggon," *United States*—*Constitution*'s sister.

At Annapolis on the 20th, all was a bustle of activity. Having only about twenty-five seamen regularly assigned to her, the commandant ordered all midshipmen aboard *Constitution* to see to her defense. Internal bulkheads were knocked down and four 32-pounders run out astern through the cabin windows to provide some firepower in the direction of the bay. Scuttling charges were laid in the magazines. Watches were set with the midshipmen about the ship to detect anyone or anything approaching from the river or the opposite shore, while others patrolled the walled grounds to provide early warning of an attack from the town.

The situation remained calm until 2:00 in the morning of the 22nd, when a midshipman on watch reported seeing a large steamer coming from the bay. The ship beat to quarters and the green youths gathered at their guns, determined to do their best. Loaded with grape, the cannon were run out. Firing locks were double checked. Slow matches were blown on to make sure the coals glowed red hot. They might get off only one salvo, but the Rebs would pay dearly in that blast of grapeshot at close range.

The steamer continued its approach, seemingly steering so as to avoid coming in way of the frigate's broadside. That she was heading for the mooring astern of "Old Ironsides" suited the defenders well, for it would mean the greatest damage from their fire. Rodgers hailed the stranger when she was about three hundred yards off, her decks seen to be packed with people. There was no answer. He hailed a second time with no better luck. One last time he called, "Ship ahoy! Keep off, or I'll sink you!" This time, he got an answer—from the recognized voice of the academy's chaplain.

When the steamer moored, it was learned that she was the ferry *Maryland*. The chaplain explained that he had been returning from leave in the North when he had found Col. Benjamin F. Butler and his Eighth Massachusetts Volunteer

Infantry at Havre de Grace (near the head of Chesapeake Bay), seeking a way to get his troops to Washington following the stoppage of the trains in Baltimore. The colonel had commandeered the ferry and sailed to Annapolis, and planned to march his men the remaining miles to the nation's capital. The citizen-soldiers were a welcome reinforcement to the harried mids.

At daylight, all the midshipmen were withdrawn from *Constitution* and placed in a defensive perimeter toward the outer walls while Butler disembarked his troops and got them into some semblance of order. Butler next agreed to help the navy get the old frigate clear of her moorings and to a position from which she could head seaward if necessary. Many of his Massachusetts troops hailed from towns along its coast, particularly the North Shore, and so had varying degrees of expertise in marine matters—many being more knowledgeable in such things than the midshipmen. Thus it was that "Old Ironsides" received a temporary crew made up of 107 soldiers from such units as the Salem Zouaves, Lynn City Guards, and the Beverley and Gloucester Light Infantry companies.

During the afternoon of the 22nd, the ship was hauled clear of her berth by *Maryland.* The frigate swung out of the channel and onto a mud bank shortly after getting under way. The grounding was of short duration, however, and she moved on down the Severn toward the bay proper, ultimately coming hard aground on the bar off Greenbury Point Light. She had almost made it to deep water, but would have to wait now for the tide's assistance; it was 10:00 P.M.

At midnight, a report was received that the rebels would be making an effort to block the outer end of the channel before daylight. This generated a new effort to get *Constitution* moving, tide or no tide. All hands were called and a kedge anchor run out with a ship's boat. Men strained at the capstan and actually got her moving, but just then a squall came up that set her still more firmly aground. As if this weren't problem enough, several ships were seen in the offing to the south, ships whose identities could not be determined in the overcast night. The ship beat to quarters, prepared for a desperate defense. Her crew might be a polyglot gang of midshipmen, militia, and Marines, but they would fight as fiercely as any crew "Old Ironsides" ever had known.

The alarm proved false. The contacts disappeared. The guns were secured. And the kedging effort was resumed. Several hours of pulling finally broke the big frigate free. At about 4:00 in the morning, the steamer *Boston* appeared, having on board the Seventh New York Regiment. With her help, *Constitution* was moved to the safety of a deep-water anchorage. *Boston* then moved in toward the

Annapolis shore to land her troops, joined by other transports bearing the First Rhode Island Artillery and other army units bound to secure the town and go on to defend Washington.

THE NAVAL ACADEMY RELOCATES TO NEWPORT

For the next couple of days, *Constitution* remained at her anchorage, taking on supplies and getting ready to go to sea. The guns removed to *Maryland* while crossing the bar were set back aboard and put in their ports. On the 25th, 140 midshipmen came aboard with their baggage and some of the educational equipment from the school. It had been decided to move them and the old frigate farther north, clear of any possible Confederate action. At 10:00 the next morning, more of her army "crew" having been transferred to normal duties, *Constitution* got under way in tow of screw gunboat uss *R. R. Cuyler* to get clear of Chesapeake Bay. Her journey to the Virginia Capes was escorted by steamer *Harriet Lane*, newly returned from her unsuccessful attempt to relieve Fort Sumter, South Carolina. *Constitution* cleared the capes still in tow on the morning of the 27th. She arrived off Governor's Island after dark thirty-six hours later, then moved to a berth at the Brooklyn Navy Yard on the 29th. There, the last two companies of soldiers left her, cheered by the midshipmen.

Secretary Welles had issued further orders concerning *Constitution*'s future as the frigate was clearing the capes: The Naval Academy was to be reestablished at Newport, Rhode Island. The steamer *Baltic*, which had been employed in carrying troops south for Washington, was detailed to take aboard all remaining academy personnel and all the furniture, books, models, and apparatus she possibly could carry.

Constitution remained in New York for about a week, not wishing to arrive in Newport much before *Baltic*. Such first class midshipmen as had not been ordered to Washington with the troops were detached for service in regular operational units. The remaining mids were permitted daily liberty ashore, by sections.[1]

The old frigate got under way in the early evening of 8 May, towed through Hell's Gate by the steamer *Freeman* and screw tug uss *Resolute*. She arrived in Brinton's Cove, off Fort Adams at Newport, at 2:00 the next afternoon. *Baltic*, with the naval and academic staffs aboard, pulled in three and a half hours later. *Constitution* announced her arrival on the morning of the 10th with a 34-gun salute to the Union.

In the days that followed, the last of the first classmen, and then the second and third classmen, were transferred for war duty. Suddenly, the fourth classmen were the "old hands." For a few months, they continued to live aboard "Old Ironsides," but took their classes in Fort Adams and paraded on its grounds. By September 1861, the government had leased the Atlantic House in downtown Newport as academy headquarters and residence for upper classmen. George Rodgers became commandant of midshipmen. Lt. Edward Phelps Lull succeeded him as the frigate's captain. The ship herself had been warped into the channel between Goat Island and the mainland and moored to the island's wharf. She became the home of some two hundred newly appointed midshipmen destined for accelerated training and assignment to a rapidly expanding navy with more responsibilities than resources. Somewhat later that fall, the frigate *Santee*, 44, one of the last pure sailing ships commissioned (1855), arrived to provide more room for the mids. She was moored just ahead of *Constitution*.

The late spring of 1862 found the Newport academy further augmented by the assignment of sloops *John Adams*, *Macedonian*, and *Marion* as underway training ships. That summer, they took the midshipmen south to view Hampton Roads, site of the recent duel between *Monitor* and *Virginia* (formerly *Merrimack*), and to Port Royal, South Carolina, site of a successful Union amphibious assault, before returning to Newport. *Constitution*, of course, remained at her wharf. Although it seems to have passed without note in the ship, during 1862 the spirit ration was forever ended in the United States Navy.

While "Old Ironsides" was seeing service inspiring and training new officers for the navy at Newport, a large ironclad steamer named *New Ironsides* was commissioned in August 1862 to carry her tradition of victorious combat into the thick of the Civil War. Displacing nearly 3,500 tons, this powerful warship had wooden sides as thick as her namesake's, but sheathed for much of its length in 4-inch iron plates; her firepower consisted of fourteen 11-inch smoothbores and two 150-pounder Parrott rifles. From January 1863 until May 1864, she saw very active service with the squadron blockading Charleston, South Carolina. Following a two-month overhaul, she was assigned to the attack force that ultimately took Fort Fisher, near Wilmington, North Carolina, in January 1865. She was considered by many to be the most powerful warship then afloat. (*New Ironsides* and "Old Ironsides" never met: The former was destroyed by fire at Philadelphia in December 1866.)

The months passed uneventfully for *Constitution* at Newport. During the fall of 1863, Lt. Henry M. Blue became captain of both stationary school ships, and in April 1864 was, in turn, relieved of the dual command by Lt. Comdr. Philip C. Johnson, Jr. He was still in command at war's end a year later.

BACK TO ANNAPOLIS

The end of the academic year in June 1865 signaled the beginning of preparations to return the Naval Academy to Annapolis. After so long at the wharf, the requirement for *Constitution* and *Santee* was for an inspection and repairs to ready them for a sea voyage. Caulkers worked to make her hull and decks tight. Divers went down on 7 July to scrape four years' accretion of marine life from her bottom; at about the same time, her guns were brought back from a battery that had been established on Goat Island. Later in the month, a cargo of unbelievable variety was brought aboard: everything from mess chests and academy furniture to eight army howitzers. On 8 August, twenty-two women and twenty children, all dependents of academy staff personnel, came on board for the trip south, which began the next morning.

It had been planned to tow the old frigate back to Annapolis, using her sails to ease the strain of the tow when possible. The steamer *Mercury* was to be the tug. On the 10th, it was seen that *Constitution* was making good six knots with her sails and was overtaking *Mercury*. As a result, the tow was dropped near sunset to permit "Old Ironsides" to set her own pace. For the remainder of the voyage, she made good between seven and nine knots by the log, and arrived in Hampton Roads shortly before midnight on the 12th. *Mercury* came in, huffing and puffing, *ten hours later.* It was quite an achievement for the sixty-eight-year-old man-o'-war.

Mercury picked up its towing bridle once more at first light on the 14th. She got *Constitution* to the entrance to Annapolis on the 16th, where the frigate's great draft again precluded her ready approach to the wharf. Guns, anchors, and chains were landed the next morning before she was *forced* alongside her assigned pier— slicing three feet into the bottom mud *at high tide.* All her ammunition was landed on the 23rd to help get her out of the mud.

During September, workmen were aboard on assignments that indicated clearly there were no plans for the ship to move in the foreseeable future. First aboard were the pipe fitters, busily making steam connections to the shore to provide heat to the ship through radiators. Later, the gas fitters came aboard to rig up gaslights in the classrooms, office, and berthing areas. A classroom "house" on her forecastle was made more weatherproof. *Constitution* had become a *structure*, a strange sort of building among a gaggle of randomly designed and built edifices dotting the academy grounds.

Diminutive Lt. Comdr. Edmund O. Matthews succeeded Johnson in both of his commands on 16 February 1866, and he, in turn, was relieved ten days later by Lt. Comdr. Thomas H. Eastman. (One is tempted to call them "Super" rather than "Skipper," for their assignment was more nearly that of a building superintendent than ship's captain, and they had additional duties, as well. As time went on, *Constitution*'s captains also were responsible for the maintenance of all the ships of the training squadron when they were in ordinary between summer cruises. All of the caretaker crews eventually lived in "Old Ironsides," only working and standing security watches in their nominal commands. In addition to the captain, *Constitution*'s own crew amounted to three or four mates, a paymaster, two or three warrant officers, and thirty to sixty enlisted men. At one point, about twenty black landsmen working in the academy mess hall also were carried on her roll.)

On the day before the 1866 graduation ceremonies, an accident occurred in *Constitution* that cast a pall over the occasion and caused postponement of the graduation "hop." While working near the anchor capstan on the gun deck, tiny Midshipman 1/c William H. Emory was hit in the legs when the chain slipped on the capstan and driven into a nearby 32-pounder long gun. The back of his skull was fractured. After having been senseless for forty-eight hours, he was pronounced dead. As his grieving father helped move the body into the mortuary, he felt a tremor in his son and subsequent ministrations brought the lad around. Emory went on to command the Second Division of the U.S. Fleet during the 'round-the-world cruise in Teddy Roosevelt's day, having risen to the rank of rear admiral.

Steadily the months slipped into years in an almost unvarying routine. The new class of midshipmen would report aboard in September. In October, hatch houses would be placed aboard to cover the ladders giving access to the interior of the ship during the winter season; in April, they would be removed. Midshipmen would be transferred to the units of the reactivated training squadron in June to spend the summer at sea, usually with ports of call in the Caribbean or northern Europe. While they were away, the members of *Constitution*'s crew would overhaul her and get set for the new cycle the following September. So shore bound had the ship become that when President Ulysses S. Grant came aboard with the Board of Visitors on an annual inspection, she was unable to fire the salute due his office.

Eastman was relieved on 6 November 1867 by Lt. Comdr. George Dewey, relative of the infamous Samuel Worthington Dewey of the Jackson figurehead caper, and himself later to become famous as the "Hero of Manila Bay" in the Spanish-American War. Dewey remained in command until 1 August 1870.

During these quiet postwar years, there occurred two deaths that essentially marked the end of *Constitution*'s glory years in living memory. In Kendall's Falls, Maine, on 15 June 1867, died William Bryant, state representative, long-time town selectman, and one of the original crewmen to serve in the ship. He probably was the last surviving "Plank Owner." His passing went without notice in the ship. Rear Adm. Charles Stewart, victor over *Cyane* and *Levant,* died at his home in Bordentown, New Jersey, on 9 November 1869. The frigate's colors were half-masted in his memory when notice was received two days later. He was the last of her hero-skippers (Preble had died in 1807, Bainbridge in 1833, and Hull in 1843).

Dewey's successor was Lt. Comdr. Henry Lycurgis Howison. For a year, Howison continued the cycle followed by his predecessors and acted as an "executive aid" to the academy superintendent. The opening and closing of each school year must have been periods of great pressure for him.

During the summer of 1871, the decision was made to end *Constitution*'s service as a school ship. Even as she rested at the wharf, ship's company began tearing down the recitation house over the main hatch and removing the study room bulkheads from the gun deck. Stores were transferred to *Santee,* lockers removed from the berth deck. Her topgallant masts and upper yards were sent down and lashed on deck, then the topmasts were lowered and housed against the main sections of each mast. Only a few sails remained to assist the tug in its effort. On 13 September, she was hauled away from the wharf and provided with an anchor and 120 fathoms of chain from *Dale.* On the 16th, she received a gig and one whaleboat for her quarter davits. A temporary crew came aboard two days later.

The navy's screw tug *Pinta* towed her away from Annapolis at 8:30 A.M. on the 20th, passing the returning training ships *Constellation* (the 1854 corvette that had succeeded to the name of the earlier frigate) and *Saratoga,* no doubt exchanging cheers with the embarked mids. After two days at anchor in Hampton Roads making final preparations for sea, *Pinta* cleared the Virginia Capes on the 23rd with the frigate in tow. *Constitution* set her main spencer to ease the strain. The pair anchored off the Delaware Capes the next evening, worked their way up to Newcastle the following day, then completed the run to Philadelphia, arriving off the navy yard in the Southwark district at noon, the 26th. Howison hauled down the commissioning pennant before dark.

ANOTHER RESTORATION

During October 1871, preliminary inactivation work was accomplished in the frigate: yards sent down, rigging landed, remaining stores and equipage transferred ashore. In November, orders came to suspend all work in her, and she was left in ordinary. Work of an unspecified nature was resumed in September 1872, then suspended once more four months later.

There were many reasons behind these start-and-stop proceedings. Firstly, no money had been specifically appropriated for the overhaul of *Constitution*. Secondly, there were the inevitable few in the hierarchy who proposed that she be scrapped, and the greater number who shouted "No!" There even was a proposal to outfit her with steam propulsion, but that was rejected as being technically impractical as well as very costly. Thirdly, no future employment had been determined; without a reason for being, monies should not be spent. And finally, the Philadelphia Navy Yard was on the verge of transferring its entire operation to League Island, but how soon this was to be accomplished and when ship work should be stopped at the old site had not been decided.

In the spring of 1873, it was agreed that *Constitution* was to be repaired and restored insofar as possible to her original appearance for the purpose of being exhibited to the public during the year of the nation's centennial (1876). In August, work resumed with the removal of the old joiner work belowdecks, and the researching and drafting of plans for the restoration. September brought the decision that she would be prepared for "yard duty" only, which probably resulted in another decision: not to restore the complex and expensive diagonal riders. In December, final preparations were made to take her out of the water. It was intended to take her up on the sectional dock on 5 January 1874, but several days of high northwest winds denied them sufficient water for the operation. Two more attempts, on the 12th and 13th, had to be stopped because of mechanical failures in the dock. A successful docking was achieved on the 27th. The dock was grounded that same day in position at the end of one of the building ways where the old frigate would be hauled ashore. This was done in a six-hour operation on 5 March.

The ship on the marine railway at the old-site Philadelphia Navy Yard about May 1875. Her outer hull planking has been removed roughly to the waterline, leaving visible the upper futtocks, top timbers, and half top timbers of her frames. This view makes clear how extremely close together the frames are: a space of only two inches was called for in Joshua Humphreys's specifications. *Official U.S. Navy photo*

Work on the ship was slow and sporadic. Gradually, she was taken down to her live oak skeleton, shorn of *everything*. The closeness of her frames, however, might have caused the casual observer to miss the fact that he was seeing a ship stripped of all her planking. In November came word that the poop cabin was to be converted to clerks' offices. By late May of 1875, she had only been planked up to the vicinity of her waterline. More and more of the yard's equipment and labor force was going to League Island, until *Constitution* remained the sole major project uncompleted. Finally, in December, she was ready to be returned to the water. On the 30th, she was moved back into the sectional dock. She lay there until 12 January 1876, when conditions were right to refloat her. Naval Constructor Philip Hichborn did the honors. The old navy yard had been formally decommissioned five days earlier.

Recognizing that working on *Constitution* to completion would delay further the final transfer of the navy yard, a contract to complete her outfitting, sparring, and rigging had been put out to bid during the latter months of 1875. Winner was Wood, Dialogue and Company of Kaighn's Point, Camden, New Jersey. On 14 March 1876, the old frigate was moved to that company's "works." Exactly what was done there is undetermined. It is known that she received two additional sets of wrought iron boat davits in the vicinity of the main shrouds. A small boiler, operating at ten to twenty pounds pressure, was installed on the forward orlop to provide heat through the radiators first emplaced at Annapolis. Much of the forward magazine became a coal bin.

There were a considerable number of visual changes to the ship during the course of this restoration that should be mentioned. The Andrew Jackson figurehead was removed and ultimately located at the Naval Academy. It had been hoped to return Hull's billet head to the ship in keeping with the directive requiring a return to her youth, but the Boston Navy Yard reported it too rotten for further use. The contractor then attempted to get the Jackson figurehead back, but its new masters refused, and so he carved a simple scroll billet head whose pattern has been followed ever since. The new trailboards differed from those emplaced in 1858 only in the substitution of a shield for the "rose," in keeping with the patriotic theme of the Centennial. The quarter galleries once again were fully glazed, but gone were the three bas reliefs from the transom—if, in fact, they ever really were installed. The stern decor was simplified to one emphasizing the eagle and six stars she has worn since then.

At the end of 1876, the navy was impatient to conclude the project and ordered her to be "completed by agreement"; that is, she would be taken back unfinished. This was done on 13 January 1877, on which date she was placed back in commission under Capt. Henry A. Adams, who also commanded the receiving ship *Potomac*. She would be used as a stationary barracks and school ship for apprentice boys right there in Philadelphia. Under a program established in 1875, boys sixteen to eighteen years old could be enlisted to serve until their twenty-first birthdays. They would be schooled in reading, writing, and arithmetic by a schoolmaster, as well as practical navigation and a technical skill by the ship's warrant and petty officers, until eighteen, when they were to be transferred to regular cruising units. Recognizing that many boys in a restricted environment could be a problem, *four* brig cells were fitted to contain the obstreperous.

From January until mid-December, *Constitution* was campus to teenage lads enlisting in the navy. There were almost daily drills in a wide variety of seamanship evolutions, both on deck and in the rigging, as well as drills at the great guns remaining on board. Matches with single sticks allowed the boys to work off their energies in personal "combat," and probably served to settle "scores," as well. Off the ship, the boys received periodic drill on the parade grounds; on other occasions, weather permitting, pulling races with the ship's boats were a happier part of their education. Crewmen and boys alike regularly overstayed their liberty and were confined or made to "toe the seam" for hours. Quarterly examinations determined the boys' progress and readiness to join the fleet.

During August and September, there was a flurry of command changes as the Office of Detail (later to be known as the Bureau of Personnel) shuffled skippers through "Old Ironsides" almost before their names could be learned by the apprentices. Capt. James A. Greer relieved Adams on 15 August and was himself relieved by Capt. Reigart B. Lowry eight days later, giving him the record for shortest term in command of *Constitution* ever. Lowry, in turn, was relieved by Comdr. Augustus P. Cooke on 5 September. Weeks later, Secretary of the Navy Richard W. Thompson made his decision in response to Congress's joint resolution of 15 December authorizing the navy to provide transportation for exhibits going to the 1878 Paris Exposition: What better ship than the fabled "Old Ironsides" to give prestige to the business?

Thus, on 24 December 1877, the big frigate began an eleven-day drydocking at Cramp and Sons to repair defective bottom planking. The "hatch house" that had been raised earlier in the year was torn down. Her heating boiler was removed. All but two of her 8-inch smoothbore guns were landed as weight compensation for the expected cargo and to permit the berthing of the crew of about 150 on the gun deck so that the berthing deck could be used for the stowage of exhibits. Similarly, since she would be carrying spar deck cargo as well, her spencer rig also was sent ashore.

FREIGHTER TO FRANCE

Capt. Oscar C. Badger, fifty-five-year-old Connecticut Yankee and veteran of both the Mexican and Civil Wars, relieved Cooke on 9 January 1878. For the next month, he and his crew of nearly 170 loaded stores, landed unnecessary gear, and got ready to load a "Noah's ark" variety of cargo that constituted the exhibit materials. The ship was moved to Philadelphia's Walnut Street Wharf on 8 February, where, for more than two weeks, the cargo was fitted into every nook and cranny in the ship. Last of the exhibits to come aboard were three pieces of railroad rolling stock, which were carefully lashed and braced on the spar deck. (What a sight that steam engine must have been on the high seas!) Last to come aboard were the thirty Marines to accompany the exhibits to Paris. Bright and early on the last day of February, the navy's screw tug *Pilgrim* towed the big frigate away from the wharf and down to the mouth of the Delaware, where "Old Ironsides" was anchored to await a fair wind. Her last trip to Europe began on 4 March as she headed out into stormy seas.

The entire passage had only one or two days where smooth seas were noted in the log. More common notations were "stormy," "heavy squalls," "very rough," and "pumped out 1 foot of water." No doubt to everyone's relief, the ship rode well while leaking much, and the train and other cargo stayed in place. On the 29th, an ordinary seaman named Young fell or was washed from the bowsprit while the ship was in a heavy gale. Badger made the difficult decision against trying a boat rescue, and all hands watched helplessly as Young swam manfully after a life buoy trailed by the ship only to tire and sink out of sight just short of it.

This easterly gale struck the ship as she was nearing the western end of the English Channel. For several days, she tacked back and forth on long reaches trying to make headway in the adverse wind and steep seas. It seemed almost as if she couldn't gain an inch. With everyone approaching exhaustion from the continuous sail handling and pumping, it was decided to take a chance and try sailing as close to the wind as possible without being beaten to pieces or driven on a lee shore. It was, in many respects, a gamble similar to that taken by Commodore Elliott in 1835 when, going to the west in these same waters, he drove her past Scilly. Once again, it was a cliff-hanger. And once again, she made it, her stout bows smashing through the swells, driven by more canvas than many would have dared to sheet home in those conditions. The sheltered peace of Carrick Bay at Falmouth allowed everyone the solid night's rest so sorely needed.

Conditions had improved sufficiently by early the next afternoon so that Badger weighed anchor and stood up the channel for Le Havre, although he still had to do so by a series of tacks back and forth across that narrowing waterway. *Constitution* was greeted off Le Havre by the tug *Jean Bart* at first light on 3 April, furled her sails, and was towed in. While attempting to get her alongside the Customs House Wharf, the pilot caused her to collide with the French steamer

326

A Most Fortunate Ship

Ville De Paris, smashing the Number 4 cutter in the after port davits. Offloading required a week, then the ship was shifted to a little-used berth where she could await the full run of the exposition and the return of the exhibits later in the year.

In May, Badger made arrangements to have the ship dry-docked to make a closer inspection of her port quarter. One plank was found to have been shattered, some caulking started, and sheathing ripped off. Additional caulking was replaced when it was found to have been poorly done by the old navy yard. She was undocked and returned to her berth on 1 June.

The months that followed were a challenge to Lt. Comdr. William H. Whiting, the executive officer, to keep the crew busy and out of trouble. In many ways, the days aboard recalled those off Philadelphia when the apprentice boys had been present, for there were frequent gun drills, cutlass drills, single stick bouts, and small arms practice. Still, liberty ashore and boredom worked their way with some men. Drunkards and deserters were common sights, being returned each morning by the French authorities. Fights occasionally broke out on board. There were at least two stabbings. Badger ordered summary courts martial regularly to deal with these infractions, and they just as regularly awarded confinement and fines to the sinful. ("Summary courts" had been established in 1855 as a replacement for the "cat." They continue to be a part of the system today.)

Month followed month until 2 December, when *Constitution* moved back to the Customs House Wharf. Two days later, recrated exhibits began arriving from Paris and were taken aboard. (Some of the crew had been sent to the French capital to help with the packing.) The arrival of crates was an almost daily occurrence until 10 January 1879, by which time about a thousand had been received. With everything accounted for and the Marine Guard returned, the old frigate left Le Havre under tow of the tug *Neptun* late on the 16th. Badger's intention was to stand nearly northward across the channel close hauled until he could change course to the west and let the easterly wind blow him straight into the Atlantic.

AGROUND

The first few hours went well, the wind steady and the sky clear. The orders were to maintain this course until 2:00 A.M., then call the captain and navigator, and change course for home. The navigator already was on deck when the appointed hour was tolled, exchanging small talk with the officer of the deck when, high above their heads and forward, could be seen what appeared to be treetops. Orders to change course were too late: Smoothly and steadily, *Constitution* slid aground, the pale expanse of one of the famous chalk cliffs not more than a hundred yards beyond her flying jib boom. She had outsailed her navigator's estimate by more than thirty miles in about ten hours.

Daylight came. Soon, a British coast guard boat appeared and informed them that they had gone aground under Bollard Head, said to be the only spot on that entire English coast out of range of a lighthouse. Word of the grounding of "Old Ironsides" soon flashed all across southern England and to London. By 10:00 that morning, five tugs were in the area, together with myriad lesser craft hoping there might be a windfall for them. But the big frigate had landed gently, remained upright, and was in no danger so long as the weather remained serene. She was, in fact, touching bottom only amidships. Lighters were brought alongside to remove the two guns and her anchor chain. The water tanks were pumped out, and an additional fifty casks were jettisoned. Several efforts to tow her off resulted only in parted hawsers. Finally, the most powerful tug present took a heavy hawser from the main masthead and began rocking her in the gently lifting swells. At 3:30 P.M., she slid off and was towed into Portsmouth Naval Shipyard. Three days later, once preparations had been made, *Constitution* was moved into Dry Dock 11 to learn the damage. Careful inspection showed only that she had lost some sheets of copper and about eighty-five feet of her false keel—nothing serious. She was refloated on the 24th. Badger had himself towed out of port by the tug *Malta* at first light on the 30th, eager, no doubt, to be clear of the shore.

RUDDER LOST

It wasn't long before those aboard knew the voyage home was going to be as uncomfortable as the outward trip had been. The strong winds that let her bowl along at ten knots on 3 February became "strong squalls" on the 5th. The barometer stood at 29.56 on the 6th (seas "rough"), dropped to 29.35 on the 7th (the ship "rolling deeply but easily"), to 28.97 on the 8th ("heavy squalls"), and to 28.70 on the 9th. But the 9th also was a day of strange peace; the proverbial calm before the storm. So rare was it that the log keeper felt compelled to write, "A remarkable instance of pleasant weather with an exceedingly low barometer." The ship soon met seas that caused her to lurch heavily. Winds were screaming out of the southeast at forty knots on the 10th as the barometer slid to a low of 28.36. Very heavy swells came barreling down on *Constitution* from the northwest. Badger had her lying on a starboard tack. Hailstones pelted the watch. On succeeding days, the barometer began to climb, but the storm in the frigate's vicinity only grew worse. Badger tried running before the wind while mountain-high seas, ofttimes clashing at cross angles, smashed at her stern. That the eighty-year-old ship withstood them as well as she did is a testimonial to those who built her those many years gone by.

During the morning watch on the 13th (not a Friday), the people on the quarterdeck noticed "frequent heavy thumps caused by seas striking stern and rudder." During the following watch, it was discovered that the rudder had been twisted from its head: It was flapping free, slamming into the hull on either side and soon loosening planking at the rudder post. Badger used one part of his crew to trim sails and maneuver the ship as best he could by that means to get her as steady as possible. The carpenter and his gang began their struggle to recover the situation aft. Their first effort was to lower anchor chain across the rudder and inch it in to stop the rudder's rampage. It was only partially successful. When the seas seemed to abate a little, men went over the stern in boatswain's chairs to bore holes forward into the rudder from its after edge. The men worked desperately, dangling perilously over the transom, where they were struck by and submerged in the angry sea, working with massive objects that could snuff them out in a twinkling at the slightest error. They could see that the upper gudgeon was weakening, that it could give way and the rudder fall clear at any time. Their calm desperation and perseverance was rewarded after twenty-three hours of effort. Into the bored holes had been driven pins to which were attached lengths of anchor chain. These were led forward on either side, where they were connected by tackles to the extreme ends of the crossjack yard, which had been lowered to rest on the quarterdeck bulwarks and stayed to immobilize it. Marines were detailed to provide muscle to each of the tackles, and by this means the ship was brought under control.

Close to noon on the 14th, *Constitution* was hailed by the British barque *Sagitta*, which offered to take off crew. Badger, not surprisingly, refused. He asked, instead, that she direct the first steamer she encountered to come to his assistance. *Sagitta* passed on. Badger set course for Lisbon, the closest port under prevailing conditions.

With the weather abating and a measure of ship control restored, "Old Ironsides" made the seven hundred miles to Lisbon in the good time of four days. A pilot and three tugs got her safely moored up the Tagus River at the end of the second dogwatch on the 18th.

Life in the Portuguese capital did not move at the same pace as it did in England. The local authorities were every bit as willing to provide assistance to the Americans, but finding the materials with which to make the needed repairs proved time consuming. The damaged rudder was unshipped and sent ashore on the 24th, but not until 10 March were they ready to dock the frigate. In the two weeks she was high and dry, new fittings were provided on the stern post and the copper in the area refurbished before a healthy rudder was installed. While they were at it, the ship also received a new maintopgallant yard. Later, during the course of back loading ammunition and stores, one of the carpenter's gang discovered rot in the jib boom, and this, too, was replaced.

Badger happily cleared Lisbon on 11 April without assistance from any steamer and hoped for a fast voyage home. He didn't get it, but neither were there any more disasters. Offloading the "New York" cargo required only six hours, but the ship remained there until 30 May. She offloaded the "private" Philadelphia exhibits on 6 and 7 June at Philips' Wharf, then shifted to the navy yard where all the government exhibits were taken off in less than eight hours. On the 21st, Badger brought her proper gun battery back aboard: eighteen 32-pounders (Model 1842). Two breech-loading 20-pounder rifles were added at the end of the summer.

Apprentice Training Ship—"Third Rate"

In July 1879, *Constitution* embarked on what was to be her final role as an active unit of the navy, that of being one of four ships assigned to the newly created Apprentice Training Squadron. An expansion of the 1875 program, the ship would carry a contingent of fifteen to eighteen year olds on minority enlistments who now were taken to sea as a part of their initial training. Only when they became adequately proficient were they transferred to regular cruising units and became eligible for advancement in the same manner as their new shipmates. Badger got her under way on 19 July and took her to New York, where she entered into a docking and overhaul while still training the youngsters. Capt. Francis H. Baker succeeded Badger in command on 2 August.

The ship was in dry dock on 7 September when Lt. Comdr. Theodore F. Jewell, the executive officer, presented Medals of Honor to Carpenter's Mate

Henry Williams and Captains of the Top Joseph Matthews and James Horton "for gallant conduct aboard this vessel the 13th Feb., last." It was they who had dared the angry sea in boatswain's chairs for so many hours. Horton's was a case of the sweet after the bitter, for he had been one of the miscreants in Le Havre, had been court-martialed as a deserter, fined three months' pay, and confined in double irons for thirty days. His return to grace had been spectacular.

The fact that the captain had not presented the medals stemmed from his sickly condition upon assuming command. So poorly was he that he had taken himself off to the hospital on 21 August. After a month's absence, it was obvious that he could not retain command. In accordance with orders, on 25 September the executive officer took command until an officer of appropriate seniority could be ordered in. Comdr. Oscar F. Stanton, who would be promoted to the rank of captain early in the new year, relieved Jewell on 1 October, as the overhaul was completing.

Constitution left New York on the 8th and was in Norfolk three days later. There, she took on another forty-eight boys. While still there on 15 November, she was again rated as "ship, second class, 20 guns."

In the evening of the 16th, 3/c Boys Eugene Nodler and Merrit Bradford attempted to desert and were captured by the ship's Marines. Bradford, however, broke away from the corporal of the guard and jumped overboard from the starboard gangway, even though he couldn't swim. Master Aaron Ward and Ship's Corporal James Thayer went in after him and kept him afloat until the ship's dinghy could get them out of the river. For his act, Thayer became the fourth "Constitution" to be awarded the Medal of Honor. Ward received a letter of commendation from the secretary of the navy; he later would serve with conspicuous gallantry in the Battle of Santiago in 1898.

From the 24th on, *Constitution* was ready to go to sea but was prevented from doing so by foul winds. She finally was able to clear on 11 December, displaying her "number" (identifying signal flags: G-Q-F-C) for the lookout tower as she passed Cape Henry, southbound for the Caribbean.

WINTER IN THE SUN

This voyage began much more auspiciously than her last, the log frequently reeling off ten knots as she swiftly left winter behind and gave the youngsters their first taste of the sea. A brief call at Guadeloupe on Christmas Eve was followed by an eleven-day visit to Fort de France, Martinique. Third Class Boy Albert Rathbun died and was buried there on 4 January 1880. Four days later, just after getting under way for Saint Croix, a summary court-martial found two guilty of sex crimes and awarded dishonorable discharges.

The stay in Frederikstadt seems to have been almost idyllic. The boys were most frequently involved in learning small boat handling, drills that were made fun by frequent pulling and sailing races. When there were infractions of the rules, the boys were punished by having to "toe the seam" (stand with one's toes carefully marking a particular caulk in the deck) for anything up to eight hours, or by missing the evening meal—a marked contrast to the "good old days" when the cat ruled. The school ship spent the entire month of February in or near Limon Bay, Colombia, an area near what later became the eastern end of the Panama Canal. There, the boys went through the school of the ship with few distractions.

Now-Captain Stanton got under way on 1 March for the return northward. Even before reaching the latitude of Cape Hatteras, Mother Nature reminded them that winter was not yet over, with strong gales, drizzling sleet, and heavy seas.

Constitution hadn't been in Norfolk long when Stanton received a letter from Como. Earl English, chief of the Bureau of Equipment and Recruiting, alerting him to an impending visit of Secretary Thompson and a party to Norfolk in the near future, and of the secretary's announced desire to visit "Old Ironsides." In a friendly suggestion that seems to presage the "Turnaround Cruises" that began nearly eighty years later, the commodore wrote, "You would appear to better advantage in the Bay than at the Wharf. Besides you might offer to get her underweigh [sic] which I think would please the Secretary and all hands." It isn't known if Stanton complied.

After a month and a half at Norfolk, "Old Ironsides" sailed on 16 May for New York, where she received a new draft of boys, and where Stanton had the "experts" do a survey of the ship to determine how badly she was aging. She got a "go" for another training cruise, but was delayed in starting it by an outbreak of scarlet fever that kept her in quarantine anchorage for most of June.

This second cruise began on 8 July when, with the assistance of tugs *George L. Garlick* and *Mary A. Hogan*, the big frigate passed northward through Hell's Gate and sailed to Gardiner's Bay, at the east end of Long Island. Operating out of there for the next twelve days, the boys were provided with training at the great guns and with small arms. Fifty-five rounds were fired from the 32-pounders, a thrill for those impressionable lads.

Following a few days at Newport, the ship went northward, visiting Bar Harbor, Maine, for a week beginning 31 July, then Halifax, Nova Scotia, for four days in mid-August before turning southward again. Brief stops at New Bedford, Massachusetts, Newport, and Lewes, Delaware, provided breaks in the trip deep into Hampton Roads and up the York River to Yorktown, where the old frigate and her young sailors provided some color to the shoreside celebrations marking the centennial anniversary of Cornwallis's surrender. As she was leaving that port, "carried away runner of Mizzen topsail halliards; the yard came down with a run carrying away the starboard yard arm at topgallant sheeve hole." She anchored for a day off Wormley's Creek to make repairs. She'd been under way again on 4 October for ten hours when "carried away maintopgallantmast four feet above the cap." She anchored again to remove wreckage and make repairs. The executive officer, Lt. Comdr. Francis W. Dickins, was injured by the falling spar and had to be transferred ashore for treatment. Following a six-week stay in Hampton Roads, the ship returned to the Philadelphia Navy Yard for overhaul. While there, on 11 November, the ship was visited by President Rutherford B. Hayes, his Cabinet, and Commodore English. This time, the she was able to fire the proper salutes.

Test borings were taken throughout *Constitution*'s hull on 15 December, which showed that the hull still was quite strong, even though it was showing signs of distortion. The rudder had to be taken ashore again for repair. She had to be caulked throughout. And her bilge pumps and heating plant needed to be overhauled. On 4 April 1881, she was moved out to anchorage in the river, pronounced fit enough to resume her relatively undemanding duties.

ACHES AND PAINS

While *Constitution* was being repaired, on 16 December 1880, she and the other apprentice training ships were organized into a "training fleet," to be home ported near Newport, Rhode Island, at Coaster's Island, where there would be established a naval training station. Both the station and the fleet were to be commanded by an officer of at least a captain's seniority. On 15 March 1881, the program was expanded to include fourteen year olds. USS *New Hampshire*, built as a ship of the line but never so employed, was ordered shifted from Norfolk to Newport to become the headquarters for the squadron.

Stanton sailed his tired ship from Philadelphia on 9 April, under orders to proceed to Washington so that his ship and crew could participate in the dedication of a memorial to Adm. David G. Farragut. They were yet two days shy of Cape Henry when both the middle and lower bobstays carried away at the bowsprit. New ones were set up the next day, and on the 17th, the frigate entered Chesapeake Bay, where the screw gunboat *Yantic*, 5, passed her a towline for the trip up the Potomac.

Constitution's deep draft precluded a simple trip to Washington, a fact that appears to have had to be relearned on this occasion. As a result, the ship herself got no closer to the capital than the waters off Piney Point, where she anchored near steam frigate *Tennessee*, 22. Her Marines and sailors went on to the celebration on board *Yantic* and the steamer *Norfolk*. She departed on 7 May as the sun rose, the middle ship in a column with sloops *Saratoga* and *Portsmouth* bound for Norfolk. There, "Old Ironsides" was taken to the yard where "yard birds" again busied themselves "hunting for rotten places." During the first week in June, iron braces were run through the ship athwartships beneath the gun deck at intervals throughout her length. These, it was hoped, would stop the tendency she was showing to sag outward.

It was during these waning days when her age was showing so badly that she became a flagship for the last time in regular service. Stephen B. Luce, first commodore of the training squadron, made her his flagship on 9 May by hoisting his broad pennant and taking up quarters in the spar deck cabin. The screw steamer USS *Powhatan* towed *Constitution* from Norfolk to Newport during the period 9–12 June. Two days after her arrival, Comdr. Edwin M. Shepard relieved Stanton. At two bells of the evening watch on 18 July, 3/c Boy C. W. Wheelock attempted to desert by swimming ashore from *Constitution*'s anchorage off Goat Island. He never made it, thereby becoming the last fatality to be logged aboard the frigate in regular service.

Parting Shot

Luce shifted his flag to USS *New Hampshire* on 9 August. Shepard got *Constitution* under way for a short training cruise on the 11th. In a series of daylight runs, he worked his way up the Sound as far as New Haven (15 August), then turned eastward, coming to anchor at New London, Connecticut, on the 26th. For the next few days, there was a gradual increase in the number of navy units until there were seven. They had come to New London to participate in a final Centennial observance: a reenactment of the British raid on the area in 1781. *Constitution* took

Private Hendrickson of Battery A, 3d Regiment, stationed at Fortress Monroe, Virginia, took this, the only known photograph of *Constitution* under sail while in regular service. She is standing in to Hampton Roads during the summer of 1881. Visible are two of the four pulling boats in quarter davits she carried as an apprentice training ship. *Official U.S. Navy photo*

the role of the enemy flagship. She fired a 17-gun salute to the governor of Connecticut in the morning, before dressing ship and firing a noon salute. In the early evening, she expended twenty-two "Coston signals" and fourteen rockets in a twenty-minute fireworks display. A 21-gun salute at sunset the next day concluded this "last hurrah."

On 11 September, the tired old frigate resumed her daylight training routine, sailing to an anchorage off New Bedford, then off Cuttyhunk, and Brenton's Reef Light, before returning to Newport. She made one more trip to New London on 2 October, remaining in that port for two weeks. The navy tug *Rocket* towed her back to Newport.

A few minutes after midnight on 3 November, *Constitution*'s career very nearly came to an end: Fire was found in the beams beneath the boiler down on the forward orlop. Alert work by ship's company prevented the situation from getting out of hand and brought the emergency to a happy conclusion within an hour. During the dogwatches the very next afternoon, the anchorage was struck by heavy squalls. *Constitution* began dragging her anchor; shortly thereafter, she went hard aground by the stern just off Goat Island. Not a leak. She was hauled off and reanchored as the sun rose the next morning.

As it turned out, the ship's moment of truth came on the 14th in the form of a Board of Inspection and Survey under the leadership of Como. Alexander C. Rhind. Their careful and thorough work resulted in what must have been an obvious conclusion: Structurally the ship was unsafe to be used at sea. The quality of work at Philadelphia during 1874–1876 evidently was so poor that, in 1881, it was almost as if it hadn't happened at all. The navy of 1881 was at a low point, perhaps its lowest ever. There was no money available for the major overhaul of a ship that ostensibly only recently had had one, especially an obsolete *wooden* ship.

END OF AN ERA

It didn't take long for the order to be issued to lay up the eighty-four-year-old frigate. On the 22nd, 49 apprentices were transferred to *New Hampshire*. In another two days, 15 crewmen and 135 more boys went to *New Hampshire*, while her 23 Marines were taken into *Minnesota*. The ship's topgallant masts were sent down because rot and splitting had been found in the maintopmast.

No record has been found of the scene when *Constitution* left Newport on 25 November 1881 at the end of a towline from the armed transport USS *Tallapoosa*. In late November, the weather on Narragansett Bay almost certainly was sharply cold. The waters were slate gray and probably choppy, little curls of foam looking like rime ice. And there went the old "eagle of the sea," her masts no longer towering to the clouds, no longer supporting glorious billows of canvas in a fresh breeze. If there were any "huzzahs," they were echoes in some old salt's mind as he watched that damned chuffing, smoking, clanking sidewheeler haul that once sleekly free hull out of sight beyond Point Judith. Shed a tear, sailorman.

Laying her up was swiftly done. Moored at the New York Navy Yard on the 27th, the powder was offloaded in the next day; the rigging began coming down on the 29th. Sails and ordnance stores went ashore on 3 December. Anchors were landed and the boats sent to the boat shed on the 5th. Her remaining yards came down on the 8th. A period of rainy weather began on the 12th. The following afternoon, she was "towed to Ordnance dock and secured under steam derrick," which began lifting out her guns in mid-afternoon. The chore was completed before noon on the 14th. It began raining again as the ship was moved to a backwater berth at the cob dock by the navy screw tug *Catalpa*. Shortly before 5:00

The hull lines of the vaunted frigate are barely visible in this view of *Constitution* as she was outfitted with a "barn" to be a receiving ship at the Portsmouth (New Hampshire) Navy Yard. A part of the sloop *Jamestown* can be seen to the right. The photo was taken sometime between 1882 and 1888. *Official U.S. Navy photo*

that afternoon, Shepard hauled down her commissioning pennant from what remained of the main mast. The fifty-four-man remnant of the crew was formed up on the dock and marched off into the wet evening to their temporary home, the receiving ship *Colorado*, a former steam frigate.

"GUARDO"

Constitution herself became a receiving ship within months of this dolorous scene at New York. Towed to the navy yard at Portsmouth, New Hampshire, she had an ugly, huge "barn" built above her hull in the final months of 1882, making her over into a barracks and assembly hall for transient sailors. Thus she stayed as months passed into years. A familiar bulk in the skyline of the navy yard, the old ship lay there, getting older and weaker. If rot appeared in her planking, other boards were nailed over it. Cement was used as patching in her bilges. How much longer she might continue to serve in that condition was anybody's guess.

The old frigate might not have looked much like herself, residing there in a backwater, but she did not entirely leave the public consciousness. Secretary of the Navy Benjamin F. Tracy, in April 1889, thought about moving her to Washington, D.C., as a replacement for USS *Dale* and received an estimate of $1,000 from the commandant of the navy yard there to make the move. The matter apparently continued under consideration into 1890, but nothing came of it, probably because of the cost of repairing and moving her.

As he himself later told it, Massachusetts Congressman John F. Fitzgerald happened to see a newspaper item sometime during 1896 that reported the old frigate was about to sink at her moorings in Portsmouth if something weren't done. Fitzgerald made a personal tour of inspection to the ship and found the report to be all too true. Upon his return to Washington, he called on Secretary of the Navy (and former governor of Massachusetts) John D. Long to see what could be done. Maintenance funds being scarce, and receiving ships being recognized as obsolete ships that would continue to be of service only so long as they didn't fall apart, Long could only say that if Congress would authorize it, the ship would be saved. Fitzgerald introduced a resolution in the House on 14 January 1897 to authorize the repair of the ship sufficient to permit her return to Boston in time for her 100th birthday. The Congress, then completing the 1897 Naval Appropriations Act, inserted a provision that the navy could use any remaining monies of the $8,000 allocated in 1894 to outfit the ship as a training site for naval militia "for such work as may be necessary for the proper care and preservation of that historic vessel." On 19 July, *Constitution* was dry-docked where, during the next twelve days, the copper was patched. Comdr. Samuel W. Very, who had made her last trip to Europe in her as a lieutenant, was placed in charge of the move and given a temporary crew of thirty sailors from the receiving ship *Wabash*. Over the protests of the New Hampshire Sons of the American Revolution and others, on 20 September 1897—one month before her centennial—she was towed back to Boston in eighteen hours by the tug USS *Leyden* to be greeted and saluted by major units of the modern navy. The Boston Navy Yard became her home where, following the celebrations in October, she settled once more into quiet erosion. The yard commandant was her former skipper, now commodore, Henry L. Howison.

CHAPTER NINETEEN

The Long Road Back

THE "HOUSE" IS LOST

Constitution's return to Boston sparked interest in her well-being among a number of historical and patriotic groups in the metropolitan Boston area, groups whose memberships included people belonging to famous families of the Revolution as well as politicians who could wield considerable power in the nation's capital. It was at the insistence of these people that Congress, on 14 February 1900, authorized the restoration of the frigate with nongovernmental funds. The Massachusetts State Society of the United Daughters of the War of 1812, under Mrs. Nelson V. Titus, took the lead in this project by kicking off a campaign to raise the $400,000 thought necessary. The program, regrettably, failed despite protracted efforts on the ladies' part.

At the end of 1903, the Massachusetts Historical Society, representing similar bodies in New England, forwarded a memorial to the Congress asking that "the necessary steps forthwith be taken for preserving the 'Fighting Frigate' of 1812; that she be renewed, put in commission as a training ship, and at suitable seasons be in the future stationed at points along our coast where she may be easily accessible to that large and ever-increasing number of American citizens who, retaining a sense of affection, . . . feel also a patriotic and an abiding interest in the associations which the frigate *Constitution* will never cease to recall." First to sign this document was Charles Francis Adams, president of the society and descendant of presidents.

In his annual report of 1905, Secretary of the Navy Charles Joseph Bonaparte (grandnephew of Emperor Napoleon) audaciously suggested that the "frigate *Constitution*, 'Old Ironsides,' being old and no longer useful, be used as a target for some of the ships in our North Atlantic fleet and sunk by their fire." When the newspapers reported the secretary's message, there was an outcry. One is worthy of mention: Moses Gulesian, an Armenian immigrant who had worked his way to wealth in his adopted homeland, offered Bonaparte $10,000 for the frigate so that she would not be destroyed. Bonaparte was restrained from implementing his proposal, and his menace to the old ship ended a few months later when he was transferred to the post of attorney general by President Theodore Roosevelt. With "Lunchbox Charlie" out of there, an amendment quickly was tacked on to the 1906 Naval Appropriations Act providing $100,000 "to repair the *Constitution* but not for active service."

Work was put in hand as soon as the bill became law. Under the direction of Naval Constructor Elliot Snow, carpenters went to work stripping away the ugly barn that had hidden the graceful lines of her hull for a quarter century. Once again the waist was open but for hammock nettings, just as it had been under Isaac Hull, and the spar deck bulwarks formed a smooth, flowing line with the cap rail enclosing the upper sides of the gun ports. Masts were restepped to the topgallants, yards sent up, and much of the standing rigging rerove. A billet head, with a dragon in the design and which was thought to reproduce the one carried in 1812, was installed in place of the curlicue model of 1876, but the stern decorations of that refit merely were refurbished.

Money being in limited supply and precise information as to their design lacking, a single battery of fifty-four "32-pounders" was produced for the ship. The guns' design was based upon data found in an eighteenth-century book on ordnance, on Theodore Roosevelt's *The Naval War of 1812* (1882), and Louis de Toussard's *American Artillerists Companion* (1811). Snow had to be content with giving the ship the aura of a man-of-war. Virtually no work was done below decks, although the camboose was relocated to its earlier position between the anchor bitts. The captain's cabin remained divided into a number of individual staterooms. The money shortage also precluded any repairs to the underwater body and only those of a limited nature were accomplished on the outer hull; the decaying stern was not touched. Therein lay the seed of future problems. Nevertheless, by the mid-summer of 1907, *Constitution* had at least the outward appearance of her old self. During Boston's Old Home Week, 28 July–3 August, Governor Guild hosted a reception on board the old frigate that was recalled as having been one of the highlights of the festivities. (The total bill for the repair came within the budget: $97,800.01.)

This 1 May 1907 photograph shows *Constitution* in the process of superficial restoration from her receiving ship days. Her waist is once again open and the bulwarks lowered to their earlier height. Unfortunately, nothing was done about the decay in the underwater body, and, before long, cement was being used to stem the leaks. *Official U.S. Navy photo*

With the ship looking somewhat as she did in her halcyon days, and a celebration of the fact having been duly conducted, *Constitution's* life settled into a quiet backwater in the Boston Navy Yard, changing locations from time to time within the yard, and being taken notice of on holidays through the flying of flags from each of her masts and ceremonies on her spar deck. A ship keeper and a sailor were her total crew. Other sailors, attached to the yard's receiving ship, *Wabash*, were assigned duties aboard her as guides, touring visitors around topsides and perhaps the gun deck, regaling them with the popular sea stories about her. In the summer months, as many as five hundred people a day paid her a call. In 1911, the rigging was extensively repaired. A year later, it was noted that the ship was making about thirty inches of water a month; by 1916, she was making twenty-five inches a *week*, and $150,000 was thought necessary to restore her to health "for a long period of years."

A Name Is Lost and Regained

On 29 August 1916, President Woodrow Wilson signed into law an authorization for the navy to build six battle cruisers. This act was of significance to "Old

Ironsides," for the name initially assigned to the lead unit was *Constitution*. Several reassignments of names were made as the contracts were awarded, however, and the name "Constitution" finally came to rest on the fifth hull, provided for in March 1917. In order to make the name available, the sailing frigate officially was renamed *Old Constitution* on 1 December of that year. The keel for the battle cruiser was laid at Philadelphia Navy Yard on 25 September 1920.

A conference called in Washington in 1921 brought together the principal naval powers of the world—England, France, Italy, Japan, and the United States—to seek a limitation to the naval programs then burgeoning in those countries in what was supposed to be an era of peace following the "war to end all wars." A treaty completed before the year was out required massive cutbacks in the fleets and building programs of England and the United States and, to a lesser extent, Japan. The American battle cruiser program was dead, although two hulls were completed as aircraft carriers, then considered to be an auxiliary type. The remainder were to be scrapped. With the final ratification of the treaty on 17 August 1923, the Navy Department immediately implemented it: Within eight days, the battle cruisers were canceled. The incomplete *Constitution* was sold "as is, where is" on the ways for $92,024.40 on 25 October, missing by just four days being a present for the 126th birthday of "Old Ironsides." To get ahead of our story a little bit, the final act in this episode occurred on 24 July 1925, when *Old Constitution* was again named *Constitution*.

If donating her name to the war effort proved to be abortive, *Constitution* made another, much more lasting contribution. The twenty-five Medals of Honor awarded to navy men during World War I were made of bronze salvaged from the old frigate, linking modern heroism with past glories.

ANOTHER RESTORATION

Exactly two weeks after the scrap sale, the Chief of Naval Operations, Adm. Edward W. Eberle, ordered the Board of Inspection and Survey to conduct a detailed inspection and provide a clear evaluation of *Constitution*'s condition, together with a recommendation for future action. The board conducted its inspection on 19 February 1924. Its report made official the deteriorating conditions obvious to the most casual observer, and much more. She was shipping water at a rate that made it mandatory that a tug come alongside every evening and pump her out. The stern was so decayed that it nearly was falling off. She

This is the original design for the 1916 battle cruisers, one of which was to be named *Constitution*. There were actually to be *seven* stacks, the second and fourth being athwartship pairs. A later version reduced the number to two broadly trucked stacks, similar to those seen in Japanese cruisers like HIJMS *Yubari*. Two hulls from this program were allocated to became aircraft carriers when the battle cruiser program was canceled, resulting in USS *Lexington* (CV-2) and USS *Saratoga* (CV-3). *Courtesy U.S. Naval Institute*

was badly distorted, so much so that her port side bulged out nearly a foot more than the starboard, the stem skewed nearly nine inches to port, and there was a fourteen-and-a-half-inch hog in the hull. All the deck beams were badly decayed at the ends and many in the center section, as well. Virtually all knees and breast hooks were shot through with dry or wet rot. The keelson was broken just abaft the foremast step. Patches of cement were present, filling rot holes in the hold ceiling planking. Nonetheless, perhaps recognizing the popular interest in the ship, the board concluded that the ship should be "rebuilt and refitted, and preserved and put in a condition for preservation for the greatest length of time practicable as a seaworthy vessel." The preliminary cost estimate was $400,000, and an immediate request for the funding was recommended as the ship was assessed as being on the verge of total ruin.

Secretary of the Navy Curtis D. Wilbur made a personal inspection tour of the old frigate in July 1924 and returned to Washington convinced of the need for immediate action. It was his feeling, however, that the cost of her restoration should be borne by the American people by a popular subscription, thereby giving them the opportunity to participate personally in the restoration of the beloved frigate and also enhance her value to them on a more intimate basis. Accordingly, he included in his next report to Congress a request for authority to restore "Old Ironsides" with monies sought by a nationwide campaign. The authorization was granted in a bill passed on 3 March 1925. A national executive committee, composed of people in the navy, government, and business, was established to coordinate the effort. The first donation, of one dollar, is said to have come from Daniel Jennings of Boston, a navy Civil War veteran.

At the Boston Navy Yard, passage of the authorization was the signal to begin preparatory work. A search was made for plans on which to base the restoration, and when a set failed to turn up, further research was undertaken to develop the data necessary to fill in the gaps (and there were many). As finally developed, the ship was restored to her approximate appearance in the 1850s, less the poop cabin. A search was begun for materials that would be needed, for it was intended, if at all possible, to use those identical to the originals. Finding the massive white oaks, the live oak, and the myriad natural knees needed was a gargantuan task that took searchers nationwide, much as had been the case in 1794, but now on a grander scale. Lt. John Abell Lord, Construction Corps, U.S. Navy, one of the few men remaining on the navy's rolls having a familiarity with wooden ship building, was assigned to superintend the project. As he and his subordinates dug more deeply into the problems of the ship, the cost estimates rose sharply. Their costing of the Board of Inspection and Survey report came to $473,725. A more extensive examination of the frigate early in 1926 raised this figure to $650,654, and it was upped again to $747,983 when suppliers began to submit bills for the unusual materials requirements for the job.

This upward spiral must have been rather disheartening to the fund-raisers as they got the campaign under way. One of the first elements of it was directed at the schoolchildren of the country during the last week of October 1925. This was under the sponsorship of the national Elks organization, and featured patriotic exercises and classroom instruction in *Constitution*'s history. In a year, the overall campaign raised $246,000 (of which $148,000 had come from the children and $31,000 from U.S. Navy, Marine Corps, and Coast Guard personnel)—just one-third of the estimated requirement.

In September 1926, it was proposed that sales of a picture of the ship by a famous artist would be a good fund-raiser. Secretary Wilbur approved, and Gordon Grant agreed to do the painting from which lithographs would be made. Priced initially at twenty-five cents a copy, it provided an important boost to the effort. More than a million were sold, and still more were given away to schoolchildren in recognition of their penny contributions. So many prints were distributed that fifty years later they could be quite readily purchased at the many flea markets in New England—but not for fifty cents. Grant's original painting, completed on 20 November 1926, was hung in the White House, where it continues on display in accordance with Grant's wishes.

Paramount Pictures assisted in bringing "Old Ironsides" into public consciousness by producing the movie "Old Ironsides," starring Wallace Beery, Charles Farrell, George Bancroft, and Esther Ralston. A richly funded picture for the time, the Maine-built ship *Llewellyn J. Morse* was altered to take the starring role, and the city of Tripoli was recreated on Catalina Island off California as the setting of the principal action. An innovation in the filming was the use of airborne radios to direct ship movements. Involving a cast of over two thousand and a fleet of nearly twenty vessels, the story was nonetheless only slightly related to the ship's history. It premiered on 6 December 1926 at the Rialto Theater in New York, with some boxes selling for one hundred dollars and more, a then-unheard-of price. The net proceeds of the night went to the restoration fund.

Used for the first time at the movie's premiere was something called "magnascope," a magnifying lens on the projector that enlarged the screened image from twelve by eighteen feet to thirty by forty feet. As the film *Constitution* swept in on "Tripoli," her image swelled and seemed to loom out over the audience. Wrote one movie critic afterwards, "[A] number of naval officers, including the Secretary of the Navy, abandoned their seats for a time being and gave a number of whoops. The scene really deserved a hand. I'll offer two to one Calvin Coolidge would have tossed off a cheer."

Back in Boston, as the year 1927 opened, Lieutenant Lord was moving nearer to the actual commencement of the restoration. The problem of materials had begun to be solved. Stocks of white oak had been located in southern Ohio and West Virginia, while white oak knees had been contracted for in Delaware. Douglas fir from the state of Washington was substituted for the long leaf yellow pine originally used in deck planking when stocks of the latter in the dimensions required were found to be inadequate. Fir similarly was substituted for white pine in the new masts. Live oak, which might have proved impossible to acquire from growing stocks, was found in Commodore's Pond on the naval air station at Pensacola, Florida. It evidently had been cut in the 1850s for an unrealized building program when that site was a shipyard; some 1,500 tons of the stuff was shipped northward.

The secretary of the navy authorized commencement of the restoration on 13 April 1927, and Lord went to work immediately, removing bulkheads and such furniture as remained in the old ship, as well as the gun battery. (In accordance with a congressional authorization of 3 March 1927, many of these materials were sold by the navy to add to the funds raised by the national committee. The wood and metal were used to produce cigarette boxes, bookends, ashtrays, medallions, picture frames, and other memorabilia.)

Constitution was moored in Dry Dock Two during 25–27 April to remove her masts and bowsprit, and to check the ship's hog. From what he saw at this time, Lord concluded that the frigate was so weak, distorted, and hogged that there was a distinct possibility she would fall apart if the dock were pumped dry. Special plans were drawn up to ensure against this disaster.

In the weeks that followed, the ship was shored thoroughly internally, using longitudinal x-bracing and slip joints worked into the cap pieces to permit adjustment as the ship came out of the water. A pyramid of heavy timbers was erected just forward of the mainmast on the spar deck, over which were run steel cables around the stem and to harpins across the stern in order to "lift" her drooping extremities and to counter the hog. About 150 tons of ballast also was embarked for this latter purpose. An eighty-foot-long "crib" was constructed to fit around the ship's bottom to cradle the sagging hull as it settled onto the blocks on the dry dock floor. And to brace the ship further, a whole forest of shoring timbers was prepared and stowed in appropriate locations about the dock. A crowd of ten thousand people was on hand when Lord carefully moved *Constitution* into Dry Dock One on 16 June 1927—eight days short of the ninety-fourth anniversary of her first entry into the same dock. Slowly pumping down the dock and checking and rechecking the old ship at every step of the way, Lord landed her successfully on the blocks, well shored and braced, without any collapse or further distortion.

The first phase of the actual restoration work consisted of removing all decayed wood in the ship. Because delays were being experienced in the delivery of large timbers, the work proceeded slowly and involved few men. Things began to move more dramatically in November when the white oak keelson timbers finally arrived—seven months late. Two large holes were cut in the frigate's bows, on either side of the stem below the berth deck level, to permit entry of these large timbers into the bowels of the ship. Through the ensuing months, the keelson was replaced and assistant (or "sister") keelsons installed to increase the ship's longitudinal strength. Working upward, short-spliced futtock sections were replaced with full-length members, a new cutwater was installed above the waterline, and the big task of totally rebuilding the stern was undertaken. By January 1929, major internal structural work had been completed to the level of the gun deck port sills. In February, the national executive committee reported that collections to date had reached $660,000 before deduction of fund-raising costs.

The work of rebuilding the hull's upper works commenced as winter turned to spring, the problem of eliminating the distortion of the one-foot skew to port demanding the best efforts of all those involved. Caulking of the underwater body was begun in midsummer and went on into the fall. On Navy Day (27 October), a large gathering watched as the newly constructed bowsprit was slipped into place. Nearly all the ceiling planking had been replaced by year's end; the outer hull planking was on to a point midway up the spar deck gun ports.

If things were going well in the ship, they weren't with the fund-raising campaign. After four years of trying, it was becoming apparent to those involved that they had gone as far as they could go, that they had entered the condition of diminishing returns. Faced with this fact, and having *Constitution* halfway to health, the Congress was prevailed upon to appropriate the monies needed to bring the project to completion. Reluctantly, in the face of the "Great Depression," an authorization for funding "up to $300,000" was approved. (The national campaign had raised a total of $942,599.23, of which $296,364.97 was eaten up by expenses. Major sources were: $165,000 from the sale of lithographs, $135,000 from schoolchildren, $126,000 from the sale of souvenirs made of *Constitution* materials, and $28,000 from bank deposit interest.)

Constitution left Dry Dock One on 15 March 1930, her hull sound and freshly coppered, and subsequently spent a day moving across the harbor to Dry Dock Three in south Boston to have her new masts stepped. In keeping with tradition and sailor superstition, coins were placed beneath each one: a five-dollar gold piece under the fore, a silver dollar under the main, and a 1797 copper penny under the mizzen.

The emphasis of the project now shifted to the internal layout and the installation of fittings. Stylistically, the design of the cabins and furnishings was that prevalent during the mid-nineteenth century, the earliest period for which Lord seems to have had information. It was, therefore, less spartan than that prevalent in the War of 1812 or earlier days. A "typical" brig was installed on the berth deck, although Lord admitted he had no evidence of one ever having been fitted in the ship.

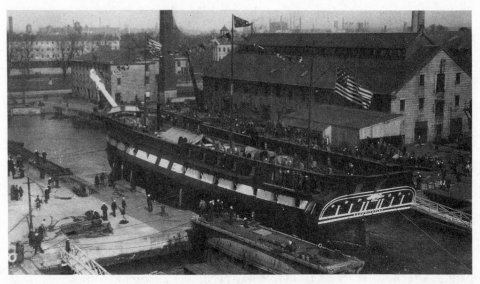

On 15 March 1930 a newly refurbished *Constitution* was towed out of Dry Dock One at the Boston Navy Yard. Funded in large part by several public fund-raising efforts, the ship had been saved from a grossly deteriorated condition and made materially healthy, although in many details her appearance was not "the original" as directed by Congress. The building to the left of the stack in 1976 became the first element of the USS *Constitution* Museum, while the one to the right now houses the staff of dedicated artisans assigned to maintain her material well-being. *Official U.S. Navy photo*

The batteries of 24-pounder long guns and 32-pounder carronades cast for the ship, while far better representations than those of 1906–1907 they replaced, still were not completely accurate for the War of 1812. Undiscovered in Navy Department files lay a drawing detailing the actual guns the ship carried in her heyday.

President Herbert Hoover entered office in 1929. His new secretary of the navy was Charles Francis Adams, the same Adams whose signature had been first on the Massachusetts Historical Society's petition more than a quarter century earlier. With Adams's advent in the department seems to have come the idea of having *Constitution*, once the restoration was completed, visit many ports around the United States so that the people who gave their money to her continued well-being could see what they had accomplished and take fresh pride in their heritage.

The prospect of voyaging in *Constitution* was taken into consideration in the internal fittings of the ship. Modern toilet facilities were adapted and installed in the bow head area, in "cabinets" forward on the gun deck, and in the quarter galleries. A modern stove was installed on the hearth of the old camboose so that the crew could be messed aboard. Water tankage and lines were installed, as was a lighting system. Provisions were made for mounting peloruses on the waist rails, port and starboard, to assist the captain in maneuvering the ship in coastal waters.

On 8 October 1930, *Constitution* made her first ceremonial trip around Boston harbor. It came about as a part of the festivities surrounding the national convention of the American Legion in the city, and for it she had the company of five cruisers, six destroyers, a submarine, and *four* tugs. The cruiser *Memphis* marked the occasion with a 21-gun salute as airplanes flew low overhead.

The remaining work went swiftly under the impetus of the forthcoming grand tour. Yards were swayed into place and rigging completed. A full set of sails was provided by a generous contributor, although there was no official intention to sail her. A crew of sailors and Marines was determined upon and orders for their transfer issued. On 14 March 1931, a set was issued for Comdr. Louis J. Gulliver, then executive officer of the cruiser *Rochester* in the Caribbean, to proceed and report as prospective commanding officer, USS *Constitution*. Gulliver had no more than sixty days in which to become familiar with his unique command and prepare for the long voyage ahead.

During the latter part of June, the ship was opened to visitors, giving the people of metropolitan Boston an opportunity to see firsthand the transformation that had taken place in "their" ship, as well as giving the new crew a chance to practice handling crowds on board. (A record 3,595 came on board on the 15th.) Two gentlemen visitors one day were seen conducting a "commissioning" ceremony of their own on the gun deck: Checking first to see if any crew member was watching, each took a hip flask from a pocket and christened the grog tub with a few drops.

On 1 July 1931, after nearly a half century in limbo, *Constitution* was recommissioned in a ceremony that gave voice to the anticipation and enthusiasm engendered during the four years of her rejuvenation. As recorded by the Boston *Evening Transcript:* "Thousands of persons, including a large number of school children, assembled for the exercises which were held on the athletic field near the pier where the historic frigate was moored. . . . After the speechmaking . . . the second part of the ceremony, the actual commissioning of the vessel, took place on the afterdeck of the *Constitution*." The total cost of the restoration was reported as $987,000.

Hardly had the festivities ended than Gulliver was preparing for the morrow's sailing. There was the usual "organized confusion" of getting aboard last-minute stores, attending to late-breaking problems, and making final checks of duty assignments for the crew of six officers, sixty sailors, and fifteen Marines. Moored nearby was the minesweeper *Grebe*, under the command of Lt. Emil H. Petri, which would provide the tow for *Constitution* on this extended tour. For the coming three years she would not only tow the old frigate from place to place: At each port she would tie up nearby and provide power to her charge.

Quietly (no official ceremonies had been laid on), *Grebe* got *Constitution* away from her berth at the yard at about noon on the 2nd. The departure time was common knowledge, however, and soon the waters were churned by craft of all sizes busy giving them a proper send-off. Outside Boston Light, the well-wishers dropped away and the ships turned north.

First port of call was Portsmouth. On hand to greet them the next morning were destroyers *Breckinridge*, *Wilkes*, and *Barney*, and Coast Guard cutters *Tampa*, *Ossipee*, and *Agassiz*. In a routine that would become all too familiar, local dignitaries were the first aboard to welcome "Old Ironsides" to their town, then the ship was opened to public visiting. That evening, a banquet was tendered, and the next day being the 4th of July, there was a mammoth parade, followed by a variety of sports programs in and around the harbor, and a dance in the evening. Civic and social groups vied with one another to do "Old Ironsides" and her men honor. Boy Scouts helped control the crowds as they waited to visit the ship and helped ensure they got up and down the often steep gangways without mishap. Nearly 31,000 people boarded the ship in the nine days of visiting during the stay, coming from miles around to take advantage of the once-in-a-lifetime opportunity.

There followed brief stops at Bar Harbor and Bath, Maine (Lord's home town), before spending a week in Portland. *Constitution* and *Grebe* headed south on a daylight trip that brought them to Gloucester on the afternoon of the 23rd. There, her arrival was announced by repeated blasts on the firehouse siren, and she was escorted into the harbor by seven Coast Guard cutters as a 21-gun salute boomed out from French 75s stationed in Stage Fort. The usual round of exercises and social events followed. One night, small pleasure boats formed a ring around the old frigate and, on signal, lighted the waters around her with a circle of red flares. A barnstorming air show added to the excitement early on another evening.

Constitution's greeting at Marblehead on the 29th was hardly less noisy, the guns of Fort Sewell providing the salute. This, of course, had been the port in which "Old Ironsides" had sought refuge from pursuing British frigates in 1814, when the countryside had rallied in readiness to defend her. On this later occasion, the Marbleheaders made sure no one could doubt their continued affection. It was an event-filled two-day visit.

Constitution and *Grebe* next proceeded through the Cape Cod Canal to New Bedford, where whaleboat races were an unusual feature of the festivities, and then on to Providence, Newport, New London, Montauk, and Oyster Bay, Long Island, site of Theodore Roosevelt's home. Insufficient water in the planned anchorage caused the frigate to anchor in a less accessible location, so that a mere four hundred people paid calls in three days.

Under way once more on 27 August, the travelers headed east around Montauk Point and then back west for New York City. This "long way 'round" was necessitated by insufficient clearances under New York's East River bridges. A few hours were spent in Gravesend Bay as a "grand entrance" was organized, then destroyers *McDougal, Porter,* and *Upshur* led the way into the Hudson River at 3:30 on the afternoon of the 29th. Three Coast Guard cutters were in column on either side, and hundreds of private and public small craft milled about the parade. *Constitution* was moored at Pier 113 at 79th Street, and one of the first to board was August F. Smith, who had been an apprentice on board half a century earlier. The cancellation of the scheduled visit to Newark (low bridges again) resulted in "Old Ironsides" remaining in the "Big Apple" until 14 September. During the extended stay, the firm of Abraham and Strauss, upon learning that Gulliver's crew was showering with a perforated bucket, donated "the very latest thing" in portable, outdoor, free-standing showers for their use. Over 102,000 people walked her decks in the fifteen days she entertained visitors.

Moving once more through waters where she had eluded an entire British squadron in 1812, the frigate rounded into Wilmington, Delaware, where Isaac Hull had scraped her bottom, welcomed aboard nearly 155,000 Philadelphians during her stay in the City of Brotherly Love, and then stopped at Newport News and Norfolk before anchoring off Yorktown, Virginia, in time to be the "star" of the celebrations commemorating the 150th anniversary of Cornwallis's surrender. Keeping her company in the stream were the battleships *Arkansas* and *Wyoming,* and the French cruisers *Suffren* and *Duquesne.*

Navy Day 1931 (27 October) found *Constitution* in Baltimore, where Secretary Adams hosted a dinner for fifty on board. The Naval Academy band provided musical entertainment. A rumor cropped up at this time that the tour would be terminated at Washington to avoid further expenses. In four days public opinion caused officialdom to deny the proposal, whether or not there was any truth to it. *Constitution* would be visiting the federal capital, but then she would go on.

Grebe towed *Constitution* to the Washington Navy Yard on 7 November after having spent four days off Annapolis so the brigade of midshipmen could visit the "eagle of the seas." President and Mrs. Hoover, together with Secretary Adams, paid an Armistice Day visit to the ship. The ship remained at the yard for eleven days.

Leaving Washington on the 18th, *Constitution* visited Wilmington, North Carolina, Charleston, and Savannah, before arriving at Brunswick, Georgia, on 12 December. Because it was from this area that the live oak had been shipped to Boston in 1795, the local populace viewed the visit as a sort of homecoming. In fact, these Georgians were vying with the residents of Annapolis and Boston to have the ship homeported with them when the grand tour ended.

Jacksonville was the next stop, and then Christmas in Miami. While his crew enjoyed the resort city, Gulliver took a few days of leave to spend the holiday with his family in Washington. New Year's Eve found the two ships at Key West.

Pensacola was the first of the Gulf ports visited, the stay lasting from 6 to 11 January 1932. The fact that the live oak had been shipped to Boston for the recent restoration from Commodore's Pond piqued local curiosity, so that over 35,000 Pensacolans came to the ship.

Following a daylight voyage, *Constitution* and *Grebe* spent a week at Mobile, Alabama. A whopping 120,000 visitors demonstrated that interest in the fabled frigate was high in the Deep South.

It was Mardi Gras week at New Orleans when the two travelers arrived following a visit to Baton Rouge. Their compatriot at Yorktown, the battleship *Arkansas,* also pulled in, and the crews had a *grand time* in the pre-Lenten madness. Nearly 200,000 visitors were received in the frigate. The pet monkey Rosie, belonging to *Grebe*'s crew, was absent upon sailing on 12 February. The gloom felt by the crew was alleviated, however, as the ships reached the mouth of the Mississippi. While they watched in disbelief, a seaplane appeared on the northern horizon, circled the ships, and landed nearby. Taxiing close to *Grebe,* the pilot delivered the errant mascot to her delighted masters.

Between 14 February and 19 March, *Constitution* and *Grebe* made calls at the Texas ports of Corpus Christi, Houston, Galveston, Beaumont, Port Arthur, and Orange. Gulliver was marshal of the Texas Independence Day parade in Galveston and laid a wreath at the Texas Heroes Monument. In Beaumont, he was taken ill and had to be hospitalized. Lt. Comdr. John H. Carson, the executive officer, became acting captain in order that the schedule of port calls could be maintained.

Carson's first chore upon leaving Orange was to see his venerable charge forty miles across Calcasieu Lake and up the Calcasieu River to Lake Charles, Louisiana, on 19 March. The more than 37,000 visitors in the ensuing three days reflected the great local interest in the ship.

Moving back into open waters on the 22nd, the ships made short visits to Gulfport, Mississippi, and Port St. Joe, Florida, before arriving at the twin cities of Tampa–St.Petersburg, where Gulliver again was in command. One of the people who came aboard here was Charles Nowack, who reported himself aboard as "Gun Captain, Gun #11," which he said he had been many years before. Despite his seventy-six years, he flitted about the ship and even headed into the rigging. His exuberance led Gulliver to caution him against further efforts. (The logs of the earlier time show that Charles Nowack had been aboard from 27 June–24 November 1881 as a 3/c Boy who had not been promoted as a result of the quarterly exams given the boys while he was there.) This port call marked the end of the Atlantic/Gulf Coast phase of *Constitution*'s grand tour.

Grebe towed "Old Ironsides" back to the Washington Navy Yard, arriving on 16 April. There they remained, but for one brief move, until 8 December, resting up and refurbishing the old frigate after the passage of more than 2 million people across her decks. The one brief trip came in mid-May when the ships moved to an anchorage off Alexandria for two days during the dedication of the Washington Masonic Memorial building. It was a time of high winds and drenching rains, and "Old Ironsides" gave everyone an unexpected thrill by dragging her anchor. *Grebe* brought her errant charge under control, however, before she could go aground down the Potomac. While resting at the nation's capital, there many changes made in the crew. Gulliver remained, but he received Lt. Comdr. Henry Hartley as executive officer, replacing the redoubtable Carson, together with other officer replacements. Hartley's young son, Henry, Jr., was christened on board 26 June. Secretary Adams hosted a Bastille Day luncheon aboard on 14 July; the guest of honor was French Ambassador Paul Claudel. President Hoover also visited the ship again before she departed.

Constitution toured the coasts of the United States in stages during 1931–1934. Here, on 21 January 1933, she is seen arriving at San Diego under tow of *Bushnell*, passing the carriers *Lexington* and *Saratoga*. These two ships began as units of the aborted 1916 battle cruiser program, which also included a new *Constitution*. The 1922 Washington Naval Treaty required most to be scrapped, but it permitted the two most advanced hulls to be completed as aircraft carriers, then considered auxiliary vessels. *Official U.S. Navy photograph*

Grebe, now commanded by Lt. Andrew Simmons, picked up the towline once more on the morning of 8 December, she and her charge heading for the Pacific. A five-day call at the U.S. naval base at Guantánamo Bay, Cuba, broke the voyage across the Caribbean to the Panama Canal. Christmas was spent at Cristóbal in the Canal Zone. *Constitution's* actual westward transit of the canal occurred between 6:00 A.M. and 3:40 P.M. on the 27th, under the care of *Grebe* and the Panama Canal tug *Gorgona*. While at Balboa, on New Year's Day 1933, President Harmodio Arias of Panama and his wife, together with U.S. Ambassador Roy T. Davis and his wife, were received on board, attended by the Canal Zone authorities.

Following some minor repairs, *Constitution*, towed by the submarine tender *Bushnell* on this 2,800-mile leg, and *Grebe* sailed into the Pacific on the morning of 7 January. The trip northward proved to be a rough one, a storm in the Gulf of Tehuantepec giving the ship a "severe wrenching" and opening many deck seams. San Diego was made safely, however, on the 21st. Here resumed the familiar sequence of port visits as the famed frigate moved steadily northward, her arrival sparking even more interest at each port than had been the case earlier in the tour. This first port call accommodated nearly 180,000 visitors, but the second, in San Pedro (harbor for Los Angeles) amassed an amazing 478,000 callers in just ten days. It is said that the waiting line was ten across and three miles long—an incredible sight. While succeeding port calls were similarly spectacular—over 375,000 in the San Francisco Bay area (including the three-millionth visitor) and more than 500,000 in the greater Puget Sound area—none matched San Pedro's "human sea." This northward trip required just five months.[1]

Constitution and *Grebe* headed south on 19 July, generally visiting smaller ports previously bypassed, although a second call in San Francisco netted another 67,000 callers, and the second stop at San Pedro another 100,000. Arriving in San Diego once more on 3 November, the two ships paused to winter over and make routine repairs. It was in San Diego that Gulliver's daughter, Grace, was married to one of the ship's officers, Wells Thompson, in ceremonies on the frigate's spar deck.

The final leg of this epic grand tour by the 136-year-old frigate began on 20 March 1934, when *Bushnell* again picked up the tow for the voyage to Balboa. *Grebe* sailed with them and resumed her familiar role after the canal was transited on 7 April. The trip essentially was over. The great enthusiasm engendered by the prospect of her visits was but a memory. People were moving on to new interests, no matter how sweet the memories were. Following two quick stops, at St. Petersburg and Charleston, home came the travelers to Boston on 7 May, fatigued from an epic towing operation of some 22,000 miles and the reception of 4,614,762 visitors into the ship's limited confines.

Gulliver hauled down the commissioning pennant on 8 June and placed *Constitution* "out of commission" but "in service," turning over responsibility for her to the "senior officer on board," Lt. Harry St. J. Butler, who had been her navigator throughout her travels.

CHAPTER TWENTY

The Second Century Completed

IN SERVICE

In placing *Constitution* "out of commission, in service," the navy was, in effect, returning the old frigate to the status she had when Isaac Hull was ordered to replace the resigned Silas Talbot in 1801: She would be assigned a small crew to oversee her day-to-day existence. This modern crew consisted of one lieutenant, one lieutenant (j.g.), one warrant boatswain, one warrant gunner, and twenty-six enlisted men. Because she was not in commission, Lieutenant Butler functioned more as a "project officer," keeping the yard commandant apprised of the ship's needs and pleading her case for money and materials. He also was responsible for the handling of visitors on board, comprising on the order of one hundred thousand a year in the 1930s, and for the support of ceremonies held on board.

One of the concerns in the ship, now that she would be essentially immobile for the foreseeable future, was to provide better facilities for her fire safety than the few hoses available. The proposal to install an automatic sprinkler system was turned down by the Bureau of Construction and Repair in June 1934 because of funding limitations. The need was recognized, however, and Butler directed to bring it up again for the next funding period.

Looking ahead to the winter, the lieutenant also requested that a heating system be installed, as his men were living aboard and New England winters could be severe. He won this proposal: A system of seven steam radiators was installed in the living areas late in October. (In February 1935, he reported that the system had to be changed, as the steam heat was causing severe drying of the timbers near the units. A humidifier was installed to ease this problem. A forced air system finally was installed in the mid-1950s.)

An inspection report dated 27 September 1935 stated that the hull and sheathing were in excellent condition. Most coamings around the spar deck hatches were rotted and needed replacement, as did three on the gun deck. The sails, still stowed on board, no longer were serviceable. On the "plus" side, the sprinkler system had just been installed, complementing the half-hourly rounds of the entire ship being made by the crew between sunset and sunrise (a practice that continued until superseded by sensor systems in 1995). Six weeks later, a letter from the yard said that deterioration in the ship was occurring more rapidly than had been estimated earlier when requesting funds for her maintenance, and indicated an additional $34,620 was necessary for caulking, replacing coamings, and renewing twenty knees and bulwark planking. Significantly, it also requested a statement of policy concerning whether just adequate repairs were to be made, or was an effort to be made to ensure historical accuracy through proper restoration. The Bureau of Construction and Repair responded on 9 December that "[I]t is considered that the vessel should be, in general, maintained as an exact replica of the original ship, both in design and materials." In practice, this meant that the ship would be kept just as she had been on completion of the previous restoration, which, as has been briefly noted, did not reflect any one period of service.

Constitution was docked briefly, 30 September–2 October 1936, while seventy-five sheets of copper at the waterline, eaten through by electrolytic action, were replaced. During the same season, considerable work was done on the port bow, where timbers around the bridle port and Number One gun port had rotted out. Nearly $30,000 was spent in these and lesser repairs.

As the years went by and insufficient monies were provided, "Old Ironsides" slowly deteriorated. Among other money-saving expedients, her yards and masts gradually were landed and her rigging reduced. The sails, which finally had been stored ashore in December 1935, rotted away without replacement or were cut up for souvenir purposes. Many, many of her smaller and more portable fittings disappeared for many reasons: Belaying pins rotted out or became mementos; muskets and cutlasses adorned offices and mantle pieces; paintings likewise went to offices and board rooms; silver went. . . . With the limited crew and the pressures of the grand tour, there never had been the opportunity to inventory and control the many objects constantly coming aboard. The reduction in personnel at the decommissioning and the easy access afforded by her being berthed amidst the hustle and bustle of a navy yard combined to make such "requisitions" possible. In a sense, it was a price paid for being so popular with the citizenry; many wanted a part of her in their everyday lives.

In 1936, navy yard Chaplain Thomas B. Thompson began a series of "Summer Sunday" services on board *Constitution,* conducted in cooperation with a variety of patriotic and fraternal organizations, which was held annually until World War II. At the conclusion of one such service, on 26 May 1940, the ashes of Lt. Charles Franz, U.S. Navy, were strewn over Boston harbor waters from the ship at the pier.

On 21 September 1938, during the course of the great hurricane that struck New England, *Constitution* broke loose from her moorings, taking Lt. (j.g.) Arthur Barrett and his crew on an unexpected voyage in the harbor. They didn't go far, however, as the winds rammed her into the destroyer *Ralph Talbot,* giving the latter a good gash. "Old Ironsides," true to her name, suffered nothing more than gouges in her hull. Crewmen from the "tin can" leaped across to help moor the errant frigate and keep her from further harm.

BACK IN COMMISSION

During the summer of 1940, President Franklin D. Roosevelt toured New England, warming up for his bid for a third term in the White House. In Newport, Rhode Island, he saw the 1854 sailing corvette *Constellation,* and in Boston, of course, he saw *Constitution,* recently moved to her now-familiar berth at Pier One. Being a long-time naval buff and a former assistant secretary of the navy, as well as an astute political leader who recognized that his country soon would be at war, Roosevelt issued an order that these two veterans of the "Old Navy" were to be placed back in commission to serve as symbolic flagships in the fleet and to inspire the citizenry to a higher sense of patriotism. The formal ceremony in *Constitution* took place just two weeks later, on 24 August, with Lt. Comdr. Hermann P. Knickerbocker in command. The ship also was assigned the unglamorous designation of "IX-21": "miscellaneous, unclassified vessel #21."

During 1941, Knickerbocker was ordered to more pressing duties, being succeeded in command by fifty-eight-year-old Clarence E. McBride, a retired lieutenant recalled to active duty. McBride previously had been a member of the caretaker crew as a chief petty officer.

A melancholy duty assigned to *Constitution* during World War II was to be the place of confinement for officers awaiting courts martial. The several gentlemen for whom this was the case were maintained in the captain's quarters, Marines from the yard barracks and members of ship's company providing the sentries at the cabin doors.

Constitution, under her new captain, Lt. Comdr. Owen W. Huff, was docked for the first time in nearly nine years during 28 July–2 August 1945. Test borings of the hull found it to be in very good condition. However, 210 sheets of copper, mostly at the waterline, had to be replaced, and the stern under the cabin required caulking.

During the evening of 7 March 1946, in a reversal of the roles in the *Ralph Talbot* collision eight years earlier, *Constitution* was rammed in the stern by navy tug *YTB-540*. In maneuvering to make its berth just behind the old frigate, the service craft's throttle became stuck in reverse, causing the mishap. Happily, damage was limited to several above-water timbers.

Constellation was moved up to Boston from Newport in October, and the two veterans existed side by side, *Constitution* the visited ship and the other providing quarters. In fact, the two ships began sharing a common captain and crew. To ease maintenance, "houses" had been built over their spar decks. Unlike the one *Constitution* had borne at the turn of the century, the new one hardly extended above the line of the bulwarks.

As the armed forces were reduced following the end of World War II, so, too, was the seniority of *Constitution*'s captain: Following Huff there came a Naval Reserve lieutenant (for a few months) and then two chief warrant boatswains. Later, junior officers in the ranks of lieutenant and lieutenant (j.g.) completing their obligated naval service filled the billet.

The United States Post Office issued a stamp commemorating the 150th birthday of "Old Ironsides" in October 1947, the only U.S. warship so honored.

In 1949, a program was begun to refurbish the ship, set her upper masts, and give her back her graceful lines. The ss *Kenyon Victory* arrived about 15 August and unloaded Douglas fir timbers from Oregon to be used in the new spars. For the next year or so, a small group of workers turned out spars, renewing almost every "stick" other than the lower masts, and the bowsprit, as well. The low "house" was removed during March 1950. In April, Chief Warrant Boatswain Knied Christensen relieved Louis Wood in ceremonies held on board *Constellation* so as not to interfere with the visitors. In September, crew members participated in the celebrations attending the yard's 150th birthday in "early Navy" uniforms prepared by the yard sail loft.

During World War II and for some years afterward, *Constitution* largely was unrigged and housed over with a low roof. This view was taken on 1 January 1950; the larboard bow of USS *Constellation*, the 1850s-vintage corvette, is just visible to the left. The two old warships, both in commission, shared a common captain for several years. *Official U.S. Navy photo*

The early 1950s found maintenance efforts shifting from the spars to the hull itself. Many areas of outer hull planking were showing signs of rot after nearly twenty-five years. At this time, the yard chose to experiment by substituting red oak for white in these planks; it was more readily available and was thought to be more easily treated with the approved preservatives of the day. Unfortunately, time proved the experiment a failure, for severe conditions of deterioration were to appear within fifteen years, and it was seen that the preservatives had inadequately penetrated the wood. The shipwrights of 1797 had recorded that red oak was the poorest of the oak family, and they were right.

At about this time, some people in the navy became concerned that several historic ships remained in the inventory, but were not specifically provided for in the budget. Monies supporting them were coming from other "pots" as skillful managers could make them available. In an effort to clarify the situation, the Congress was approached for a decision as to the future of these units and, if the navy was to continue their maintenance, the funds with which to do so. The ships in question were *Constitution,* the sole survivor of the original six; *Constellation,* the corvette constructed, in part, with timbers from the earlier frigate of the same name; *Hartford,* Admiral Farragut's flagship at Mobile Bay; *Olympia,* the flagship of Commodore Dewey at Manila in 1898; and the battleship *Oregon,* which had made a dramatic high-speed transit around the Horn during the Spanish-American War. A bill signed into law by President Eisenhower on 23 July 1954 directed the navy to retain *Constitution* and restore her, insofar as possible, to her "original appearance, but not for actual service." House Speaker John McCormack also had included a provision that Boston was to be her home port: the only time Congress has directed the navy on this subject. *Constellation* was to be turned over to a nonprofit organization in Baltimore and *Hartford* was to go to a similar group in Mobile. If arrangements like these could be made for *Olympia* and *Oregon* within six months, they too were to be transferred. *Constellation* and *Olympia* did find new homes in Baltimore and Philadelphia, where they are moored today. *Hartford* was destroyed in a tragic fire at Norfolk before she could head south. *Oregon's* remains finally became part of a breakwater, her passing mourned only by a few ship buffs. *Constitution's* captain, now Lt. Charles W. Morris, was reduced to having just one ship.

In the postwar years, two events have come to be thought of as traditional in "Old Ironsides": Easter sunrise services and the annual "turnaround cruises." The earliest mention found of the religious service is on 16 April 1953, when Methodist Bishop John Wesley Lord officiated. Begun primarily for the naval personnel and their families, it has come gradually to include any of the general public wishing to attend; for more than fifteen years, the service was broadcast locally by one of Boston's radio stations. The turnaround cruise likewise evolved from very modest beginnings when, in the 1950s, the ship randomly was turned around at her berth to evenly weather her wooden hull. Sometimes she was turned once a year, sometimes twice, and sometimes not at all—and never with passengers until 20 November 1959. The commandant of the First Naval District, Rear Adm. Carl F. Espe, was the official host for the hardy few males who came; Lt. Edward J. Melanson was in command. A note of that period in the headquarters files has been found that recommended, "for the record," that if guests are to be invited again, a better season of the year be chosen for the cruise. The event evolved in the 1960s to where, by 1965, upwards of four hundred men were invited by the commandant for an annual trip under tow down the harbor and back, upon completion of which each was issued a florid certificate attesting to the fact that they had been under way in "Old Ironsides." In 1971, the publicity given the presence of a female stowaway—Ruby Litinsky, a journalist from Peabody, Massachusetts—ended this demonstration of male chauvinism, and each subsequent cruise has sought to make the opportunity available to a wider number of citizens.

Backtracking for a moment, *Constitution* was dry-docked in 1957 for most of the month of March in order to replace 390 sheets of copper and inspect the hull, which required no work. She was docked again from 3 December 1963 to 25 March 1964 for similar work, although at this time it was found necessary to replace the cutwater, as well. This particular overhaul figured in two significant decisions that indicated clearly the frigate was from another age. In September 1962, following no response to two calls for rigging hemp, the decision reluctantly was taken to substitute polypropylene in all future work. And in November 1964, again in response to difficulty in finding proper materials, the decision was taken to use laminated timbers when adequate natural timbers could not be obtained at reasonable prices.

If the spars and yards were holding up well, and the underwater body was too, the outer and ceiling planking and the decks were not. The red oak employed in the sides, as noted earlier, was inadequate to the task. The steady flow of visitors across the decks, handling fittings and often climbing on them, took a steady toll—in some ways, it was far harder service than fighting British frigates. (*Constitution* had 175,000 visitors in 1950, 342,000 in 1960, and would nearly double that figure again in 1970.) It was evident to Rear Adm. Joseph C. Wylie shortly after he became district commandant in 1969 that the time for another major restoration was near. Through his efforts, the navy's Board of Inspection and Survey made another visit to inspect and report.

ANOTHER RESTORATION

The inspection took place in August 1970 and the report issued on 1 September. The board found that "the repairs and alterations . . . [needed] . . . are not disproportionate to the value of the ship"—no one expected them to say otherwise—but her routine maintenance had been "neither adequate nor effective." The sum of the report was that the ship should be refurbished from keel to main truck, and it was estimated that $4.2 million would be needed to do the job. Delays in getting congressional authority for the money precluded a start on the work in 1972. With the nation's bicentennial coming up in 1976, consideration was given to dividing the work into two phases: the dry-docking phase to be completed *before* the celebrations and the rest of the work to be done afterward. The steady diminution in the value of the dollar decided the issue, resulting in a continuous program designed to minimize any limiting effect on the ship's availability for the big year.

Wylie also concluded that one of the reasons *Constitution* had gotten into such condition was that she had not had an officer of sufficient experience and seniority in command, one who was sensitive to maintenance problems and who had the "horsepower" to get things taken care of. His campaign in this regard resulted in a policy change whereby henceforth the captains of "Old Ironsides" would be officers of the rank of commander, with about two decades of service behind them.

Constitution was dry-docked from April 1973 to April 1974. During that time, one-sixth of the outer underwater hull planking was replaced and the whole hull recoppered. (The white oak used came mainly from the area around Piqua, Ohio, after a strenuous search for adequate stands of timber.) While this work was going on outside, another crew of craftsmen labored deep in the ship to restore her forward structure, which was settling badly. Sections of the keelson and nearby deck beams had to be replaced; an entire new step for the foremast was needed, as well. Having accomplished that, the team worked progressively up through the ship's bow structure, overcoming the sagging induced by the large weights exerting severe pressures through long lever arms in this area. Structurally it was, perhaps, the most significant element of the restoration.

Ashore, in the rigging loft of a nearby building, yet a third crew labored to refurbish or replace the miles of rigging required by the ship, and similarly to renew the yards and spars. (Only the lower mainmast had been left in the ship as she lay in the dock.) On a floor below, other men worked over the ship's guns, replacing rotted carriages.

Amidst all this activity came the disconcerting announcement that the Boston Navy Yard, as an economy measure, was to be shut down as of 30 June 1974. Moving quickly, those concerned with *Constitution*'s welfare organized from the existing yard workforce an identifiable "*Constitution* Restoration Group" that would continue in being until the scheduled end of the restoration two years later. In addition, equipments were consolidated into one building adjacent to the dry dock so that the work of decommissioning the yard would not conflict with or be delayed by the frigate's overhaul.

Constitution came out of dry dock on 25 April 1974 and was moved to a fitting-out pier. Many of the artifacts previously in her were set up in a temporary museum nearby, and a viewing platform had been erected from which visitors could get a view of the ship and the work in progress. In July, the work of restepping her masts and restoring her top-hamper began. In September, it was realized that virtually all the ceiling planking above the spar deck would have to be replaced, contrary to earlier evaluations. A special effort was made to accomplish both of these jobs before winter's bitter cold and snows came on. It was a very busy time for the workforce and for the new captain, Comdr. Tyrone G. Martin, who had taken over from Comdr. Thomas Coyne in early August.

President Gerald R. Ford on 1 October signed into law a bill authorizing creation of the Boston National Historical Park. Pertinent to *Constitution* was the provision transferring about thirty acres of the now-defunct navy yard to the National Park Service, including her normal berth, Dry Dock One, and the building housing her artisans' shops. For the first time, she would be berthed in a setting with an historical theme, rather than existing amidst the conflicting priorities and programs of an operating shipyard. Other elements of the geographically dispersed park include the Old North Church, Paul Revere House, Faneuil Hall, the Old State House, and the Old South Meeting House. The ship, however, remained a part of the regular navy, her commission unimpaired.

By February 1975, most of the work was done per the schedule, and the ship was returned without fanfare to her normal berth. Between then and 14 March, "Old Ironsides" was a beehive of activity. Her guns were swung back aboard and emplaced. Crewmen returned the bulk of the six thousand items removed two years earlier to their proper places about the ship and completely painted the interior. Regular watches were resumed on board. On 14 March, with Secretary of the Navy J. William Middendorf II and other dignitaries in attendance, *Constitution* formally reopened to visiting. Virtually all of the planned internal work had been completed.

The remainder of the month was spent erecting staging and making other preparations for what was then thought to be the last major job: replanking the outer hull above the waterline. This would involve the removal of over 440 lengths of rotted red oak and replacing them with "custom tailored" white oak—something like a giant jigsaw puzzle. Through the expertise and teamwork of the restoration workforce, it all went smoothly.

The summer of 1975 was a time of some redirection in the restoration as Martin, after nearly a year of study, concluded that more effort should be put into returning the ship to her earlier appearance rather than merely replacing wood parts as found. In a detailed report to the Chief of Naval Operations (CNO), he recommended that a long-term, open-ended program be established to move in the direction of *Constitution*'s 1812 appearance (her most famous era) in the spirit of the oft-repeated congressional directive. He included a listing of about two dozen projects within the scope of this theme, each one based on cited historical references. The CNO approved the plan before the year was out and directed that the projected rebuilding of the bow head area be accomplished before the major restoration period ended.

A lesser project that came up during the summer of 1975 had to do with whether or not the ship's guns could be used for firing salute charges. Martin arranged for an informal feasibility study to be done by the navy's Ordnance Laboratory, and as the determination was positive he was ready to get the necessary modifications made when it became known that the reigning monarch of England would visit Boston during the main bicentennial celebrations the following year.

On 1 September, Secretary Middendorf issued a directive canceling the "IX-21" hull number *Constitution* had borne for more than three decades. This he did in response to the suggestion from the captain that a ship of her prestige needed nothing more than her name to identify her.

As the workforce pressed on with the hull replanking, the rebuilding of the head, and the construction of all-new quarter galleries, management was wrestling with the problem of what was to happen when the particular project ended. After weeks of careful study, the proposal was made that a full-time restoration and maintenance group of a dozen artisans be established to ensure the material well-being of "Old Ironsides" for all time. The evident merit of the proposal almost completely precluded its disapproval, and the only real question was whether or not to begin the program as soon as the restoration period ended. After some discussion, it was decided to begin its operation the day after the restoration was over, so that skilled men would not be lost and there would be no deterioration in the ship to "catch up" on. It happened just that way on 1 July 1976.

More than 895,000 people visited *Constitution* during the nine and a half months she was open in 1975. As winter 1976 turned to spring, it was obvious to all concerned that there would be at least as many in the new year. All of these people not only were able to tour the ship in the accustomed manner, they also could view the rebuilding process at close range and, sometimes, talk directly with the craftsmen as they plied their traditional trades.

THE NATION'S BICENTENNIAL

The USS *Constitution* Museum opened its doors for the first time on 8 April 1976, and for the first time the fabled frigate had associated with it a facility dedicated to helping people know her as well as they wished. The foundation that backed the museum, a private nonprofit organization, had been the inspiration of Wylie when he was commandant, and after his retirement he and other dedicated citizens formally had incorporated themselves for the purpose in 1972. With the help and cooperation of the navy, the National Park Service, and many interested private individuals, it had been possible to remake the old (1833) dry dock machinery building into a proper museum.

A month after the museum opened, there occurred another ceremony that looked to the frigate's future. On navy-owned land near Crane, Indiana, a white oak grove spread over some 25,000 acres formally was dedicated to the sole use of *Constitution,* when and as such timbers would be needed. The days of tedious searches for prime white oak appear to have been ended by this act.

Events of the bicentennial year crowded in upon one another. On 17 June, *Constitution* conducted her first turnaround cruise since 1972, with youngsters from thirty-three friendly nations as her special guests. On the nation's 200th birthday, *Constitution*'s newly returned, modified 24-pounders boomed out a 21-gun salute at high noon in honor of the occasion. Nearly ninety-five years had passed since last they had been heard, and a more appropriate occasion there never would be. On 10 July, "Old Ironsides" was the official host ship for the visit of many of the world's remaining "Tall Ships" to Boston and led them in a majestic sea parade up the harbor, her guns firing at one-minute intervals as hundreds of thousands of people watched and cheered from every possible vantage point.

The culminating event of the season—one that, in a sense, makes *Constitution*'s story come full circle—took place on Sunday, 11 July 1976. Under way

Constitution and HMY *Britannia* on 11 July 1976 on the occasion of Queen Elizabeth II's participation in national bicentennial observances. The queen and her consort visited "Old Ironsides" that afternoon, then hosted a reception for their Boston hosts on board the royal yacht that evening, an event concluded by a "retreat" performed by the Royal Marine Band. *Author's collection*

promptly at 8:00 that morning with her attendant tugs, the old frigate moved smartly to a position just inside the Boston Light where, at twenty minutes past nine, the 24-pounders roared out yet another 21-gun salute as a large, sleek, dark-blue yacht slid swiftly past: The royal yacht *Britannia* was bearing Queen Elizabeth II and Prince Philip into Boston for a one-day visit. Flags snapped smartly in the wind, and the royal craft appeared and moved on almost before anyone knew it—almost before "Old Ironsides," swinging quickly to keep the proper bearing, could complete her salute. The smoke still was heavy in the air when a message flashed between ships: "Your salute was magnificent—Britannia sends." The gunners were proud as peacocks.

Later that afternoon, the royal couple visited *Constitution* and spent more than half an hour in a nearly private tour of the ship. The crew wondered what it was going to be like, since the ship's reputation is based largely on victories over units of the Royal Navy. The royal visitors exhibited a keen interest in everything about the ship, including *Guerriere*'s mirror and the long guns bearing the monogram of King George III, and acknowledged that the two countries were not always as friendly as they were on the present occasion. (A crew member later was heard to swear as gospel that, when the queen was shown the King George guns she turned to the prince and said, "I say, Philip, we really must talk to the Secretary about these foreign arms sales when we get home!" Another story is born.) Upon their departure from the frigate, the crew demonstrated their admiration for the royal visitors when they leaped into the shrouds and Sr. Chief Boatswain's Mate Walter R. Gross shouted, "Three cheers for the Queen, lads! Hip, hip, hooray! Hip, hip, hooray! Hip, hip, hooray!"

"Hip, hip, hooray," indeed—for *Constitution* and her men. While Martin became the first skipper since Charles Stewart to be decorated for his performance in office, the ship herself received her first-ever official recognition for superlative performance of duty, a Meritorious Unit Commendation, in this instance for her contribution to the celebration of the nation's 200th birthday.

A QUIET PERIOD

As the events of the bicentennial subsided into memory, the pace in and around the ship gradually returned to the quieter routines known in the years prior to 1973. Visitation, which had peaked in 1976 with 911,243 people coming aboard from every state in the Union as well as nearly a hundred foreign countries, returned to a more normal level of around 600,000 in 1977. A major difference from earlier years, however, was the fact that the maintenance of the old warrior was constant and coordinated.

During this period, one old navy practice was revived and several "traditions" begun. On 11 November 1976, the daily custom of firing morning and sunset guns was reinstituted. And with the 1977 turnaround cruise was begun the practice of scheduling this event on Independence Day and having the ship fire the navy's national birthday salute at high noon. Too, it became policy to invite all living former captains of the ship to participate.

Ever since her return to Boston in 1934, *Constitution* had been subordinate to the commandant, First Naval District. When a navy reorganization closed down the local district headquarters in 1977, at Martin's recommendation the ship was

A gathering of captains. Left to right can be seen the 60th, 51st, 59th, 57th, and 58th captains of *Constitution* as they join together in celebration of the ship's 184th birthday in October 1981. *Author's collection*

subordinated to the director of naval history, and so gained a superior whose primary responsibilities were historic in nature.

Martin's tour in command ended on 30 June 1978, one of the longest on record at that point. At the parting, he was presented with an antique master key to the ship's locks, a new tradition symbolizing that "Old Ironsides" always would welcome a former captain's return. Assuming command was Comdr. Robert L. Gillen, a native of Charlestown, Massachusetts, and a special duty officer not normally eligible to command a ship. His assignment was the result of his specific request because he had been born and reared in Charlestown, that part of Boston in which the ship was moored.

The 1978 turnaround cruise nearly saw the end of the 4th of July "tradition" when rain and high winds made it prudent not to sail that day. Gillen turned the ship the following morning in an unannounced, abbreviated voyage with a number of surprised and delighted tourists aboard who had expected merely to tour the ship at pierside. The following year's cruise was back on track and had as honored guest former House Speaker John McCormack, observing the 25th anniversary of the law he had sponsored requiring the navy to preserve *Constitution* and specifying Boston as her permanent home port.

In one way, the year 1980 echoed the bicentennial: On 30 May *Constitution* once again led the "Tall Ships" in parade in Boston harbor, this time in celebration of the city's 350th birthday. She also did her traditional turnaround five weeks later. Gillen was succeeded in command by Comdr. Herman O. Sudholz on 28 September.

May 1982 saw the realization of a goal set several years earlier in the waning days of the restoration: the publication by the navy of the "USS *Constitution* Maintenance Manual." Recognizing that many of the skills involved and knowledge gained through problems solved during the course of that work would be lost over time, the compilers of the manual sought to perpetuate the expertise and understanding of those involved for future generations of shipwrights and sailors charged with the responsibility of protecting this living symbol of our naval heritage.

During this same period, another of the projects of the long-term restoration program was begun. Norfolk Naval Shipyard undertook to create the molds and cast two 32-pounder carronades in accordance with a recently rediscovered contemporary scale drawing of the weapons that originally had been cast by Henry Foxall in 1808. Funding precluded manufacturing a greater number, but commitment to the program was viewed as more important than seeking a large one-time outlay.

Sudholz remained in command until 22 June 1985, a tour that may have been the longest ever, perhaps even exceeding McBride's, which spanned World War II. He was succeeded by Comdr. Joseph Z. Brown, who proved to be a most popular captain with both the crew and the visiting public. Shockingly, he died suddenly in his office on 8 July 1987, the victim of a heart attack. Comdr. David M. Cashman was ordered in to succeed his friend with whom he had, on an earlier occasion, lightheartedly discussed following him in command. On 22 July 1990, Cashman took as his wife Bobbi Bishop of Boston; it was the first time a *Constitution* captain was married on board ship.

During this same period, concern for the ship's health was heightened when it was found that the hog, relatively stable for some years, was once again on the increase. In an effort to slow the process, the rudder was removed, along with

24-pounders from the captain's cabin and forward on the gun deck. Ninety tons of lead ingots were placed in the bilges amidships. These actions reduced the rate by 50 percent, but obviously did not represent a solution. Discussions among experts and interested parties resulted in a variety of proposals for a permanent "fix." These included everything from placing the ship high and dry in a cradle, as was done with HMS *Victory*, to installing a sort of cantilever girder atop the sister keelson, to providing additional support to the ends of the ship by a system of "balloon" pairs connected by cables passing beneath the ship. The decision was made to schedule a dry-docking of the ship primarily to make a thorough inspection of her underwater structure as a basis on which to develop a corrective strategy.

A NEW DEAL

This was a period in the U.S. Navy's history when, as a result of the collapse of the Soviet Union, a major reorganization and "down-sizing" was begun. In Boston, the office of the supervisor of shipbuilding, which had provided planning and design support for *Constitution*, as well as another small naval administrative organization in the area, was slated for closure. Rather than have the design function move to an area remote from the ship, the billets assigned to the administrative organization were reassigned to the director of naval history, and the cognizant planners and designers from the supervisor's office transferred to those billets. The result was the establishment, on 25 October 1991, of the Naval Historical Center Detachment, Boston, combining these new people with the former Maintenance and Repair Facility established in 1976. For the first time, planning, design, and the actual workforce—some twenty-one permanent staff—were in one organization under one head. And, just as importantly, in a move harkening back to a recommendation made by Martin in 1976, included on this staff was an historian whose job it would be to gather and maintain documentation on the ship's structure and the methods used to create and maintain her over the years. Consistent historical restoration and maintenance of the ship were a fact, at last.

With the ship's bicentennial in the near future, it was thought prudent to put *Constitution* in dock and check her well-being in anticipation of increased activity during that period. Dry-docked in September 1992, in what was intended to be a twelve- to fifteen-month "dry-docking and inspection," discovery that the diagonal riders called for in Joshua Humphreys's 1794 design actually *had* been

The newly reinstalled diagonal riders, looking forward on the starboard side. The upper ends are cut like "birds' beaks" to fit the lower after edges of the deck beams. The snaky lines on the diagonal in the foreground are tar runs, not defects in the wood. *Courtesy Naval Historical Center Detachment, Boston*

installed led to a reorientation of the program and an extension of the docking period when model tests and computer analysis verified the validity of the idea. In addition to allowing the keel yet again to settle into a nearly straight line largely free of "hogging," work went forward to reinstall the entire system of diagonal riders, standard knees, thick planks, stanchions, and scarphed spirketting the designer had called for. It was a much stronger "Old Ironsides" that returned afloat in September 1995.

Perhaps inspired by the success of this restoration project, the artisans went forward with a second program to restore the berth and orlop decks to their 1812 configuration, even as visiting continued, and included in the planning was consideration of making new areas of the ship accessible to visitors.

During the summer of 1996, *Constitution* made a total of ten "turnaround cruises," each of which bore lucky lottery winners from five different states of the union. Unmistakably, "Old Ironsides" was ready for her third century of service to the country.

Afterword

[T]he ship! Never has she failed us! Never has her crew failed in showing their allegiance and belief in the country they served, or the honor they felt, in belonging to the ship that sheltered them, and on whose decks they fought, where many gave their lives. To have commanded the Constitution is a signal honor; to have been one of her crew, in no matter how humble a capacity, is an equal one. Her name is an inspiration. Not only do her deeds belong to our Naval record, but she herself is possessed of a brave personality. In light weathers, in storm or hurricane, or amid the smoke of battle she responded with alacrity and obedience, and seemed ever eager to answer the will of her commander. May the citizens of this country, in gratitude, see that she, like her namesake and prototype, will never be forgotten. Her commanders in the future, as in the past, will see to it that her flag never shall be lowered. She was conceived in patriotism; gloriously has she shown her valor. Let her depart in glory if the fates so decree; but let her not sink and decay into oblivion.

COMO. WILLIAM BAINBRIDGE (1831)

Notes

CHAPTER ONE

1. Both the British and French navies had used short riders, vertical and diagonal, between decks and in ships' holds for years. The use of diagonal riders extending upward from the keelson to berth deck beams was introduced into the British navy by Sir Robert Seppings and first adopted in *Tremendous*, 74, in February 1811; it became common practice in all new Royal Navy vessels after Seppings became surveyor of the navy in 1813. Seppings, however, was forced to employ a system using shorter timbers because England's supply of great timbers such as used by Humphreys had long since been depleted.

2. William P. Bass has done an exhaustive comparison of the *Terrible* drawing and dated, signed drawings by both Fox and Doughty, which clearly shows that Humphreys's original hull form was used without variance by his copyists. This, in the present writer's opinion, eliminates Fox from any credit for the design of the 44s. Fox subsequently designed frigates *Crescent* (for Algiers), *Philadelphia*, and *John Adams*, as well as brigs *Wasp* and *Hornet*, and two gunboats. He served as an appointed naval constructor from 1804 until 1809, when he was summarily discharged, in part because of continuing conflict with the commandant of the Washington Navy Yard, Capt. Thomas Tingey. The success and fame of the 44s only increased the acrimonious relationship between Fox and Humphreys, and it was continued by succeeding generations on both sides. The course of events detailed here is based on contemporary correspondence and records, and ignores later allegations. Doughty, appointed naval constructor briefly in 1804 and more permanently in 1813, later designed the liners *Columbus* and those of the *North Carolina* class, together with most frigates after 1812, *Alligator* class sloops, *Argus* and *Wasp* class sloops of war, and gunboats and row galleys. He served until 1837.

3. The ten names submitted, in order, were *United States, Constitution, President, Congress, Constellation, Defender, Fortitude, Perseverance, Protector,* and *Liberty.* The president merely underlined the first five and returned the list to Secretary Pickering. (Naming of the sixth unit authorized apparently was delayed because it was not planned to begin her construction until after John Morgan completed cutting the live oak in Georgia. *Chesapeake* finally was selected.) The source of the last three names in the Pickering list can be identified, for they were among forty names sent to the Secretary by Humphreys on 20 February. His other proposed names were

Ardent, Intrepid, Formidable, Defiance, Fame, Resolution, Modeste, Prudent, Reasonable, Enterprize, Active, Robust, Thunderer, Vengeance, Terrible (the name on the original draft for the 44s), *Invincible, Tartar, Republican, Independence, Convention, Virtuous, Justice, Senator, Representative, Negociator* [sic], *Franklin, Hancock, Lawrence, Green, Mercer, Montgomery, Putnam, Warren, Biddle, Rhode Island, Connecticut, Jersey, Delaware, Carolina,* and *Georgia.*

CHAPTER TWO

1. Louis Alexis de Courmont, son of a noble French family, was sent to the United States to avoid the excesses of the French Revolution. Ultimately, he served in the U.S. Navy for over twenty years, being attached to the New Orleans station during the War of 1812 and attaining the rank of master commandant before returning to France in the early 1820s.

CHAPTER FOUR

1. The guns were numbered in pairs beginning with the fowardmost pair on the gun deck and going aft on that deck, then from forward aft on the spar deck, though not necessarily in a continuous sequence (e.g., in 1809, the numbering ran 1–15 on the gun deck and 31–42 on the spar deck)—however it suited the captain.

CHAPTER EIGHT

1. The schooner to which Hull refers has not been identified and may have been a misidentification or a curious "hanger on"—or both, on different occasions. The brig with the British squadron, noted later, was *Emulous,* 12, until earlier that day the USS *Nautilus.* She was the first ship lost by either side in the war; her former commanding officer, Lt. William M. Crane, and 106 crewmen, were imprisoned in *Africa.* She had served with *Constitution* off Tripoli in 1804.
2. According to observers in the British ships, most of these shots actually went *over* their target and splashed on the far side, out of sight of the Americans. One is said to have landed on deck without significant damage.

CHAPTER NINE

1. Hull's yawing first one way and then the other to avoid being raked was interpreted by the Briton as being attempts by his enemy to gain a raking position astern of *him,* hence the repeated reversals of course and alternating broadsides. In other words, each was trying to prevent what the other, in fact, was *not* attempting to do.

CHAPTER TEN

1. Three eyewitnesses in *Constitution*—Surgeon Amos A. Evans, Midshipman Henry Gilliam, and Boatswain's Mate James Campbell—later wrote separately that the reason Bainbridge headed to seaward was because the contact was thought to be a 74, and that he doubled back

when it became apparent that she really was a frigate. If true, it was a prudent course of action, but certainly not the stuff popular heroics are made of. Bainbridge, ever sensitive to his image, found "nobler" motives for the maneuver when the time came to write his report, stating that he hadn't wanted neutral territorial waters providing a safe haven for his opponent.

2. Ironically, this double wheel, the ship's first, had not been aboard long. Examination of extant battle bills—Preble (1804), Rodgers (1809), and Bainbridge (1812)—found only two men assigned versus four in the last instance, indicating that either Hull, most likely during the Washington Navy Yard overhaul, or Bainbridge at Boston had made the change from a single wheel.

3. The commodore's first wounding had been caused by a piece of copper (possibly from the railing around the companionway hatch) that had buried itself in the quadriceps muscle a few inches above the knee. The second actually consisted of several contusions caused by splinters. Evans enlarged the first on 8 January, found the metal shard and removed it, and sewed the edges of the wound together. No complications occurred, and Bainbridge healed fast. The contusions responded quickly to what was little more than first aid.

4. Because Bainbridge's battle bill is in the archives of the Naval Historical Center, it is possible to determine the distribution of American casualties in this engagement: Four were wounded on the forecastle, and six killed and eight wounded on the quarterdeck; below, there were one killed and four wounded each in First and Second Divisions, and two wounded in Third; aloft, one was killed and four wounded in the main top. Ironically, Daniel Hogan, the sailor who returned an ensign to the foremast in the midst of the *Guerriere* fight, had fingers shot off both hands on this occasion.

Chapter Eleven

1. Whipple did not see *Constitution* again for six months, for although Sir George Beckwith, governor of Barbados, treated him with due respect, Rear Admiral Dunham, commanding the squadron based there, refused to accept the cartel and permit the young officer to leave the island until he was satisfied that *Constitution* no longer was in the area. After three months and three weeks, Whipple was permitted to seek transport to regain his duty station. He made it by 14 August.

2. Jones's ready agreement with Bainbridge's recommendation for an official investigation may have been facilitated by his displeasure over the way Stewart had pressed him regarding officers and men for *Constitution* the previous summer, causing, the Secretary felt, unnecessary expenditures of limited funds purely to satisfy a captain's wishes. So strongly had he reacted, in fact, that he had made it, as he said, an "inflexible" policy never to do it again. Too, Jones had been given some reason to believe that Stewart was at least partially responsible for the deplorable condition of *Constellation*, which was reported to him some months after Stewart's transfer to *Constitution*.

3. Rodgers's cruise, at the outset of the war, had lasted eighty-one days. His five-ship squadron, in a sweep of European waters, captured a privateer, a letter of marque, and six merchantmen, of which at least two were scuttled. Capt. David Porter's epic Pacific cruise in *Essex* during 1812–1814 never exceeded sixty days at sea without some replenishment from ashore.

4. Some accounts state that Stewart actually got sternway on the ship, but this seems unlikely given the swift sequence of events. What is more likely is that *Constitution* rapidly decelerated, causing her surprised foe to move forward on her larboard side, well within lethal range of the American batteries.

5. The "gunades" had been among sixty-six captured by the Portsmouth, New Hampshire, privateer *Fox* in the British brig *Stranger* and sent safely into Salem, Massachusetts, in September 1814, from whence Stewart acquired them, replacing four carronades on the spar deck. These guns, shorter than long guns (and 875 pounds lighter) but longer than carronades, had been designed by Sir William Congreve (the younger; of rocket fame) and first produced in 1814. They were mounted on regular ship carriages like conventional long guns to permit ready shifting from one side of the ship to the other. Stewart had installed one on the forecastle and the other on the quarterdeck.

Chapter Thirteen

1. Beecher used as his model a painting by President Jackson's nephew-in-law, R. E. W. Earle, entitled "Hermitage Scene" (1826), which shows Jackson, planter's hat and cane in hand, with "Hermitage" plantation in the background.

Chapter Fourteen

1. Elliott was restored to duty as commandant of the Philadelphia Navy Yard in 1844; he died there the following year.

2. Claxton's death also terminated the proceedings against Buchanan.

Chapter Fifteen

1. During her month in New York, *Constitution* had many visitors. In a vein that would be familiar to her modern crew, carpenter Henry G. Thomas noted: "Most of the time . . . we have been trying to see that none of the many visitors we received will get hurt or lost. This has become somewhat of nuisance as many ask and repeat again the same question, 'Is this the same old *Constitution* that won so much fame in the war?' The men have generally remained hospitable towards them and have tried to explain everything to them that is worth knowing."

2. These orders are curious in that they represent the allocation of a ship to a circumnavigation over and above those units assigned to the East India Squadron that routinely completed their tours by circumnavigation, making many of the same port calls. It may be that Percival wished, as his final sea duty, to sail around the world in the navy's most famous ship and that acting Secretary David Henshaw, a fellow Bay Stater, acceded to the old salt's desires.

3. Midshipman Meriwether Patterson Jones, son of Como. Thomas ap Catsby Jones, recalled Percival's words in his journal: "You are guilty of having made use of the following language on the afternoon of the day you returned on board from shore at Majunga: 'You were confined for acting like a man and that old jack the son of a bitch struck you and you would have knocked him down, if you had a chance.' You continually repeated the language and said that

the Captain could only punish you and for that you did not care a d——d. You again said that you attempted to strike him while on shore and would have done so if it had been <u>Jesus Christ</u>."

4. The Cochin emperor at this time was Thieu Tri, and he had a history of threatening missionaries with death if they didn't leave his country. For Lefevre, it was his second expulsion.

CHAPTER EIGHTEEN

1. Fifteen-year-old Midshipman Douglas Cassel, writing to his mother at the time, reported the situation a little differently: "I wish the Government was a little better off for the reason that though they allow us liberty they can affords [sic] us no money at present. I have not been in the city yet, for the simple reason that to save my soul (after staying aboard ship for so long) I could not walk a mile, and have no money to pay my fare."

CHAPTER NINETEEN

1. The West Coast phase was not without its "moments." While in San Pedro, on 10 March, a ten-second earthquake shook the ship and severed all electrical connections with the pier. On 6 April, in San Francisco, she was subjected to a ship-clearing bomb threat that proved to be a hoax. And in Portland or Astoria, a nude dancer at a stag party for the officers so upset the straightlaced "Uncle Henry" Hartley that he stomped out in a huff.

Glossary

Baker's pumps a more efficient type of pump than the chain pumps with which the ship originally was fitted.

Barque a three-masted vessel, square-rigged on the two forward masts, but fore-and-aft rigged on the mizzen.

Bear up course so that she runs more nearly *with* the wind.

Beat to quarters the drummer's particular signal for all hands to go to their battle stations.

Best bower the anchor on the starboard bow; the "bower" was carried to larboard and a "sheet" anchor on either side of the waist.

Billet head bow ornamentation other than a figurehead; usually a scroll.

Binnacle a stand in which the compass is suspended, usually in gimbal rings so that it remains horizontal.

Bitts strong wooden uprights used for securing heavy ropes, such as anchor cables.

Blister to apply a strong poultice that will cause the skin to blister, thereby drawing the bad "humors" from the body.

Boarded his fore tack hauled in the tack of a square sail in order to sail closer to the wind.

Bobstay a rope used to confine the bowsprit of a ship downward to the cutwater.

Boggin lines rudder chains.

Boomkin a short boom at either side of the bow or stern used to take either a foresail tack or a main brace.

Bowline the line attached to the leach rope of a square sail, and leading forward; used to hold the weather side of a close-hauled sail forward and steady, enabling the ship to sail as close to the wind as possible.

Bowse ("bouse") to haul downward on a particular rope.

Brace rope attached to a yard; used to adjust the yard in the horizontal plane.

Breasthook a thick, curved timber fastened across the inside of the stem holding the bows and sides together.

Breeching tackle a rope used to secure a cannon, and to prevent it from recoiling too much when fired.

Brig a two-masted vessel, square-rigged on both masts; also, a ship's jail.

Bulkhead a vertical partition between two decks; a wall.

Cable's length one hundred fathoms (two hundred yards).

Camboose (also caboose) the galley; the cook's stove.

Carlings short, fore-and-aft timbers placed for reinforcement between deck beams.

Catharpins ropes under the fighting tops bracing the lower end of the futtock shrouds.

Cathead a short, strong boom on either bow used to suspend an anchor clear of the hull for letting go, or upon weighing.

Ceiling the inner, horizontally laid layer of timber in a ship's hull.

Chandler a supplier of ship's stores.

Channels (from "chain wales") broad and thick planks projecting horizontally from the ship's side, abreast of, and somewhat behind, the masts; provide a greater span for the supporting mast shrouds.

Charlie Noble nickname for the galley smokestack.

Clear for action preparations for battle short of actually stationing the men at their posts.

Close reefed said of sails when all the reefs (q.v.) have been taken in and the sails can be reefed no further.

Colt a short length of rope with one or more knots in it; used in place of the cat-o'-nine-tails as an alternate form of flogging.

Cooper barrel maker.

Copal a hard, transparent resin; used in varnishes.

Cordwainer leather worker.

Coxswain the petty officer in charge of a boat's crew; usually the steersman.

Cutwater the foremost part of the stem, forming a curved leading edge that parts the water as the ship advances.

Deadeye a round or pear-shaped block pierced with three holes, used mainly in standing rigging to set up shrouds.

Doublings those areas where two sections of mast overlap.

Dress ship a full display of flags to honor a person or event; sometimes called a "rainbow."

Fathom a unit of measure: six feet.

Fidded home locked into place with a square pin having a shoulder at one end; akin to a modern cotter pin.

Fine in terms of bearing, a small amount; a few degrees; less than a point (q.v.)

Fire ship an expendable vessel filled with combustibles and sailed to the enemy by a volunteer crew that sets the final course to target, ignites the materials, and abandons it in a small boat.

Fish a long, convex piece of wood designed to reinforce a damaged mast or spar; a splint.

Fish hoop the iron band used to bind together the segments of a "made up" mast.

Forcing pump a pump mounted on the channels (see entry on page 382) and drawing water directly from the sea.

Freeboard the height of the upper deck above water.

Futtock one of the middle sections making up a frame, or ship's "rib."

Futtock shrouds those short shrouds running downward and inward from the fighting tops.

Galley the camboose; the cook's stove; also, a long, low craft powered by a single bank of oars and a sail.

Galliot a small, speedy sailing vessel with oars for auxiliary power.

Gammoning rope or chain lashing staying the bowsprit to the knee of the head to hold the bowsprit down against the upward pull of the forestay.

Gig the ship's boat particularly reserved for the captain's use.

Grog a drink of watered rum served in the Royal Navy after 1740. The U.S. Navy issued it initially, but soon substituted bourbon for the rum, calling it "Bob Smith," after the navy secretary who ordered the change.

Guardo a receiving ship; a floating barracks.

Gudgeon metal clamp bolted to the sternpost. Pintles (see entry on page 385) on the rudder fit into corresponding holes in the gudgeons, thus hinging the rudder to the sternpost.

Gurnet a small, narrow channel dangerous to navigate owing to current and numerous rocks.

Harness cask the large cask kept on deck near the camboose in which the daily salted meat ration was leached in fresh water prior to cooking.

Helm down to turn the wheel in the leeward direction, i.e., "helm a-lee," causing the ship's bow to swing toward the wind.

Helm up turn the wheel to windward, causing the ship's head to turn downwind.

Hog the result of stress on a ship's hull, causing it to droop fore and aft.

Holystone soft, white sandstone used to scrub a ship's decks.

Hove to trimming sails so the ship is making no headway; stopped.

Hull down on the horizon with only masts and sails showing.

Hulled shot in the hull below the waterline, usually at point-blank range.

Hundredweight 112 pounds.

In ordinary a ship essentially ready for use, but with only a caretaker crew aboard and in need of stores and rerigging.

In stays a ship headed directly into the wind; usually a transitory condition when going from one tack to another and not one desired otherwise.

Joggling shaping the surfaces of two adjacent, irregularly shaped timbers so that they fit closely together.

Joiner a craftsman who makes furniture and installs cabins and other light wood structures in a ship.

Jorum a drinking bowl.

Kedging to move a ship, usually in harbor, by taking a light anchor out ahead with a boat, dropping it, and winching up to it; repeating the process in succession using two anchors in order to move the ship when wind and tide are adverse or nonexistent.

Keelson a timber bolted to the keel above, or on either side of that timber, to strengthen it.

Kentledge pig iron ballast.

Kid a container in which rations were carried.

Knee a large angled piece of timber with one arm bolted horizontally to a beam and the other to the ship's side, for the purpose of strengthening the sides against sudden shock.

Knighthead the heavy balks of timber on either side of the stem that support the bowsprit laterally.

Laid up not in use; the ship is unrigged and dismantled.

Larboard the left-hand side of a ship as one stands on deck facing the bow.

Lateen yard a long spar hoisted obliquely to a mast, usually with the shorter, lower end forward of the mast.

Lay to to be under way with no motion through the water.

Ledge a piece of timber placed athwartships between beams to provide additional support.

Leech the edge of a sail.

Let fly releasing the sheets completely, as quickly as possible.

Lifting a sail bellying upward in the wind with its sheets slackened.

Log the ship's "diary," its official operating record; also, a device used to measure a ship's speed through the water.

Luff to come closer to the wind; also, a tackle comprised of line, a single block, and a double block.

Mess a group of persons eating together.

Messenger a rope or chain used to connect a number of objects while maintaining intervals between them.

Missed stays when a ship fails to complete tacking from one side to the other.

Mould a pattern made of thin, flexible wood.

Oakum a substance made by unravelling old rope and used principally for caulking seams.

On a taut bowline sailing close-hauled to the wind.

Orlop lowest deck in a warship; usually, a partial, or platform, deck.

Partners timber framework strengthening the deck where it is pierced by a mast or other structure.

Pintle the vertical bolt attached to the forward edge of the rudder that fits into the hole in the "gudgeon" attached to the aft side of the sternpost to form a hinge.

Plank sheer the uppermost plank running along the top timbers of a ship's frame.

Point an arc of 11.25 degrees.

Polacre (also polacca or "polacky") a Mediterranean three-master, square-rigged on the fore and main, but with a lateen sail on the mizzen with a square sail above it.

Port word officially substituted for *larboard* (see entry on page 384) in the U. S. Navy in February 1846 to end confusion with "starboard."

Press of canvas all sails set and drawing well.

Purchase the mechanism by which mechanical advantage is gained.

Quasi-War defensive action taken by President John Adams to protect American commerce from French depredations, 1798–1801.

Rake to fire one's broadsides down the length of an enemy's ship, either from ahead or astern.

Razee to cut down the spar deck of a vessel, reducing her freeboard; a ship of the line might be converted into a heavy frigate in this manner; the designation of such a ship.

Reef to reduce sail area by gathering up a portion of the sail and securing it by means of reef points (short tie lines) fitted in two or three rows across the face of a sail.

Reefer a midshipman; also, an officer's peacoat.

Scantling any piece of timber of a particular standard square-section.

Scarph (also scarf) a method of joining the ends of two pieces of timber in a line by tapering an overlapping joint so that there is no increased thickness in that area. A scarph may be "locked" by cutting the pieces to fit together like pieces of a jigsaw puzzle.

Schooner a fore-and-aft rigged sailing vessel having anywhere from two to seven masts.

Sheer the longitudinal curve of the ship's decks or sides.

Sheet a rope fastened to one or both of the lower corners of a sail.

Shoe a false keel installed on the underside of the keel as an expendable shield in the event of grounding.

Skulking acting in a furtive manner, usually in an area wherein the suspect is not normally authorized access.

Sky poles short, light masts affixed to the after sides of the topgallant masts to accommodate the skysails (those carried above the royals).

Sloop a single-masted vessel carrying a large fore-and-aft mainsail and a single head sail.

Soundings waters that can be plumbed with a deepsea lead, commonly less than one hundred fathoms.

Spirketting the planks forming a fillet between a deck and the side of a ship rising above it.

Spitkit any small, nondescript craft.

Starboard the right-hand side of a ship as one stands on deck facing the bow.

Staysail any triangular sail hoisted on a stay abaft the foremast or mainmast.

Steerage that area of the ship containing the midshipmen's berthing.

Stepped installed a mast in its seat ("step").

Strake a line of planking running along a ship's side.

Stunsail contraction of "studdingsail": light sail extended, in light or moderate breezes, beyond the skirts of the principal fore and main mast sails.

Supercargo an officer charged with the commercial affairs of a merchant ship.

Tack to work a ship to windward by alternately taking the wind from one side and then the other; also, a rope used to confine the foremost lower corners of the courses (fore and main sails) in a fixed position.

Taffrail an ornamental rail along the upper edge of the stern.

Taken aback stopped short, as by an unexpected, sudden shift of the wind.

Tender any small vessel or craft used in support of a man-of-war; also said of a ship with marginal stability.

Tinker a sheet-metal worker.

Tompion a plug used to stop the mouth of a cannon when not in use.

Trafficker a ship carrying on a trade in a particular item, usually contraband.

Transom the vertical face of a ship's stern.

Tried on a bowling to sail as close to the wind as possible.

Trim the difference in draft readings at the bow and stern; the attitude of a ship as she rests in the water.

Truck the circular wooden cap on the uppermost masthead.

Tumblehome the inward slope of a ship's side above its widest breadth.

Veer see **wear**.

Waist that part of a ship between the forecastle and quarterdeck; roughly the middle.

Wales heavy fore and aft timbers in the side planking of a ship, particularly beneath the gun ports.

Wardroom the common room for commissioned officers, both lounge and dining room.

Weather gauge the upwind position relative to another ship.

Wear to put a ship on the other tack by turning her *away* from the wind.

Wind (rhymes with "mind") **ship** pivot a vessel end for end, usually with a system of anchors and cables.

Woulding to reinforce a mast or spar by tightly winding a rope around it. A fish (see entry on page 383) is often woulded to a damaged mast.

Xebec a craft native to the Barbary pirates, characterized by an unusually long overhang, fore and aft, by low freeboard, and employing a mix of square and lateen sails.

Bibliography

Abbreviations used in this section

CAPT: Captain
CARP: Carpenter
CDR: Commander
CHAP: Chaplain
CHCONST: Chief Naval Constructor
COL: Colonel
COMO: Commodore
CONST: Naval Constructor
CPO: Chief Petty Officer
CWO: Chief Warrant Officer
DLC: Library of Congress
DNA: National Archives
GPO: Government Printing Office
HSP: Historical Society of Pennsylvania
JDLP: John D. Long Papers
LCDR: Lieutenant Commander
LT: Lieutenant
LTJG: Lieutenant (j.g.)

MHS: Massachusetts Historical Society
MIDN: Midshipman
MSTR CMDT: Master Commandant
NHC: Naval Historical Center
PMIDN: Passed Midshipman
PRO: Public Records Office (UK)
PRBP: Paul Revere Business Papers
PURS: Purser
PVT: Private
RADM: Rear Admiral
RG: Record Group
RN: Royal Navy
SBP: Samuel Brown Papers
SLG MSTR: Sailing Master
SURG: Surgeon
USNI: U.S. Naval Institute
USSCM: USS *Constitution* Museum
2LT: Second Lieutenant

CHAPTER ONE

American State Papers, vol. 1. Papers 2, 3, 5–9, 12, 25, and 34. Washington: Gales and Seaton. 1834.

Brewington, M. V. *Shipcarvers of North America*. New York: Dover Publications, Inc. 1962.

Bryant, William. Letter Copy Book. Private collection.

Chapelle, Howard I. *The History of the American Sailing Navy*. New York: Bonanza Books. 1949.

Letter, Furnace Hope to Timothy Pickering, 23 Nov 1795. John Carter Brown Library, Brown University.

Letter, Tench Coxe to fifteen iron masters, 26 May 1794. RG45 (M47, roll 1), DNA.

Letters, Tench Coxe to Henry Knox, 7 Jun and 30 Dec 1794. RG45 (M47, roll 1), DNA.

Letters, Tench Coxe to Paul Revere, 16 Jun, 21 Jul, and 10 Nov 1794. RG45 (M47, roll 1), DNA.

Letter, Tench Coxe to Paul Revere, 5 Sept 1794. PRBP, MHS.

Letters, Tench Coxe to Samuel Hughes, 16 Jun and 18 Aug 1794. RG45 (M47, roll 1), DNA.

Letter, Tench Coxe to Brown and Francis, 20 Jun 1794. RG45 (M47, roll 1), DNA.

Letter, Tench Coxe to Alexander Hamilton, 25 Jun 1794. RG45 (M47, roll 1), DNA.

Letter, Tench Coxe to twenty-six addressees, 30 Jun 1794. RG45 (M47, roll 1), DNA.

Letters, Tench Coxe to all navy agents, 5 Jul and 31 Dec 1794. RG45 (M47, roll 1), DNA.

Letter, Tench Coxe to Robert Coleman, 11 Jul 1794. RG45 (M47, roll 1), DNA.

Letter, Tench Coxe to M. De Rancy, 22 Jul 1794. RG45 (M47, roll 1), DNA.

Letter, Tench Coxe to Elijah Phelps, 21 Aug 1794. RG45 (M47, roll 1), DNA.

Letter, Tench Coxe to John Chester, 25 Sep 1794. RG45 (M47, roll 1), DNA.

Letter, Tench Coxe to Nathaniel Cushing, 25 Sep 1794. RG45 (M47, roll 1), DNA.

Letter, Tench Coxe to John Blegge, 24 Dec 1794. RG45 (M47, roll 1), DNA.

Letter, Tench Coxe to Gardiner and Oldden, 3 Feb 1795. RG45 (M47, roll 1), DNA.

Letters, Nathaniel Cushing to SecNav, 19 Oct 1819 and 8 Dec 1825. RG45 (M124, roll 85, vol. 5, and roll 103, vol. 7), DNA.

Letter, William Doughty to Henry Knox, 8 Feb 1796. Henry Knox Papers, Pierpont Morgan Library, New York.

Letter, Alexander Hamilton to Paul Revere, 23 Jul 1794. PRBP, MHS.

Letter, Samuel Hodgdon to Henry Knox, 4 Jan 1794. RG45 (M739, roll 1), DNA.

Letter, Samuel Hodgdon to Paul Revere, 24 Mar 1796. PRBP, MHS.

Letter, Joshua Humphreys to Robert Morris, 6 Jan 1794 [misdated 1793], Joshua Humphreys Papers, Letterbook, 1793–1794, HSP.

Letter, quartermaster general of Massachusetts to the state General Court, 7 Feb 1800. Massachusetts State Library.

Letter, quartermaster general of Massachusetts to the governor, 7 Jan 1805. Massachusetts State Library.

Letter, Paul Revere to Tench Coxe, 31 Jul 1794. PRBP, MHS.

Letter, Paul Revere to Henry Jackson, 28 Oct 1797. PRBP, MHS.

Letter, MIDN John Roche to his father, 19 Jun 1798. Robert Rogers Collection, William L. Clements Library, University of Michigan.

Letters, SecWar to George Claghorn, 23 Apr and 12 Sep 1796; 29 Jul 1797. RG45 (M739, roll 1, DNA.

Letter, SecWar to Josiah Fox, 16 Jul 1794. RG45 (M739, roll 1), DNA.

Letter, SecWar to Tench Francis, 29 Jun 1795. RG45 (M739, roll 1), DNA.

Letter, SecWar to Caleb Gibbs, 31 Dec 1794. RG45 (M739, roll 1), DNA.

Letter, SecWar to governor of Massachusetts, 30 May 1798. RG45 (M739, roll 1), DNA.

Letter, SecWar to James Hacket, 1 Apr 1794. RG45 (M739, roll 1), DNA.

Letter, SecWar to House of Representatives, 22 Mar 1798. RG45 (M739, roll 1), DNA.

Letters, SecWar to Joshua Humphreys, 28 Jun, 24 Jul, and 1 Aug 1794. RG45. (M739, roll 1), DNA.

Letters, SecWar to Henry Jackson, 28 Aug 1794 and 18 Oct 1796. RG45 (M739, roll 1), DNA.

Letter, SecWar to naval agents, Boston, New York, and Norfolk, 29 Nov 1794. RG45 (M739, roll 1), DNA.

Letters, SecWar to CAPT Samuel Nicholson, 18 Mar and 17 May 1798. RG45 (M149, roll 1), DNA.

Letters, SecWar to Paul Revere, 4 Mar, 17 Jun, and 30 Jul 1794; 3 Apr and 8 Sep 1795. PRBP, MHS.

Letters, SecWar to the secretary of the treasury, 21 Apr and 25 Jun 1794; 20 Sep 1796. RG45 (M739, roll 1), DNA.

Letter, SecWar to George Washington, 14 Mar 1795. Manuscript Division, DLC.

Letter, SecWar to John Wharton, 12 May 1794. RG45 (M739, roll 1), DNA.

Navy Department. *Naval Documents Relating to the Quasi War with France.* Vol. 1. Washington: GPO. 1935.

————. *Naval Documents Relating to the Barbary Wars.* Vol. 1. Washington: GPO. 1939.

Smelser, Marshall. *The Congress Founds the Navy.* South Bend, Indiana: University of Notre Dame Press. 1959.

Tucker, Glenn. *Dawn Like Thunder.* New York: Bobbs-Merrill Co., Inc. 1963.

Chapter Two

Bryant, William. Letter Copy Book. Private collection.

Grant, Bruce. *Isaac Hull: Captain of "Old Ironsides."* Chicago: Pellegrini and Cudahy. 1947.

Letter, Henry Knox to CAPT Samuel Nicholson, 28 Dec 1798. Henry Knox Papers, MHS.

Letters, Benjamin Stoddert to CAPT Samuel Nicholson, 15, 18 (2), and 28 May 1799. RG45 (M149, roll 2), DNA.

McKee, Christopher. "*Constitution* in the Quasi-War with France: The Letters of John Roche, Jr., 1798–1801." *The American Neptune,* Apr 1967.

Navy Department. *Naval Documents Relating to the Quasi War with France.* Vols. 1 and 11. Washington: GPO. 1935.

————. *Barbary Wars: Personnel and Ships Data.* Washington: GPO. 1945.

"Peter St. Medard" Log, USS *Constitution,* 1 Dec 1798–15 Feb 1800. USSCM.

Chapter Three

Brown, Samuel. Miscellaneous papers. MHS.

Fowler, William M., Jr. *Silas Talbot: Captain of Old Ironsides.* Mystic: Mystic Seaport Museum. 1995.

Grant, Bruce. *Isaac Hull: Captain of "Old Ironsides."* Chicago: Pellegrini and Cudahy. 1947.

Letter, Nathan Levy to CAPT Silas Talbot, 24 Nov 1799. Silas Talbot Papers. G. W. Blount White Library.

Letter, CAPT Samuel Nicholson to LT John Blake Cordis, 27 Dec 1798. Silas Talbot Papers, G. W. Blount White Library.

Letter, SecNav to CAPT Silas Talbot, 4 Dec 1799. Silas Talbot Papers, G. W. Blount White Library.

Letters, SecNav to CAPT Silas Talbot, 3 and 25 Jul 1799. RG45 (M149, roll 2), DNA.

Letters, CAPT Silas Talbot to Stephen Higginson & Co., 12 Jun 1799, 14 Jul and 5 Nov 1800. Silas Talbot Papers, G. W. Blount White Library.

Letter, CAPT Silas Talbot to LT Isaac Hull, 11 Sep 1800. Silas Talbot Papers, G. W. Blount White Library.

Letter, CAPT Silas Talbot to Nathan Levy, 24 Nov 1799. Silas Talbot Papers, G. W. Blount White Library.

Letter, CAPT Silas Talbot to Dr. Edward Stevens, 23 Mar 1801. Silas Talbot Papers, G. W. Blount White Library.

Log, USS *Constitution*, 6 Dec 1798–20 Oct 1800. RG45 DNA.

Navy Department. *Naval Documents Relating to the Quasi War with France.* Vols. I-VII. Washington: GPO. 1935–1939.

Record of Courts Martial and Courts of Inquiry. RG45 (M273), DNA.

Valle, James E. *Rocks and Shoals.* Annapolis: USNI. 1980.

CHAPTER FOUR

Anonymous (Henry Mercier). *Life in a Man-of-War.* Boston: Houghton, Mifflin Co. 1927.

Anonymous. *Man-of-War Life.* Cincinnati: Moore, Wilsatch, Keys and Co. 1856.

Bell, Frederick J. *Room To Swing a Cat.* New York: Longmans, Green and Co. 1938.

Crumpacker, CDR J. W. "Supplying The Fleet For 150 Years." USNI *Proceedings*, Mar 1941.

Naval Regulations, 1802. Annapolis: USNI. 1970.

Oliver, CAPT Frederick L. "Prize Money." USNI *Proceedings*, Oct 1946.

Skillman, CDR J. H. "Eating Through The Years." USNI *Proceedings*, Mar 1941.

U.S. Frigate *Constitution* General Harbor Routine. Undated, but probably 1850s. Personal copy.

CHAPTER FIVE

Cooper, James Fenimore. *Naval History.* New York: Mason, Baker, & Pratt. Ca. 1861.

Letter, SMSTR Nathaniel Haraden to COMO Edward Preble, 22 May 1803. MHS.

Letters, COMO Edward Preble to Samuel Brown, 27 May and 18 Jun 1803. MHS.

Letters, SecNav to Samuel Brown, 10 Dec 1801; 10 Apr, 28 May, and 30 May 1803; 2 Jun 1804. SBP, MHS.

Letter, SecNav to Stephen Higginson, 31 Oct 1800. RG45 (M209, roll 1, vol. 3), DNA.

Letter, SecNav to F. Johonot, 3 May 1808. RG45 (M209), DNA.

Letters, SecNav to Paul Revere, 18 Apr and 3 Jul 1803. RG45 (M209), DNA.

Letter, SecNav to Governor Caleb Strong, 18 Jul 1802. MHS.

Letter, Governor Caleb Strong to Quartermaster General Amasa Davis, 19 Jan 1804. MHS.

Log, USS *Constitution*, 16 Aug 1803–6 Mar 1804. RG45, DNA.

McKee, Christopher. *Edward Preble.* Annapolis: Naval Institute Press. 1972.

Navy Department. *Naval Documents Relating to the Barbary Wars.* Vols. II–IV. Washington: GPO. 1940–1942.

Paullin, Charles Oscar. *Commodore John Rodgers, 1773–1838.* Annapolis: USNI. 1967.

Summary account, USS *Constitution* Overhaul, 31 Dec 1803. SBP, MHS.

Tucker, Glenn. *Dawn Like Thunder.* New York: Bobbs-Merrill Co., Inc. 1963.

CHAPTER SIX

Chapelle, Howard I. *The History of The American Sailing Navy.* New York: Bonanza Books. 1949.

Cooper, James Fenimore. *Naval History.* New York: Mason, Baker, & Pratt. Ca. 1861.

Letters, COMO Hugh Campbell to SecNav, 10 Jul (2), 8 Sep (2), 1 (2), 3, and 15 Oct, 5 Nov, and 20 Dec 1806; 26 Jan (2), 1, 15, 17 (3), n.d., and 8 Apr, 12 May, 15 Aug, 3 Sep, 14 Oct, 30 Nov, and 3 and 12 (2) Dec 1807. RG45 (M125, roll 5,) DNA.

Letters, CAPT Isaac Chauncey to SecNav, 22 and 26 Dec 1807. RG45 (M125, roll 8), DNA.

Letter, LT David Porter to Charles Goldsborough, 21 Apr 1806. RG45 (M147, roll 1), DNA.

Letters, COMO John Rodgers to SecNav, 10 Jan, 17 and 24 Mar, 26 May, and 10 Jun 1806. RG45 (M125, rolls 4 and 5), DNA.

Letters, SecNav to COMO James Barron, 26 May 1806 and 17 Jan 1807. RG45 (M147, roll 7), DNA.

Letters, SecNav to COMO Hugh Campbell, 21 Apr, 20 and 23 Oct, and 26 Nov 1807. RG45 (M147, roll 7), DNA.

Letter, MSTR CMDT John Smith to SecNav, 14 Oct 1807. RG45 (M147, roll 7), NA.

McKee, Christopher. *Edward Preble.* Annapolis: Naval Institute Press. 1972.

Navy Department. *Naval Documents Relating to the Barbary Wars.* Vols. IV–VI. Washington: GPO. 1942, 1944(2).

Paullin, Charles Oscar. *Commodore John Rodgers, 1773–1838.* Annapolis: USNI. 1967.

Records of Courts Martial and Courts of Inquiry. RG45 (M273), NA.

Chapter Seven

American State Papers, vol. I. Washington: Gales and Seaton. 1834.

Brewington, M. V. *Shipcarvers of North America.* New York: Dover Publications, Inc. 1962.

Grant, Bruce. *Isaac Hull, Captain of "Old Ironsides."* Chicago: Pellegrini and Cudahy. 1947.

Journal, MIDN Frederick Baury, 5 Jul 1811–21 Jun 1812. MHS.

Journal, USS *Constitution,* 20 Jul–12 Nov 1809. Rodgers Family Papers, DLC.

Journal, David Bailie Warden, 1 Aug–6 Sep 1811. MHS.

Letters, CAPT Isaac Chauncey to SecNav, 22 and 26 Dec 1807. RG45 (M149, roll 7), DNA.

Letter, CAPT Isaac Hull to SecNav, 31 Mar 1809. RG45 (M125, roll 14), DNA.

Letters, COMO John Rodgers to SecNav, 1, 17, and 24 Mar, 12 and 29 Apr, 5 and 14 May, 23 Jun, and 14 Jul 1808; 5, 13, and 16 Feb, and 3, 13, 17, and 25 Mar 1809. RG45 (M125, rolls 12 and 14), DNA.

Letter, SecNav to all captains, 29 Feb 1808. RG45 (M149, roll 8), DNA.

Letter, SecNav to James Beatty, 22 Apr 1812. RG45 (M209), DNA.

Letter, SecNav to Amos Binney, 22 Apr 1812. RG45 (M209), DNA.

Letters, SecNav to COMO Hugh Campbell, 26 Nov and 3 Dec 1807. RG45 (M149, roll 7), DNA.

Letters, SecNav to CAPT Isaac Chauncey, 8 and 26 Dec 1807. RG45 (M149, roll 7), DNA.

Letter, SecNav to Henry Foxall, 18 Mar 1808. RG45 (M209), DNA.

Letter, SecNav to George Harrison, 22 Apr 1812. RG45 (M209), DNA.

Letter, SecNav to COL Samuel Hughes, 18 Sep 1807. RG45 (M209), DNA.

Letters, SecNav to CAPT Isaac Hull, 7 May, 22 Aug, and 24 Oct 1810; 3 May 1811. RG45 (M149, roll 9), DNA.

Letters, SecNav to COMO John Rodgers, 6 Oct 1808; 2 Feb (2), 12 and 19 Jul, 1 and 6 Aug, 21 Sep, 21 Nov, and 13 Dec 1809; 2 Jun, 21 Jul, and 28 Dec 1810; 26 Feb, 3, 19, 22, and 29 Jul, and 8 Aug 1811; 26 Feb and 17 Mar 1812. RG45 (M149, rolls 8 and 9), DNA.

Letter, SecNav to John Strickler, 18 Mar 1808. RG45 (M209), DNA.

Letter, Thomas Y. Sprogell to SecNav, 2 Sep 1810. RG45 (M148, roll 8), DNA.

Log, USS *Constitution*, 17 Jun 1810–31 Jan 1812. RG45, DNA.

——, 1 Feb–13 Dec 1812. RG45, DNA.

Navy Department. *Naval Documents Relating to the Barbary Wars.* Vol. VI. Washington: GPO. 1944.

Paullin, Charles Oscar. *Commodore John Rodgers, 1773–1838.* Annapolis: USNI. 1967.

Records of Courts Martial and Courts of Inquiry. RG45 (M273), DNA.

Chapter Eight

Forester, C. S. *The Age of Fighting Sail.* Garden City, New York: Doubleday and Co., Inc. 1956.

Grant, Bruce. *Isaac Hull: Captain of "Old Ironsides."* Chicago: Pellegrini and Cudahy. 1947.

Journals, MIDN Frederick Baury, 5 Jul 1811–21 Jun 1812 and 24 Jun–27 Oct 1812. MHS.

Letter, Charles L. Davis to SecNav, 20 Jul 1812. RG45 (M124, roll 50), DNA.

Letters, CAPT Isaac Hull to SecNav, 27 Jun and 21 Jul 1812. RG45 (M125, roll 24), DNA.

Letter, LT Charles Morris to LT John O. Creighton, 19 Jun 1812. Private collection.

Letter, W. Wilson & Sons to SecNav, 30 Jul 1812. RG45, DNA.

Log, USS *Constitution,* 1 Feb–13 Dec 1812. RG45, DNA.

Roosevelt, Theodore. *The War of 1812.* 3d ed. New York: G. P. Putnam's Sons. 1910.

Smith, Moses. *Naval Scenes in the Last War.* Boston: Gleason's Publishing Hall. 1846.

Chapter Nine

Claxton, LT C., RN. *The Naval Monitor.* 2d. ed. London: A. J. Valpi. 1833.

Court Martial Record, CAPT James R. Dacres, RN, 2 Oct 1812. PRO (ADM 1/5431).

Forester, C. S. *The Age of Fighting Sail.* Garden City, New York: Doubleday and Co. 1956.

Grant, Bruce. *Isaac Hull: Captain of "Old Ironsides."* Chicago: Pellegrini and Cudahy. 1947.

Journal, MIDN Frederick Baury, 24 Jun–26 Oct 1812. MHS.

Journal, SURG Amos A. Evans, 11 Jun 1812–15 Feb 1813. Private collection.

Letter, 2LT John Contee, USMC, to Lewis Bush, 13 Sep 1812. Private collection.

Letter, MIDN Henry Gilliam to CAPT William Jones, 7 Sep 1812. Georgia Historical Society.

Letter, Charles W. Goldsborough to SecNav, 7 Oct 1818. RG45 (M124, roll 94), DNA.

Letter, CAPT Isaac Hull to COMO John Rodgers, 2 Sep 1812. RG45, DNA.

Letter, CAPT Isaac Hull to Benjamin Silliman, 29 Oct 1821. Yale University.

Log, USS *Constitution,* 1 Feb–13 Dec 1812. RG45, DNA.

Log, USS *Constitution,* 1–29 Aug 1812. Huntington Library.

Mahan, CAPT Alfred T. *Sea Power in Its Relations to the War of 1812.* Boston: Little, Brown and Co. 1905.

Maloney, Linda M. *The Captain from Connecticut: The Life and Naval Times of Isaac Hull.* Boston: Northeastern University Press. 1986.

Morris, COMO Charles, Jr. *Autobiography.* Annapolis: USNI. 1881.

Paullin, Charles Oscar. *Commodore John Rodgers, 1773–1838.* Annapolis: USNI. 1967.

Roosevelt, Theodore. *The Naval War of 1812.* 3d. ed. New York: G. P. Putnam's Sons. 1910

Smith, Moses. *Naval Scenes in the Last War.* Boston: Gleason's Publishing Hall. 1846.

U.S. Congress. *Annals of the Congress of the United States.* 12th Congress, Second Session.

Chapter Ten

Court Martial Record, LT Henry Ducie Chads, RN, 23 Apr 1813. PRO (ADM 1/5435).

James, William. *Naval Occurrences.* London: T. Egerton. 1817.

————. *The Naval History of Great Britain.* London: Bladwin, Craddock, and Joy. 1824.

Journals, MIDN Frederick Baury, 24 Jun–26 Oct 1812 and 28 Oct 1812–16 Feb 1813. MHS.

Journal, SURG Amos A. Evans, 1 Jun 1812–15 Feb 1813. Private collection.

Letter, CAPT William Bainbridge to John Bullus, 23 Jan 1813. Maine Historical Society.

Letters, CAPT William Bainbridge to SecNav, 2 and 13 Sep, 24 Oct 1812; 13 Apr 1813. RG45 (M125, rolls 25 and 27), DNA.

Letter, CAPT William Bainbridge to William Jones, 5 Oct 1812. William Jones Papers, HSP.

Letter, William Ferson to SecNav, 11 Oct 1838. RG45 (M124, roll 164, vol 288), DNA.

Letter, MIDN Henry Gilliam to CAPT William Jones, 16 Feb 1813. Georgia Historical Society.

Letter, CAPT Isaac Hull to SecNav, 1 Sep 1812. RG45 (M125, roll 25), DNA.

Letters, SecNav to CAPT William Bainbridge, 9 Sep and 2 Oct 1812. RG45 (M149), DNA.

Letters, SecNav to George Harrison, 10 and 16 Sep 1812. RG45 (M209), DNA.

Long, David F. "Bainbridge and His Navy." Manuscript. 1978. Published as *Ready to Hazard.* Hanover, New Hamphshire: University Press of New England. 1981.

Mahan, CAPT Alfred T. *Sea Power in Its Relations to the War of 1812.* Boston: Little, Brown and Co. 1905.

Roosevelt, Theodore. *The Naval War of 1812.* 3d ed. New York: G. P. Putnam's Sons. 1910.

Chapter Eleven

Cooper, James Fenimore. *Naval History.* New York: Mason, Baker, & Pratt. Ca. 1861.

Court Martial Record, CAPT Lord George Douglas, RN, 1815. PRO (ADM1/5449).

Court Martial Record, CAPT George Thomas Falcon, RN, 1815. PRO (ADM1/5449).

General Order, CAPT Charles Stewart to crew, 23 Feb 1815. DNA.

Humphreys, CHAP Asheton Y., USN. "Recapitulatory Journal." Manuscript. Lilly Library, Indiana University.

James, William. *Naval Occurrences.* London: T. Egerton. 1817.

Letters, CAPT William Bainbridge to SecNav, 21 Feb, 14 Mar, 18 Apr, 3 May, 22 Jun (2), 21 Aug, 15, 24, and 25 Sep 1813; 2, 9, 21, and 29 May, 2 and 23 Jun, 1, 3, 6, 7, and 29 Jul, 15 Aug, 6, 13, and 25 Sep, and 11, 20, and 25 Oct 1814; 11 and 17 Dec 1814. RG45 (M125, rolls 26–31 and 36–41), and (M148, roll 31), DNA.

Letter, U.S. Naval Observatory to author, 1 Apr 1993.

Letter, CAPT Charles Morris to CAPT Charles Stewart, 7 Dec 1813. RG45 (M125, roll 33), DNA.

Letters, SecNav to CAPT William Bainbridge, 24 Jan, 8 Mar, 21 Apr, 16 Jul, 1 and 14 Aug, 19 and 30 Sep 1814. RG45 (M149, roll 11), DNA.

Letter, SecNav to CAPT Isaac Chauncey, 14 Feb 1815. RG45 (M149, roll 12), DNA.

Letter, SecNav to LT Beekman V. Hoffman, 15 Apr 1815. RG45 (M149, roll 12), DNA.

Letters, SecNav to CAPT Isaac Hull, 31 May 1814 and 25 Jan 1816. RG45 (M149, rolls 11 and 12), DNA.

Letter, SecNav to CAPT Robert T. Spence, 31 Mar 1814. RG45 (M149, roll 11), DNA.

Letters, SecNav to CAPT Charles Stewart, 18 and 23 May, 25 Jun 1815. RG45 (M149, roll 12), DNA.

Letter, CAPT Charles Stewart to CAPT Charles Morris, 17 Dec 1813. RG45 (M125, roll 33), DNA.

Letters, CAPT Charles Stewart to SecNav, 5 and 25 Dec 1813; 4 and 18 Apr, 10 Aug 1814; 2 [?] May 1815. RG45 (M125, rolls 33, 35, 38, and 44), DNA.

Logs, USS *Constitution*, 31 Dec 1813–3 Apr 1814 and 18 Dec 1814–16 May 1815. RG45, DNA.

Log, HMS *Pique*. PRO (ADM51/2695).

Mahan, CAPT Alfred T. *Sea Power in Its Relation to the War of 1812*. Boston: Little, Brown and Co. 1905.

Martin, CDR Tyrone G. "The *Constitution* Connection." *Journal of Erie Studies*, Sep 1988.

Napier, LT Henry Edward, RN. *New England Blockaded 1814*. Salem, Massachusetts: Peabody Museum. 1939.

National Intelligencer (Washington), 23 May 1815.

Preble, George Henry. "History of the Boston Navy Yard." Manuscript. New England Historical Genealogical Society.

Price, Norma Adams, ed. *Letters from Old Ironsides, 1813–1815*. Tempe, Arizona: Beverly-Merriam Press. 1984.

Roosevelt, Theodore. *The Naval War of 1812*. 3d ed. New York: G. P. Putnam's Sons. 1910.

The War. Vol. I, no. 45 (27 Apr 1813), and vol. II, nos. 92 (22 Mar 1814) and 97 (26 Apr 1814). New York: S. Woodworth & Co.

Chapter Twelve

Geisinger, LT David. "Notes of a Cruise on board the United States Ship *Constitution*." Manuscript. MHS.

General Order, 12 Mar 1825. RG45 (M149, roll 15), DNA.

Journal, PVT William Fleming, USMC, 2 Sep 1824–4 Jul 1828. USSCM.

Journal, MIDN Richard L. Page, 23 Feb 1826–30 Mar 1828. University of North Carolina Library.

Journal, MIDN Philip Augustus Stockton, 29 Oct 1824–31 Dec 1826. USSCM.

Letter, commandant, USMC, to CAPT Richard D. Wainwright, 21 Mar 1821. RG45, DNA.

Letter, CAPT John Downes to CAPT John Rodgers, 11 Aug 1829. RG45 DNA.

Letter, SLG MSTR Briscoe Doxey to CAPT John Rodgers, 1 Jun 1821. RG45, DNA.

Letter, MIDN Samuel F. Dupont to his father, 19 Apr 1821. Eleutherian Mills Library.

Letters, MIDN Samuel F. Dupont to his mother, 19 Apr, 28 Jul 1821, and 12 Apr 1822. Eleutherian Mills Library.

Letters, MIDN Samuel F. Dupont to his brother Charles, 5 Jun, 10 Dec 1821, and 18 Mar 1822. Eleutherian Mills Library.

Letter, Chief Clerk Charles Hay to SecNav, 4 Jun 1824. RG45 (M124, roll 99, vol. 3), DNA.

Letters, CAPT Isaac Hull to CAPT Stephen Decatur, 6 Nov 1819; 16, 17, and 23 Feb, 23 Mar, 3, 11, 13, 14, and 30 Apr 1821. RG45, DNA.

Letters, CAPT Isaac Hull to CAPT John Rodgers, 12 and 30 Mar, 6 Aug, 18 Nov, and 1 Dec 1817; 24 Jan, 12 Mar, and 17 Jun 1818; 6 May, 29 Jun, 4 Oct, and 10 Dec 1819; 25 Apr, 3 and 8 May, 14 Jun, 3, 15, and 21 Jul, 22 Sep, 11 Oct, 5, 6, and 27 Nov, 4, 7, 11, 21, and 24 Dec 1820; 12 Feb, 10 Apr 1821. RG45, DNA.

Letter, CAPT Isaac Hull to SecNav, 25 Feb 1819. RG45 (M125), DNA.

Letter, Samuel Humphreys to CAPT Isaac Hull, 20 Sep 1819. RG45, DNA.

Letter, COMO John Marston to Mrs. Samuel F. Dupont, 21 Jul 1866. Eleutherian Mills Library.

Letters, CAPT Daniel T. Patterson to SecNav, 25 Nov 1826; 5 Mar, 8 and 27 Aug 1827; 19 Jul 1828. Daniel Todd Patterson Papers, Manuscript Division, DLC.

Letter, LT John Percival to CAPT John Rodgers, 15 May 1821. RG45, DNA.

Letter, CAPT David Porter to CAPT Isaac Hull, 19 Aug 1817. RG45, DNA.

Letter, Robert Potts to SecNav, 24 Mar 1828. RG45 (M124, roll 113, vol. 3), DNA.

Letter, MIDN John Reed, Jr., to his father, 24 Aug 1816. HSP.

Letters, CAPT John Rodgers to CAPT Isaac Hull, 25 Jul 1815; 24 Jul 1816; 14 Apr 1817; 27 Apr 1818; 21, 24, and 26 Jun and 10 Sep 1819; 17 Apr, 2 May, 20 and 25 Jul, 27 Sep, 31 Oct, 10, 21, and 24 Nov 1820; 15 Jan, 16, 22, and 23 Feb, 11 and 15 Apr 1821. RG45, DNA.

Letter, CAPT John Rodgers to LT Richard Winter, 6 Jul 1815. RG45, DNA.

Letter, SecNav to CAPT William Bainbridge, 5 Jul 1815. RG45 (M149, roll 12), DNA.

Letter, SecNav to CAPT Thomas Macdonough, 19 Oct 1824. RG45 (M149, roll 15), DNA.

Letters, SecNav to CAPT John Rodgers, 29 Aug, 1 and 2 Sep 1825. RG45 (M149, roll 16), DNA.

Letter, LT William Shubrick to CAPT Charles Stewart, 1 Jun 1815. RG45, DNA.

Letter, CAPT Charles Stewart to CAPT John Rodgers, 29 Jun 1815. RG45, DNA.

Letter, Dr. Spencer C. Tucker to author, 14 Jun 1985.

Logs, USS *Constitution*, 10 Apr 1821–22 May 1824 and 28 Oct 1824–6 May 1826. RG45, DNA.

Niles' Weekly Register, 30 Nov 1823.

Paullin, Charles Oscar. *Commodore John Rodgers, 1773–1838*. Annapolis: USNI. 1967.

———. *History of Naval Administration, 1775–1911*. Annapolis: USNI. 1968.

Valle, James E. *Rocks and Shoals*. Annapolis: USNI. 1980.

CHAPTER THIRTEEN

Board of Naval Commissioners circulars issued 16 May 1825 and 29 Mar 1830. RG45, DNA.

Jarvis, Russell. *Life of Commodore Elliott*. Philadelphia: Howes. 1835.

Letters, CONST Josiah Barker to CAPT Jesse Elliott, 23 Jun, 30 Aug, and 24 Dec 1834. RG45, DNA.

Letters, CAPT John Downes to CAPT John Rodgers, 11 Aug 1829, 10 Apr 1835, 1 Feb 1836, and 19 Apr 1837. RG45, DNA.

Letters, CAPT Jesse Elliott to CAPT John Rodgers, 24 Jun, 23 Nov, and 6 Dec 1833; 8 Jan, 14 Feb, 1 and 21 Mar, 2 and 8 May, 23 Jun, 26 Oct, 22 and 27 Dec 1834; 5, 13, and 26 Jan, 9 and 14 Feb 1835. RG45, DNA.

Letter, CHCONST Samuel Humphreys to CAPT Jesse Elliott, 16 Sep 1833. RG45, DNA.

Letter, CAPT Charles Morris to CAPT Jesse Elliott, 3 Sep 1834. RG45, DNA.

Letters, CAPT Charles Morris to CAPT John Rodgers, 19 Jul, 1 Nov 1828; 28 Aug, 27 Sep 1830; 24 Feb, 4 Apr, and 14 Dec 1831. RG45, DNA.

Letter, J. K. Paulding to SecNav, 14 Mar 1835. RG45 (M124, roll 147, vol. 247), DNA.

Letters, CAPT John Rodgers to CAPT William Bainbridge, 15 Sep, 4 Dec 1832; 4, 17, and 23 Apr 1833. RG45, DNA.

Letters, CAPT John Rodgers to CAPT Jesse Elliott, 28 May, 23 Jun, 16 and 19 Aug, 9 and 20 Sep, 5 Dec 1833; 24 Feb, 13 and 24 Mar, 9 and 21 Apr, 7 May, 2 Jul, 20 Sep, 9, 15, 19, and 27 Dec 1834; 8 Jan 1835. RG45, DNA.

Letters, CAPT John Rodgers to CAPT Isaac Hull, 25 and 26 Jun 1821. RG45, DNA.

Letter, CAPT John Rodgers to CAPT Charles Morris, 18 Aug 1830. RG45, DNA.

Letters, CAPT John Rodgers to SecNav, 20 Sep 1830 and 31 Aug 1833. RG45, DNA.

Letters, SecNav to CAPT Jesse Elliott, 9 and 20 Feb 1835. RG45 (M149, roll 23), DNA.

Letters, SecNav to CAPT John Rodgers, 17 and 30 Aug 1830. RG45 (M149), DNA.

Letters, MSTR CMDT John Smith to CAPT John Rodgers, 19 and 28 Apr 1833. RG45, DNA.

Letter, CAPT Charles Stewart to CAPT Charles Morris, 22 Sep 1830. RG45, DNA.

Letter, MSTR CMDT Thomas W. Wyman to CAPT John Rodgers, 28 Dec 1832. RG45, DNA.

Pinckney, Pauline A. *American Figureheads and Their Carvers.* New York: W. W. Norton & Co. 1940.

Speech of Com. Jesse Duncan Elliott, USN, Delivered in Hagerstown, Md., on 14th November 1843. (With Appendices and Addenda.) Philadelphia: G. B. Zieber & Co. 1844.

Chapter Fourteen

An eyewitness. "Old Ironsides on a Lee-Shore." *The Parlor Annual and Christian Family Casket,* vol. 4, 1846.

Anonymous (Henry Mercier). *Life in a Man-of-War.* Boston: Houghton, Mifflin Co. 1927.

Brewington, M. V. *Shipcarvers of North America.* New York: Dover Publications, Inc. 1962.

Edward C. Anderson Papers, Southern Historical Collection, University of North Carolina Library.

Johnson, Robert Erwin. *Thence Round Cape Horn.* Annapolis: USNI. 1963.

Journal, PMIDN Frank A. Bacon, 1835–1836. Western Reserve Historical Society.

Journal, MIDN William P. Buckner, 26 Mar 1844–30 Apr 1845. USSCM.

Journal, LT William Henry Kennon, 1839–1840. Private collection.

Letters, COMO Alexander Claxton to Francis Sorrel, 13 Jan, 24 Mar, and 11 May 1839. U. S. Naval Historical Foundation.

Letter, LT C. H. McBlair to SecNav, 5 Dec 1838. RG45 (M124, roll 165, vol 289), DNA.

Letter, MIDN Joseph W. Revere to his aunt, 5 and 6 Nov, 5 Dec 1835. MHS.

Letters, SecNav to PMIDN Charles C. Barton, 3 Dec 1838 and 13 Mar 1839. RG45 (M149, roll 28), DNA.

Letter, SecNav to SURG Thomas J. Boyd, 14 Mar 1839. RG45 (M149, roll 28), DNA.

Letters, SecNav to COMO Alexander Claxton, 31 Dec 1838; 21 Feb, 7 Mar, 1 Apr, 8 and 9 May 1839. RG45 (M149, roll 28), DNA.

Letters, SecNav to COMO Jesse D. Elliott, 13 Mar 1835, 1 Oct 1836, 16 Mar and 1 Nov 1837; 18 and 28 Aug, 5 Sep and 15 Nov 1838; 21 Feb and 2 Mar 1839. RG45 (M149, rolls 23 and 25–28), DNA.

Letter, SecNav to LT Charles G. Hunter, 23 Nov 1838. RG45 (M149, roll 28), DNA.

Letters, SecNav to COMO Edmund P. Kennedy, 6 and 8 Sep, 6 Dec 1842. RG45 (M149, roll 35), DNA.

Letters, SecNav to CAPT Foxall A. Parker, Sr., 27 Apr, 9 and 25 May 1842. RG45 (M149, roll 34), DNA.

Letters, SecNav to CAPT Edward R. Shubrick, 4 Mar and 27 Apr 1842. RG45 (M149, roll 34), DNA.

Letters, SecNav to COMO William B. Shubrick, 1 Jul 1842 [2]. RG45 (M149, roll 34), DNA.

Letter, SecNav to LT Henry A. Steele, 13 Nov 1838. RG45 (M149, roll 28), DNA.

Letters, SecNav to COMO Charles Stewart, 21 Sep, 13 and 24 Dec 1842. RG45 (M149, roll 35), DNA.

Letter, SecNav to CAPT Daniel Turner, 25 Feb 1839. RG45 (M149, roll 28), DNA.

Letter, CAPT Lewis Warrington to CAPT John Downes, 11 Dec 1841. RG45, DNA.

Log, USS *Constitution*, 5 Jul 1837–9 Aug 1838 (partial). USSCM.

Log, USS *Constitution*, Mar 1839–16 May 1841, 17 May–12 Nov 1841, and 22 Jun 1842–16 Feb 1843. RG45, DNA.

Paullin, Charles Oscar. *Paullin's History of Naval Administration, 1775–1911*. Annapolis: USNI. 1968.

Semi-Monthly Reports of Repairs, Gosport Navy Yard, 1 Nov 1841–15 Apr 1842. RG45 AR, Box 93, Folder 4, DNA.

Speech of Com. Jesse Duncan Elliott, USN, Delivered in Hagerstown, Md., On 14th November, 1843 (with Appendices and Addenda). Philadelphia: G. B. Zieber & Co. 1844.

Valle, James E. *Rocks and Shoals*. Annapolis: Naval Institute Press. 1980.

Chapter Fifteen

Dunn, CAPT Lucius C., USN (Ret). "The United States Navy and the Open Door Policy." USNI *Proceedings*, Jan 1949.

Hanks, CAPT Robert J., USN. "Commodore Lawrence Kearney, the Diplomatic Seaman." USNI *Proceedings*, Nov 1970.

Johnson, Robert E. *Thence Round Cape Horn*. Annapolis: USNI. 1963.

———. *Far China Station: The U.S. Navy in Asian Waters, 1800–1895*. Annapolis: Naval Institute Press. 1979.

Journal, MIDN William P. Buckner, 26 Mar 1844–30 Apr 1845. USSCM.

Journal, LT John B. Dale, 29 May 1844–27 Sep 1846. New England Historical Genealogical Society.

Journal, MIDN Meriwether Patterson Jones, 20 May 1844–5 Jul 1846. DNA.

Journal, MIDN Lucius M. Mason, 8 Aug–14 Dec 1844. DNA.

Journal, MIDN Colville Terrett, 1 Oct 1845–15 Sep 1846. DNA.

Journal, CARP Henry G. Thomas, 26 Mar 1844–26 Sep 1846. Private collection.

Letter, Board of Naval Commissioners to Yard commandants, 19 Jan 1842. RG45, DNA.

Letter, MIDN John E. Hart to his sister, ? [date not legible] Sep 1846. USSCM.

Letter, Charles Haswell to SecNav, 22 Jul 1845. RG45, DNA.

Letters, CAPT John Percival to SecNav, 6 and 21 Jun 1845. RG45 (M125, roll 322), DNA.

Letter, J. C. Reinhardt to Samuel S. Haldeman, 24 Aug 1846. Academy of Natural Sciences Library, Philadelphia.

Logs, USS *Constitution*, 26 Mar 1844–30 Nov 1845 and 1 Dec 1845–5 Oct 1846. RG45, DNA.

Paullin, Charles Oscar. *American Voyages to the Orient, 1690–1865*. Annapolis: USNI. 1971.

Stevens, Benjamin F. *A Cruise on the Constitution*. New York: United Service Magazine. 1904.

———. "Around the World in the U.S. Frigate Constitution in the Days of the Old or Wooden Ships." *United Service Magazine*, vol. 5 (1905).

"The Noble Seamen of our Navy." *Nautical Magazine*, Dec 1845.

Chapter Sixteen

Brewington, M. V. *Shipcarvers of North America*. New York: Dover Publications, Inc. 1962.

Chief, Construction, Equipment, and Repair. Order. 1846. DNA.

Emmons, LT George F. W. *The Navy of the United States from the Commencment, 1775 to 1853.* Washington: Gideon and Co. 1853.

Langley, Harold D. "An American Surgeon and His Papal Patient: Notes from the Papers of Charles Fleury Bien-Aime Guillon." *Fugitive Leaves,* Fall 1994.

Letters, chief, Bureau of Construction, to commandant, Boston Navy Yard, 25 Aug, 13 Dec 1847; 12 Jan, 30 Mar, and 27 Jun 1848. DNA.

Letters, CAPT John Gwinn to his wife, 27 Jan, 10 and 22 Mar, 20 Apr, 3, 8, 14, and 22 May, 25 Jun, 6 Jul, and 8 Aug 1849. Manuscript Division, DLC.

Letter, COMO Charles W. Morgan to SecNav, 17 Sep 1849. NHC.

Logs, USS *Constitution,* 9 Oct 1848–12 Oct 1849 and 13 Oct 1849–16 Jan 1851. RG45, DNA.

Navy Department. *Annual Report.* 1850. DLC.

Phelps, COMO Thomas S. "A Reminiscence of the Old Navy." *United Service Magazine,* Aug 1882.

Chapter Seventeen

Duke, CDR Marvin L. "The Navy Founds a Nation." USNI *Proceedings,* Sep 1970.

Journal, Edward Cobb, commander's clerk, USS *Constitution,* 22 Dec 1852–2 Jun 1855. USSCM.

Letter, Joseph H. Nicholson to Eliza Anne ? [last name not given], 30 Mar–10 Apr 1853. NHC.

Logs, USS *Constitution,* 22 Dec 1852–23 Dec 1853, 24 Dec 1853–21 Sep 1854, and 22 Sep 1854–14 Jun 1855. RG45, DNA.

Morison, Samuel Eliot. *"Old Bruin": Commodore Matthew Calbraith Perry, 1794–1858.* Boston: Little, Brown and Company. 1967.

Paullin, Charles Oscar. *History of Naval Administration, 1775–1911.* Annapolis: USNI. 1968.

Tucker, Spencer C. "The Dahlgren Boat Howitzer." *Naval History,* Fall 1992.

Valle, James E. *Rocks and Shoals.* Annapolis: Naval Institute Press. 1980.

Watmough, PURS James H. Outgoing Letterbook, 25 Mar 1853–10 Jul 1855. Bancroft Library, University of California (Berkeley).

Chapter Eighteen

Anonymous. *Attractive Bits Along the Shore.* Portland, Maine: H. Wilbur Hayes. Ca. 1895.

Boston *Globe* (evening edition), 21 Sep 1897.

Brewington, M. V. *Shipcarvers of North America.* New York: Dover Publications, Inc. 1962.

Davis, William H. "'Old Ironsides' in Chancery." USNI *Proceedings,* Jun 1941.

Evans, RADM Robley D. *A Sailor's Log.* New York: D. Appleton and Company. 1901.

George Henry Preble's Naval Scrap Book. MHS.

Gleaves, RADM Albert. *The Life of an American Sailor: Rear Admiral William Hemsley Emory, United States Navy.* New York: Geo. H. Doran Co. 1923.

———. *Life and Letters of Stephen B. Luce, Rear Admiral, U.S. Navy.* New York: G. P. Putnam's Sons. 1925.

Journal, Sailmaker Charles E. Tallman, USN. Private collection.

Letter, Commandant, New York Navy Yard to CAPT Oscar F. Stanton, 4 Jun 1880. G. W. Blount White Library.

Letter, COMO Earl English to CAPT Oscar F. Stanton, 26 Apr 1880. G. W. Blount White Library.

Letter, Otis G. Hammond to SecNav, 22 Apr 1897. JDLP, MHS.

Letter, COMO Henry L. Howison to SecNav, 22 Apr 1897. JDLP, MHS.

Letter, George H. Jenkins to SecNav, 30 Jan 1890. NHC.

Letter, COMO Stephen B. Luce to CAPT Oscar F. Stanton, 22 Apr 1881. G. W. Blount White Library.

Letter, Mrs. Willard E. Mattson to author, 15 May 1978.

Letter, R. W. Meade to F. D. Wilson, 1 May 1889. NHC.

Letter, Franklin D. Roosevelt to F. Alexander Magoun, n.d. RG45 AR, Box 92, B to C, DNA.

Letter, CAPT R. W. Meade to SecNav, 22 Mar 1889. RG45 AR, Box 108, Folder 3, DNA.

Letter, Lillie B. (Mrs. Nelson V.) Titus to SecNav, 7 Oct 1897. JDLP, MHS.

Letter, SecNav to Henry Bainbridge, 30 Apr 1897. JDLP, MHS.

Letter, SecNav to William E. Barrett, 29 Jul 1897. JDLP, MHS.

Letter, SecNav to William E. Chandler, 30 Apr 1897. JDLP, MHS.

Letter, SecNav to Jacob Emerson, 16 Oct 1897. JDLP, MHS.

Letter, SecNav to E. H. Goss, 12 Apr 1897. JDLP, MHS.

Letters, SecNav to COMO Henry L. Howison, 30 Sep 1897 (2). JDLP, MHS.

Letter, SecNav to Eugene A. Perry, 5 Oct 1897. JDLP, MHS.

Letter, SecNav to William Reynold, 29 Sep 1897. JDLP, MHS.

Letter, SecNav to Miss E. F. Sohier, 29 Sep 1897. JDLP, MHS.

Letter, SecNav to C. A. Sollowney, 12 May 1897. JDLP, MHS.

Letter, SecNav to Lillie B. (Mrs. Nelson V.) Titus, 27 July 1897. JDLP, MHS.

Letter, SecNav to Lillie B. (Mrs. Nelson V.) Titus, 7 Oct 1897. JDLP, MHS.

Letters, SecNav to Roger Wolcott, 23, 28, and 30 Apr, 1 May 1897. JDLP, MHS.

Letter, Naval Constructor Elliott Snow to chief, Bureau of Construction and Repair, 16 Jan 1904. RG19, Entry 83, Box 10, DNA.

Logs, USS *Constitution*, 1–25 Aug 1860; 1 Mar 1865–14 Feb 1866; 9 Apr–14 Oct 1866; 15 Oct 1866–31 Mar 1867; 1 Apr–15 Sep 1867; 16 Sep–18 Dec 1867; 19 Dec 1867–29 Dec 1868; 30 Dec 1868–14 Jan 1870; 15 Jan 1870–16 Jan 1871; 17 Jan–26 Sep 1871; 19 Jul 1877–19 Jan 1878; 20 Jan–25 Jul 1878; 26 Jul 1878–31 Jan 1879; 1 Feb–15 Jul 1879; 16 Jul 1879–21 Jan 1880; 22 Jan–24 Jul 1880; 25 Jul 1880–4 Feb 1881; 5 Feb–21 Aug 1881; 22 Aug–14 Dec 1881. RG45, DNA.

Longacre, Edward G. "Flight From Annapolis." *Manuscripts*, vol. XXXIII, no. 2 (Spring 1981).

Mager, Chief Warrant Carpenter Philip T. Undated statement. Author's collection.

Magruder, P. H. "Naval Academy Practice Ship." USNI *Proceedings*, May 1934.

———. "The U.S. Naval Academy and Annapolis during the Civil War." USNI *Proceedings*, Aug 1945.

Navy Department. *Official Records of the Union and Confederate Navies in the War of Rebellion.* Washington: GPO. 1921.

Nicolosi, Anthony S. "The Founding of the Newport Naval Training Station, 1878–1883, an Exercise in Naval Politics." *The American Neptune*, Fall 1989.

"Old Ironsides." *Harper's Weekly* (Supplement), 10 July 187? [date not legible].

Routine and Orders for the United States School Ship *Constitution*. MHS.

Stockton, CAPT Charles H. "Recollections of My Life Afloat and Ashore from the Beginning to My Arrival in Rio de Janeiro in 1866 Based on Journals, Letters, etc., etc., etc., Part I." Manuscript. U.S. Naval War College Museum.

The Congressional Medal of Honor: The Names, The Deeds. Forest Ranch, California: Sharp & Dunnigan Publications. n.d.

Thompson, M. S., comp. *General Orders and Circulars Issued by the Navy Department from 1863 to 1887.* Washington: GPO. 1887.

Vallette, Henry M. "History and Reminiscences of the Philadelphia Navy Yard." Potter's *American Monthly Magazine,* Jan–Oct 1876.

RADM (Cameron MacRae) Winslow's Address. Undated. New York Historical Society.

CHAPTER NINETEEN

Albright, Charles Leonard. *The East Coast Cruise of the U.S. Frigate Constitution.* Richmond, Virginia: Press of the Dietz Printing Co. 1934.

Andrews, RADM Philip. "The 'Old Ironsides' Campaign." USNI *Proceedings,* Oct 1926.

Brewington, M. V. *Shipcarvers of North America.* New York: Dover Publications, Inc. 1962.

Downin, CDR Jack. "'Lunchbox Charlie' Bonaparte." USNI *Proceedings,* Aug 1976.

Krafft, Herman F. "New Lease on Life for Old Ironsides." USNI *Proceedings,* Oct 1925.

Letters, Lewis N. Finney to Lillie B. (Mrs. Nelson V.) Titus, 9 and 13 Nov 1899. JDLP, MHS.

Letter, SecNav to O. H. Cook, 24 Jan 1898. JDLP, MHS.

Letter, SecNav to Edward H. Rogers, 29 Dec 1898. JDLP MHS.

Letters, SecNav to Lillie B. (Mrs. Nelson V.) Titus, 11 Jan 1898, 28 Aug and 25 Oct 1899. JDLP, MHS.

Letter, SecNav to the Senate Committee on Appropriations, 2 Feb 1916. DNA.

Letters, Lillie B. (Mrs. Nelson V.) Titus to SecNav, 22 Oct 1897, 8 Jan 1898, 14 Dec 1899, ? ? [date not legible] 1901, and 4 Jan, 18 Feb 1902. JDLP, MHS.

Logs (monthly), USS *Constitution,* 1 Jul 1931–8 Jun 1934. RG45, DNA.

Lord, LT John A. "U.S.S. CONSTITUTION RESTORATION, 1927–1930." Typed, duplicated report. n.d. USSCM.

Martin, CDR Tyrone G. "The New *Constitution.*" Unpublished manuscript. Author's collection.

"Memorial To the Senate and House of Representatives of the United States" from the Massachusetts Historical Society. 30 Dec 1903. MHS.

"'Old Ironsides' Asail On The Silv'ry Screen." *The Literary Digest,* 1 Jan 1927.

Paramount Pictures. "Old Ironsides." Souvenir movie program. n.d. USSCM.

Royal, RADM William F. Telephone conversation with author, 20 Dec 1979.

Scrapbooks maintained by ship's company during the 1931–1934 grand tour. USSCM.

Snow, RADM Elliot. "The Battery of 'Old Ironsides.'" *Army Ordnance,* vol. VI, no. 33 (Nov–Dec 1925).

The Youth's Companion (New England ed.), 6 Jun and 8 Aug 1907 issues.

CHAPTER TWENTY

Boston *Globe* (morning eds.), 15 Jun, 30 Sep 1936; 27 May, 24 Aug 1940; 8 Mar 1946; 24 Jun 1971.

Boston *Herald,* 26 May 1939.

Boston Naval Shipyard *News,* numerous issues, 1949–1967. Boston National Historical Park.

Boston *Post,* 21 May 1940.

Correspondence and/or conversations with CPO Jerry P. Knickerbocker (nephew of LCDR Hermann P. Knickerbocker, Captain, 1940–1941); CDR Owen W. Huff (Captain, 1946–1947); CDR Louis E. Wood (Captain, 1947–1950); CWO4 Knied H. Christensen (Captain, 1950–1952); CDR Albert C. Messier (Captain, 1952–1954); LCDR Charles W. Morris (Captain, 1954–1957); David G. O'Brien (then LTJG; Captain, 1957–1959); CAPT Edward J. Melanson (Captain, 1959–1960); CDR Victor B. Stevens, Jr. (Captain, 1960–1963); John C. Kelleher (then LT; Captain, 1963–1965); CDR Hugh A. Moore (Captain, 1969–1970); CDR John D. McKinnon (Captain, 1971–1972); CDR Thomas Coyne (Captain, 1972–1974); CDR Robert L. Gillen (Captain, 1978–1980); CDR Herman O. Sudholz (Captain, 1980–1985), CDR Joseph Z. Brown (Captain, 1985–1987); CDR David M. Cashman (Captain, 1987–1991); CDR Richard B. Amirault (Captain, 1991–1995); CDR Michael C. Beck (Captain, 1995–); and the men of the USS Constitution Maintenance and Restoration Facility: Donald A. Turner (Head), Joseph Brodeur, Clarence Gaudet, John McLean, John Paula, Daniel Scully, Domenic Silvaggio, Frank Stachowski, Anthony Vitale, Richard Wallace, Iggy Wencek, and Ralph Yarn; and its successor, the Naval Historical Center, Boston, particularly Charles Deans, Patrick Otton, and David G. Mullins.

Files of the Public Affairs Office, First Naval District.

Letter and photograph files of USS Constitution.

Martin, Tyrone G. "The Rejuvenation of 'Old Ironsides.'" Paper presented to the New England Section, Society of Naval Architects and Marine Engineers, Jan 1977.

———. "Maintaining 'Old Ironsides.'" Paper presented at the Bath Marine Museum Symposium on American Maritime History, May 1977.

Personal participation by the author, 6 Aug 1974–30 Jun 1978.

Personal recollections and memorabilia of ship's company, USS Constitution, Aug 1974–Jun 1978.

USS Constitution Maintenance and Restoration Facility. "Record of Work Accomplished by Shop 64 on USS Constitution, January 1927–June 30, 1972." Unpublished report in facility files.

Witherell, Peter W. "A Study of Wooden Ship Hogging—The USS Constitution." Paper presented at the Ancient Interface XVI Symposium on Sailing, Oct 1986.

Index

Abbott, N.H.M., 308–9

Abo, 288

Abraham and Strauss, 351

Acasta, 191, 204

Accra, Ghana, 305

Acteon, 262

Acton, John, 100

Adam, Po, 275

Adams, Charles F., 339, 348, 352–53

Adams, Henry A., 324–25

Adams, John, 13, 15, 17–19, 27, 44, 63

Adams, 64, 85, 94, 124, 130

Adelina, 154

Adiona, 154

Adrianna, 185

Aegina Island, 230

Aeolus, 145–46, 150, 155

Africa, 145, 150, 155

Agassiz (u.s. Coast Guard cutter), 350

Alcmene, 284

Alcott, Midshipman, 132

Alexandria, Egypt, 253, 292–93

Alexandria, Virginia, 140, 142–43, 353

Alexis, Louis, 26

Alfred, 117

Algeciras, Spain, 126, 223

Algiers (Algeria), 82, 85, 91, 95, 123–24, 208, 215, 217–18, 222, 228, 302

Alicante, Spain, 125

Allegheny, 293

Allen, Peter, 49

Allen Gardner, 309

Alliance, 1, 3

Amalia, 47

Amazon, 96

Ambriz, Angola, 306

America, 269

American, 25

Amory, William, 31, 49, 56, 58

Amphitheatre, 54–56, 59–60

Amsterdam, Netherlands, 136

Anaconda, 193

Anacostia, 313

Anderson, Edward C., 253–55

Andromache, 62, 64

Annalaboo, Sumatra, 275

Annapolis, Maryland, 129, 134, 143–45, 311, 314–17, 319, 321, 352

Annobon Island, 308

Antigua Island, 37

Arab, 191

Arethusa, 64

Argo, 41

Argus, 90, 95, 100–101, 103, 105, 106, 108–10, 119, 123, 128–30, 133, 166, 212

Arias, Harmodio, 354

Arkansas, 352

Armstrong, James, 244

Athens, Greece, 229–30, 252

Augusta, 54, 58, 61, 64

Austin, William, 61
Avenger, 154–55
Aylwin, John C., 179

Baalbek, Lebanon, 254
Bacchante, 160
Bache, George M., 288–89
Bacon, Frank A., 252
Badger, George, 254
Badger, Oscar C., 325–30
Bahamas Islands, 152, 187
Baie Citron, Santo Domingo, 58
Bainbridge, Joseph, 104
Bainbridge, William, 48–49, 83–84, 92, 96,
    98, 120, 167, 169–70, 177–82, 188–91,
    206, 212–14, 220, 228, 235–36, 240, 246,
    276, 321, 373; awarded gold medal, 180;
    biographic sketch, 168; defeats *Java*, 171–76
Baker, Francis H., 330
Baker, George S., 313
Balboa, Canal Zone, 354–55
Ballard, Henry E., 194, 202, 204
Baltic, 317
Baltimore, Maryland, 6, 11, 13–14, 62, 139,
    141, 316, 352, 361
Baltimore, 28
Bancroft, George (actor), 345
Bancroft, George (secretary of the navy), 311
Bandar Seri Begawan, Brunei, 278
Barbados Island, 185–86
Barbo tribe, 303–5
Barcelona, Spain, 298
Bar Harbor, Maine, 333, 350
Barker, Josiah, 211, 233–34, 238, 241, 245
Barlow, Joel, 12, 82, 134–35, 137, 139
Barnegat Inlet, New Jersey, 299
Barney, Joshua, 54, 163
Barney, 350
Barnhouse, Augustus, 222
Barnstable, Massachusetts, 267
Barret, James, 141
Barrett, Arthur, 358
Barron, James, 121, 125, 127, 167

Barron, Samuel, 109–10, 112, 115, 117–19,
    121, 124
Barry, John, 3, 10, 30, 34–35, 37–39, 41, 212
Bastard, John, 145
Bates, James, 28–29
Bath, Maine, 154, 350
Baton Rouge, Louisiana, 352
Beale, Richard C., 31
Beaumont, Texas, 353
Beaussier, Bonaventure, 99, 110
Becton, 218
Beecher, Laban S., 237, 239–41
Beery, Wallace, 345
Beirut, Lebanon, 252
Bellona, 261
Belvidera, 145–48, 150, 155
Bembatooka, Madagascar, 273
Bennett, John, 49
Bently, Samuel, 17
Berceau, 269–70, 274
Bermuda Island, 152, 187, 189, 192
Biddle, James, 284
Biddle, Nicholas, 244
Bight of Leogane, Haiti, 52–54, 58, 60
Bingham, William, 12–13
Bishop, Bobbi, 370
Blakesley, A., 218
Bliss, Daniel, 139
Blue, Henry M., 319
Boerum, William, 254, 256
Bollard Head, England, 328
Bolton, William, 292
Bonaparte, Charles J., 339–40
Bonaparte, Joseph, 63
Bonaparte, Mrs. Jerome, 139
Bonaparte, Napoleon, 139, 214, 290, 306, 339
Bon Homme Richard, 162
Bonne Citoyenne, 171, 178–79
Borer, 296
Boss, Edward, Sr., 54
Boston, Massachusetts, 1, 6, 7, 10–13, 17–18,
    20–21, 23–24, 27, 29–31, 37, 39, 42, 46,
    62–63, 65, 87–88, 125–28, 130, 132–33,

141, 151–52, 161, 163, 165–66, 179–80,
184, 187–92, 195, 206, 208, 211–12, 218,
232–47, 289, 338–39, 344–45, 347, 349,
352, 355, 358–59, 361, 366–67, 369–70
Boston, 316
Boston *Advertiser*, 234
Boston *Evening Transcript*, 349
Boston Manufacturing Company, 10
Boston Navy Yard, 25, 40, 242, 291, 324, 338,
341, 344, 348, 363
Boston, uss (1799), 45, 48–50, 52, 54
Boston, uss (1826), 245, 284
Bosworth, Nathaniel, 47
Bouldfern, Francis, 49
Bourne, Sylvanus, 136
Brackett, Benjamin, 47
Bradford, Merrit, 331
Brailsford, Joseph, 133
Branch, John, 233–34
Brandywine, 226, 227, 264–65
Breckinridge, 350
Brett, Edward, 273–74
Brice, John W., 253
Brittania, 367
Broke, Philip B.V., 145
Brook (Brooks), William, 35
Brooke, James, 278
Brooklyn (New York) Navy Yard, 299, 317
Brown, Jacob, 61
Brown, John, 42
Brown, John (1798), 24
Brown, Joseph Z., 370
Brown, William, 61
Brunswick, Georgia, 352
Bryant, William, 321
Bryson, Joseph, 299
Buchanan, Franklin, 311
Buchanan, George, 177
Buchanan, McKean, 257, 261
Buenos Aires, Argentina, 195
Bullus, John, 180
Bullus, Oscar, 256
Bulwark, 190

Burne, John (aka William Wallace), 138
Bush, William S., 158, 162
Bushnell, 354, 355
Busuttil, Salvatore, 97
Butler, Benjamin F., 315–16
Butler, Harry St. J., 355–56
Byron, George, 216
Byron, Richard, 145, 147

Cabo da Gata, Spain, 92, 298
Cabo de São Roque, Brazil, 205
Cabo Frio, Brazil, 179
Cabot, George, 18
Cadiz, Spain, 97, 124, 216, 219, 253
Cagliari, Sardinia, 124
Callao, Peru, 259–61
Cambrian, 276
Camden, New Jersey, 324
Camille, 261
Campbell, Hugh G., 85, 94, 123, 125–28; bio-
graphic sketch, 124
Canaris (Greek admiral), 230
Canton, China, 283–85
Cape Ann, Massachusetts, 28, 184, 187, 190
Cape Charles, Virginia, 46
Cape Coast Castle, Ghana, 305, 307
Cape Cod, Massachusetts, 40, 152, 184, 190
Cape Finisterre, Spain, 193
Cape Francois, Haiti, 49–50, 52–56, 58–61,
64–65
Cape Hatteras, North Carolina, 46, 288, 332
Cape Henry, Virginia, 24, 27, 331, 334
Cape Horn, Chile, 258, 262, 288
Cape Mensurado, Liberia, 300
Cape Palmas, Liberia, 303, 307–8
Cape Passaro, Sicily, 102
Cape Race, Newfoundland, 155
Cape St. Vincent, 91
Cape Samana, Santo Domingo, 58
Cape Spartel, Morocco, 93
Cape Verde Islands, 202
Carey, James, 35
Carleton, 160

Carlotta, A., 227

Carmick, Daniel, 56

Carney, Dennis, 24

Carolina Augusta, 275

Carrick Bay, England, 326

Carson, John H., 353

Carteret, 37

Cashman, David M., 370

Cass, Lewis, 237, 253–54

Cassimere, 193

Catalano, Salvatore, 98

Catalpa, 336

Catharine, 186

Cathcart, James L., 1, 83, 85, 100

Catherine, 83

Cavalier, Samuel, 52

Cavally River, Liberia, 304

Cecil Iron Works, Maryland, 128

Celia (brig), 92–93

Chads, Henry D., 175, 178–79, 276

Chanticleer, 230

Chaplin, William C., 277–79

Charleston, South Carolina, 7, 24, 28, 62,
     165, 184, 187, 189, 318, 352, 355

Charlestown, Massachusetts, 369

Chauncey, Charles W., 252, 265

Chauncey, Isaac, 109–10, 127

Chedullah, Rajah, 275

Cheevers, James, 179

Cheevers, John, 179

Chenango, 288

Cherbourg, France, 135–39

Chesapeake, 85, 125–28, 168, 183

Chesapeake Bay, Virginia, 47

Chilia, 261

Chios Island, 217

Christensen, Knied H., 359

Chronicle, 15

Cinderella, 299

Cira Island, 252

Civitavecchia, Italy, 252

Claghorn, George, 6, 15–17

Claudel, Paul, 353

Claxton, Alexander, 257, 259–60

Cleopatre, 285

Cobb, Edward, 308

Cochrane, John, 128

Cochrane, Thomas J., 285

Colhoun, John, 252

Collier, George, 191, 204

Collins, Isaac, 56

Collins, James, 49

Colorado, 337

Columbia, 264–65

Columbia Iron Works, D.C., 128

Columbian Centinel, 15, 17

Columbine, 185

Columbus, 214, 234, 241–44, 268, 284

Comte de Beaujolais, 17

Conde de Jozal, 306

Confidence, 298–99

Congress, 45, 117, 122–23, 166, 190–91, 206,
     219, 270

Connally, John, 38

Connell, James, 30

Conover, Thomas, 298; biographic sketch, 297

Constantinople (Istanbul), Turkey, 83, 168,
     223, 228, 231, 253

Constellation, USS (1798), 14–15, 20, 22, 24, 42,
     62, 82, 85–86, 115, 117–18, 120–24, 182,
     284, 299

Constellation, USS (1855), 321, 358–59, 361

Constitution: alterations to, 128, 132, 134–35,
     169, 210, 290, 301, 311, 324, 340, 365; as
     apprentice training ship, 324–25, 330–34;
     authorization for, 3; award to, 368; cap-
     tures by, 25–27, 32–33, 38, 47, 55–57, 115,
     118, 129, 185–86, 192, 194–95, 306;
     chased, 143–51, 187–88, 203–5; circum-
     navigation by, 268–89; collisions, 218,
     298–99; "crossing the line," 269–70;
     design of, 5; diagonal riders in, 5–9, 371;
     dry-dockings, 237–43, 266, 325, 338,
     346–47, 357, 362–64, 371–72, 373; fig-
     urehead beheaded, 243–44; groundings,
     61–62, 224, 284, 316, 327–28, 334–35;

gun batteries, 19, 90, 117, 128, 154–55, 160, 176, 184, 199, 209–10, 245, 265–66, 291, 330, 340, 348, 366; hauled out, 312, 322–23; heaving down, 88–90, 141, 209; launching, 14–17; name changes, 341–42; organization, 70–76; original appearance, 67–70; with paddle wheels, 211, 212–13; as receiving ship, 337–38; as stationary school ship, 312–22; versus *Cyane* and *Levant*, 195–99; versus *Guerriere*, 155–59; versus *Java*, 171–76

Constitution (proposed), 341–42, 343

Cook, Joseph J., 277

Cooke, Augustus P., 325

Cooke, James W., 277

Cooke, Simeon, 60

Coolidge, Calvin, 345

Coombs, William, 141

Cooper, William (1799), 52

Cooper, William (1812), 139

Cordis, John B., 20, 30–31, 44–45

Corfu Island, 252

Cork, Ireland, 193

Cornè, Michel Felice, 69, 105, 157, 165

Corpus Christi, Texas, 353

Courageux, 136

Cowes, England, 298

Coxe, Charles D., 222

Coyne, Thomas, 364, 369

Crane, Indiana, 366

Crane, William M., 231

Creighton, John O., 220, 222

Crescent, 82

Cristóbal, Canal Zone, 354

Crofford (Crawford), Lewis, 139

Cumberland, 302

Curtis, Asa, 172

Curtis, Joseph W., 277, 287

Curtis, Roger, 137–38

Cushing, Nathaniel, 10

Cyane, HMS, 197, 198–200, 201, 202–4, 206, 292

Cyane, USS, 220, 222–23, 287, 300, 321

Dabney, Frederick, 268–69

Dacres, James R., Jr., 145–46, 160–63, 194

Dale, John B., 268, 277, 280, 283

Dale, Richard, 19–20, 42, 83–85, 90, 118, 168

Dale, 301, 321, 338

Damascus, Syria, 254

Dardanelles, Turkey, 228

Dauphin, 1

Davidson, Pliny, 53

Davis, George, 122

Davis, John, 98

Davis, Roy T., 354

Deal, England, 136

Deane, 23

Dearborn, Henry, 65

DeBlueg, Arthur, 277

DeCamp, John, 306

Decatur, James, 104

Decatur, Stephen, Jr., 98, 104–5, 110, 114–15, 117, 167, 180, 183, 208, 220

Decatur, 155

Defield, Jesse, 49

De Gregorio, Marcello, 97

Delancy, James, 170

Delaware, 263

De Luria, R.L. d'Abun, 273

Demerara Island, 186

Den Helder, Netherlands, 136

Dent, John H., 96–97, 100

Deptford, England, 7

Derne, Libya, 119–20, 130

Detroit, Michigan, 164, 181

Dewey, George, 242, 321, 361

Dewey, Samuel W., 242–44, 321

Diana, 269

Dickens, Francis W., 333

Dickerson, Mahlon, 244

Dighton, Massachusetts, 41

Dix Cove, Ivory Coast, 305

Dodge, Charles J., 239, 247

Dodge, James, 122

Dolphin, USS (1821), 23

Dolphin, USS (1836), 301

Dom Pedro II, 263
Doughty, William, 7, 10
Douglas, George, 199, 202–3
Doxey, Briscoe S., 211, 213, 215, 219
Duc de Chartres, 17. *See also* Louis Philippe
Duc de Montponsier, 17
Duke of Beresford, 194
Duilius, 283
Dupetit-Thouars, George, 26
Duquesne, 351
Duvall, Marius, 277

Eagle, 36–37, 39, 124
Eames, Samuel, 189
Eastman, Thomas H., 320–21
Eaton, William, 85, 119–20
Eberle, Edward W., 342
Eddy, Luther, 46, 48, 59
Edwin, 226
Eisenhower, Dwight D., 361
El Dorado, 310
Eleanor (or *Ellen*), 178
Elizabeth, HMS, 194
Elizabeth (schooner), 53
Elizabeth (transport), 300
Elizabeth II, 367
Elk, 160
Elliott, George, 91
Elliott, Jesse D., 236, 237–50, 252–56, 267,
    290, 326
Ellis, Powhatan, 257
Ellsworth, Oliver, 63
El Mina, Ghana, 305
Emmerton, 273
Emory, William H., 320
Emulous, 150
Endicott, Andrew, 7
Endymion, 195
English, Earl, 332–33
Enoch Turley, 289
Enterprize, USS (1799), 55, 83–86, 90, 95,
    97–103, 105, 109–10, 115, 121, 123–24,
    130, 182, 206

Enterprize, USS (1831), 263
Ephesus, Turkey, 230
Erie, USS (1814), 219–20, 222–23, 226, 227, 229
Erie, USS (1843), 270, 287, 292
Espe, Carl F., 361
Essex, 83–84, 87, 119–21, 123–24, 128–29, 135,
    154, 168–70, 179, 203, 207, 262, 296
Esther, 55–56
Evans, Amos A., 162, 178
Experiment, 52, 54, 59, 106

Fabian, 288
Falcon, Gordon T., 198, 202–3
Fama, 195
Farquhar, Richard, 97
Farragut, David G., 334, 361
Farrell, Charles, 345
Fayal, Azores, 268–69
Ferdinand II, 294
Fernando de Noronha Island, 170
Fernando Po Island, 305
Ferrolana, 310
Fields, Ambrose, 132
Fischer, Christian, 274
Fisher, Anton Otto, 149
Fitzgerald, John F., 338
Flushing, Netherlands, 136
Flynn, Daniel, 59
Ford, Gerald R., 364
Fort Independence, Massachusetts, 246
Fortress Monroe, Virginia, 335
Fort Washington, Virginia, 140
Fox, Josiah, 7, 82
Foxall, Henry, 370
Francis, Samuel, 132
Franklin, 121, 123
Franz, Charles, 358
Freeman, 317
Freeman, Daniel (Andrew), 59
Friendship, 275
Fritt, Michael, 285
Frolic, HMS, 212–13
Frolic, USS, 291

Fuller, George, 285
Funchal, Madeira Island, 269, 303
Furnace Hope, Rhode Island, 10, 14, 19

Gaeta, Italy, 294
Galt, John Minson, 27
Galveston, Texas, 353
Gambia River, 309
Ganges, 19–20, 60, 212
Gardiner's Bay, New York, 332
Garretson, Isaac, 136
Gavino, John, 92
Gay, John, 38
Geddes, Henry, 53
Geisinger, David, 217
General Greene (revenue cutter), 24
General Greene, USS, 48, 50–53, 55, 140
General Washington, 41
Genoa, Italy, 214–15, 252, 297–98
George, 303
George L. Garlick, 332
Georgetown, Maryland, 18
George Washington (frigate), 34–35, 42, 83, 168
Ghent, Belgium, 193, 206
Gibbs, Caleb, 6
Gibraltar (British colony), 84–86, 92–95, 97, 99–100, 118, 123–24, 195, 199, 214–19, 222–23, 225–26, 228, 231–32, 251–53, 298, 302
Gillen, Robert L., 369, 370
Gilliam, Henry, 159
Gilliland, Samuel, 132
Gloucester, Massachusetts, 350
Golconda, 129
Gordon, Charles, 116
Gore, John, 95
Goree, Senegal, 309
Gorgona, 354
Gosport, Virginia, 11
Governor Jay, 24
Grahway tribe, 307
Grant, Gordon, 344–45
Grant, Gough W., 271

Grant, Ken, 175
Grant, Ulysses S., 320
Great Inagua Island, 53
Grebe, 350, 352–55
Grebo tribe, 303–5
Greenbury Point Light, Maryland, 316
Greene, Pitt Barnaby, 171
Greenleaf Point, D.C., 142
Greer, James A., 325
Grenada Island, 186
Gross, Walter R., 368
Groton Heights, Connecticut, 133
Guadeloupe Island, 34–35, 37, 47–48, 331
Guantánamo Bay, Cuba, 354
"Guerriere," 194
Guerriere, HMS, 145–47, 150, 153, 155, 157, 160–65, 176–79, 194, 303, 308–9, 368
Guerriere, USS, 220
Gulesian, Moses, 340
Gulfport, Mississippi, 353
Gulliver, Grace, 355
Gulliver, Louis J., 349–53, 355
Gwinn, John, 292–97; biographic sketch, 291

Hackett, James, 3
Half Cavally tribe, 307
Halifax, Nova Scotia, 145, 152, 160, 183, 191, 333
Hamdullah, 82
Hamilton, Alexander, 6–7
Hamilton, Archibald, 132
Hamilton, Paul, 131, 134, 140, 142, 144, 151, 164, 167–68
Hamilton, Robert W., 37, 58–59
Hamouda Pasha, Bey of Tunis, 82
Hampton, Virginia, 255
Hampton Roads, Virginia, 26, 45–47, 129–30, 132, 263, 318–19, 321, 333, 335
Hancock, John, 36
Handy, John, 61
Hannah, 93
Haraden, Nathaniel, 30, 66, 88, 100, 102, 106, 114, 140–41
Harding, Abraham, 139

Hardison, Jonathan, 61

Hardy, Thomas M., 190

Harriet Lane, 317

Harrison, William, 193

Hart, John E., 289

Hartford, 361

Hartley, Henry, Jr., 353

Hartley, Henry, Sr., 353

Hartt, Edmund, 6, 66

Haskins, Asa, 52

Hassan Bashaw, 82

Hassan Pasha, 82

Havana, Cuba, 28, 49, 55, 60, 257, 310

Havannah, 137–38

Haverford, Pennsylvania, 4

Havre de Grace, Maryland, 316

Hawke, 41

Hayes, Rutherford B., 333

Hazard, 214, 218

Hellas, 230

Herald, 20, 31, 36, 50, 55–56, 60, 65

Hercules, 268

Hichborn, Philip, 323

Higginson, Stephen, 20, 37, 63

Hill, Henry, 171

Hislop, Thomas, 176, 178–79

H. N. Gambrill, 306

Hodgdon, Samuel, 18

Hodgkinson, John, 15

Hoffman, Beekman V., 194, 198, 204

Hogan, Daniel, 156

Holland, Thomas, 137–38

Holmes, Oliver W., Sr., 234

Honolulu, Hawaii, 286–87

Hoover, Herbert, 348, 352–53

Hornet, USS (1804), 119, 121

Hornet, USS (1805), 123–26, 135, 166, 169–71, 178–79

Horton, James, 331

Hotspur, 139

Houston, Texas, 353

Howard, Cornelius, 34

Howison, Henry L., 321–22, 338

Huff, Owen W., 359

Hughes, Thomas, 52

Hull, Isaac, 31–32, 36, 38, 63, 66, 90, 95, 129, 131–41, 152, 153, 154–55, 161–69, 180–82, 206, 209–12, 227, 237–38, 240, 321, 324, 340, 351, 356; avoids capture, 143–51; awarded gold medal, 165; biographic sketch, 130; cuts out ex-*Sandwich*, 56–58; defeats *Guerriere*, 155–59

Hull, William (*Constitution*'s captain), 181

Hull, William (Isaac's brother), 152

Humphreys, Ashton Y., 191, 194, 202

Humphreys, Joshua, 4–5, 7, 9–12, 238, 323, 371

Humphreys, Samuel, 238

Hunter, Bushrod, 256

Hunter, Charles G., 254

Hunter, William M., 205–6

Huntington, Jedidiah, 7

Hydra Island, 217

Iggulden, Edward, 136

Inconstant, 200, 202, 205

Independence (Russian ship), 187

Independence, USS, 191, 209, 234, 242–43, 296

Industry, 23

Intrepid, 98–99, 110, 112–14

Invincible, 48

Irvine, John, 162

Isaac Jeames, 310

Isabella, Santo Domingo, 55

Israel, Joseph, 112

Itapecuru River, Brazil, 205

Izard, Ralph, Jr., 98

Jackson, Andrew, 226, 236–44, 246–48, 251, 271, 275–76, 290, 293, 297, 299, 321, 324

Jackson, Henry, 6, 20

Jacksonville, Florida, 352

Jaffa, Palestine (now Israel), 252–53

Jamestown, 289, 297, 337

Jarvis, John Wesley, 153, 167, 221

Jarvis, Philip, 31

Jarvis, William, 118

Jason, 154
Java, HMS, 175–80, 276
Java, USS, 231
Jay, James, 136
Jay, John, 13
Jean Bart, 326
Jefferson, Thomas, 65, 83, 94, 127–28
Jeffries, John, 141
Jeffry and Russell, 14
Jennings, Daniel, 344
Jerusalem, Palestine (now Israel), 253
Jericho, Jordan (now Israel), 253
Jewell, Theodore F., 330–31
John Adams, 42, 85–86, 92, 94, 109, 111, 115,
    117, 121, 182, 251, 252, 303, 318
John Hancock, 303
John P. Kennedy, 303
Johnson, James, 28
Johnson, Philip C., Jr., 319–20
Johnson, William, 258
Jones, George, 227
Jones, Jacob, 213, 214–17, 219–20, 226, 291;
    biographic sketch, 212–13
Jones, John P., 19, 44, 162
Jones, Peter, 141
Jones, Thomas, 38
Jones, William, 181, 183, 188–89
Josef, 195, 204
Julia, 193
Junon, 187, 190

Kabenda, Angola, 306
Kamehameha III, 287
Karamanli, Hamet, 97, 119–20
Karamanli, Yussuf, 82–83, 97, 119
Kearney, Lawrence, 284, 287
Kenyon Victory, 359
Key West, Florida, 352
Khosrew (Capudan Pasha), 224–25, 228–29
Kingman, Isaac, 156
King's Roads, Massachusetts, 20, 29, 42
Kinney, William, 141
Kinsale, Ireland, 193

Knickerbocker, Hermann P., 358
Knowles and Thayer, 238
Knox, Henry, 2–4, 6–7, 11
Knox, Thomas, 88
Kosciusko, Tadeusz, 139
Kuala Batu, Sumatra, 275

La Amazonas, 194
Lady Warren, 154
Lafayette, Marquis de, 139, 226
Lagos, Nigeria, 305, 307–8
Lake Charles, Louisiana, 353
Lambert, Henry, 178–79
Lambert, Thomas R., 254
Lampedusa Island, 96
Larache, Morocco, 93–94
La Spezia, Italy, 292–94, 297–98, 302
Law, Richard, Jr., 53–54, 60
Lawrence, James, 134, 169–71, 178
Laws, Alexander, 98
Leander, 190–91, 204
Lear, Tobias, 91, 95, 119–20, 122–23
Le Croyable, 168
Lee, Charles, 27
Lee, James, 308
Leeds, William, 261
Lefevre, Dominique, 279, 283
Leghorn, Italy, 83, 85–86, 95, 123, 125–26,
    214, 216–18, 252, 292, 297, 302
Le Havre, France, 248, 326–27, 331
Lelah Eisha, 82
Leonard, Charles, 62
Leopard, 125, 128, 168
Le Rusé, 107
Lesbos Island, 217
Levant, HMS, 197, 199–200, 201, 202–4, 206,
    292, 321
Levant, USS, 265, 287
Levy, Nathan, 50
Lewes, Delaware, 333
Lewis, Charles, 285
Lexington, 4
Leyden, 338

Libreville, Gabon, 305
Lille Belt, 135
Limon Bay, Colombia, 332
Lincoln, Abraham, 314
Lincoln, Henry, 242–43
Lincoln, Levi, 237
Lincoln, William, 242–43
L'Insurgente, 32–33, 117
Lisbon, Portugal, 118, 124, 193–94, 252–53,
    329–30
Litinsky, Ruby, 362
Little, George, 45, 48, 50
Liverpool, England, 129, 195
Livingston, Edward, 247–48
Livingston, Robert, 99
Llewllyn J. Morse, 345
Lloyd, David, 218
Lockhart, David, 224
Logis, Charles, 2
Lohman, Henry, 285
London, England, 137, 162, 328
London Times, 165
Long, John D., 338
Longley, John, 53
Lord, John A., 344–47
Lord, John W., 361
Lord Nelson, 192
Lornson, James, 139
Los Angeles, California, 355
Los Island, 307
Louisa, 23
Louis Philippe, 248, 284, 290
L'Ouverture, Toussaint, 51
Lovely Ann, 185–86
Lowry, Reigart B., 325
Luce, Stephen B., 334
Ludlow, Charles, 126
Lull, Edward P., 318
Lynnhaven Bay, Virginia, 47, 125

Macao, 284–85
Macdonough, Thomas, 207, 221, 222–23,
    225–27, 296; biographic sketch, 220

Macedonian, HMS, 212
Macedonian, USS, 234, 265, 308, 318
Macta, 309
Madden, Edward, 95
Madeira Island, 195, 255, 307, 309
Madison, Dolly, 139
Madison, James, 2, 88, 128, 143
Madison, John R., 154–55
Madrid, Spain, 219
Mahmoud II, 223
Mahomet Ali, 253
Maidstone, 53, 91, 152
Maimona, 91
Maio Island, 202
Majunga, Madagascar, 273
Málaga, Spain, 86, 124–25, 217–19, 223
Maley, William, 52, 54
"Malimba" (Mayoumba, now Mayumba),
    Gabon, 306, 308
Malta, 328
Malta Island, 84–86, 95–97, 99–102, 110,
    115–18, 120–21, 123–24, 126, 217–18, 229,
    254, 292–93
Manila, Philippines, 286
"Maranham" (Maranhão Island), Brazil, 205
Marblehead, Massachusetts, 187–88, 351
Margaret Hugg, 288
Maria, 1
Marion, 263, 301, 318
Marks, Lanson, 133
Mars, 139
Marseilles, France, 253–54, 297
Martin, Caleb, 132
Martin, Tyrone G., 364–65, 368, 369, 371
Martinique Island, 38–39, 332
Martin Smith, 265
Mary A. Hogan, 332
Maryland (ferry), 315–17
Maryland, USS, 117
Mason, Lucius M., 275
Mastico, 97–98, 112
Matthews, Edmund O., 320
Matthews, Joseph, 331

Mayo, Isaac, 301, 302, 303–8, 310
Mazatlán, Mexico, 287
Mazopha, 288
McBlair, Charles H., 256
McBride, Clarence E., 358, 370
McCauley, Charles S., 310, 315
McCauley, Constitution S., 292
McCauley, Daniel S., 292–93
McCauley, Frances A., 292
McCormack, John, 361, 370
McDonald, Patrick, 141
McDougal, 351
McHenry, James, 13–14, 17–19, 21–22
McLeod, Daniel C., 253, 277
Medusa, 95
Melanson, Edward J., 361
Memphis, 349
Merchant, 313
Mercury, 319
Merrimack, USS (1798), 35, 37
Merrimack, USS (1856), 318
Meshuda, 84–86, 92–94
Messina, Sicily, 99–101, 123, 125, 217, 222–23,
    252, 294–96
Metany, Zanzibar Island, 274
Miami, Florida, 352
Middendorf, J. William II, 364–65
Milos Island, 217, 228–31, 252
Minnesota, 336
Mirboha, 92–94
Mississippi, 264, 294
Missouri, 264
Mobile, Alabama, 352, 361
Mogador, Morocco, 93
Mohammed Selawy, 93
Mona Passage, 186
Monitor, 318
Monohain, John, 305
Monrovia, Liberia, 303, 307–8
Montague, 171, 178
Monterey Bay, California, 287
Monticristi, Santo Domingo, 48–49, 52, 58–59
Montor, Rufus, 58

Moody, Thomas, 52, 61
Moore, James, 31
Moore, John, 288
Morgan, Charles W., 132, 294, 296
Morgan, John T., 7, 10
Morris, Charles, Jr., 98, 137–40, 143, 147,
    154, 158, 165, 176, 226, 234–35, 263
Morris, Charles W., 361
Morris, Richard V., 85–86, 92, 94, 118
Morris, Robert, 4
Mosquito, 185
Mozambique, 272–73
Muller, F., 147
Murad Rais, 84
Murray, Alexander, 62, 85
Murray, Dennis, 53
Muscat, Sultan of, 274
Mytilene, Tenedos Island, 228–29

Nantasket Roads, Massachusetts, 29, 40, 42,
    65, 132, 152
Nantucket Island, 145, 151
Naples, Italy, 86, 100, 116, 123, 216–17, 252,
    294–97
Napoli de Romania (Nauplia), Greece, 224,
    230, 252
Nash, Thomas, 6
National Intelligencer, 206
Nautilus, 90, 92, 94–97, 99–103, 105, 109, 112,
    115, 119, 121, 123, 135, 150
Naval Historical Center Detachment, Boston,
    371
Navarino, Greece, 231
Nazareth, Palestine (now Israel), 254
Nelson, Charles, 215
Nelson, Constitution Jones, 215
Nelson, Horatio, 190
Nelson, Hugh, 219
Nelson, Thomas, 29
Neptun, 327
Neutrality, 38
Newark, New Jersey, 351
New Bedford, Massachusetts, 333, 335, 351

Newburyport, Massachusetts, 55
Newcastle, Delaware, 132, 322
Newcastle, England, 154
Newcastle, 191, 204
New Hampshire, 333–34, 336
New Haven, Connecticut, 334
New Ironsides, 318
New London, Connecticut, 7, 128, 132, 213, 334–35, 351
New Orleans, 55, 212, 352
Newport, Rhode Island, 24, 87, 128, 189, 317–18, 333–36, 351, 358–59
Newport News, Virginia, 351
New York (city and state), 6–7, 23, 42, 47, 90, 128–29, 133, 136, 144–45, 151–52, 165, 167, 180, 182, 186, 193, 204, 206, 208, 220, 239, 246–47, 249, 257, 260, 262, 266–67, 273, 276, 279, 284, 301, 303, 317, 330–32, 337, 351
New York, 85, 92, 94
New York Navy Yard, 127, 247, 336
Nicholson, James, 23
Nicholson, John, 23
Nicholson, Joseph H., 301–2
Nicholson, Samuel, Jr., 27
Nicholson, Samuel, Sr., 6, 16–20, 24, 25, 28–31, 35–45, 63, 66, 70, 95, 140; biographic sketch, 23; takes ex-*Carteret*, 38; takes ex-*Spencer*, 32–34; takes *Niger*, 25–27, 29
Niese, John, 134
Niger, 26–27, 29
Niles' Weekly Register, 235
Nissen, Nicholas C., 120
Nodler, Eugene, 331
Nonsuch, 168, 215–19
Norfolk, Virginia, 26, 27, 125, 139, 182, 245, 255–56, 265–66, 331–32, 334, 351, 361
Norfolk Navy Yard, 264, 266, 315, 370
Norfolk (steamer), 334
Norfolk, USS, 48–49
North Carolina, 223, 226, 227, 228–29, 231, 267
Nos Bey Island, 273
Nowack, Charles, 353

Nymph, 55–57
Nymphe, 190

Oakly, Isaac, 215
O'Bannon, Presley N., 119
O'Brien, Richard, 1, 85, 100–101, 109–10
Offley, David, 224, 230
Old Constitution, 342
Olympia, 361
Ontario, 214–19, 222–23, 225–26, 227, 229
Orange, Texas, 352
Oregon, 361
Ormerod, Richard, 185
Ossipee (U.S. Coast Guard cutter), 350
Otho (Greek king), 252
Oyster Bay, New York, 351

Packett, John H., 133
Paine, Amasa, 268, 274, 276, 278
Paine, John S., 215
Paine, Phillip, 36
Paixhans, Henri J., 265
Palermo, Sicily, 100, 125, 252, 296
Palmerston, Lord, 249
Panama Canal, the, 332, 354
Paramount Pictures, 345
Paris, France, 136–37, 139, 248, 327
Parker, Foxall A., Sr., 264, 265
Parker, George, 176
Parker, Josiah, 13–14
Paros Island, 223, 228, 230
Passandava Bay, Madagascar, 273
Patapsco, 53
Patterson, Daniel T., 225, 227, 229–32, 252; biographic sketch, 226
Patterson, Elizabeth, 139
Paulding, James K., 259
Pawcatuck, Rhode Island, 133
Payta, Peru, 260
Peacock, 267
Pennsylvania, 265–66
Pennsylvania Academy of Fine Arts, 230
Penrose, James, 4

Pensacola, Florida, 345, 352
Pensacola Navy Yard, 315
Penshaw, James, 170
Percival, John ("Mad Jack"), 241, 266, 267, 268–77, 284–88; biographic sketch, 267; in Vietnam, 278–83
Perry, Christopher R., 48, 53–54
Perry, Oliver H., 188–89, 207, 236, 257
Perry, 301
Petri, Emil H., 350
Philadelphia, 1, 2, 4–7, 10–11, 13, 17, 21, 36–37, 40, 47, 51–52, 60, 62, 129, 141, 165, 182, 226, 230, 318, 322, 324, 326–27, 330, 333, 336, 351, 361
Philadelphia Navy Yard, 291, 322–23, 333, 341
Philadelphia, 83–84, 90, 92, 95–98, 109–10, 120–21, 168, 212–13, 220, 226
Phillips, Henry, 61
Phillips, Isaac, 28
Phoenix, 186
Pickering, Timothy, 10–11, 27, 29, 51
Pickering, 36, 87
Pictou, 185–86
Pierpoint, William E., 139
Pigot, 41
Pilgrim, 326
Pinkham, R. R., 258
Pinta, 321
Pioneer, 270
Piqua, Ohio, 363
Pity, James, 24, 30
Pius IX, 294, 295
Plymouth, England, 7, 249
Pocock, Nicholas, 177
Poinsett, 263
Polly, 37
Pomone, 155
Porpoise, 227, 229, 231
Port Arthur, Texas, 353
Porter, David, 54–55, 60, 154, 169–70, 296
Porter, David D., 227, 312–13
Porter, 351
Portland, Maine, 350

Port Mahon, Minorca, 214–19, 226–27, 229, 231, 251–55, 292
Porto Grande, Cape Verde Islands, 303, 307, 309
Porto Praya, Cape Verde Islands, 201–2, 204, 206, 303, 307
Port Republicain, Haiti, 60
Port Royal, South Carolina, 318
Port St. Joe, Florida, 353
Portsmouth, England, 137
Portsmouth, New Hampshire, 3, 6, 11, 17, 45, 82, 190–91, 310, 338, 350
Portsmouth, Virginia, 6
Portsmouth (England) Naval Shipyard, 328
Portsmouth (New Hampshire) Navy Yard, 220, 311, 337
Portsmouth, 287, 334
Potomac River, 140
Potomac, 252, 263, 275, 291, 324
Pottinger, Robert, 189
Powhatan, 334
Preble, Edward, 87, 88, 90–103, 116–17, 121, 140, 144, 209, 214, 291, 321; assaults Tripoli, 104–15; awarded gold medal, 115; biographic sketch, 86–87
Preble, Jedidiah, 86
President, HMS, 261–62
President, USS, 83–84, 115–16, 118–21, 129–30, 133–35, 156, 166, 168–69, 182, 186, 191
President Roads, Massachusetts, 62, 151, 166, 169
Presque Isle, Pennsylvania, 181–82
Preston, William B., 295
Prince de Neufchatel, 191
Prince Rupert's Bay, Dominica, 30, 34–36, 39
Princeton, 292
Principe Island, 308
"Propello marino," 211–12
Protector, 3, 86
Providence, Rhode Island, 10, 42, 351
Provincetown, Massachusetts, 191
Psyttaleia Island, 230
Puerto Plata, Santo Domingo, 55–57, 59
Puerto Rico Island, 39
Puna, Ecuador, 260

Quantico, Virginia, 140
Queen Victoria, 263
Quincy, Massachusetts, 27

Ralph Talbot, 358–59
Ralston, Esther, 345
Ramillies, 190
Randolph, 4–5
Raritan, 270, 271
Rathbun, Albert, 332
R. B. Forbes, 289
Read, George C., 143–44, 159, 162, 226–27
Read, John, 134
Read, William, 20, 27
Rebecca, 163
Redpole, 137
Regulator, 184
Reinhart, J. C., 271, 277–78
Renomée, 176
Resolute, 317
Retaliation, 168
Revenge, 133
Revere, Paul, 12, 18, 276
Rhind, Alexander C., 336
Rhodes, Foster, 266
Richmond (brig), 273
Richmond, USS, 53, 58–60, 64
Ridgely, Charles G., 247, 263
Rigaud, André, 60
Ringgold, Cadwalader, 303
Rio de Janeiro, Brazil, 171, 257–58, 260, 263,
    269–71, 284, 288
Rio de la Plata, 200, 262
Roberts, Joseph J., 300
Robinson, Edward, 286
Robinson, John, 46, 49
Robinson, Thomas, 108
Rochester, 349
Rocket, 335
Rodgers, Christopher R.P., 308
Rodgers, George W., 313, 315, 318
Rodgers, John, 86, 92–93, 118–24, 127–28,
    129, 130–33, 140, 144–45, 152, 154, 166,
    169, 180, 213, 222–29, 231, 235, 237, 243,
    245–46; biographic sketch, 117
Rodgers, Richard, 132
Roosevelt, Franklin D., 358
Roosevelt, Theodore, 340, 351
Rose, 129
"Rosie," 352
Ross, Malcolm, 200
Rowan, James H., 296
Rowan, John, 294–95
Rowe, John, 98
Royal Oak, 135
R. R. Cuyler, 317
Rudd, John, 302–4, 308–9; biographic sketch,
    301
Russell, Benjamin, 17
Russell, Charles C., 31, 50, 56
Russell, Jonathan, 137

Sackett's Harbor, New York, 181–82
Sagitta, 329
St. Augustine's Bay, Madagascar, 272
St. Croix Island, 332
St. Helena Island, 170–71, 306–7
St. Iago, Santo Domingo, 56
St. John's, Newfoundland, 154, 192
St. John's Island, 154
St. Louis, 258
St. Nicholas Mole, Haiti, 51–52, 54, 59,
    64–65
St. Simon's Island, Georgia, 10
St. Thomas Island, 186
Salamis, Greece, 230
Sale, Morocco, 93
Salem, Massachusetts, 87, 154–55, 187, 273,
    275
Sally, 56–58
Samana Bay, Santo Domingo, 58
Sambas River, Borneo, 276
Samos Island, 230
Sanderline, Reuben, 179
Sandford, Thomas, 56
San Diego, California, 354–55

Sandwich, 57–58

San Francisco, California, 355

San Jacinto, 310

San Juan, Puerto Rico, 206

San Pedro, California, 355

Sans Pareil, 302

Santa Cruz, Teneriffe (Tenerife) Island, 269

Santa Margaretta, 36

Santee, 318–19, 321

São Iago Island, 202

São Luís, Brazil, 205

São Paulo de Loanda (Luanda), Angola, 306, 308

São Salvador (Bahia), Brazil, 170–71, 176, 178–79

São Tomé Island, 305

Sarah, 263

Saratoga, 321, 334

Savannah, Georgia, 7, 24, 184, 352

Savannah, 286

Sawyer, Herbert, 145

Sawyer, William, 224

Scammel, 36

Scios (Chios) Island, 230

Scilly Islands, 249

Scourge, 100–101, 103

Schuykill, 10

Selawy, Mohammed, 93–94

Serapis, 162

Serra, Dahomey, 307

Sever, James, 16–17, 45

Shannon, 145, 148, 150, 155

Shark, 251, 252, 287

Sharkey, Robert, 28

Shaw, William, 52

Shediac Harbor, New Brunswick, Canada, 154

Shepard, Edwin H., 334, 337

Sherry, James, 310

Shubrick, Edward R., 264–65

Shubrick, John T., 164, 169, 264

Shubrick, William B., 199, 203, 264

Sidon, Lebanon, 252

Simmons, Andrew, 354

Simpson, James, 91–94

Singapore (British colony), 275–76, 279, 284

Sinoe, Liberia, 303

Siren, 90, 94–95, 98–100, 102, 105, 115, 117, 121, 123, 128, 182, 267

Skjoldebrand, 82

Skillens, John, 12, 66

Skillens, Simeon, 12, 66

Skinner, William, 299

Sloan, John, 224

Sloat, John D., 286–88

Smith, August F., 351

Smith, Moses, 155, 162

Smith, Robert, 65–66, 85–86, 88, 90, 95, 98–99, 109, 118, 123–25, 127

Smith, Thomas, 58

Smith, William, 61

Smyrna (Izmir), Turkey, 217, 224, 230–31, 252

Sophia, 83

Snow, Elliott, 340

Somers, Richard, 101, 104–6, 112, 114–15, 125, 183

Souda Bay, Crete, 252

Southard, Samuel, 221, 223, 226

Spark, 214

Spartan, 155

Spencer (British merchant ship), 33–34

Spencer, HMS, 190

Sprague, John, 49

Stanton, Oscar F., 331–32, 334

Starkey, Thomas, 277

Sterett, Andrew, 84

Stevens, Edward, 49–51

Stewart, Charles, 94, 98, 107, 167, 182, 183, 184–86, 191–94, 200, 202–3, 205–6, 240, 264, 292, 321, 368; avoids capture (1814), 187–88; avoids capture (1815), 203–5; awarded gold medal, 206; biographic sketch, 182; court of inquiry, 189–90; defeats *Cyane* and *Levant,* 195–99

Stewart, George, 204

Stoddert, Benjamin, 18, 20–21, 24, 26–27, 30, 36–37, 39–42, 44–45, 47, 51, 53, 58, 62–63, 65, 184

Strain, Isaac G., 271, 277, 281
Stringham, Silas H., 301–2
Sudholtz, Herman O., 369, 370
Suffren, 351
Sullivan, Richard, 24
Sully, Thomas, 183
Sultana, 218
Summer, Increase, 15
Susanna, 195, 200, 206
Swain, Charles, 30
Swords, James W., 224
Sylph, 3–7
Syracuse, Sicily, 95–96, 98–102, 110, 117, 121, 123–26, 218, 222–23, 227
Syrene, 48

Tagus River, 194
Talbot, Cyrus, 45
Talbot, Silas, 36, 39, 42, 43, 44–66, 70, 95, 140, 185, 356; biographic sketch, 41
Talcahuano, Chile, 260–61
Tallapoosa, 336
Talleyrand, Prince, 17
Tampa (U.S. Coast Guard cutter), 350
Tampa–St. Petersburg, Florida, 353, 355
Tangier, Morocco, 91–94, 118, 199, 223, 252, 302
Taylor, Thomas M., 268
Taylor, William, 215
Tenedos Island, 228
Tenedos, 187, 190
Teneriffe (Tenerife) Island, 303
Tennessee, 334
Terrett, Colville, 277
Tetuan, Morocco, 94
Texel, Netherlands, 136
Thayer, Cotton, 31
Thayer, Ephraim, 12, 66
Thayer, James, 331
Thetis, 261
Thompson, Archibald, 49
Thompson, Richard W., 325, 332
Thompson, Robert, 129–30

Thompson, Smith, 211
Thompson, Thomas B., 358
Thompson, Wells, 355
Ticknor, George, 17
Tiger, 194
Titcomb, Michael, 45
Titus, Mrs. Nelson V., 339
Tobago Island, 186
Torrey, Joseph, 31
Toulon, France, 252, 297
Tourane (Da Nang), Cochin China (Vietnam), 279
Townsend, James, 145, 150
Tracy, Benjamin F., 338
Transfer, 100
Traveler, 95
Tripoli, Libya, 82–86, 95–102, 106–7, 110–11, 115, 117–21, 123, 125, 127, 168, 215, 220, 253, 292–93, 345
Tripoli, Syria, 252, 254
Tripoli, 84, 106
Trippe, John, 104–5
Tristan da Cunha Island, 272
Troude, Aimable-Giles, 136
Trumbull, 59, 61–62, 64
Truxtun, Thomas, 24, 42
Tunis, Tunisia, 82, 100–101, 120–22, 124, 218, 222–23, 228, 231, 253, 294, 301–2
Turk, William, 226
Turks Island, 23
Turner, Daniel, 259, 261–62; biographic sketch, 256–57, 263
Tweed, 288

United States, 15, 20, 22, 30, 34, 36–37, 39, 63, 129, 166, 182, 184, 207, 212, 251, 252, 254, 299, 315
Upshur, Abel P., 263–65
Upshur, John H., 314
Upshur, 351
Uras (Round) Island, 224
USS *Constitution* Museum, 240, 348, 366

Vallette, Elie A. F., 226–27
Valparaíso, Chile, 170, 203, 258, 260–62, 288
Van Buren, Martin, 237, 244
Vandalia, 291
Venerable, 206
Vera Cruz, Mexico, 257
Vermont, 240
Very, Samuel W., 338
Ville de Paris, 327
Virginia, CSS, 318
Virginia, USS, 240
Virginia (revenue cutter), 27
Vixen, 90, 92, 95–101, 103, 105, 107–10, 118, 120, 123, 128
Volontaire, 194
Vourla Island, 224, 228–30, 252

Wabash, 338
Wadsworth, Henry, 112
Wallace, William (aka John Burne), 138
Ward, Aaron, 331
Warner, Nehemiah, 61
Warren, 287
Warrington, Lewis, 266
Washington, George, 2–3, 6, 11–13, 139, 216
Washington, D.C., 88, 94, 97, 122–23, 127, 130, 139, 143, 151–52, 164, 169, 182, 209, 211, 239, 241, 244, 284, 317, 333–34, 338, 341, 343, 352
Washington (D.C.) Navy Yard, 140, 211–12, 225, 237, 246, 352–53
Washington (brig), 288
Wasp, 126, 128–29, 212–13
Watson, James, 46
Wave, 299
Welles, Gideon, 315, 317
Welsh, Stephen, 179
Weri, William, 141
West, Edward, 38

West, William E., 302
Weston, John P., 274
Wharton, John, 4
Wheeler, Hugh, 303
Wheelock, C. W., 334
Whipple, Pardon M., 186
Whiting, William H., 327
Wilbur, Curtis D., 343–44
Wilkes, 350
Willard, George, 214
William, 178
William and Mary, 118
Williams, Henry, 331
Williams, John F., 3
Williams, Thomas (1799), 46, 52
Williamsburg, Virginia, 26–27
Wilmington, Delaware, 131, 351
Wilmington, North Carolina, 352
Wilson, Peter, 299
Wilson, Woodrow, 341
Winnegance, 307
Winthrop, 86
Wise, Henry A., 268–70, 288
Wolfe, Peter, 275
Wood, Louis, 359
Wood, Dialogue and Company, 323
Woodbury, Levi P., 237, 247
Wormley's Creek, Virginia, 333
Worthington, Thomas B., 215
Wylah, Sumatra, 275
Wylie, Joseph C., 362–63
Wyoming, 351

Yantic, 334
Yorktown, Virginia, 333, 351–52
Young, Charles, 106
YTB-540, 359

Zanzibar Island, 273

ABOUT THE AUTHOR

Comdr. Tyrone G. Martin was a career surface warfare officer who served in both the Korean War and the war in Vietnam. He commanded two destroyers prior to taking command of the *Constitution* in 1974. That tour in command resulted in Commander Martin's becoming the first of the frigate's captains since 1815 to be decorated and in the ship receiving her first official unit commendation.

The first edition of *A Most Fortunate Ship* was awarded a George Washington Honor Medal by the Freedom Foundation at Valley Forge. Commander Martin has also written *Undefeated* and *Creating a Legend*, as well as numerous contributions to, among others, such journals as the U.S. Naval Institute's *Proceedings* and *Naval History*, and *American Neptune*. He received the USS *Constitution* Museum's Samuel Eliot Morison Award in recognition of his efforts in naval history. Currently, Commander Martin is working on seven other book projects at his home on Devil's Ridge in North Carolina's Blue Ridge Mountains.